9/08

THE BORDER BETWEEN THEM

THE BORDER

BETWEEN THEM

VIOLENCE AND RECONCILIATION

ON THE KANSAS-MISSOURI LINE

Library of Congress Cataloging-in-Publication Data

Neely, Jeremy, 1975–
    The border between them : violence and reconciliation on
the Kansas-Missouri line / Jeremy Neely.
        p. cm.
    Summary: "Jeremy Neely recounts the exploits of John
Brown, Wililam Quantrill, and other notorious guerrillas, as
well as the stories of everyday people who lived through the
conflict that marked the terrible first act of the American Civil
War. He then examines how emancipation, industrialization,
and immigration eventually eroded wartime divisions"—
Provided by publisher.
    Includes bibliographical references and index.
    ISBN 978-0-8262-1729-5 (hard cover : alk. paper)
  1. Kansas—History—Civil War, 1861–1865—Social aspects.
2. Missouri—History—Civil War, 1861–1865—Social aspects.
3. United States—History—Civil War, 1861–1865—Social
aspects.   4. United States—History—Civil War, 1861–1865—
Biography. 5. Kansas—Boundaries—Missouri. 6. Missouri—
Boundaries—Kansas. 7. Violence—Kansas—History—19th
century. 8. Violence—Missouri—History—19th century.
9. Reconciliation—History—19th century.   I. Title.
    E508.N44 2007
    973.7'309781—dc22   2006101813

Designer: foleydesign.net
Typesetter: BOOKCOMP INC.
Printer and Binder: Thomson-Shore, Inc.
Typefaces: Birch and Palatino

*The University of Missouri Press offers its grateful acknowledg-
ment to an anonymous donor whose generous grant in support of
the publication of outstanding dissertations has assisted us with
this volume.*

TO ANGIE AND OWEN

CONTENTS

LIST OF TABLES   ix

ACKNOWLEDGMENTS   xi

NOTE ON STATISTICAL TABLES AND METHODS   xv

INTRODUCTION   1

ONE. DRAWING THE PERMANENT FRONTIER   7

TWO. TO SETTLE THE SLAVEHOLDING FRONTIER   24

THREE. ON THE BORDER OF WAR   60

FOUR. "'REVENGE' WAS THE WATCHWORD"   96

FIVE. A BORDER RECONSTRUCTED   132

SIX. "THAT THE DISPUTE HAS TWO SIDES IS EVIDENT"   171

SEVEN. THE BORDER OF THE CORN BELT   202

CONCLUSION. THE BORDER RECONCILED AND REMEMBERED   233

APPENDIX: TABLES   253

BIBLIOGRAPHY   269

INDEX   291

TABLES

1. Nativity of Missouri Border Population, 1850   253
2. Distribution of Occupations, Missouri Household Heads, 1850   254
3. Nativity of Households with Parents of Kansas-Born Children, 1854-1860   255
4. Nativity of Settlers, Kansas Border Counties, 1860   256
5. Nativity of Total Population, Kansas and Missouri Border Counties, 1860   256
6. Distribution of Occupations, Missouri Border Counties, 1850-1880   257
7. Distribution of Occupations, Kansas Border Counties, 1860-1880   258
8. Nativity of Southern Heads of Household, Kansas Border Counties, 1860   259
9. Results of Missouri Gubernatorial Election, 1860   259
10. Religious Affiliation along the Kansas-Missouri Border, 1870   260
11. Nativity of Missouri Border Population, 1870-1880   261
12. Nativity of Kansas Border Population, 1870-1880   262
13. African American Border Population, 1860-1870   263
14. School Attendance Rates, Kansas and Missouri Children, 1850-1880   263
15. Average Annual Investment in Implements, 1850-1880   264
16. Acreage Ratios for Major Grain Crops, Kansas Farms, 1872-1896   265
17. Proportion of Improved Land in Major Grain Crops, 1880   265

18. Fencing Preferences of Kansas Settlers, 1883   266
19. Border Farmers Who Built Fences, by Tenure, 1880   266
20. Results of Presidential Elections, Missouri-Kansas Border
Counties, 1868-1896   267

ACKNOWLEDGMENTS

*I*t gives me great pleasure to acknowledge the many people and institutions whose assistance and support made this book possible. The Frank F. and Louise I. Stephens Scholarship and Fellowship provided by the Department of History at the University of Missouri allowed me to dedicate several months toward preparing the manuscript that eventually grew into this book. A Supreme Court of Missouri Historical Society fellowship gave me the valuable opportunity to explore the judicial records housed at the Missouri State Archives. The generous help of Shelly Croteau, Patsy Luebbert, Lynn Morrow, Kenneth Winn, and the archives' reference staff made each trip to Jefferson City both productive and enjoyable. In addition to the Local History Department of the Springfield–Greene County Library, which handled my interlibrary loan requests with great efficiency, I would like to thank the staffs at the repositories where most of the research for this project was done: the Kansas State Historical Society in Topeka; the State Historical Society of Missouri in Columbia; the Kenneth Spencer Research Library at the University of Kansas; the Library of Congress and the National Archives Building in Washington, D.C.; the National Archives and Records Administration reading room in Kansas City, Missouri; and the Western Historical Manuscripts Collections at the University of Missouri–Columbia and the University of Missouri–Kansas City. Linda McCurdy helped me obtain copies of the Missouri militia papers that are housed at Duke University's Rare Book, Manuscript, and Special Collections Library. Arnold Schofield, historian at the Fort Scott National Historic Site, introduced me to several sources from the territorial period in Kansas. I am especially grateful to Terry Ramsey and Patrick Brophy of the Vernon County Historical Society in Nevada, Missouri, for publishing the John Dryden diary, fielding my many questions, and sharing their passion for the border area's history. James Shortridge, professor of geography at the University of Kansas and a native of Cass County, graciously shared his knowledge about the western border and many details concerning his family's history there. Thanks to the extraordinary genealogical research that Larry Wendt has published on the Internet, I was able to locate at least one family that settled briefly along the border before emigrating to points farther west.

I would like to thank Beverly Jarrett and Jane Lago at the University of Missouri Press for taking an interest in my work and shepherding this book toward completion. I am indebted to Annette Wenda for her keen copyediting skills, which prevented an embarrassing array of errors from reaching this book's other readers. I appreciate Susan Ferber's willingness to produce the splendid maps for this book on such short notice. Two anonymous readers offered suggestions and criticisms that helped make this study much stronger.

Many people at the University of Missouri provided valuable assistance during my time there. Within the Department of History, the cheerful help of Nancy Taube made my life and every other graduate student's life immeasurably easier. The comments, criticisms, and thoughtful service that Mark Carroll, Mary Neth, and LeeAnn Whites gave as members of my committee have helped this become a much better book. I extend special thanks to the two teachers whose extraordinary contributions made this book possible. Back in the fall of 1996, when I had the very good fortune to enroll in undergraduate courses taught by Susan Flader and Walter Schroeder, I could not have imagined the profound impact that these two scholars would have on my intellectual development. Professor Schroeder was the first person to suggest that I think about graduate school, and he planted the seed of curiosity that grew from an undergraduate thesis into this book. Professor Flader guided this project from start to finish, provided unflinching support and peerless editing skills, and has been everything that one could ever hope for in a graduate adviser.

I extend heartfelt thanks to Bryce Oates, Jenny Czyzewski, Heath Oates, Chris Rees, Paul Russell, Heather Russell, Braden Russell, Kurt Neely, Brittany Lowenstein, Billy Lowenstein, Sam Brewster, Adam Whitesell, Bethany Whitesell, Karen Whitesell, Dana Whitesell, Tom Sowell, Chloe Sowell, and Noah Sowell. By sharing their homes, tables, and babysitting skills, or simply making me laugh, these folks made research and writing an even greater pleasure. To my family I offer my deepest gratitude and appreciation. I thank my grandparents, James and

Helen Hill and John and Dorothy Neely, for always being proud of me, and my parents, Bob and Kathy Neely, for their support and encouragement. This book is dedicated to my wife, Angie, whose love and faith sustained me through its completion, and to my son, Owen, who makes our little farm feel like the luckiest place on the border.

NOTE ON STATISTICAL TABLES AND METHODS

Much of the social and economic analysis presented in this study draws upon an extensive sample of the federal census manuscripts produced in the six border counties from 1850 to 1880. I conducted a systematic sample of the population schedules to produce a sample population of roughly equivalent size for each county and decade. The sampling variable chosen for each county and decade depended on each county's total population at that time and was selected to arrive at a sample population of between 250 and 300 households. In a county with a frontier population of some 800 households, for example, I sampled one of every three households; in a more developed county with more than 5,000 households, I included a smaller proportion of households—perhaps one in every seventeen. By selecting households at a constant interval, each border household had an equal probability of being selected. Although sampling procedures cannot reflect the full complexity of a total population, the construction of representative samples offers an efficient and consistent methodology that facilitates thorough historical analysis. Upon completion, the population sample included more than 25,000 individuals.

The samples taken from the different kinds of census schedules (population, agriculture, and slave) recorded most of the details noted by enumerators. For the population samples, which have been abbreviated as Census-Pop, I included the name, age, gender, occupation, property holdings, birthplace, education, race, and marital status, whenever indicated. The agriculture schedules, or Census-Ag, provide a wealth of data on the production of border farms, revealing the acreage (improved, unimproved, and woodland) and value of farmland; investments in implements, fencing, and wages; livestock holdings; crop production and acreage; domestic production of butter, cheese, and home manufactures;

and the market value of the farm and its products. The less detailed slave manuscripts provide the names of slave owners and the number, age, and sex of their slaves. Unlike the population samples, the samples of the slave and agriculture manuscripts were not systematic. I studied these schedules after finishing with the population manuscripts and instead focused on individuals who had already been identified in the population sample. Integrating the variables found in each of the various manuscripts illuminated the ways that wealth and nativity shaped farming strategies, production totals, and tenure along the western border. In addition to examining people as they appeared in different manuscript schedules, close attention was paid to the individuals and families that happened by chance to reappear in the samples of different decades. These individuals—and particularly those who appeared in at least two decades and those who migrated across the state line—offer instructive examples of the broader trends that were reshaping the border.

Some readers may question why this study does not use the decennial state censuses that were first conducted in Kansas in 1865, especially when studies by James Shortridge and other Kansas scholars demonstrate the usefulness of these state manuscripts. Consistency is the primary reason. Using the federal census allows a parallel examination of Kansas and Missouri counties at a common point in time. There are no comparable state censuses available for Missouri counties in 1865, 1875, or 1885.

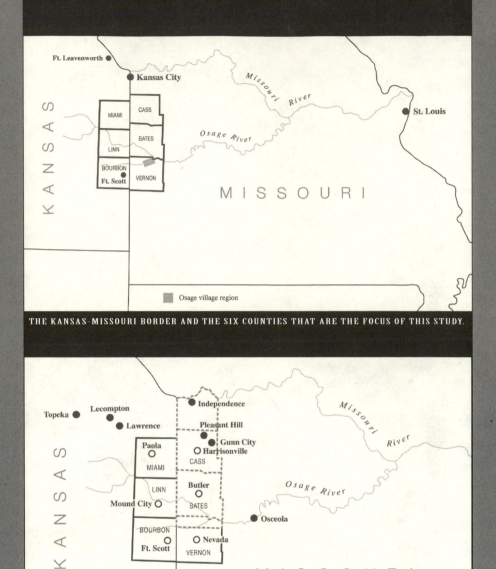

Ft. Leavenworth

Kansas City

St. Louis

Missouri River

Osage River

KANSAS

MIAMI | CASS

LINN | BATES

BOURBON | VERNON
Ft. Scott

MISSOURI

Osage village region

THE KANSAS-MISSOURI BORDER AND THE SIX COUNTIES THAT ARE THE FOCUS OF THIS STUDY.

Topeka Lecompton Independence

Lawrence Pleasant Hill

Paola Gunn City
MIAMI Harrisonville
CASS

KANSAS

Butler
LINN BATES
Mound City Osceola

BOURBON
Ft. Scott Nevada
VERNON

Missouri River

Osage River

MISSOURI

○ County seat

------ Area affected by Order Number 11

 Wilson's Creek Battlefield

THE KANSAS-MISSOURI BORDER DURING THE CIVIL WAR ERA.

THE BORDER BETWEEN THEM

At least three times each year, once in the fall and twice or more during the following winter, several thousand midwesterners file into large public spaces to participate loudly and vicariously in what some fellow congregants consider a tradition consecrated by history. At the center of these boisterous secular gatherings are the annual contests between the men's basketball and football teams from the flagship universities of Kansas and Missouri. Whether clad in the black and gold of the Missouri Tigers or the Kansas Jayhawks' crimson and blue, many players, coaches, alumni, and fans mark these grand occasions as the most important days on their school's athletic calendar. The Missouri-Kansas games boast an intensity and competitiveness that are common to collegiate rivalries across the United States, yet the quality of the games themselves cannot account for the level of passion, and in many cases obsession, among the supporters of each school. Ask loyal Jayhawks or Tigers, and they will likely say that the series remains so spirited because of the history between Kansas and Missouri—a storied history on the playing fields, yes, but more important, the states' violent history on the field of battle.[1]

The Missouri-Kansas rivalry can indeed be described as the peculiar product of modern athletic fandom and murky historicism. The reasons that people choose to identify with a certain institution or team can be elusive and complex, though they are often influenced by ties of kinship, geography, class, culture, and history. For fans of the Tigers and Jayhawks, it is one particular period of history—the nearly decadelong conflict that

1. The first Kansas-Missouri football game took place in 1891, making the schools' rivalry the second oldest in the United States—behind Minnesota and Wisconsin, which first played a year earlier—and the oldest west of the Mississippi River.

festered along the border between Kansas and Missouri in the mid-nineteenth century—that explains, justifies, and animates this passionate rivalry. From 1856 to 1865, people in western Missouri and eastern Kansas engaged in some of the worst guerrilla fighting ever witnessed on American soil, robbing, whipping, and killing their neighbors in a vicious cycle of retaliatory violence and intimidation. The border war reached a terrible climax on an August morning in 1863 when guerrillas from Missouri ambushed the sleeping town of Lawrence and killed more than 180 men and boys. Days later, Union soldiers, many of them Kansans, executed an order to depopulate several western Missouri counties, plundering and burning as they went. The popular mythology of this border war, which predated and helped ignite the national Civil War, holds a prominent place in the universities' rivalry, even after more than a century. University administrators from Kansas and Missouri in 2001 decided to market the schools' competitions in all varsity sports as part of an annual "Border War" contest. (Three years later, school administrators renamed the series the "Border Showdown," a move that chagrined students at both schools.)[2] If anything, this official sanction was a shrewd marketing approach, for it merely validated what countless fans already knew: the past is ever present within the Missouri-Kansas rivalry, as every game, race, and match is itself a renewal of the century-old fight between people along the state line.

A great many of the men and women who experienced the actual border war would no doubt find a small measure of irony in the aggressive historical posturing that surrounds today's rivalry. As they passed through middle age and into the twilight of their lives, the border conflict's veterans, victims, and other longtime settlers along the state line showed themselves to be more interested in sectional reconciliation than in perpetuating the antagonisms of their youth. Having endured the most violent and tumultuous period that their states would ever know, these survivors preferred to leave cross-border hostilities buried in the past, along with the disputes over slavery and secession. By the 1890s, several people in each state even spoke openly about having become friends with former foes living across the border. Other survivors, to be sure, still held on to the hard feelings that the war had fostered, and as they passed on tales of bitterness about vile Missourians or no-good

2. "MU, KU Headed for a 'Showdown,'" *Columbia Daily Tribune,* October 5, 2004; "Students Wage Campaign for 'War,'" *Columbia Daily Tribune,* October 24, 2004; "'Border War' No More," *Lawrence Journal-World,* October 5, 2004; "KU Student Leader Wants to Revive 'Border War,'" *Lawrence Journal-World,* October 22, 2004.

Kansans to their children and grandchildren, the historical grist that today fuels the MU-KU rivalry began to spread. One could easily fill bookshelves with works that cover the two most widely known (and reviled) border warriors, abolitionist John Brown and guerrilla William Quantrill, but much less is known about the ordinary people who settled along the state line, lived through the terrors of the border war, and then carried on to rebuild their lives and communities.[3] This book uncovers those stories and illuminates the possibilities and limits of postwar reconciliation. At the close of the nineteenth century, many Kansans and Missourians could look at the border between them as a symbol of peaceful reunion; for others, memories of its violent past lived on, making reconciliation an ever elusive prospect.

The chapters that follow thus examine the story of the border and its changing historical meanings. During the first two-thirds of the nineteenth century, no other geographical boundary in the United States stood at the center of as many major controversies and questions as did the border between Missouri and Kansas. Slicing invisibly across the rolling prairies of the lower Missouri Valley, the boundary was a compelling reflection of the nation's shifting priorities and the tensions that often accompanied those changes. The western boundary of Missouri was conceived amid the American expansion into the trans-Mississippi West; under the terms of the Missouri Compromise that had been set forth by Congress, this new line marked the northwestern limit of slavery's expansion into the territory acquired in the Louisiana Purchase. The U.S. Army later infused the border with additional significance, designating it as part of a "permanent Indian frontier" that separated the lands occupied by whites and Native Americans. By the mid-1850s, those meanings were discarded, and the border became an explosive political fault line and the first real battleground in the ideological struggle over whether freedom or slavery would prevail in the western territories. Free-soil partisans won that struggle, but the onset of the national Civil War further sharpened the divisions along the border, which now separated a staunchly Unionist state from a divided state with strong Southern sympathies.

By the end of the border war, the Kansas-Missouri line was the most pronounced political, ideological, and cultural divide in the entire

3. Notable biographies include David S. Reynolds, *John Brown, Abolitionist: The Man Who Killed Slavery, Sparked the Civil War, and Seeded Civil Rights;* Stephen B. Oates, *To Purge This Land with Blood: A Biography of John Brown;* James C. Malin, *John Brown and the Legend of Fifty-six;* Edward E. Leslie, *The Devil Knows How to Ride: The True Story of William Clarke Quantrill and His Confederate Raiders;* and Albert E. Castel, *William Clarke Quantrill: His Life and Times.*

nation.[4] In no other place did such embittered enemies, having fought for close to ten years, live in such close proximity. Yet on the other hand, the fierceness and duration of the border conflict masked the similarities between the populations in each state, many of which would become steadily more apparent during the postwar period. The populations of western Missouri and eastern Kansas were not altogether different. Most settlers along the border had emigrated from states west of the Appalachians, and the continued immigration of western families—especially those from the lower Midwest—would reduce the border's demographic contrasts even more. The war had reshaped the racial composition of the rural borderland, helping hundreds of Missouri slaves escape to freedom in Kansas, but many white citizens came to regard emancipated African Americans with a common mixture of ambivalence and contempt. White majorities in Kansas and Missouri, for example, were reluctant to extend voting rights to their black neighbors, even when those men had been among the first African American soldiers to face combat in the entire war. The issue of railroad expansion, meanwhile, introduced questions of taxation that subverted old partisan identities and instead united settlers according to class interests. Railroad projects nurtured new alliances between wealthy developers in each state and stimulated the spread of agrarian capitalism. Farmers responded to market opportunities in a consistently similar fashion, by raising greater amounts of corn and livestock, and thereby brought the area within a new region, the Corn Belt, that transcended political geography. Each of these developments further blurred the differences between settlers in Kansas and Missouri and soon called into question whether their shared border remained a meaningful boundary at all.

This book looks in particular at the countryside that lay south of the big bend in the Missouri River, where there was no natural boundary separating Kansas and Missouri. Unlike the area to the north of Kansas City, where the meandering Missouri River was a barrier to marauding guerrillas, the counties to the south straddled a nearly imperceptible open boundary, a fact that helped make cross-border guerrilla raids a regular yet unpredictable part of life for nearly a decade. As a result, the greatest destruction during the border war fell upon the people and communities situated near this open line. The massacres near Pottawatomie Creek and the Marais des Cygnes River took place in this part of Kansas and helped to reinforce the territory's dark nickname, Bleeding Kansas.

---

4. Such an assertion can be found in John C. Hudson, "North American Origins of Middlewestern Frontier Populations," 401–2.

Years later, travelers appended an equally grim label—the Burnt District—to the adjacent Missouri counties that had been depopulated and devastated by the Union army's General Order No. 11. Whereas most of the histories that have been written about this area focus largely on the violent incidents of this extraordinary period, this book puts the border conflict in a broader historical context by also looking at the more peaceful, though never tranquil, periods that came before and after it.

Several kinds of primary sources provide the evidential foundation for the chapters that follow. The manuscripts that were left behind by people who lived along the border are the most engaging and revealing materials within this book. Diaries, letters, and other private papers breathe life into the history of the borderland by giving voice to the attitudes, fears, ambitions, and memories of its people. The men and women who produced these manuscripts represented a wide cross section of rural society, having come from varied regional and ideological backgrounds. Abolitionist dairy farmers John and Sarah Everett penned some of the most interesting letters from the Kansas side of the border. The Everetts migrated to Kansas shortly after the territory was opened with the expressed purpose of making it a free country. Even within Osawatomie, a noted hotbed of antislavery sentiment, few neighbors could match their zeal or their prolific capacity to document the territory's troubles for relatives living in the East. John Dryden, a farmer living in rural Vernon County, Missouri, offered an equally compelling view of the border war from the opposite side of the state line. Living in a county dominated by Democrats and Confederate sympathizers, Dryden was an outspoken and nonpartisan Unionist whose unpopular views made him a repeated target of guerrilla violence. He survived the Civil War and continued to keep a journal for the next twenty years, providing a remarkable record of the political, economic, and environmental challenges that confronted border farmers during the postwar period. It should be noted that within these manuscripts, the voices of several groups of people remain muted. Prior to the border war (and to a lesser extent in the decades thereafter), many men and women could not read or write, as illiteracy was widespread among people who lacked access to schooling, such as women, African Americans, and poor farmers. Furthermore, not everyone who could write took the time to record their daily activities or their views on the border war, politics, or culture.[5]

Newspaper editors, on the other hand, made it their business to sound off on those topics and many others; their published observations

5. Floyd C. Shoemaker, "Missouri's Proslavery Fight for Kansas, 1854–1855," 221, notes the lack of primary sources from Missouri.

represent the second group of primary sources behind this book. Nine-teenth-century newspapers did not always provide a representative view of local opinions and instead reflected the values and prejudices of their middle-class proprietors. In addition to being better educated than many of their neighbors, these editors typically stood among the most opti-mistic boosters in a community and were quick to celebrate the spread of railroads, industrial capitalism, and bourgeois Victorian culture. These weeklies occasionally included letters from disgruntled farmers or other alternate perspectives, but dissenting voices were usually excluded, lest traces of conflict harm a community's reputation in the eyes of critical rivals. Local newspapers nevertheless remain useful sources for studying the public discourse and week-to-week events of border life.

Historical analysis of census data, meanwhile, helps to illuminate the impact of immigration, industrialization, and the other major social and economic changes that reshaped life along the Kansas-Missouri line. This book draws upon my extensive sample of federal census manuscripts from 1850 to 1880, which includes more than twenty-five thousand indi-viduals from both states. Population manuscripts contain a wealth of data for each man, woman, and child who settled along the border, revealing their birthplace, age, gender, race, wealth, occupation, and level of educa-tion. Taken in ten-year intervals, census enumerations offer imperfect snapshots of a frontier population in flux, but this sample is large enough that it traces many families across multiple decades. In addition, informa-tion within the Census Bureau's agriculture and slave manuscripts offer important insights into the changing nature of farming and slavery. Chap-ters One and Six draw upon separate samples of these manuscripts to reconstruct the farm strategies adopted by producers in each state.

Various other primary documents support this book. During the late nineteenth and early twentieth centuries, groups of old-stock settlers pub-lished local histories that shed light on the development of several border communities. These sources were published only a few decades after the war, and most contain detailed reminiscences of the border counties' oldest inhabitants. Unabashedly triumphant and self-congratulatory in nature, local histories also included biographies of many well-to-do citi-zens. In addition, farm records and statewide government reports docu-ment the expansion of agricultural and industrial production. Finally, local court records reveal the judicial and administrative priorities of offi-cials who often busied themselves prosecuting gamblers and drunkards in an era known for its extraordinary violence.

DRAWING THE PERMANENT FRONTIER

*A*s winter gave way to spring in March 1838, brothers Leonard and Samuel Newitt Dodge seemed perhaps the most unlikely Indian fighters on Missouri's western border. Sixteen years earlier, their father, the Reverend Nathaniel B. Dodge, had led a band of twenty-five northern evangelists to the nearby Marais des Cygnes River on an errand of spiritual salvation and cultural uplift. Acting under the auspices of the United Foreign Society of New York, the Reverend Dodge and company settled at a ford in the river's forested bottomlands and there established Harmony Mission, the first Indian mission school in Missouri. The missionaries located the school some ten miles from the principal village of the Osage Indians and dedicated themselves to transforming their indigenous neighbors into good Christian farmers. When the missionaries began work in the largely unsettled valley of the upper Osage River, neither Leonard nor Newitt, as the younger brother came to be known, had grown to maturity, though the former, who by then had reached his late teens, was much closer than his infant brother. The Dodges were clustered within a community of faithful reformers at the western limits of white settlement and thus came of age in a rather extraordinary frontier setting. At Harmony Mission, the brothers attended school, worked the model farm, and worshiped at church services alongside their parents' Osage charges, thereby developing an intimacy with the Osages that was uncommon even in the Missouri backcountry.[1]

The Dodge family arrived at a moment when the Missouri border represented the rapidly changing margin of the American settlement frontier. They encountered a prairie landscape that was hardly an untouched wilderness, having been transformed and exploited for centuries by its Osage inhabitants; nor were the local tribes foreign to the white traders and hunters who had first entered the area many years earlier. By the second decade of the nineteenth century, the Osages had signed a series of treaties with the United States in which the tribes surrendered most of their former homeland to U.S. authorities. According to these treaties, the western border formalized the partition of Indians and whites in the Osage valley, as the boundary marked the line between Indian Territory and the new state of Missouri. The border and Harmony Mission, which sat just a few miles to the east, were striking contrasts of white attitudes toward Native Americans, the former having been created to maintain their separation, the latter devoted to transcending that very division.[2]

By the late 1830s, the Dodge brothers occupied a world that was strikingly different from that of their youth. Harmony Mission had finally closed in 1835, its proprietors having surrendered in a losing fight against geographic reality and Osage apathy. Disease, intertribal warfare, and the loss of hunting grounds had accelerated the Osages' decline and signaled the demise of the mission. With the dispossession of the Osages and the mission's failure, new kinds of opportunities came to the former missionaries and other white settlers. Shortly after the mission closed, the Dodge men—Nathaniel, Leonard, and Newitt—seized upon the chance to acquire the first-rate lands abandoned by Native Americans, and by 1836 each had moved south to settle upon claims along the Marmaton River in present-day Vernon County.[3]

In spite of the government's intentions, the effectiveness of the western border as a cultural barrier between Indians and whites was neither immediate nor complete. Conflicts over access to natural resources underscored this volatile social reality. Even after the Osages had removed to Indian Territory, they continued to maintain their right to hunt in their traditional homeland, alleging that such rights had been endorsed by the 1808 treaty signed between tribal elders and U.S. authorities. Missouri

1. *History of Vernon County, Missouri,* 159–60; Mrs. W. W. Graves, "In the Land of the Osages—Harmony Mission," 409–15.

2. Floyd C. Shoemaker, *Early History of Halley's Bluff, Osage Indian Villages, and Harmony Mission,* 16–18.

3. Graves, "Land of the Osages," 417.

settlers disputed such claims, and following a subsequent treaty in 1825, which explicitly denied the tribe access to its former lands, they threatened violent retaliation against Native American hunting forays into the state. By denying Osage hunters access to the deer and other animals that had long sustained their fur trade with Europeans and Americans, the treaties of 1808 and 1825 disrupted both the subsistence patterns and the commercial ties that had enabled the tribe's nearly century-long dominance in the valley.[4]

Several Osage men returned to the site of their former villages in the difficult winter of 1838, starving and searching for food. Finding neither charity nor game sufficient to feed their families, the Osages turned to foraging upon the Missourians' livestock, which according to frontier custom had been turned loose to subsist on the mast and nuts of the nearby stream valleys. The Osages captured and slaughtered several hogs and then hastened a retreat back across the state line. Later that day, farmer Jesse Summers discovered the animal entrails that had been discarded upon the snow-covered ground, and a group of thirteen men quickly organized to apprehend the stock thieves. Pursuing the trail of viscera, the Missourians located the Osage hunting party in the marshy bottoms of Island Slough, near the mouth of Walnut Creek.[5]

The two parties, each armed with guns, regarded one another with a mistrust born both of need and of cultural misunderstandings over sovereignty and rights of property. The Osages maintained that in their treaties with the Americans they had sold the land but had not surrendered their right to the game upon it. White settlers, meanwhile, rejected this distinction and were particularly outraged at what they saw as a blatant and unforgivable theft of personal property.[6] Interpreter Newitt Dodge, having learned the Osage dialect during his childhood at Harmony Mission, voiced the settlers' demands, saying, "You have killed our hogs; we want the men who did it. Give them up to us that they may be punished." According to the Missourians' account of the exchange, an Osage warrior responded defiantly, "The men who killed your hogs are here, but before you get them you will have to get me. Come on if you want to fight. I am not afraid to die." Sources suggest that the warrior then began loading his gun, but Leonard Dodge, his weapon already loaded and primed, fired first, hitting his target in the shoulder. Falling to

4. Willard H. Rollings, *The Osage: An Ethnohistorical Study of Hegemony on the Prairie-Plains*, 220–80.
5. *History of Vernon County*, 159–62.
6. John Joseph Mathews, *The Osages: Children of the Middle Waters*, 574–76.

the ground, the wounded warrior attempted to prime his gun but died after a quick shot by Newitt Dodge struck him in the neck. In the clash that followed, at least three Osage hunters and one Missourian, the Dodges' brother, Nathaniel Jr., were killed.[7]

In the wake of the bloody disturbance, alarmed locals circulated rumors that the skirmish portended a broader Osage attack upon the Missouri settlements. Determined to preserve order on the state's frontier, Missouri governor Lilburn W. Boggs ordered a five hundred–member militia from Jackson and Lafayette Counties to move southward to protect whites along the border.[8] Local rumors of Osage aggressions, as it turned out, had been exaggerated, and the threat to the border proved more imaginary than real. Captain E. V. Sumner of the Seventh U.S. Dragoons, whose cavalry battalion had been sent from Fort Leavenworth to eliminate the Native American threat, reported that his three companies failed to find a single Native American. Furthermore, local histories indicate that the militiamen had committed perhaps even more depredations upon the settlers than had the Indians.[9]

Although many elements of the clash between white farmers and Osage hunters—murder, theft, vigilantism, assertions of military abuse—foreshadowed the bloody calamities that would afflict the area in years to come, the experiences of Leonard and Newitt Dodge also illustrated the dramatic shift in American-Osage relations along the early Missouri border. White attitudes and strategies regarding the native inhabitants of the Osage valley had changed over their century-long engagement and varied by cultural group, but, as the Dodge family history reveals, the most significant upheavals occurred within a single generation of American settlers. The French, the first group to make contact with the tribe, had regarded the Osages as indigenous allies to be used for commercial and diplomatic advantage; the Spanish, on the other hand, had later regarded them as unruly subjects who flouted royal control. Early Americans entertained similarly diverse opinions of the Osage country. Some sought to exploit the fur trade initiated by the French, whereas a small group of

7. *History of Vernon County*, 160.

8. It would not be the only time during 1838 in which Governor Boggs would rely on the threat of force to subdue a reportedly unruly minority group. On October 27, Boggs issued an "Extermination Order" against the state's Mormon settlers. The violence that flared between old-stock Missourians and Mormon residents of Jackson County in the early 1830s had a lasting impact on the country to the south. Several Mormons reportedly had lived near the current border between Cass and Bates Counties, along a tributary of the South Grand River, which locals would name the Mormon Fork.

9. Mathews, *Osages*, 574–76; Rollings, *Osage*, 280.

others, including the Harmony Mission evangelists, saw minds and fields to be cultivated and souls to be redeemed. When the Osage refused to adopt the beliefs and practices of the white missionaries, Christian paternalism gave way to impatience and hostility, and a great many settlers and government leaders alike came to see the Osages as, at best, pitiful dependents incapable of self-protection or, at worst, incorrigible obstacles to western expansion.

By the 1830s, such thinking found expression in a "permanent" frontier that sought to keep Indians and whites separated along the Missouri boundary. Below the confluence of the Missouri and Kansas Rivers, this border was an artificial and almost invisible boundary, cutting southward across the rolling prairie landscape. The Indian-white frontier was by no means a permanent boundary, as it would be abandoned after barely a decade. Its short existence provided a telling lesson about the malleability of political borders and the contested meanings that were ascribed to them. Under the terms of the Missouri Compromise, Missouri's western boundary also had represented the outer margin of slavery, yet with increasing sectional hostility between advocates and opponents of slavery's expansion, the survival of that boundary, too, came into question.[10]

When the Osages settled in the lower Missouri River valley in the early sixteenth century, they became the earliest in a succession of peoples to migrate to the area from eastern North America. Within a century, the Osages dominated the broad expanse of prairies and plains that lay between the Ozark Plateau and the Great Plains, an area that today encompasses large parts of Kansas, Missouri, and Oklahoma. The dominance of the Osages resulted partly from the flexible subsistence strategies the tribe adopted in response to their location near the ecotone where eastern hardwood forests yielded to western grasslands. The Osages situated their principal villages on the elevated tallgrass prairie above the "Place-of-the-Many-Swans," the low, marshy confluence where the Marais des Cygnes (or "Marshes of the Swans," as the French translated the Osage dialect), Marmaton (another name of likely French origin), and Little Osage Rivers joined to form the Osage River.[11] The villages' location

10. Michael A. Morrison, *Slavery and the American West*, 45–52.

11. Explanations vary for the etymology of the Marmaton, or Marmiton, as it is sometimes spelled. John Rydjord notes, "The name might refer to pots and pans [*marmite*], to the little scullion who cleaned pots and pans [*marmiton*], or to prairie dogs acting like little monkeys and called *marmots*" (*Kansas Place Names*, 114). See also W. O. Atkeson, *History of Bates County, Missouri*, 287.

within this edge habitat offered the advantages of diverse plant and animal life from the nearby prairie and forest ecosystems.[12]

To seize upon the country's varied resources, the skilled hunters, gatherers, and farmers of the Osages divided their seasons among these habitats. The tribe, but especially the women, devoted the spring months to planting and tending gardens in the rich silt loam of the lowland soils near their prairie villages. By the early summer, the Osages left their villages and crops for the semiarid plains, where the men hunted and the women and children dressed the buffalo that would sustain the tribe during the coming winter. In the fall they returned to harvest the crops from their eastern gardens and then retreated in smaller groups to the forests of the Osage valley for the winter, as local game and stored foodstuffs would support the tribe through the following spring. The material simplicity of Osage culture helped make such mobility possible, and although the tribe generally kept its villages in the Place-of-Many-Swans, the depletion of soil fertility, pasture, or firewood occasionally forced the tribe's members to shift their village sites.[13]

Wide-ranging incursions into territories claimed by rival tribes enabled the Osages to thrive but also drew the ire of potential enemies, both indigenous and European, at the margins of the nation's broad domain. The tribe's location near the great waterways that coursed through the midsection of North America, however, made them strategic allies to the French traders who ventured up the Mississippi and Missouri Rivers in the early eighteenth century. The French and the Osages developed a mutually beneficial relationship that grew out of complementary needs. The French desired trading partners who could provide furs, pelts, and labor, as well as loyal Indian allies who could thwart British expansion beyond the Mississippi. The Osages in turn welcomed the weapons and other manufactured goods traded by the French. Formed of necessity, the two groups' generally friendly relationship was preserved through economic self-interest and cross-cultural cooperation, and it likely approximated something akin to the French-Indian "middle ground" of the Ohio valley. Moreover, this alliance reinforced the Osages' hegemony over the prairies and made them, in effect, gatekeepers to the peoples, resources, and lands of the West and Southwest.[14]

12. Graves, "Land of the Osages," 409; Rollings, *Osage*, 1, 21–22.
13. Charles J. Mann, Allen L. Higgins, and Lawrence A. Kolbe, *Soil Survey of Bates County, Missouri*, 15–21; Mathews, *Osages*, 140; Rollings, *Osage*, 21–22, 68–72.
14. Mathews, *Osages*, 141; Rollings, *Osage*, 7–9. For the "middle ground" concept, see Richard White's excellent work *The Middle Ground: Indians, Empires, and Republics in the Great Lakes Region, 1650–1815*.

The earliest French forays into Osage territory demonstrated the close connection between their commercial and diplomatic intentions. By the early eighteenth century, the French-controlled Company of the West had gained considerable influence over the lower Louisiana Territory and sought to strengthen its trade with the Indians of the trans-Mississippi West and to develop new ties with the Spanish in New Mexico. Violent raids by the Comanche and other southwestern tribes, however, threatened the company's goals for New Mexico. In 1719, Louisiana governor Jean-Baptiste de Bienville granted the company's request to send a small expedition under Lieutenant Charles Claude du Tisne to forge an alliance with these western Indians. Du Tisne's first venture up the Missouri River later that year failed, having faltered somewhere near present-day Saline County. After returning to Kaskaskia, the young Canadian regrouped, and his second effort proved successful, though the overland journey through the rugged St. Francois Mountains and the forests of the northern Ozarks was no less arduous.[15]

When du Tisne's group reached the Osage villages near the Marmaton River in present-day Vernon County, they became the first whites to reach the rolling grasslands of the modern Kansas-Missouri border. Du Tisne's company received an inauspicious welcome. Greeting the travelers with suspicion, Osage warriors allowed the Frenchmen to pass through, but only after surrendering several of their weapons. The Osages further complicated the French expedition by dispatching messengers to the Pawnee, the tribe's ancient rivals on the buffalo plains to the west, and informed them that the advancing Europeans intended to capture and enslave them. Alarmed by the rumored attack, the Pawnee halted du Tisne's advance and forced him to retreat back down the Missouri to the Illinois country.[16] The Osages' rough treatment of their first European visitors could have inhibited the development of any future alliances, but the false warning issued to the Pawnee was a measure of shrewd diplomacy. The deceit undermined the possibility of French alliances with Plains tribes, and the Pawnee's predictably hostile reaction made the Osages' own brusque welcome almost hospitable by comparison.

Therefore, although du Tisne never succeeded in reaching the Paducas, the information gathered by his expedition opened the Osage country to European traders. Subsequent decades witnessed the arrival of *coureurs du bois* (runners of the woods) and other fur traders of French

15. F. Shoemaker, *Early History,* 5–7; Mathews, *Osages,* 178–81.
16. Graves, "Land of the Osages," 410; James R. Christianson, "The Early Osage— 'Ishmaelites of the Savages,'" 5–6.

descent. At least one source indicated that French entrepreneur Philippe Renault, who had developed the lead mines at Mine La Motte in eastern Missouri, came with a small group of miners to the Place-of-the-Many-Swans to assess its mineral prospects but departed shortly thereafter.[17] In their exchanges with the French, the Osages favored guns and durable metal goods that replaced existing utensils commonly made of wood, in addition to other items, such as textiles, mirrors, or jewelry, which they could not make themselves. Food, horses, and Indian slaves, which were seized by Osage warriors from the Pawnee and other neighboring tribes and then sold to the French, were important trading goods, but the items desired most by French traders were deer skins. Although deer pelts usually fetched low prices, the animals were plentiful and easily taken in the woods and prairies of the Osage valley.[18]

The lucrative French trade triggered profound changes in the Osages' subsistence patterns. The most significant change involved the commodification of deer, as the development of the European fur trade transformed the Osages' concepts of use and value. Traditionally, the two concepts were closely intertwined, for deer had little extrinsic value other than their usefulness as a source of food or clothing. Prior to their interaction with the French, the Osage had little incentive to hunt more animals than they needed. The commercial exchange with the French, however, affixed to deer new values that were relative to the prices of certain mercantile goods. The worth of a slain deer was no longer limited to the usefulness of its hide and meat but instead was linked to its value as a commodity that could be traded to Europeans for guns or other manufactured goods. With value dislodged from use, the desires of tribal members to acquire such goods soon joined the subsistence needs of the tribe as the driving forces behind Osage hunting expeditions.[19]

The successful commercial exchange with the French created new opportunities for social advancement among the Osages, yet it also had serious implications for the political stability of the nation. The fur trade in particular transformed the class structure of Osage society. Despite the wealth and prestige that some Osages gained through their commercial exchanges, they nevertheless remained shut out of positions of political leadership, which were traditionally determined by heredity and not by

17. Graves, "Land of the Osages," 410.
18. Mathews, *Osages*, 185; Rollings, *Osage*, 84–95, 109.
19. William Cronon, *Changes in the Land: Indians, Colonists, and the Ecology of New England*, 97–100. For the cultural implications of transforming animals into resource commodities, see Carolyn Merchant, *Ecological Revolutions: Nature, Gender, and Science in New England*, 30–68.

material or class status. Many of these ambitious yet politically frustrated Osages created positions of authority for themselves by breaking away from the tribe and establishing independent Osage bands to the south of the tribe's Great Village. In addition, the expansion of the fur trade also aggravated the Osages' relations with their indigenous neighbors to the west. They had initially acquired horses by exchanging European goods with western tribes, such as the Caddos and Wichitas, but by the late 1720s, this exchange could no longer satisfy growing trade demands. The Osages therefore turned to raiding the villages of their western rivals for the slaves, horses, and furs that would allow them to buy even more guns and ammunition.[20]

Although the transition from French to Spanish authority in Louisiana in the 1760s brought a notable change in imperial attitude and policy, the shift had little effect upon life in the Osage valley other than to reinforce already established trade networks. A series of trade regulations issued by territorial governor Alejandro O'Reilly, the Spanish governor of Louisiana, beginning in 1769 demonstrated the new regime's intention to control its Osage subjects. Two major changes—the prohibition of the Indian slave trade and a reduction of the trade in firearms—signaled O'Reilly's hopes to limit warfare among the western tribes and to contain the military threat posed by Osage raiders. Neither of these reforms was strictly enforced, and the trade in guns and slaves thus continued. A more threatening sanction came in 1790, when officials forbade all trade in the Osage country. This policy soon proved unenforceable by imperial officials in St. Louis, especially given the number of traders already in the area and the Osages' determination to disregard any restrictions. Spanish officials later ordered that the Osage trade could be resumed, but only with traders licensed by colonial authorities.[21]

The reversal of Spanish policy represented a tacit acknowledgment of the importance of the Osage trade to the economy of St. Louis, the seat of government for Upper Louisiana. Not long after Auguste Chouteau founded St. Louis in 1764, his half brother, Pierre, began trading at the Osage villages and eventually took an Osage wife. Responding to Spanish concerns about the intractably aggressive Osages, the Chouteaus offered to build and operate a fort near the Osage villages in exchange for exclusive trading privileges with the tribe. Spanish authorities, eager to establish order and convinced of the Chouteaus' close economic and

20. Rollings, *Osage*, 11, 122–23.

21. Mathews, *Osages*, 242; Rollings, *Osage*, 131–53, 179; Donald W. Meinig, *The Shaping of America: A Geographical Perspective on 500 Years of History*, 2:60.

kinship ties to the villages, accepted the deal, and in May 1794, Baron de Carondelet, governor-general of Louisiana, granted the Chouteaus a six-year trading monopoly. Fort Carondelet, as the new garrison had been christened, was the only fort established in western Missouri under the Spanish regime.[22] Governor Carondelet declared the efforts at the fort a "complete success." He reported, "The savages have let our settlements alone during this year . . . so much that they have not committed one murder, and on the other hand have restored various arms and horses which their war parties have stolen."[23]

The peace that apparently had been achieved in the villages belied the destabilizing challenges that lay before the Osage nation. To meet European traders' growing demands for furs, Osage hunters intensified their efforts in the eastern woodlands, but the decline in deer populations there made the tribe only more dependent on raids against the Plains Indians and buffalos in the West. In addition to the increased warfare in the West, the Osage nation also struggled with its own internal fissures. The Chouteaus' alliance with Osage leaders of disputed political legitimacy exacerbated the growing divisions within tribal society. The political chaos that steadily enveloped the Osages took another turn with the transfer of the Spanish trading monopoly to Manuel Lisa in 1802, but Lisa's short-lived tenure ended with the Louisiana Purchase of the following year. The Chouteaus, meanwhile, survived the multiple transfers of national sovereignty with their political influence intact, as the United States designated Pierre as its agent for the Osage nation.[24] For the Osages, however, such transfers portended significant changes for their own sovereignty over traditional homelands.

When the United States assumed control of Louisiana, its goals of promoting peace and commercial stability in the Osage country mirrored those of the French or the Spanish. The leaders of the young republic understood that the Osage, though politically fractured and constantly warring with western rivals, remained the most powerful Indian nation of the prairie-forest margin. To cultivate friendly relations with the Osages and neighboring tribes, an expedition under Zebulon Pike set out to explore the largely unknown lands of Louisiana that lay to the south and west of the Missouri valley. When Pike's company reached the location of Fort Carondelet on August 17, 1806, few vestiges of the fort

22. Mathews, *Osages*, 295–96; Rollings, *Osage*, 175–77; Shirley Christian, *Before Lewis and Clark: The Story of the Chouteaus, the French Dynasty That Ruled America's Frontier*, 94–95.

23. F. Shoemaker, *Early History*, 10.

24. Rollings, *Osage*, 175–213; Christian, *Before Lewis and Clark*, 114–15.

remained. On the east bank of the Osage River they discovered a cluster of ten French houses occupied only by a French-speaking Sac Indian and his Osage wife. The Americans continued across the prairie for more than nine miles before they arrived at the principal "village of the Grand Osage," where they were greeted warmly and entertained for nearly a fortnight.[25] Pike was struck by the splendor of the landscape, which he described as "one of the most beautiful the eye ever beheld," as well as its practical advantages of available water and timber. "The extensive prairies crowned with rich and luxuriant flowers," he wrote, "presented to the warm imagination the future seats of husbandry, the numerous herds of domestic animals, which are no doubt destined to crown with joy these happy plains."[26] The vision conjured by Pike's "warm imagination" offered a telling glimpse of the impending changes that awaited the Missouri territory, for it would be American farms and ranches—and not the semipermanent villages at the Place-of-the-Many-Swans—that would soon dot the prairie landscape.

As Pike continued his journey westward, the advance of backcountry settlers presented only a distant challenge, but the immigration of eastern Native American tribes into the trans-Mississippi West posed an immediate threat to Osage hegemony. The millions of acres acquired in the Louisiana Purchase, inhabited for the moment by scattered Indian tribes, provided the U.S. government with a convenient dumping ground for the other indigenous peoples who were being removed from land east of the Mississippi River. Competition from the hunters in these powerful, well-armed nations resulted in the collapse of the Osage fur trade. Before long, the tribe itself came under attack, as Pottawatomi raiders killed thirty-four women and children in a single raid of an undefended Osage village. Desperate for assistance, the Osages sought protection from an unlikely ally, the U.S. government, which had relocated the eastern tribes but was determined to keep peace among western Indians. American assistance and protection came at a steep price, as the Osages quickly learned.[27]

American officials and Osage leaders agreed in 1808 upon a treaty in which the Osages surrendered nearly all of their claims in the Missouri and Arkansas River valleys, an area of nearly fifty million acres. One of the treaty's central goals was to reduce the intertribal warfare that continued to

25. Stephen G. Hyslop, "One Nation among Many: The Origins and Objectives of Pike's Southwest Expedition," 7–11; Francis A. Sampson, "Glimpses of Old Missouri by Explorers and Travelers," 83; Meinig, *Shaping of America*, 2:71.

26. Zebulon Montgomery Pike, *The Journals of Zebulon Montgomery Pike, with Letters and Related Documents*, 2:21–22.

27. Rollings, *Osage*, 220–21, 260.

plague the western frontier. Under its terms, the United States established a fort on the Missouri River to police and protect the Osages, who pledged they would no longer attack or retaliate against the eastern tribes, thereby rendering themselves wards of the U.S. government. In addition to providing cash annuities, the Americans also agreed to furnish the Osages with a grain mill, a blacksmith, farming implements, and a trading post. Misunderstandings of language and culture, or even deception, may have marred the treaty negotiation. Some Osages did not favor giving up hunting rights in their traditional homelands, but several tribal leaders, heeding the advice of the tribe's agent, Pierre Chouteau, agreed to the treaty's terms.[28]

The limited assistance that the U.S. government promised to the Osages proved short-lived, as the trading posts at Fort Osage and the Marais des Cygnes were both closed by 1822. Furthermore, the State of Missouri, which had gained admission to the Union the previous year, exhibited little interest in supporting the displaced indigenous peoples who had recently lived within its boundaries. The Osages consequently turned to other sources for relief. Having learned of missionary efforts to assist the Arkansas tribes to the south, an Osage delegation traveled to Washington, D.C., in 1821 to seek the help of the United Foreign Mission Society, an evangelical body whose support from the Presbyterian, Dutch Reformed, and Associate Reformed Churches had been recently buoyed by a ten thousand–dollar congressional appropriation to teach agriculture, reading, writing, and arithmetic to Native American children.[29]

When the party of missionaries departed for the Osage villages in the spring of 1821, they may not have fully appreciated the challenge of transforming their seminomadic hosts into sedentary Christian farmers. Composed of sixteen men, fifteen women, and sixteen children, the traveling party was a select group, having been chosen from a pool of more than one hundred volunteers; it included ministers, teachers, artisans, farmers, and a physician, several of whom had been college educated, and thus represented a broad cross section of northeastern society. Their long journey to the Missouri wilderness was slowed by sandbars, striking boatmen, and a visit in St. Louis with William Clark and the Chouteaus, who instructed the missionaries about their Native American hosts. By August

28. Mathews, *Osages*, 390; Rollings, *Osage*, 225–27; Walter A. Schroeder, "Populating Missouri, 1804–1821," 276–77; Margot Ford McMillen, ed., *"Les Indiens Osages:* French Publicity for the Traveling Osage," 298–300; Christian, *Before Lewis and Clark,* 155–62.

29. Jules de Mun, *Journals of Jules de Mun*, 15; Graves, "Land of the Osages," 410–12; Mathews, *Osages*, 526–27; Rollings, *Osage*, 260–61.

1821, the party finally settled in the Osage valley at a site approximately ten miles from the tribal villages, and here it established Harmony Mission, the first Indian school in Missouri. Although the location offered close proximity to the Osages, the mission sat in poorly drained lowlands, a fact that likely contributed to the spate of illnesses that soon afflicted the missionaries. Within the first month, the party had been so severely weakened by fevers, ague, and other malarial symptoms that barely a quarter of the men were healthy enough to work.[30]

Once the missionaries returned to good health, they struggled to reshape the subsistence strategies of the hundreds of Osage families who remained in the area.[31] During their first spring at the mission, they planted a four-acre garden and sowed forty acres of corn with hopes of demonstrating to indigenous observers the efficacy of white farming practices. The tribe itself had been successfully cultivating the area's dark loam soils for well over a century, but the missionaries nonetheless criticized several elements of Osage agriculture. The small Osage gardens were unfenced, unlike the neat enclosures favored by Anglo-American farmers, and were typically maintained by the women of the tribe. In addition, the village gardens were left untended during the summer months when the tribe relocated to its western hunting grounds. The missionaries received little help in reforming the Osages' farming practices from the white fur traders of western Missouri who encouraged and depended upon the tribe's summer hunting raids into the western prairies and plains. Despite the missionaries' admonitions and the continued decline of the fur trade, the Osages generally refused to abandon their traditions of cyclical mobility in favor of settled agriculture.[32]

Although the classrooms at Harmony Mission sabbath school fostered opportunities for cross-cultural intimacy by bringing together Osage youth and the missionaries' own children, the school superintendent, Nathaniel Dodge, found it challenging to reshape the beliefs of his Osage neighbors. The school enjoyed regular attendance from at least a dozen Osage students, some of whom came to embrace Christianity. One local history, however, concludes that the mission school was a practical failure, given the native pupils' reluctance to share their education back in the tribal villages.[33] One story illustrates the missionaries' struggle to

---

30. Graves, "Land of the Osages," 412–15.
31. The population of the Osage villages in 1815 was estimated to be between three hundred and four hundred families (de Mun, *Journals*, 26).
32. F. Shoemaker, *Early History*, 20; Rollings, *Osage*, 260–61.
33. Bates County Old Settlers Society, *The Old Settlers' History of Bates County, Missouri: From Its Settlement to the First Day of January, 1900*, 22.

produce converts in the Osage country. Preaching to an Osage audience one Sunday, a missionary began to relate the biblical account of Jonah and the whale. His translator, William Shirley Williams, who had married an Osage woman and had lived with the tribe for more than fifteen years, objected to the story, arguing that it would destroy the listeners' confidence in the speaker. The missionary rejected this advice and continued with the story, which Williams obediently translated. After hearing the tale, an Osage chieftain rose and before he walked away announced, "We know [you] will lie, but this is the biggest lie we ever heard."[34]

The Harmony evangelists enjoyed limited success during their decadelong work along the Missouri border, but the mission was ultimately undone by geographic reality as much as Osage indifference. The continued relocation of Osage families to reservations farther south and west meant that even fewer members of the tribe remained near the traditional villages at the Place-of-Many-Swans. What's more, disease and continuous warfare against their indigenous rivals dramatically reduced the Osages' numbers—in the summer of 1834 cholera claimed four hundred lives—and by the mid-1830s their departure from their Missouri homelands was nearly complete. Consequently, the United Foreign Mission Society abandoned Harmony Mission in 1835 and sold its buildings to the federal government for a substantial sum of eight thousand dollars. Their evangelical mission abandoned, the Reverend Dodge and other missionaries dispersed to establish homesteads in the wooded valleys along the Osage River and its tributaries.[35]

The failure of Harmony Mission and the dispossession of the Osages dovetailed with the prevailing attitude and policy toward Native Americans that were held by the U.S. government, which increasingly favored geographic separation of Indians and whites over attempts at cultural assimilation. The removal of indigenous peoples to separate, specially designated territories had many precedents in the history of North America. As far back as 1763, British and American authorities had attempted to manage immigration by demarcating Indian reserves and prohibiting white settlement therein. The removal of Native Americans gained renewed momentum in the 1820s and 1830s with the relocation of the Wyandots, Delawares, Pottawatomis, and Shawnees, who had been

34. Mathews, *Osages*, 527. For a thorough analysis of the Osages' responses to Christian missionaries, see Willard H. Rollings, *Unaffected by the Gospel: Osage Resistance to the Christian Invasion (1673–1906), a Cultural Victory.*

35. Christianson, "Early Osage," 14; Rollings, *Osage*, 279; Bates County Old Settlers Society, *Old Settlers' History*, 23; Graves, "Land of the Osages," 417; McMillen, *"Les Indiens Osages,"* 299.

moved from their homelands in the Ohio valley, onto western reserves carved out of lands forfeited by the Osages. Christened "Indian Territory," the land beyond the western borders of Missouri and Arkansas in effect became a dumping ground for the eastern tribes that had been displaced by treaty, force, and the Indian Removal Act of 1830.

Federal authorities conceived of this longitudinal boundary as a permanent Indian frontier, designed to separate Indian space in the West, where the semiarid plains were deemed unfit for farming, from white space in the developing East. In order to preserve the coexistence of Indian and white cultures and to regulate interactions along this cultural frontier, Congress passed the Trade and Intercourse Acts of 1834. These acts prohibited white settlement on Indian lands, barred the sale of firearms and alcohol, and stipulated that whites conducting business with Indians must first obtain a federal license. In addition, the legislation authorized the U.S. military to enforce these regulations and to keep peace along the vast frontier that stretched nearly from the Canadian border to the Red River valley in the South.[36]

Authorities faced a daunting challenge in attempting to police this long border, where, as in the case of the Osage country, there were often no natural barriers. In reality, the frontier never achieved a hard-and-fast separation of Indians and whites. Some hunters and traders maintained existing relationships, and elsewhere there remained the potential for violence between displaced tribes and the settlers who had seized their lands. The bloody feud that erupted between the Osage hunting party and white settlers in the spring of 1838 offered a clear example of this danger. In 1836, Secretary of War Lewis Cass had proposed that the U.S. government construct a series of forts, bound together by a network of military roads, to patrol and pacify the permanent frontier, but only in 1842 did General Zachary Taylor appoint a commission to build a military post to defend the western frontier that lay between Forts Leavenworth and Gibson.[37]

The army founded Fort Scott in 1842 but did not finish building it for another eight years, when the post's original peacekeeping mandate no longer seemed as relevant. Perched on a high bluff overlooking the Marmaton River, the fort had been situated on lands that were promised to but never occupied by various Indian tribes from New York. The

36. Meinig, *Shaping of America*, 2:77–101; H. Craig Miner, *Kansas: The History of the Sunflower State, 1854–2002*, 33–34.

37. Louise Barry, "The Fort Leavenworth–Fort Gibson Military Road and the Founding of Fort Scott," 115; Bernice C. Shackleton, *Handbook on the Frontier Days of Southeast Kansas*, 68–69.

mounted companies of the First Dragoons who manned the fort spent a considerable amount of time patrolling the frontier to settle intertribal disputes, but by 1850 the threat of Indian depredations against white settlers in Missouri, which had been the post's principal raison d'être, declined significantly.[38] Most of the Osages now lived well south of the Place-of-the-Many Swans; the few who remained were largely dependent upon American trade and protection against relocated eastern tribes. Sergeant John Hamilton recalled that he never witnessed an Indian raid during his stay at Fort Scott and that the tribes rarely approached the garrison, "only to come in and beg some provisions, tobacco, & co."[39] In addition, the authority of the military patrols was circumscribed by the guidelines set forth in the Trade and Intercourse Acts, which granted jurisdiction over liquor trade violations to civilian officials. Fort Scott's soldiers thus found themselves engaged in a variety of other missions. Dragoons, for example, were used to guard the trade caravans that followed the nearby Santa Fe Trail from Independence, Missouri, to New Mexico. In 1847, the army sent most of the soldiers stationed at the fort to fight in the Mexican War. On March 30, 1853, the military ceased operations at the fort. Because the lands upon which the fort was built were still reserved for the New York tribes and thus off-limits to American settlers, the area surrounding the fort saw little immediate development, and the fort's buildings fetched auction prices between $300 and $505 each, well under the value of similar buildings east of the border.[40]

Unlike previously established western posts, Fort Scott was built with the sole purpose of maintaining the permanent Indian frontier. Its brief initial incarnation, however, had the ironic effect of stimulating the expansion of American settlements in western Missouri. A number of soldiers remained in the area, as did the fort's sutler, Hiero T. Wilson, who, in anticipation of future development, shrewdly purchased the blacksmith shop and other completed buildings. The fort had maintained a close economic relationship with the area's settlers from its inception. The post offered a convenient market where cash-poor pioneer families could exchange food, labor, and supplies with soldiers who almost always paid in hard money. Perhaps no settler benefited more from the army's investment at Fort Scott than George Douglass. A Virginian by

38. Daniel J. Holder and Hal K. Rothman, *The Post on the Marmaton: An Historical Resource Study of Fort Scott National Historic Site*, 9–10.

39. Hamilton to O. Diffenback, April 25, 1872, John Hamilton Papers, Collection 668, Kansas State Historical Society, hereafter cited as KSHS.

40. Barry, "Founding of Fort Scott," 128; Holder and Rothman, *Post on the Marmaton*, 9, 25–61.

birth, Douglass parlayed his familiarity with the Osage country—he had helped to find a suitable location for the post just miles upstream from his home on the Marmaton—into a lucrative army contract for livestock and forage, which helped him to become one of the wealthiest men along the western border.[41]

A portion of the soldiers, traders, and missionaries who passed through the Osage country eventually chose to remain there. Those who did were a motley mix of antebellum American society, arriving from the North and the South, rich and poor, in families and as individuals, and with ambitions that varied accordingly. Given their northeastern birth and college educations, the proprietors of Harmony Mission initially shared little in common with the immigrants from the backcountry of the trans-Appalachian West. In time, however, they and their children came to adopt many of the attitudes, values, and farming practices trans-planted by the settlers from Kentucky, Tennessee, and Virginia who pre-dominated in the Osage valley. The western border of Missouri thus came to represent the northwesternmost extension of an Upper South frontier society dominated by subsistence-oriented farmers. More than 70 percent of border households traced their roots to southern states, and most of these immigrants came from the Upper South, as table 1 (Nativ-ity of Missouri Border Population, 1850) illustrates. One particular south-ern institution, the ownership of African American slaves, held only a marginal presence in this frontier society, yet its expansion behind the western border—but not beyond—would prove to have profound impli-cations for the state's inhabitants.[42]

41. J. B. Johnson, ed., *The History of Vernon County, Missouri, Past and Present*, 188; Holder and Rothman, *Post on the Marmaton*, 1, 68–70; Earl Arthur Shoemaker, *The Per-manent Indian Frontier: The Reason for the Construction and Abandonment of Fort Scott, Kansas, during the Dragoon Era*, 1.

42. Wilbur Zelinsky analyzes the lasting cultural and social significance of early settlers in his discussion of the "doctrine of first effective settlement" (*The Cultural Geography of the United States*, 13). For more on this subject, see Raymond D. Gastil, *Cultural Regions of the United States*, 26–27. For an excellent analysis of Upper South influence throughout rural Missouri, see R. Douglas Hurt, *Agriculture and Slavery in Missouri's Little Dixie*.

T W O

TO SETTLE THE SLAVEHOLDING FRONTIER

❧

L ike the other family members whom Cecil Ball had come to see in
1837, his uncle Nathaniel Dodge could readily vouch for the
prospects that awaited enterprising immigrants along Missouri's
western border. Sixteen years earlier, Dodge led the group that founded
the first Indian school in Missouri, at Harmony Mission. After declining
attendance ultimately spelled the demise of that effort in 1835, he and his
adult sons, along with the remaining members of the missionary company, scattered throughout the Osage valley and laid claim to the best
lands the country had to offer. These excellent claims boasted the necessary makings of a successful homestead—access to timber, pasture, and
water, plus fertile soil that had already been cleared and worked by its
previous native occupants. The Dodges were no doubt eager to share
news of their excellent claims with eastern kinfolk, and within two years
Ball joined them on a visit to the frontier. Whereas ties of kinship had first
lured the twenty-seven-year-old to Missouri, it was the pull of opportunity, the chance to make his fortune and enjoy the full liberties afforded a
western man, that promised to bring the visitor from Massachusetts back
for good.[1]

The time that Ball spent ambling through the prairies and woods
around his family's new homes left an indelible impression, as barely a
year passed before the young man journeyed to the western border yet

1. *History of Vernon County,* 386–88.

again, this time to stay. Not long after arriving in 1839, he agreed to purchase the mill that Daniel Austin, a former member of the Harmony Mission company, had established along the Little Osage River. The new owner rebuilt the mill and eventually constructed a country store nearby. These properties became the commercial hub for settlers in the surrounding countryside, and neighbors soon affirmed the owner's prominence by dubbing the surrounding settlement Balltown. In 1851 the successful merchant laid out a new town, which he called Little Osage, and there established the first post office in the area that would later become Vernon County.[2] Three years later Ball snapped up an additional eight thousand acres of land in the bottoms along the Osage and its tributaries, a purchase that helped make him one of the richest landowners in southwest Missouri. Within two decades the New Englander had fulfilled the economic potential of western migration as well as any man he knew.[3]

Few households in rural western Missouri would ever match Ball's wealth, but many settlers shared a similar faith in the economic independence that could indeed be wrung from the "Missouri country." Despite failing in his endeavors as a frontier teacher and sawmill proprietor, Allen Ward remained undaunted about his prospects in western Missouri. Writing to his family back in Indiana, he explained, "I still think it is the best country I have found for the poor man whether laborer or mechanic or a man with a small capital can generally invest it in such a manner here that he can realize more profits from it than in most other places."[4] The significance of property ownership within the agrarian society of antebellum Missouri was difficult to overstate. As table 2 (Distribution of Occupations, Missouri Household Heads, 1850) illustrates, more than 90 percent of household heads in Cass and Bates Counties were farm owners, tenant farmers, or farm laborers. Property ownership was a standard toward which all farm households aspired and was a goal that most families could realistically expect to achieve, as three-fourths of the country's households owned at least some appreciable property. Most of these farms were small in size, generally with fewer than fifty improved acres, but large enough to provide a modest subsistence for a typically large frontier family. Property ownership, however, was not

2. Ibid., 159, 387–88.
3. Betty Harvey Williams, *Bates County, Missouri, Swamp Land Sales, 1854–1855*, 3–31. Ball's real wealth was listed at $70,600 in 1860, or nearly twice the amount of the next wealthiest owner in Bates, Cass, and Vernon Counties (author's sample, U.S. Bureau of the Census, Manuscript Census, Missouri, Bates, Cass, and Vernon Counties, Schedule I [Population], 1850, 1860, hereinafter cited as Census-Pop).
4. Ward to parents, December 21, 1850, Allen T. Ward Papers, KSHS.

simply the basis of personal wealth and subsistence in the pioneer West; widespread republican beliefs also held that such ownership was the foundation upon which a citizen's independence and virtue rested.[5]

Although it is unknown whether Ward's parents or sister soon joined him, many of the countless dispatches that frontier settlers sent back east helped to lure other family members to the raw but promising West. Indeed, as Ball's experience showed, kinship ranked alongside the desire for economic advancement as one of the most powerful forces behind one's decision to relocate. Migration and settlement often were joint endeavors in which the combined efforts of family members lessened the burdens of overland travel. Such chain migrations offered many obvious advantages. On a practical level, families who migrated or settled in large groups not only enjoyed greater security but also could pool their resources and labor to build homesteads more efficiently. In addition, family migrations also helped settlers to uphold long-standing social traditions, preserve bonds of intimacy, and maintain connections with the familiar in a land that was new.[6]

The prospects that a given household would succeed, much less survive, the isolation and material hardship of the western frontier, depended largely on the cooperation of the men and women living within it. Despite such necessary cooperation, striking inequalities often characterized the relationship between the sexes in pioneer households. Women occupied a subordinate social and economic position that was generally shaped by their relationships to male relatives. Relatively few married women owned property.[7] According to the 1850 census, only one in twelve homes along the border had a female head of household, and most of these women were widowed mothers. That only one of the women sampled, thirty-nine-year-old farmer Christina Osborne, was listed as having an occupation says less about her uniqueness than it does about the narrow opportunities that women faced beyond the farm household. The fact that almost all women were described as having no employment also suggests that census enumerators undervalued the economic worth of women's contributions as domestic producers. In addi-

5. Bill Cecil-Fronsman, "'Death to All Yankees and Traitors in Kansas': The *Squatter Sovereign* and the Defense of Slavery in Kansas," 145.

6. For competing interpretations about the significance of kinship on frontier migration and settlement, see Carolyn Earle Billingsley, *Communities of Kinship: Antebellum Families and the Settlement of the Cotton Frontier*, 42–76; Joan Cashin, *A Family Venture: Men and Women on the Southern Frontier*, 4–8, 32–98; and John Mack Faragher, *Sugar Creek: Life on the Illinois Prairie*, 56–60.

7. Cashin, *Family Venture*, 4; John Mack Faragher, *Women and Men on the Overland Trail*, 187.

tion to their vital, if often overlooked, assistance on the farm, women were often responsible for generating much of the household's limited cash income through their production of butter and household manufactures, which were produced in more than three-fourths of border homes.[8] Ann Dobbins, a widowed mother of six, reflected upon a predicament common in frontier households: "Money was scarce and goods high. As far as that was concerned it didn't bother us any, for we had plenty of cotton, hemp, flax and wool, a loom, wheel, and other necessaries, and we well understood the art of converting it into cloth, and, therefore, our family fared well."[9]

Most settlers endured, for varying lengths of time, a kind of transitory poverty upon arriving in western Missouri. The majority of households had most of their wealth invested in land, and the purchase, improvement, and payment of taxes on these claims left families with little cash on hand. Labor therefore became the most important resource in a household's effort to meet its subsistence needs. Because hired hands were understandably scarce in an area where land was plentiful, frontier families were often quite large.[10] Although few Missouri families would have as many children as Joseph and America Christopher's eleven, that couple was not unusual in counting three adult children as members of its household. The five oldest sons of Henry Cook, for example, continued living and working as farm laborers within the family's Bates County home, even though all were twenty years or older.[11]

Western Missouri's earliest settlers kept their limited labor resources in mind when selecting the land on which they could most efficiently establish a homestead. Located at the margin of American settlement, this prairie environment that pioneers encountered offered the basic ingredients of subsistence agriculture: good soils, adequate trees and rainfall, plentiful grasses for livestock, and an abundance of available and cheap land. The country was by no means a wilderness, despite some old-stock settlers' eventual recollections to the contrary. Over several centuries, the Osages and other Native Americans had actively transformed their environment through burning, hunting, forestry, and planting. Fires set by

8. Census-Pop, Missouri, Bates and Cass Counties, 1850; Glenda Riley, "'Not Gainfully Employed': Women on the Iowa Frontier, 1833–1870," 237; Sandra L. Myres, *Westering Women and the Frontier Experience, 1800–1915*, 138–56; Susan Sessions Rugh, *Our Common Country: Family Farming, Culture, and Community in the Nineteenth-Century Midwest*, 67.

9. Bates County Old Settlers Society, *Old Settlers' History*, 208.

10. Myres, *Westering Women*, 160. For the centrality of the family to the rural political economy, see Faragher, *Women and Men*, 40–44.

11. Census-Pop, Missouri, Bates and Cass Counties, 1850, 1860.

several generations of Osages had promoted the growth of the area's characteristic prairie grasses, such as big bluestem, by retarding the spread of young trees and other woody vegetation beyond narrow stream valleys. Prior to white settlement, these broad prairies covered more than three-fourths of the border landscape, and in many places a person could walk for miles without seeing a single tree. The intricate prairie-forest ecosystem also supported a rich diversity of animal species, including deer, turkey, buffalo, elk, rabbit, bear, and a host of waterfowl, although by 1830 white observers had already noted a diminution in the variety and extent of local game.[12]

The wooded valleys that lined the margins of the tallgrass prairie proved to be an attractive location for most early settlers. The grassy uplands and forested bottoms of this environment were recognizable to many families migrating from the Ohio valley. The Osage plains of western Missouri and eastern Kansas sat at the southwestern corner of the Prairie Peninsula, a vast interior grassland that stretched from Ohio in the east to Minnesota in the north.[13] The border counties therefore offered one of the last places where westering immigrants could find a familiar mix of prairies and hardwood forests. The appeal of the prairie-forest mix grew from its practical advantages as much as its cultural appeal. This landscape offered settlers superior access to timber, water, and pasture, and thus lessened the labor demands of establishing a farm. Samuel Newton, one of the settlers at Harmony Mission, wrote that their location afforded "excellent timber in abundance" and "first rate prairie for plowing, pasturing, and mowing." Although the dense sod of the tallgrass prairies was difficult to plow, the wooded soils that the Osages had farmed for centuries were fertile and easily tilled. Excellent pasturage could be found in the nutritious native grasses of the nearby prairies, which area settlers would continue to use as a common range through the early 1870s.[14]

The prairie-forest margin that attracted early settlers was well suited to the extensive agricultural practices that immigrants from the Upper South brought with them. Corn and hogs, the twin staples of Upper South agriculture, were easily adaptable to frontier conditions in that they each could thrive without extraordinary investments of labor and

12. Zelinsky, *Cultural Geography*, 16; Walter A. Schroeder, *Presettlement Prairie of Missouri*, 2–12.

13. Edgar Nelson Transeau, "The Prairie Peninsula."

14. Quote from F. Shoemaker, *Early History*, 18; Terry G. Jordan, "Between the Forest and the Prairie"; Douglas R. McManis, *The Initial Evaluation and Utilization of the Illinois Prairies, 1815–1840*, 27–29; Schroeder, *Presettlement Prairie of Missouri*, 18–20.

capital. Raising hogs on a pioneer homestead, for example, required only a crude pen where the animals could be enclosed for fattening. For most of the year these hardy, even aggressive, animals were turned loose to forage on the nuts and mast of the nearby woods. Corn production, meanwhile, required a significant exertion of labor only at certain times in the growing season, such as planting, laying by, and harvesting. The corn crop could then be used either to feed the pioneer family, for whom cornbread was a steady if mundane part of the everyday diet; to produce distilled whiskey; or to fatten livestock, which in turn would be processed and sold at market for a small profit.[15]

Because they were so easily grown, corn and hogs quickly became an indispensable part of pioneer agriculture. Four out of every five border households raised hogs, with most owning at least a couple dozen, and the proportion of settlers growing corn was even higher, reaching nearly 100 percent in Cass County. The remarkable homogeneity of agriculture in frontier Missouri extended to the production of secondary crops and livestock. Almost every household had at least a few horses and beef cattle and a couple of cows for milking, and most also owned some sheep, which could satisfy a family's demand for wool, and perhaps another beast of burden, such as a mule but more likely an ox. Farmers' heavy reliance on the common pasture of the unbroken prairies may be inferred by the limited cultivation of hay, which was harvested on barely one-quarter of the border's farms. In addition to occasionally tending a garden, or less frequently an orchard, the majority of settlers supplemented the corn-hog regime with a secondary grain crop, such as oats or wheat.

The primitive sameness of frontier agriculture did not extend to levels of farm production. The amount of livestock and crops that a particular family could produce was limited by the quality and quantity of land and technology at its disposal, as well as the number of hands available to operate it. Most families along the border owned at least fifty dollars' worth of farming implements, and typically worked claims of at least forty improved acres. Such an investment was typically sufficient to meet the subsistence needs of an average-size household. The farm operated by Henry Cook and his five sons provides a useful illustration of the diversified subsistence strategy that many settlers pursued. In 1849, the Cooks improved half of their acreage, raising corn (harvesting a disappointing

15. Bates County Old Settlers Society, *Old Settlers' History*, 35; Rugh, *Our Common Country*, 19; Allan G. Bogue, *From Prairie to Corn Belt: Farming on the Illinois and Iowa Prairies in the Nineteenth Century*, 69; Hurt, *Agriculture and Slavery*, 125–27; Terry G. Jordan, *North American Cattle-Ranching Frontiers: Origins, Diffusion, and Differentiation*, 202–4.

150 bushels), oats, peas, beans, and flax on seventy acres, and turned out their thirty cattle, twenty-five hogs, and seven sheep on their unimproved lands and the adjacent prairie. In addition to the vegetables harvested from their family's five-acre garden, Sarah Cook also produced two hundred dollars' worth of butter and cheese, which could be either consumed within the home or sold locally.[16]

Evidence from the western border suggests that subsistence-level production was a matter of circumstance as well as choice. The pace of railroad expansion in Missouri remained slow and uneven through the 1850s, and the state's two major rivers, the Mississippi and the Missouri, remained its primary arteries of transportation. The relative isolation of the rural Osage valley delayed its economic development. Farmers in Cass and Bates Counties were more than a long day's trip from the closest port on the Missouri, and steamships could generally navigate the low, serpentine channel of the Osage River only as far upstream as Warsaw, which was more than a county away. One nineteenth-century account described the result of the pioneers' isolation: "They made but little attempt to raise more than was sufficient for their needs, as they were too distant from market, and transportation too laborious and costly to dispose of any surplus to advantage."[17] Given the high cost and difficulty of overland travel, settlers like Daniel Young, who raised fifteen acres of corn, fifteen hogs, and half as many cattle, apparently had little incentive to expand their farms. What little surplus they did produce was typically exchanged in neighboring villages or in the county seats of Harrisonville or Butler.[18]

In spite of the area's remoteness, Ball and many other commercially minded farmers found themselves drawn to widening regional markets. George Douglass, for example, capitalized on his trading contracts with Fort Scott to build an extensive mixed-grain, livestock business of nearly seven hundred animals.[19] Even after the fort was closed, Douglass remained a wealthy trader of horses, asses, cattle, and hay, in addition to his endeavors as a land speculator. North Carolina immigrant Jerry Jackson owned the second-largest stock-breeding operation in Bates County,

16. Author's sample, U.S. Bureau of the Census, Manuscript Census, Missouri, Bates and Cass Counties, Schedule II (Agriculture), 1850, hereinafter cited as Census-Ag.

17. Bates County Old Settlers Society, *Old Settlers' History*, 35–36.

18. Gerard Schultz, "Steamboat Navigation on the Osage River before the Civil War"; Schroeder, "Populating Missouri, 1804–1821," 289.

19. Census-Ag, Missouri, Bates and Cass Counties, 1850, 1860. In 1850, Douglass owned 50 horses, 50 asses, 110 milk cows, 16 oxen, 550 beef cattle, 20 sheep, and 200 hogs.

although it was barely one-fourth the size of Douglass's ranch. The two most valuable farms in Cass County belonged to James M. Simpson and Violine Fleming, and were likewise devoted to livestock feeding. These four farms were the Osage country's most profitable early examples of the commercial mixed-grain and livestock farming that later became known as Corn Belt agriculture.[20]

All of these profit-minded farmers were also linked by another notable factor: they were among the small number of slave owners along the western border. These slaveholding farmers were not the first people in the area to own human chattel, as the Osages and French had engaged in the trade of Indian slaves more than a century earlier. In 1850, few households in Bates and Cass Counties owned slaves, and the average slaveholding was small, at just over three. Slaves constituted only a small proportion (9.6 percent) of the border area's population, compared with 13 percent statewide and as much as 30 percent in some counties along the Missouri River. There was a predictably strong link between wealth, nativity, and slave ownership, that is, slave masters were likely to have been born in the South and to possess more wealth than their non-slave-owning neighbors. Although the border's largest slave owners—Douglass, Jackson, Fleming, Simpson, William Palmer, and Hannah Tarkington—were all southerners by birth, some prominent masters like Cecil Ball had emigrated from the free states of the North.[21]

Most slave-owning households in the Osage valley bore little resemblance to the large plantations of the Deep South, where the intensive production of cash crops like cotton and tobacco relied on large numbers of slave laborers. Historians customarily distinguish the planter class as those households that owned twenty or more slaves, yet only one person along the border—George Douglass, who owned two dozen slaves—met this statistical threshold.[22] The few details that can be gleaned about his slaves illustrate the labor demands of the largest farms on the Missouri frontier. Seven of Douglass's slaves were adult males, ranging in age from twenty to forty-five; four were adult women, all in their twenties, and the remaining thirteen slaves were children under the age of ten. The

20. John C. Hudson, *Making the Corn Belt: A Geographical History of Middle-Western Agriculture*, 7.

21. Author's sample, U.S. Bureau of the Census, Manuscript Census, Missouri, Bates and Cass Counties, Slave Schedules, 1850, hereinafter cited as Census-Slave. For the significance of slavery in moving farmers from subsistence to commercial production, as well as the disproportionate influence of slave owners in antebellum Missouri, see Hurt, *Agriculture and Slavery*, 222.

22. Ira Berlin, *Many Thousands Gone: The First Two Centuries of Slavery in North America*, 8–13.

men were likely expected to perform the same kinds of manual tasks, such as working in the fields or tending to livestock, that a hired hand would do. Several characteristics of the plantation system, most notably the hierarchical organization of slave labor and the clear separation of blacks' and whites' social worlds, were foreign to frontier agriculture, as slaves often worked side by side with their masters. Such close proximity also extended from the fields to the home, where slave women also produced domestic goods, such as homespun cloth, and performed multiple household tasks, such as laundry, cleaning, and cooking. Such efforts often made it possible for white women to focus on child care and the production of domestic goods. Some masters hired out their slaves to neighboring farms; Robert D. Means sent his slave, Jim, to work for James and Allen Ellis at a charge of forty-five dollars per year. Others, like slave-owning merchant Frank Chilton, may have employed slave labor in nonagricultural capacities.[23]

Slaves were a means to multiple ends for their Missouri owners. Although human chattel surely increased farm output, helping many households move from subsistence production to commercial agriculture, slave ownership also was a clear expression of power and status within a dynamic frontier society.[24] It was the ownership of slaves, as much as the wealth generated by his mill, store, and lucrative speculative developments, that marked Ball as a person of wealth and influence. He owned five slaves in 1850—an adult woman and three grown men, as well as a young boy. This number was dwarfed by the holdings of a great many families in the cotton South but was still larger than that of almost every other slave owner on the western border. New England birth had made Ball a statistical minority in a rural society in which the sons and daughters of Kentucky, Virginia, and Tennessee predominated; the possession of slaves marked him as one of its elite. In a dynamic and patriarchal frontier society populated largely by southern emigrants, slave ownership was a mark of ascendance, proof positive of a man's achievement and authority.[25]

Few border settlers owned slaves in 1850, a fact that enhanced the elite standing of area masters. For every Cass County household that owned

23. Census-Slave, Missouri, Bates and Cass Counties, 1850; Miscellaneous Papers, Slavery File, 1860, Vernon County Historical Society, hereinafter cited as VCHS. For a discussion of nonagricultural slave labor, see Meinig, *Shaping of America*, 309–10.

24. For a deft explication of the economic, social, and ideological significance of slave ownership and "ascendance" in antebellum Missouri, see Christopher Phillips, *Missouri's Confederate: Claiborne Fox Jackson and the Creation of Southern Identity in the Border West*, 39–52.

25. Census-Slave, Missouri, Bates County, 1850.

slaves that year, there were ten more that did not; to the south, in Bates County, only one in twenty households owned slaves.[26] These counties and others that lined the Missouri border were among the last sparsely settled places where westering masters could legally immigrate with their slaves. A great many slaveholders, along with those who aspired to such status, located near this frontier because it afforded such opportunity. Even so, economic considerations limited the proportion of slaveholding households. Most settlers lacked the means to become a slave owner at the midpoint of the nineteenth century. The average total wealth of households in Bates and Cass Counties was less than five hundred dollars, or just below the cost of an adult slave. Yet over the next decade, as border settlers saw their personal wealth double and even triple, many more households joined the class of local slaveholders and thereby demonstrated that chattel bondage was expanding along, not receding from, the border.[27]

Slavery's expansion during the 1850s evinced both popular acceptance of the institution and many white settlers' interest in becoming masters themselves. Statewide census figures obscured the spread of slavery along the western border. Missouri's total population had swelled in the decades that followed statehood, but the proportion of African American residents had actually declined from 18 percent in 1830 to 10 percent thirty years later. In the Osage valley, meanwhile, slavery was gaining a stronger foothold. The number of slaves employed and their value continued to grow from 1830 to 1860. During the last decade, both the number of slaves and the percentage of households that owned slaves doubled in Bates and Cass Counties. Immigrants from the Upper South, most of them owning a single slave, fueled much of this increase. The average slaveholding in border counties increased slightly but still remained relatively small. The border's wealthiest master, George Douglass, was again a notable exception; his slaveholding increased from twenty-four to thirty-eight. Taken together, this evidence demonstrates that by the end of the 1850s, the peculiar institution was an expanding—not vanishing—part of society in the Osage valley.[28]

26. Ibid., Bates and Cass Counties, Slave Schedule, 1850.

27. Census-Pop, Missouri, Bates and Cass Counties, 1850, 1860. In 1850, the average value of households in Bates and Cass Counties was $309 and $490, respectively; ten years later, it jumped to $865 and $1,537. Median property values experienced a similarly large increase, going from $150 to $400 in Bates and from $240 to $600 in Cass. Slave owners at the 1855 Lexington Convention estimated the value of western Missouri's 50,000 slaves at $25 million; these figures put the average price of slaves at around $500. See *Liberty Weekly Tribune*, July 20, 1855.

28. Hudson, *Making the Corn Belt*, 118; Census-Slave, Missouri, Bates, Cass, and Vernon Counties, 1850, 1860.

Many of the poor whites who had not joined the growing ranks of Missouri slaveholders found no reason to question their neighbors' enslavement of African American men, women, and children. Racial prejudice linked masters and non–slave owners in common ideological cause and provided the foundation upon which white settlers constructed their identities as independent men. Racism pervaded nearly every corner of the United States, but it assumed a singular potency in slave states such as Missouri, where it shaped how whites looked upon both their human chattel and themselves. From the vantage point of proslavery whites, race, not economic class, was the primary mark of an individual's status. Even though vast differences in wealth separated masters and poor whites, their shared skin color rendered them political equals. That only degraded blacks were slaves further reinforced this privileged status.[29]

This white man's democracy—and that it truly was, denying political equality to either women or blacks—offered limited room for black liberty. The will drafted by Vernon County settler James Moore reveals how the discretion of local whites shaped the boundary between slavery and freedom for African Americans. Moore stipulated that his lone slave, Anthony, was to be freed only if he "behaves himself." If the executors of Moore's estate determined that he had behaved badly, Anthony would be sold back into slavery for the rest of his life. Despite a paucity of records relating to manumission in western Missouri, it is evident that very few free blacks lived along the border, for the 1860 census counted only thirteen among a combined three-county population of almost twenty-two thousand. The tiny minority who lived in the area found their lives circumscribed by white authorities. Freedman David Mitchell, for example, was required by law to petition the county court in Butler for permission to live in Bates County. Mitchell gained legal authorization to settle there only after paying a sizable bond and presenting a reliable witness who could attest to the rectitude of his character.[30]

The economic boom that had spurred slavery's expansion was itself fueled by the Missouri border's role as the jumping-off point for western expansion. The Santa Fe, California, and Oregon Trails all originated near the state's western boundary, and the trailhead at Independence, a town that was a day's ride from the Osage River, developed a thriving trade among merchants, outfitters, freighters, and overland emigrants. The estab-

29. Cecil-Fronsman, "'Death to All Yankees,'" 144–45; Drew Gilpin Faust, *The Creation of Confederate Nationalism: Ideology and Identity in the Civil War South,* 10; Eric Foner, *Free Soil, Free Labor, Free Men: The Ideology of the Republican Party before the Civil War,* 261–86.

30. Moore Papers, Slavery File, VCHS; Bates County Court, Minutes, 1858.

lishment of the earliest Texas cattle trails, one of which cut a northeasterly swath across the Osage plains, proved to be a boon for Missouri livestock traders. Border settler Jonathan Newberry recalled that the cattle trade between Missouri farmers and California emigrants brought "thousands of dollars of gold coin" into local hands, thereby bringing "prosperous times" to the area.[31] At the same time, hundreds of Missouri settlers joined the frenzied quest for gold in the hills and streams of California. Most adventurers failed to uncover the mineral wealth they set out to find. "Like many others fortune failed to smile upon me in that country," wrote miner-cum-physician R. H. Hogan. "Consequently I had to resort to something for a living and thought the practice of medicine would suit me as well as anything else." D. C. Hunter's experiences in California had a lasting imprint upon his Missouri community. The county clerk was so impressed by his time in Nevada City that he suggested it as the name for the town that would become the seat of Vernon County, and the name stuck.[32]

The lure of ever greater opportunity reshaped the population of the western border, drawing new families to the region and encouraging others to move on. The westering journeys of the Cockrill family testify to the dynamic character of the area's fluid population. Traveling as a family, the Cockrills emigrated from Kentucky to the country that would become Bates County sometime around 1839. Barely ten years later, James Cockrill, a recently widowed thirty-seven-year-old laborer, joined his brothers-in-law, Henry Beaver and William Boyd Hagans, and set out with William's son, Oscar, for the gold fields of California. The group's efforts at provisioning hungry miners with beef proved successful, and the Hagans established ranches near Sacramento and Petaluma, just to the north of San Francisco Bay. After making repeated trips to and from Missouri, returning with a herd of cattle to supplement the Hagans' inferior Spanish stock, James fell ill and died of smallpox. In the spring of 1853, however, a party of 125 individuals from the neighborhood of Pleasant Gap, led by the Hagans and James's younger brother, Larkin, departed from the border town of West Point for California. Five months later, the party arrived nearly entirely intact before its members dispersed to individual homesteads throughout northern California.[33]

31. Bates County Old Settlers Society, *Old Settlers' History*, 122.
32. Hogan to Albert Badger, September 23, 1852, Badger Papers, VCHS; J. Johnson, *History of Vernon County*, 438. Local voters shortened the town's name to Nevada in 1869.
33. For details about the California experiences of the Cockrill family and its traveling party, I am indebted to Larry Wendt, who made much of his genealogical research, including William H. Zilhart, "Ledger of My Travels from Missouri to California," 1853, available on his Web page, http://cotati.sjsu.edu/cockrill/Home.html. Census-Pop, Missouri, Bates County, 1850.

Although some families were willing to make the arduous thousand-mile trek across the continental interior, other would-be emigrants set their sights just beyond the state line. Existing laws, however, prohibited permanent settlement in this territory, which had been set aside for various Native American tribes who had been removed from eastern states. With no place for westering migrants to settle legally short of California or Oregon, the Missouri border became, as one geographer describes it, a demographic dam that held back the swelling tide of an expanding American population.[34] What's more, the Missouri Compromise had long ago stamped the western border as the legal margin of the slave-holding frontier. Under the terms of that agreement, which covered the vast territory acquired in the Louisiana Purchase, Congress declared that slavery was legal within the new state of Missouri but forbidden above its southern boundary of 36° 30'.

Political pressure to open the unorganized "Nebraska country," as contemporaries described the broad grassland stretching northward from Texas, came from a variety of sources besides westering migrants. Its principal supporters were advocates of the myriad proposals to establish a transcontinental railroad through the region. This group included Stephen A. Douglas, an Illinois Democrat who had helped to secure the passage of the Compromise of 1850 and who hoped to see Chicago become the terminus for a transcontinental route. When Douglas presented a bill providing for the organization of Kansas and Nebraska Territories before the Senate Committee on Territories in January 1854, he understood the success of the measure depended on the support of his party's powerful southern delegation, which was likely to oppose the formation of new free territories. Eager to maintain peace between the competing sectional interests in his own party, he therefore agreed to extend popular sovereignty to the territories and thereby abandon the Missouri Compromise. Most southerners, doubtful that slavery would take root in either Kansas or Nebraska, reacted with ambivalence to Douglas's concession because they realized that if a large number of slaves were to be brought into the new territories, they would come with owners from Missouri.[35]

Missourians, especially those living in the state's western counties, had long taken an interest in the development of the adjacent territories. Profit-minded citizens maintained that a transcontinental railroad, which would

34. Schroeder, "Populating Missouri, 1804–1821," 292.
35. Morrison, *Slavery and the West*, 45–52, 110–25; David Potter, *The Impending Crisis, 1848–1861*, 157; David D. March, *The History of Missouri*, 2:841.

be preferably routed through this central corridor via St. Louis, would benefit the state's farmers and businessmen. With no natural boundary separating the Kansas Territory from the Osage plains of western Missouri, this was an attractive country through which the Missouri Pacific Railroad could expand. Local farmers also recognized the agricultural potential of the area just beyond the open state line and saw few geographic differences between its undulating grasslands and wooded valleys and their own fertile country. Those who had passed through the land that would become eastern Kansas understood that it scarcely resembled the "great American desert" described by traveler Stephen Long. Missouri politicians likewise saw the development of the neighboring territories to be an attractive political issue. Douglas's bill received nearly unanimous support from the state's congressional representatives.[36]

The enduring popularity of proslavery politicians such as David Rice Atchison reflected Missourians' keen interest regarding the status of slavery in the western territories. Atchison himself owned only one servant, but his fierce defense of slaveholders' liberties elicited broad approval from common whites and masters alike. The Platte County senator and his constituents understood that should slavery be permanently excluded from Kansas, as it had been in Illinois and Iowa, and as the 1821 compromise had ordained, the slave state of Missouri would be surrounded by free soil on three of its four sides. Many slaveholders in western Missouri resented having another free-soil boundary and regarded the prospect of a free Kansas, where slaves could quickly escape to freedom, and the presence of slave-stealing abolitionists as a real threat to their economic interests. The state legislature had passed a resolution in January 1849 supporting the abrogation of the Missouri Compromise and in favor of "squatter sovereignty."[37] Such a measure not only aimed to protect the rights and interests of a defensive slave-owning society but also affirmed a commitment to local self-government that resonated strongly with citizens of the Jacksonian era. Old-stock settlers in western Missouri identified so strongly with the western expansion of slavery that just months after former president Martin Van Buren was nominated as a Free-Soil candidate in 1848, they renamed Van Buren County after Democratic standard-bearer Lewis Cass.[38] The principle of popular sovereignty, as

36. William E. Parrish, *David Rice Atchison of Missouri: Border Politician*, 86–93; Jay Monaghan, *Civil War on the Western Border, 1854–1865*, 4.

37. Phillips, *Missouri's Confederate*, 182–84; F. Shoemaker, "Missouri's Proslavery Fight," 222–23.

38. O. P. Williams, *The History of Cass and Bates Counties, Missouri*, 93–95. For the organization of the Free-Soil Party, see Foner, *Free Soil*, 152–53.

Atchison, Cass, and other Democrats well understood, appealed to democratic sensibilities of western settlers by promoting the virtue of local decision making. Breaking from the precedent of congressional intervention set forth in the Northwest Ordinance and Missouri Compromise, popular sovereignty recognized the ability and right of western citizens to decide their affairs for themselves.[39]

After months of impassioned congressional debate, President Franklin Pierce signed Douglas's bill, the Kansas-Nebraska Act, on May 30, 1854. The act passed through the Senate by a margin of 37 to 14, but the narrow vote in the House, where the bill was approved 113 to 100, revealed the nation's sharp political divisions. The abrogation of the Missouri Compromise outraged abolitionists and other northern leaders who had considered its latitudinal boundary of 36°30' a sacrosanct principle of sectional cooperation. It also intensified antislavery sentiments among northerners, driving many free-soil Democrats into the ranks of the new Republican Party. Opponents of slavery regarded the extension of popular sovereignty to the Kansas and Nebraska Territories as a challenge from the slaveholding South, and William Seward, an antislavery senator from New York, framed the terms of the ensuing struggle when he declared, "Come on, then, gentlemen of the Slave States; since there is no escaping your challenge, I accept it in behalf of the cause of freedom. We will engage in competition for the virgin soil of Kansas, and God give the victory to the side that is stronger in numbers as it is in right."[40] For all of their rhetorical zeal, Seward and his peers could not have easily foreseen the viciousness of the conflict that was set to unfold a thousand miles to their west.

Born from the opening of a closed geopolitical boundary, this conflict was at first partisan and demographic in nature, a contest to be determined by the side, slave or free-soil, that could send the most settlers to Kansas. On a most basic level, it was a struggle to control territory, and there would be a clear economic basis to the disputes between many immigrants. At the same time, differences over slavery magnified otherwise mundane quarrels over land and resources into bloody conflicts.[41] In the period that followed the opening of Kansas Territory, the untold fights that originated over settlers' rights to land, water, and livestock mirrored the quarrels over basic resources that had accompanied the settlement of

39. Morrison, *Slavery and the West*, 99–123; Nicole Etcheson, "The Great Principle of Self-Government: Popular Sovereignty and Bleeding Kansas," 16–17.

40. Potter, *Impending Crisis*, 160–77. See also Oates, *Purge This Land*, 80–82.

41. Malin, *John Brown*, 498; March, *The History of Missouri*, 2:848–57; Miner, *Kansas*, 54–58.

other frontier areas, including western Missouri. The battle for Kansas that was waged among settlers, squatters, speculators, and rival town companies often resembled the competition for land that invariably followed the spread of the settlement frontier.[42] Yet in the headlong rush to settle Kansas, the fight over rights to land and water involved much more than that; for many pioneers, the opportunity to establish a successful claim represented a chance to strike a political blow for the cause of slavery or freedom, depending on a settler's point of view. The competition for Kansas, as the people who waged it understood, was an opportunity to help settle the divisive political question that had cleaved Americans into antagonistic proslavery and antislavery sections. Ideological, economic, and personal motivations were often therefore overlapping and inseparable parts of the Kansas conflict. Partisans on each side believed that this struggle involved more than a contested boundary between slavery and freedom; indeed, it amounted to a fight for the political, moral, and economic future of both the West and the entire republic.[43]

Distressed by the repeal of the Missouri Compromise, northern antislavery activists attempted to seize an early advantage in mobilizing for the settlement contest. Weeks before Douglas's legislation was signed into law, northerners had already organized several emigrant-aid companies to foster Kansas's development as a free territory. On April 26, 1854, the Massachusetts legislature approved the charter for the most famous of these groups, the Massachusetts Emigrant Aid Company (later renamed the New England Emigrant Aid Company) and set its capital stock at a maximum of five million dollars. Led by Eli Thayer, the company sprang forth from a fusion of ideological and economic motivations, as it merged antislavery sentiment with the speculative aspirations of frontier land development. Thayer hoped that an infusion of New England homesteaders, reaching perhaps twenty thousand emigrants per year, and the establishment of planned Yankee communities not only would serve to advance the free-soil movement in the West but also would return a handsome profit to the company's stockholders in the East. The swift formation of other well-organized and -financed associations in New York and

---

42. Kevin J. Abing, "Before Bleeding Kansas: Christian Missionaries, Slavery, and the Shawnee Indians in Pre-territorial Kansas, 1844–1854," 69; Miner, *Kansas*, 57. Among works that emphasize the importance of economic factors in the Kansas conflict, the most outstanding are still Malin, *John Brown*; and Paul Wallace Gates, *Fifty Million Acres: Conflicts over Kansas Land Policy, 1854–1890*. For another work that supports this position, see G. Murlin Welch, *Border Warfare in Southeastern Kansas, 1856–1859*.

43. Morrison, *Slavery and the West*, 151–65.

Washington, D.C., indicated the determination of antislavery interests to seize a quick victory for the cause of freedom in Kansas.[44]

Although northeastern emigration societies provided only a minor portion of the early settlers in Kansas—the territorial census of 1855 shows that New England natives composed just 4.3 percent of the population—their influence clearly outweighed what their limited numbers suggested.[45] To attract settlers to a largely undeveloped area, these associations carried out the basic promotional function of spreading information about its climate, soils, topography, and market prospects in florid terms. What distinguished the promotions put forth by antislavery societies from those of other emigrant companies, of course, was the fervor and ideological nature of their message. In fact, the success of the antislavery organizations resulted in part from their ability to propagandize the settlement of Kansas as a contest between divergent and antagonistic civilizations. They celebrated the free-soil effort and the transplantation of northern schools, churches, and industry as a nineteenth-century recapitulation of a familiar American narrative of progress. Northern colonizers hoped that by re-creating the very best elements of a free society, they would give Kansas an identity that was sharply different from the slave state of Missouri. Antislavery settlers and writers were quick to denigrate Missourians as backward "pukes" who embodied the cultural and moral decay that had been wrought by slavery and that now threatened the western territories. Such contrary portrayals of free-soil and proslavery societies framed the basic terms of the Kansas conflict for many northerners.[46]

The free-soil ideology involved both a sharp critique of slavery and a parallel affirmation of the North's own dynamic capitalist society. The attack on human bondage and the southern society that it supported was grounded in both moral revulsion of slavery and northerners' own values and attitudes toward work. Slavery, its opponents contended, was not only brutally inhumane but also an inherently flawed system of labor that degraded slaves and denied them any fruits of their labor. Free-soil critics also maintained that the dignity of hard work, so celebrated and rewarded in the industrializing North, was not appreciated in the slaveholding

44. F. Shoemaker, "Missouri's Proslavery Fight," 226–27; Monaghan, *Civil War*, 6; Potter, *Impending Crisis*, 199–201.

45. Nicole Etcheson, *Bleeding Kansas: Contested Liberty in the Civil War Era*, 37.

46. For northern image making in Kansas, see Gunja SenGupta, *For God and Mammon: Evangelicals and Entrepreneurs, Masters and Slaves in Kansas, 1854–1860*, 3–4, 80–91. For negative stereotypes of Missourians developed by opponents of slavery, see Michael Fellman, *Inside War: The Guerrilla Conflict in Missouri during the American Civil War*, 21–22. Myres discusses similar stereotypes among westering migrants (*Westering Women*, 98–130).

South, where manual labor carried a heavy racial stigma. Furthermore, poor white farmers faced limited opportunities for advancement within a slave economy. Adherents of the free-soil ideology feared that the extension of human chattel into Kansas would threaten the economic independence of farmers and laborers who would be locked in unfair competition against masters who exploited and degraded their slaves. Antislavery settlers in Kansas thus hoped to confine chattel bondage within its previous boundaries, behind the Missouri border.[47]

As ardent opponents of slavery, John Everett and his wife, Sarah, were typical of early abolitionist settlers in Kansas. Each came from a family of outspoken antislavery leanings. John's father, Robert, was a Congregational minister who had published a Welsh translation of *Uncle Tom's Cabin* and a magazine, *Y Cenhadwr Americanaidd* (The American Messenger), that promoted parallel reforms of abolition and prohibition. Inspired by the urgency of the antislavery effort in Kansas, the young couple abandoned their original plans of settling in Minnesota in order to assist the free-soil cause to the south. The initial journey to Kansas began inauspiciously, and John Everett described the slow passage from St. Louis to Kansas City in the fall of 1854 as "the most unpleasant 4 days I ever journeyed." Like other eastern immigrants, he was struck by the peculiar nature of western people. Some looked upon these backcountry inhabitants with both regard and contempt; Pennsylvanian Joseph Trego, for example, noted, "They are very clever folks and as pleasant as they can be, but they are of the 'Hoosier' stripe and of course not company for us." Among the eastern natives who managed to pick up the frontier dialect was New Yorker J. S. West, who would later write, "I had to learn the Kansas language, and found that a pail was a bucket, afternoon was evening, sunrise was sunup, bread was light bread, hot biscuits was bread, Johnny cake was corn bread, a fish spear a gig, a spider a skillet, and a ramrod a gunstick."[48]

Everett, however, found the unrefined behavior of Missourians especially jarring. "I do not remember hearing a man speak on the boat whose conversation I watched at all who did not swear," he wrote to his brother, Robert. "The cabin presented a continual scene of card playing from beginning to end." At the same time, the Everetts marveled at the ability of Missourians and other westerners to "settle right down, build their

---

47. Foner, *Free Soil*, 4–15, 47–59.

48. John Everett and Sarah Everett, "Letters of John and Sarah Everett, 1854–1864, Miami County Pioneers," 4 (letter of John Everett to Robert Everett, October 21, 1854); Trego, "The Letters of Joseph H. Trego, 1857–1864, Linn County Pioneer," 117; J. S. West, "Early Days in Drywood," 353.

cabins, fence and break up their fields and drop their corn, before you hardly know they are here." Upon establishing their claim, the antislavery couple found themselves better suited to frontier life than many other emigrants from the Northeast. At least half of the "Eastern people," by their estimate, left Kansas within months of arriving, unaccustomed to the rigors and necessities of living in the West.[49]

The influx and rapid departure of such antislavery immigrants confirmed Missourians' darkest suspicions about eastern abolitionists' intentions for Kansas. From a proslavery perspective, newcomers who relied on the assistance of emigrant-aid companies were dependent men who had no legitimate rights in Kansas Territory. The writings of Benjamin Stringfellow, editor of the stridently partisan *Squatter Sovereign* newspaper, typified the characterizations of such "hirelings." Emigrant-aid colonists, he wrote, "are mostly ignorant of agriculture, picked up in cities and villages, they of course have no experience as farmers, and if left to their unaided resources—if not clothed and fed by the same power which has effected their transportation—they would starve." Productive property was a necessary element of personal independence and republican virtue; people who did not own and could not improve their property were neither honorable, independent, nor manly.[50]

Proslavery critics spared the great many free-soil immigrants who came to Kansas on their own accord without receiving a dollar of emigrant aid–company support. These settlers came primarily from the free states of the Ohio valley and, as native westerners, were generally better acquainted with the demands of frontier life and agriculture than their Yankee peers. Some Missourians declared themselves ready to accept free-state emigrants who, unlike abolitionists and "hirelings," were industrious, self-reliant, and, most important, respectful of slaveholders' rights. "If Kansas could be peopled by honest citizens of the free States," wrote Stringfellow, "and if it were made a free State by such people, who were always willing to protect the rights of their neighbors, the Country, would have nothing to fear."[51]

49. Everett and Everett, "Letters of John and Sarah Everett," 4, 25 (John Everett to Robert Everett, October 21, 1854; John Everett to Father, January 25, 1855).

50. Quote from Cecil-Fronsman, "'Death to All Yankees,'" 148; Christopher Phillips, "'The Crime against Missouri': Slavery, Kansas, and the Cant of Southernness in the Border West," 73; Kristen Tegtmeier Oertel, "'The Free Sons of the North' versus 'The Myrmidons of Border-Ruffianism': What Makes a Man in Bleeding Kansas?" 176–84; James C. Malin, "The Proslavery Background of the Kansas Struggle," 286–94; F. Shoemaker, "Missouri's Proslavery Fight," 230–31.

51. Cecil-Fronsman, "'Death to All Yankees,'" 146.

Missouri residents, for their part, had demonstrated a facility for identifying and claiming the best lands in eastern Kansas well before the territory was formally opened in the spring of 1854. In the country south of present-day Kansas City, where no natural barrier inhibited entry into Kansas, many individuals had easily slipped across the state line to establish illegal claims on the adjacent Indian reserves. Missouri settlers had long regarded the territory to the west as their own special domain, and, with no obstacles to stop them from breaching the permanent frontier, many people traveled, hunted, and traded with the soldiers and Indians across the western border. By the summer of 1854, many of the Missourians who were intimately familiar with this neighboring country moved quickly to capitalize on the decisive advantage that geographic proximity afforded them. The reduced presence of eastern Indian tribes, which were relocated yet again through a new series of federal treaties, was more an inconvenience than a legal or physical threat to white squatters. The process of staking a claim for many would-be settlers was itself quite simple. Some Missourians were content to carve notches on nearby trees, position a few rails on the ground, and post a notice warning that potential trespassers might be shot.[52]

Missourians feared that free-soil settlers were not content to deny slaveholders' liberties in Kansas but instead would undermine them east of the border, either by assisting fugitives or by invading the state to steal slaves themselves. More than two hundred slave owners converged upon the Missouri town of Lexington in July 1855 to express their outrage at the gathering antislavery threat. Attendees came from twenty-six counties; Cass sent thirteen participants, two of whom, W. H. Russell and Gilford D. Hansborough, were elected to leadership positions. The eighth resolution passed at the Lexington convention illuminated the dangers its members saw in their zealous free-soil neighbors. The slave property of western Missouri, they declared, was "not merely unsafe but valueless, if Kansas is made the abode of an army of hired fanatics, recruited, transported, armed and paid for the special and sole purpose of abolitionising Kansas and Missouri." A local newspaper affirmed the convention's opposition to the "mad schemes of abolitionists" and its determination to "act harmoniously together . . . and refrain from any lawless proceedings."[53]

Although unburdened by masters' financial anxieties, nonslaveholders shared their open hostility toward "fanatical" abolitionists. Racist

---

52. Malin, "Proslavery Background," 286–94; F. Shoemaker, "Missouri's Proslavery Fight," 230–31; March, *The History of Missouri*, 2:842.

53. *Liberty Weekly Tribune*, July 20, 1855; Phillips, *Missouri's Confederate*, 204.

sensibilities and antislavery assertions of moral superiority over southerners strengthened the bond between slaveholders and poor whites in Missouri. Many poor farmers defended slavery because they believed that an institution with such clear racial boundaries—after the dispossession of the Osages, only black people were held in bondage—preserved their own tenuous status in society. Slavery was the cornerstone of a racially based social hierarchy that put common whites on an equal political footing with wealthy slaveholders. Any threat to slavery was thus a danger to the egalitarian standing they enjoyed along the border.[54]

Missouri settlers established secret defensive organizations, such as the Sons of the South, Friends of Society, and Blue Lodges, to protect their claims from encroachment by free-soil immigrants. Families who were unwilling to emigrate but nonetheless wished to see Kansas become a proslavery territory also worked to support these organizations. In Vernon County, the "stay-at-home" council formed by fifty Nevada residents joined nearby groups in Balltown and Montevallo to send money, arms, and ammunition across the state line. Missourians also established emigrant-aid societies, much like their northern antislavery counterparts, that would assist settlers in relocating to Kansas.[55]

Proslavery settlers in Kansas dominated the territory's earliest elections, yet their questionable tactics triggered an immediate backlash, and thus began a seemingly endless drama of electoral controversy and confusion. The earliest controversies stemmed from disputes about the legal requirement that eligible voters needed to be residents of Kansas, as citizens disagreed sharply about the exact definition of "residence." Settlers who held a narrow construction of the law believed that eligibility required clear proof of residence, but proving ownership of real property remained somewhat problematic, as various Indian tribes still held legal title to land within the new territory. Other people maintained that only permanent settlers had the right to vote. Many individuals, however, insisted that an intention to settle, rather than actual proof, was a sufficient measure of residence, and voters therefore needed to spend only a few moments in Kansas and profess their intent to remain in order to be eligible.

In the election to decide Kansas's delegate to Congress, which was held on November 29, 1854, proslavery candidate J. W. Whitfield, who had recently lived across the border in Jackson County, Missouri, received 2,258 of the 2,833 votes cast. Whitfield owed his striking margin

54. Cecil-Fronsman, "'Death to All Yankees,'" 144–45; Morrison, *Slavery and the West*, 4–5, 115.

55. J. Johnson, *History of Vernon County*, 225.

of victory to the estimated 1,700 Missourians who had come into the territory on the day before and the day of the election in order to cast their votes. Although some of these voters were new arrivals who had come to Kansas with an intention to settle, others returned across the border soon after casting their ballot. Whitfield probably would have won without the participation of nonresident voters, as proslavery settlers outnumbered free-soil residents at the time.[56]

The next election, in which Kansas voters chose their representatives for the territorial legislature, proved more consequential than the first. On March 29, 1855—the day before the election—a large body of armed Missourians, led by Senator David Rice Atchison and future governor Claiborne Fox Jackson, crossed into Kansas, determined to elect a solidly proslavery majority. The territorial census, which had been conducted a month before the election, put the territorial population at 8,600. Of that total, 2,905 were eligible to vote, but in the final tally some 6,307 votes were cast, with 5,427 going to proslavery candidates. Between four and five thousand Missourians cast votes, with some claiming to be Kansas residents and many others again making no such pretense. The results from the Fort Scott electoral district, where there were only 100 legal voters, further illustrated the magnitude of the electoral fraud that was apparently carried out by proslavery voters. Proslavery candidates S. A. Williams and J. C. Anderson were elected with 315 votes apiece, whereas their free-soil opponents, John Hamilton and William Margraves, each received just 35 votes.[57]

Outraged free-soil settlers denounced the egregious behavior that led to results that they considered fraudulent. Witnesses claimed to have seen Missourians vote repeatedly, donning different hats and coats to change their appearances while election judges turned a blind, and perhaps complicit, eye. Proslavery voters in some districts reportedly used threats of violence to intimidate free-soil partisans and thereby suppressed the turnout for antislavery candidates. Accusations and examples of voting irregularities and outright fraud were not unique to Kansas Territory, however, and instead afflicted elections throughout antebellum America, especially in frontier districts where citizens from different regional backgrounds clashed over standards of acceptable civic decorum.[58]

Territorial governor Andrew H. Reeder, who had been appointed by President Pierce, struggled to defuse the free-soil outcry that followed the

56. Ibid., 223; Etcheson, *Bleeding Kansas,* 54.
57. J. Johnson, *History of Vernon County,* 223; F. Shoemaker, "Missouri's Proslavery Fight," 326–29.
58. Etcheson, "Great Principle," 16–20.

March vote. Reeder certified the election results from most of the districts despite the widespread evidence of vote fraud, but responded to free-soil protests of electoral impropriety by ordering that a special election be held in May for six districts. Missourians abstained from this election, recognizing that the legislature's proslavery majority could later remove any free-soil candidates elected in the six disputed districts. After free-soil candidates had indeed been elected, the territorial legislature, once it convened in July, voided the May results and instead seated the proslavery members-elect who had been chosen in March. Days later, the three remaining free-soil representatives resigned, giving proslavery forces unanimous control of the Kansas legislature.[59]

Thanks to the Kansas-Nebraska Act, legislators in Kansas enjoyed a greater degree of self-government than authorities in previous territories. In addition to letting settlers choose between slavery and freedom, the act also exempted the territorial legislation passed in Kansas from congressional approval.[60] Unencumbered by the oversight of authorities in Washington, D.C., the proslavery legislature quickly enacted several policies that further aggravated free-soil settlers. One of the first acts of the "Bogus Legislature," as the body became known to its critics, was the wholesale adoption of the revised laws of Missouri, in which it simply substituted the words *Kansas* for *Missouri* and *Territory* for *State*. Having adopted Missouri's slave statutes, the legislature also implemented a slave code that was even more severe than the recently passed federal Fugitive Slave Act. Albert Richardson, an Englishman traveling through the West, described the punitive elements of the territory's harsh slave code, writing, "They made it an offense punishable by death to harbor or assist runaway slaves and rendered any man, woman, or child, circulating anti-slavery publications, or denying the right to hold slaves in the Territory liable to imprisonment for five years." In addition to disqualifying antislavery citizens as jurors in slavery suits-at-law, the code also disfranchised individuals who refused to take an oath supporting the fugitive slave law or the Kansas-Nebraska Act. A proviso that all local officials were to be appointed by the legislature—and not elected locally—further reinforced the legalized persecution of free-soil settlers.[61]

The measures of the territorial legislature elicited mixed responses from citizens in Missouri. Slave owners in the state's western counties

---

59. Ibid., 20–21; Holder and Rothman, *Post on the Marmaton*, 75.
60. Etcheson, "Great Principle," 17.
61. Richardson, *Beyond the Mississippi: From the Great River to the Great Ocean*, 41–42; F. Shoemaker, "Missouri's Proslavery Fight," 339; Miner, *Kansas*, 54–55.

approved of the harsh slave code and trusted that it would check any threats to their human property. Other Missourians, including several Whigs and Benton Democrats, deplored the seemingly unlawful excesses of the territorial elections and feared they might bring greater instability to the state's western border. Free-soil emigrants and abolitionist editors were incensed by the behavior of the proslavery partisans, whose electoral shenanigans and legislative abuses had the unintended effect of animating the antislavery cause and stimulating even more free-soil migration. Such actions also eroded the already slim chances for compromise between advocates of slavery and freedom and instead contributed to the early radicalism of the free-state effort in Kansas.[62]

Free-soil emigrants responded to what they regarded as an illegitimate Lecompton administration by framing a rival authority of their own in late 1855. At the convention that met in Topeka, they ratified a constitution that prohibited slavery and arranged for an election to determine the governor and representatives for their own territorial government. Conducted in January 1856, that election—boycotted by proslavery Missourians—witnessed the triumph of gubernatorial nominee Charles Robinson and an entire slate of free-state candidates. Proslavery citizens who described themselves as the Law and Order Party dismissed the Topeka movement as a "treasonable" attempt to subvert popular sovereignty.[63] For free-soil settlers, however, the differences between the two rival governments were clear. John Everett maintained that whereas the "Bogus Legislature was the result of a gigantic and well planned fraud . . . carried by an invading mob," the free-state legislature "was the result of the unbiased and free vote of the people." Not all free-soil emigrants endorsed the Topeka legislature as strongly as Everett. Some vacillating citizens tried to straddle the partisan fence, prepared to support whichever faction triumphed; others believed that forming a rival government might alienate federal officials. Such arguments proved correct, as the extralegal maneuverings of the Topeka faction found limited support in Congress, which denied its petition to enter the Union as a free state.[64]

Free-soil disagreements over the Topeka government illustrated the diversity of the antislavery movement's constituent elements in Kansas. Abolitionists constituted only a small portion of free-soil immigration,

62. Etcheson, *Bleeding Kansas*, 96; March, *The History of Missouri*, 2:844.

63. Etcheson, "Great Principle," 20–21.

64. Everett and Everett, "Letters of John and Sarah Everett," 143 (John Everett to Father, July 10, 1856); Malin, *John Brown*, 113; Monaghan, *Civil War*, 34–46; March, *The History of Missouri*, 2:845. For an insightful analysis of the complexity and diversity of northern antislavery organizations, see SenGupta, *For God and Mammon*, 10–27.

but this powerful and vocal minority, which included Charles Robinson and Amos A. Lawrence, an associate of Eli Thayer and namesake of the free-soil Kansas town, wielded considerable influence over the Topeka convention. Most Kansas emigrants wanted to avoid the stain of political extremism associated with abolitionism. John Everett affirmed this in Osawatomie: "The community here are [sic] very nearly united on the free-state question. But the majority would dislike and resent being called abolitionists." Although free-soil settlers wished to exclude slavery from the territory, their fight was less about abolishing slavery where it existed than it was about preserving the western territories for white Americans of ordinary means. Albert Richardson described such feelings when he suggested that most free-state advocates "warred not against slavery in the abstract, only slavery in Kansas." Many free-state emigrants, Richardson continued, were "frightened by the mere mention of that mysterious specter, 'negro equality.'"[65]

Opposition to slavery did not thus translate into sympathy for African Americans. James Lane, an Indiana native and future Kansas senator, once exclaimed bluntly, "I look upon this nigger question just as I look upon the horse or the jackass question. It is merely a question of dollars and cents." For Lane, the nonextension of slavery became an issue of political expediency, and his assertion of free-soil principles made him one of the most powerful men in Kansas. The proposed Topeka constitution illustrated the paradoxical racial attitudes of its free-state framers, as it not only excluded the scourge of slavery from Kansas but also prohibited free blacks from settling in the territory. The apparent contradiction of these provisions was not lost on antislavery minister Samuel Adair. "Their free soil is free soil for white, but not for the black. They hate slavery, but they hate the Negro worse," wrote Adair. "The ignorance of some of these men is most profound."[66]

The Topeka constitution's "Black Law" reflected the pervasiveness of racism in the trans-Appalachian West. There were several legal precedents for such a discriminatory measure. Laws that provided for the exclusion of free African Americans had found widespread support in Illinois, Indiana, and other western states. In Missouri, the nonenforcement of a constitutional exclusion clause was a necessary, although often

65. Everett and Everett, "Letters of John and Sarah Everett," 25 (John Everett to Father, January 25, 1855); Albert E. Castel, *A Frontier State at War: Kansas, 1861–1865*, 40; Richardson, *Beyond the Mississippi*, 43.

66. SenGupta, *For God and Mammon*, 64. See also William G. Cutler, *History of the State of Kansas*, 2:1102; and Everett and Everett, "Letters of John and Sarah Everett," 25 (John Everett to Father, January 25, 1855).

overlooked, part of the compromises that had secured its admission to the Union. Iowa passed a free-black exclusion bill in 1851, and voters in Illinois and Indiana supported exclusion measures by margins of approximately three to one. Widespread western racism may be attributed to the fluid nature of frontier society. There was likely an economic dimension to the prejudices of white farmers and laborers who wished to avoid competing for land and work with free blacks. White settlers also wished to limit opportunities for advancement by free African Americans, who posed a potential challenge to their own social status and prerogatives.[67] An account published on the editorial page of a Fort Scott newspaper illuminated white anxieties about a racially integrated frontier society. Printed under the headline, "AMALGAMATION," the story detailed the recent visit of a biracial couple who had come to town to reclaim the wife's son, George, who remained in the possession of a local slaveholder. Although the newspaper's publisher was taken aback by the rare appearance of a white husband and a black wife walking along the town's main roads, the spectacle of the husband carrying their mixed-race infant was deemed particularly offensive. "It was," the writer huffed, "a disgusting sight."[68]

The mutual antipathy toward free African Americans that was shared by proslavery and free-soil settlers illuminated the complex role of race in the territorial crisis. The Kansas struggle brought into question the fate and place of African Americans in western society, with one faction endorsing their continued enslavement and the other preferring the general exclusion of blacks—free and slave alike—from the developing territories. Such a question at the same time was inextricably bound with a dispute about which of the rights enjoyed by white Americans would be privileged in the West: the right to own slaves or the right to labor as independent producers, unburdened by the competition of slaveholding peers.[69] The paradoxical similarities of shared racial prejudices did not lessen the fervor of the slavery debate in territorial Kansas, however. The issue of slavery still framed the territory's basic social and political divisions and gave an uncommon intensity to otherwise ordinary disputes.

Missteps by federal lawmakers aggravated the controversies over land that followed the opening of the Kansas Territory and thus increased the

67. Malin, *John Brown*, 512–13; Eugene H. Berwanger, *The Frontier against Slavery: Western Anti-Negro Prejudice and the Slavery Extension Controversy*, 43–45; Foner, *Free Soil*, 261–86; Hudson, *Making the Corn Belt*, 123; SenGupta, *For God and Mammon*, 99–100.

68. *Fort Scott Democrat*, November 3, 1860.

69. Etcheson, *Bleeding Kansas*, 71–79.

likelihood that disagreements could erupt into violent feuds. By the time congressional debate had ended and President Pierce signed the Kansas-Nebraska Act, hundreds of people had already slipped across the state line to establish claims in the new territory. At that moment, however, none of the land in eastern Kansas was actually available for purchase. Most of the territory was still legally owned by the Indian tribes who had been resettled there in an elaborate patchwork of reservations. Returning these lands to federal possession and moving them onto the market required that the U.S. government first surrender its treaty-bound obligations to the Miami, Shawnee, Pottawatomi, and the various confederated tribes who were all scattered throughout eastern Kansas. In dealing with the Osages in Missouri, the government had shown its willingness to forsake existing policy in order to accommodate the expansion of the settlement frontier, and the status of relocated tribes would be only a slight obstacle to the organization of Kansas Territory. Federal authorities finalized the hurried purchase of most of the Indian lands by the end of 1854, and nearly ten thousand Native Americans, their treaties now extinguished, were relocated yet again, to the Indian Territory south of Kansas.[70]

The few Indian reserves that were not promptly dismantled became the setting for some of the territory's most confusing and contentious claim warfare. Some Native Americans were not quick to leave the lands that the government had promised to them, and several continued to live on the reserves allotted to the Miami and the tribes from New York. Although these lands, which lay in the upper Osage valley just across the Missouri line, would not be officially opened for settlement for years, they were quickly overrun with white immigrants, most of them Missourians, by the spring of 1855. Federal authorities ordered these early settlers to withdraw but made few efforts to remove them, perhaps because the recent closing of nearby Fort Scott had made threats of military intervention difficult to enforce. The shrinking number of Native Americans who remained suffered widespread harassment from white squatters, who destroyed the homes of several Miami and drove many others from the territory.[71]

Since clear legal title could not be had until the Kansas lands actually went up for sale, settlers' claims were only as secure as their ability to resist the encroachment of competitors. Like-minded immigrants found

---

70. Cutler, *History of Kansas*, 2:875–76; Gates, *Fifty Million Acres*, 7–15; James A. Rawley, *Race and Politics: "Bleeding Kansas" and the Coming of the Civil War*, 82–83; Abing, "Before Bleeding Kansas," 69.

71. Gates, *Fifty Million Acres*, 27–33; Holder and Rothman, *Post on the Marmaton*, 76.

greater strength in numbers, and settlers' organizations, such as the secretive "dark lantern lodges" of proslavery partisans, helped to defend the claims of their individual members against claim jumpers and trespassing interlopers. Roaming about on horseback, these armed groups also became notorious within free-soil circles for terrorizing newcomers who were suspected of holding antislavery sentiments; in some cases, northern birth was enough to make a person a potential target. Proslavery settlers employed a variety of tactics, including robbery and arson, to intimidate their rivals. In the first few years of Kansas's settlement, proslavery men succeeded in forcing a large number of free-soil immigrants to flee the area, having already gained control of the eastern and most heavily settled part of the territory.[72]

Antislavery critics derided the members of such gangs as "border ruffians," a term that proud Missourians initially disdained. Englishman Thomas Gladstone embraced the term to describe the rough proslavery partisans he encountered on a trip through the territory. The "lawless mob" consisted of "drunken, bellowing, blood-thirsty demons." The men were "for the most part of large frame, with red flannel shirts and immense boots worn outside their trousers, their faces unwashed and unshaven . . . wearing the most savage looks, and giving utterance to the most horrible imprecations and blasphemies; armed, moreover, to the teeth with rifles and revolvers, cutlasses and bowie-knives." Defensive Missouri citizens dismissed the epithet as the mark of condescending outsiders. "We do not deserve this appelation [sic]," claimed Atchison. "Those of us who are called the 'Border Ruffians' are men of property, of education—the best kind of men. We are the men who will submit to no wrong."[73]

Outnumbered by their proslavery rivals, free-soil settlers were acutely aware of their vulnerable position as a political minority. "Free men here," John Everett concluded, "are treated just as negroes are at the South." Everett's own experiences, however, revealed that mistreatment sometimes came from unexpected sources within the antislavery faction. During his initial visit to Kansas in late October 1854, the Michigan native found a promising claim and enlisted John Serpel, a Quaker of professed antislavery feeling, to build a cabin that would be occupied in the coming spring, once Everett had returned with his wife and children. The following spring, after completing a difficult journey on which one of their two

72. F. Shoemaker, "Missouri's Proslavery Fight," 232; Holder and Rothman, *Post on the Marmaton*, 80.

73. Thomas H. Gladstone, *The Englishman in Kansas; or, Squatter Life and Border Warfare*, 40–41; Parrish, *David Rice Atchison*, 188–89.

children died, the Everetts were stunned to discover not only that the cabin had been built and then granted to another family but also that their claim had been jumped by Serpel and O. C. Brown, the free-soil founder of Osawatomie. Like several other would-be speculators, Brown and Serpel were attempting to maintain four or five claims apiece, an action that the Everetts regarded as "plainly illegal, wrong, and not to be tolerated." They then moved to a neighboring claim, only to find that it, too, had been preempted. Finally, John and Sarah resigned themselves to squatting upon a third site, which was one of Brown's speculative hold-ings, and paid $62.50 for the primitive, windowless log cabin that sat on it. John defended their move as a just exercise of paternal duty. He wrote, "I do not think it is my duty to turn out of my path for those who are ille-gally speculating in the public lands. This claim was not the one [Brown] intended for his family, but one intended for speculative purposes. Our neighbors, generally, particularly the more intelligent and manly, say that we are right, and should stick to it."[74]

Had the Everetts decided to take legal action against Serpel or Brown, they were unlikely to have found favorable recourse from strongly parti-san proslavery authorities. Local judges, who generally sympathized with the Lecompton legislature, almost invariably sided with proslavery litigants. Free-soil settlers living near Fort Scott charged that Joseph Williams, a judge in the Third Judicial District, unfairly issued writs of trespass against immigrants who had allegedly squatted on the claims of proslavery settlers. In addition, antislavery men were arrested and jailed on trivial or unsubstantiated charges, and those who were granted bail typically had to pay exorbitant costs. Convinced they could find no jus-tice under the "bogus" officials, free-soil settlers in southeastern Kansas followed the example set by the Topeka legislature and established their own local institutions to protect their rights and property. The formation of "squatters courts," which were composed largely of free-soil judges and juries who issued binding settlements for quarreling neighbors, posed a direct challenge to the legitimacy of the established proslavery authorities.[75]

The effort to make Kansas a slave territory was bolstered in early 1856 by the organized influx of hundreds of southern colonists under the lead-ership of Major Jefferson Buford, a slave-owning attorney from Eufaula,

74. Everett and Everett, "Letters of John and Sarah Everett," 32, 4–11 (John Everett to Father, June 1856; to Sarah Everett, October 28, 1854; to Robert Everett, April 28, 1855; to Father, June 25, 1855).
75. Malin, *John Brown*, 30; Holder and Rothman, *Post on the Marmaton*, 80.

Alabama. In November 1855, Buford had declared his intention of direct-ing a proslavery expedition to Kansas in an open letter that was pub-lished by the local newspaper and distributed throughout the South. The operation, he explained, required "three hundred industrious, sober, dis-creet, reliable men capable of bearing arms" who were willing to travel north and "to do something for Kansas—something toward holding against the free-soil hordes." This colonization scheme offered lucrative inducements, such as free passage, a forty-acre homestead, and one year's support for each settler. In order to finance the effort, Buford pledged to spend more than twenty thousand dollars of his personal fortune, a sum that he had raised from the sale of forty slaves. He also lobbied unsuc-cessfully for an appropriation of twenty-five thousand dollars from the Alabama legislature. Buford's expedition traveled under banners that read "Kansas" and "The Supremacy of the White Race," and reached southeastern Kansas in May 1856. The party's arrival heartened the local proslavery majority, who were almost certainly quick to overlook any similarities to free-soil colonization efforts of the near past.[76]

Alarmed free-soil partisans feared that the colonists signaled a broader mobilization of slaveholding interests in the Deep South. Upon hearing of Buford's plan, Eli Thayer, the founder of the New England Emigrant Aid Society, enlisted 165 antislavery men, each of whom was armed with a Sharps rifle, to travel to Kansas to counteract the growing proslavery con-tingent.[77] Although the ascendancy of the proslavery majority justified Thayer's concern, any fear about an organized southern campaign in Kansas was largely overblown. Limited evidence indicates that the Buford organization, which was smaller and much slower to materialize than the northeastern antislavery emigration societies, was one of the few southern emigration schemes that actually sent settlers to Kansas. Most proslavery settlers came directly from Missouri, not from the Deep South, and emi-grated on their own accord, rather than as a part of a well-coordinated plan. At the same time, it should be noted, most free-soil immigrants also came independently, not as part of an antislavery emigrant-aid company, as many Missourians suspected.

On May 21, 1856, proslavery partisans, most of them Missourians, attacked the Douglas County town of Lawrence, a noted stronghold of antislavery feeling. Pressed into service by proslavery sheriff Samuel J. Jones, this group had been authorized by a local grand jury to subdue the

76. Walter L. Fleming, "The Buford Expedition to Kansas"; Monaghan, *Civil War*, 101.
77. Fleming, "Buford Expedition," 41.

nuisance posed by the New England Emigrant Aid Company hotel and the town's two free-soil newspapers, the *Herald of Freedom* and the *Kansas Free State.* Jones's posse, which was led by Atchison and included several Missourians, ransacked both papers' offices, destroyed the presses, and tossed the type into a nearby river. The men looted and vandalized several other buildings throughout Lawrence and burned the home of free-soil governor Charles Robinson. Lawrence, more than any other place, had come to represent for proslavery partisans those men whose claims upon Kansas were deemed illegitimate and dangerous to slaveholders' interests. Most of the attackers were products of a southern culture that upheld a community's right to expel those who challenged established norms and behaviors. Proslavery editor Benjamin Stringfellow had framed the contours of such popular authority, writing, "We as a general thing, disapprove of lynch law, and are the last to justify people in taking the law into their own hands. . . . But there are in certain cases in which a community are [sic] justifiable in resorting to *any means* to protect themselves and punish offenders." A subsequent editorial suggested that antislavery settlers shouldered the blame for the proslavery faction's turn to violent means. "Although we preferred Kansas being made a Negro slave State," Stringfellow wrote, "we never dreamed is making it so by the aid of bowie-knives, revolvers, and Sharp's Rifles, until we were threatened to be driven out of the Territory, by a band of hired abolitionists, bought up and sent here to control our elections, and steal our slaves and those of our friends in adjoining states."[78]

The sack of Lawrence pushed the divided territory to the brink of open warfare, yet it was a momentous event not simply because of the damage that was inflicted. In fact, none of the town's inhabitants had been killed or seriously injured. Instead, the raid's larger significance came from its galvanizing impact on a recent emigrant named John Brown, who would soon become one of the most legendary and controversial figures in Kansas history.[79] When Brown first came to Kansas in the fall of 1855, he may have seemed, to an unknowing observer, not much different from other free-soil emigrants. Like many others, he came west to join his family, as his five sons had established a claim in Kansas several weeks earlier. For a man who by his midfifties had failed in repeated business ventures and struggled to escape bankruptcy, the West may indeed have

---

78. Cecil-Fronsman, "'Death to All Yankees,'" 151; Oertel, "'Free Sons of the North,'" 180–81.

79. Parrish, *David Rice Atchison,* 199–203; James C. Malin, "Judge Lecompte and the 'Sack of Lawrence,' May 21, 1856," 465–67; March, *The History of Missouri,* 2:846.

been a place to start over or escape creditors. During stays in Ohio and New York, the elder Brown had performed a variety of jobs, working as a tanner and then a farmer, teacher, stock breeder, and postmaster; in Kansas Territory, a frontier environment wracked by land disputes, he quickly found employment as a competent surveyor. The presence of his half sister, Florella, and her husband, Samuel Adair, who had settled in Osawatomie, may also have influenced the decision to emigrate and establish a claim just northwest of town. In that particular family, however, bonds of kinship and ideology were closely linked. The Adairs were graduates of Oberlin College, the first American college to admit women and one of the earliest to admit African Americans, and had come to Kansas for the same principal reason as Brown: to block the spread of slavery into the western territories.[80]

The eruption of the Kansas crisis had whipped John Brown's indignation over slavery into a righteous fury and convinced him that the defeat of slavery required action, even violence. Brown's zealous antislavery convictions grew from several sources, particularly from his experiences with the Underground Railroad in rural New York, where he learned firsthand of slavery's brutality and came to abhor its destructive impact on slave families. Such moral revulsion was reinforced by his belief that slavery violated God's Commandments as well as the basic precepts set forth in the Declaration of Independence. In fact, it was the fervent religiosity of Brown's Calvinist faith that set him apart from most free-soil settlers. He firmly believed not only that Kansas would be the setting of an inevitable clash between slavery and freedom but also that he had been divinely chosen to carry out this holy war against slaveholders. From Brown's perspective, if the campaign of moral denunciation waged by William Lloyd Garrison and other pacifist abolitionists had not rid the United States of slavery, then he, an enforcer of divine will and inspiration, would take up this fight.[81]

John Brown was therefore no ordinary immigrant; he came west prepared for violence, having procured a cache of guns and broadswords during his journey through Ohio. He did not commence his war against the proslavery forces upon arriving in the Kansas Territory, however. Working under the pseudonym Shubel Morgan, he maintained a low profile through the spring of 1856. Although rumors of slave-hunting forays

80. Reynolds, *John Brown, Abolitionist*, 36, 132–33; Malin, *John Brown*, 10; Castel, *Frontier State*, 40; Oates, *Purge This Land*, 86.

81. Reynolds, *John Brown, Abolitionist*, 4, 41; Oates, *Purge This Land*, xvii, 151; Bertram Wyatt-Brown, *Yankee Saints and Southern Sinners*, 97–127; Potter, *Impending Crisis*, 211–13.

and the harassment of free-soil settlers by proslavery gangs stirred his anger, Brown was roused to action only after hearing of the sack of Lawrence by Sam Jones's men. Three nights later, on May 24, he led a party of eight men southward to Pottawatomie Creek. Near Dutch Henry's Crossing, Brown's men dragged five unarmed proslavery settlers from their homes and murdered them, mutilating several of the bodies with razor-sharp cutlasses. Four of the five victims were affiliated with the strongly partisan territorial district court; none was a slave owner. None of the killers was ever convicted for the attacks, although an irate mob apprehended and eventually released two of Brown's sons. The older Brown escaped to carry on with his personal crusade against the proslavery settlers, a campaign that, according to Kansas critics, soon devolved into horse stealing and highway robbery.[82]

The murders near Dutch Henry's Crossing prompted widespread condemnation from both proslavery and free-soil settlers in southeastern Kansas. Three days after the killings, neighbors along Pottawatomie Creek gathered in Osawatomie to express their disapproval of Brown and his men. To prevent the recurrence of such bloodshed, the bipartisan meeting elected a committee dedicated to bringing the murderers to justice. Settlers also passed a series of resolutions in which they agreed to "lay aside all sectional and political feelings and act together as men of reason and common sense. determined to oppose all men who are so ultra in their views as to denounce men of opposite opinions." This impulse for reconciliation, however, failed to produce a lasting peace. Proslavery demands for retaliation and the accumulation of bitter feelings on both sides undermined the difficult search for common ground in southeastern Kansas. Authorities in Lecompton intensified their campaign against the free-state Topeka movement and arrested many of its leaders, including Governor Robinson, for treason. Among the free-soil leaders imprisoned in makeshift prisons and army camps was free-soil settler Henry Williams, the elected secretary of the Pottawatomie committee.[83]

The sack of Lawrence and the murders at Dutch Henry's Crossing were a grim turning point in the contest for Kansas and marked the beginning of open civil war throughout the territory. On the northeastern border of Kansas, David Rice Atchison and other supporters of the

82. Reynolds, *John Brown, Abolitionist*, 149–74; Malin, *John Brown*, 759; Potter, *Impending Crisis*, 212–13. For the recollections of one man who claimed to have participated in Brown's summer banditry, see William W. Caine to F. G. Adams, February 28, 1889, Caine Correspondence, KSHS.

83. H. Williams, "Letters of a Free-State Man in Kansas, 1856," 166–67; Oates, *Purge This Land*, 140.

proslavery Law and Order Party closed the Missouri River to free-state traffic.[84] In the territory's southeastern counties, the partisan fighting was even more intense. The May 1856 attacks gave a newfound ferocity to the struggle and set in motion a pattern of retaliatory guerrilla violence that would continue almost unabated for nearly a decade. Proslavery men led raids from Missouri into Kansas with greater frequency and boldness, and free-soil Kansans responded in kind by attacking proslavery settlers on both sides of the state line. Brutal and domestic, the partisan violence in Kansas Territory was waged in and upon settlers' households, and nearly every home seemed to become a potential target. By stripping away the conventional boundaries of the territorial struggle, the attacks of May 1856 also drew into the fray a number of violent outlaws, most seeming to profess no clear preference about the extension of slavery. For such criminals, the eruption of guerrilla warfare presented an opportunity to rob, steal, and settle grudges.[85]

The war of retribution continued with rumors of a broad proslavery assault upon Osawatomie, the town regarded as John Brown's seat of support. Shortly after the Pottawatomie massacre, the town's inhabitants circulated an anxious rumor that Buford and his southerners would soon kill every free-soil settler in the area. Although the feared massacre never materialized, fears of a proslavery attack proved to be justified in early June, when a band of between 250 and 400 proslavery men, led by Missourian John Reid and former Indian agent George W. Clarke, converged on Osawatomie. The proslavery men easily defeated the free-soil settlers' hastily mustered defenses and then turned to plundering what guns, horses, and money they could find. Before leaving, the invaders also set fire to most of the buildings. Aside from the substantial property damage, there were apparently few casualties, as most families had managed to take refuge in the safety of nearby woods and fields. Proslavery gangs followed the Osawatomie attack with similarly destructive raids on the Linn County village of Sugar Mound and other free-soil havens.[86]

The spring and summer of 1856 marked the high point of the proslavery faction's dominance in Kansas. Proslavery figures maintained control

---

84. Parrish, *David Rice Atchison*, 205.

85. Malin, *John Brown*, 589; Marvin Ewy, "The United States Army in the Border Troubles, 1855–1856," 392.

86. Everett and Everett, "Letters of John and Sarah Everett," 31 (John Everett to Father, June 1856); Cutler, *History of Kansas*, 2:876–77, 1103–4; Malin, *John Brown*, 217; Monaghan, *Civil War*, 81. That Everett and his wife, who lived some two miles outside of Osawatomie, only heard about the attack two days later suggests that the raid was confined to the town itself.

of the federally recognized territorial legislature, occupied the most attractive lands, and had effectively cowed, imprisoned, or expelled many of their free-soil rivals. The administrations of Franklin Pierce and his Democratic successor, James Buchanan, together provided a sympathetic federal ally for the Lecompton authorities. The U.S. military, charged with the difficult task of keeping the peace in Kansas, struggled to maintain a neutral position and often served to reinforce the dominance of proslavery authorities. Secretary of War Jefferson Davis rejected inquiries about the potential intervention of U.S. troops following the Lawrence raid and the Pottawatomie murders, and federal soldiers thus did little to prevent the harassment of free-soil settlers at Osawatomie. In July, the proslavery territorial authority relied on the U.S. Army to disperse the Topeka legislature at gunpoint.[87]

The violent events of May 1856 were a critical factor in moving the nation ever closer to sectional rupture. The sack of Lawrence showed that the struggle for Kansas was not simply a contest of words and ideologies but had instead deteriorated into open armed conflict. The next day, Representative Preston Brooks of South Carolina violently assaulted Charles Sumner in the chamber of the U.S. Senate. Sumner, a senator from Massachusetts, had days earlier issued a series of vitriolic speeches, collectively titled *The Crime against Kansas*, that criticized slavery in general and mocked Senator Andrew P. Butler, a relative of Brooks, in particular. The antislavery press seized upon the attacks on Sumner and Lawrence as examples of menacing southern aggressiveness. Southerners, meanwhile, widely cheered Brooks's defense of his cousin's honor and mailed him dozens of canes to replace the one broken during the assault.[88]

The murders along Pottawatomie Creek were May's most shocking and polarizing episode of political violence. For whites in Missouri and the South, the audacity and brutality of the killings confirmed deep-seated fears about the abolitionist movement, proving that antislavery fanatics were indeed a radical threat to their own lives and property. The slave revolts of Denmark Vesey and Nat Turner, as well as the successful revolution that Toussaint-Louverture waged in Haiti, had long fueled insecurities about racial violence among white southerners, but the bloodshed of that May night in Kansas provoked even greater alarm. There, in the grassy hills and woods of the Osage valley, were white men

87. Everett and Everett, "Letters of John and Sarah Everett," 143 (John Everett to Father, July 10, 1856); Malin, *John Brown*, 88; Ewy, "Border Troubles," 388–99.

88. Reynolds, *John Brown, Abolitionist*, 178; Potter, *Impending Crisis*, 208–24; Lloyd Lewis, "Propaganda and the Kansas-Missouri War."

who had shown themselves willing to kill over the issue of slavery. The Pottawatomie massacre, along with the Lawrence raid and the Sumner-Brooks affair, not only deepened the divide between antislavery interests in the North and slavery's defenders in the South; such events also roused once impassive observers hundreds of miles away, confronting them with the magnitude of the ideological gulf between proslavery and free-soil partisans. The middle ground of political moderation, which had made sectional compromise possible for more than a half century, had begun to shrink more rapidly than ever.

The struggle over Kansas had also reshaped the meaning of Missouri's western border. Once the Kansas-Nebraska Act had broken the dam that held back the flow of westering migrants, a wave of settlers—some anti-slavery easterners, most proslavery Missourians—surged across the state line to claim the territory's best lands. In addition, that boundary no longer limited the spread of slavery, and with the proslavery movement in ascendance, the slaveholding frontier was poised to spread as far across the Kansas plains as settlers wanted to take it. The proslavery faction's goal of establishing a slave-owning society, such as the one in Missouri that had lured Cecil Ball west decades earlier, appeared to be within its reach, but a conclusive political triumph remained elusive. The murders at Pottawatomie Creek and the survival of an extralegal free-state authority in Topeka demonstrated the fervor and persistence of its antislavery rivals. An even greater challenge to proslavery dominance came from the increasing number of free-soil immigrants, whose ranks included both newcomers and exiled settlers who were determined to retake their claims. The violent spring of 1856 had kindled a flame within the tinder-box of partisan hostilities, and in the months to come, winds of retribution promised to ignite an even wider conflagration.

THREE

ON THE BORDER OF WAR

I t took the man from Kentucky less than a week to forsake the rolling prairies he found in western Missouri for the country across the state line. In hindsight, there was little surprise to the immigrant's decision, for he had come to Missouri with hopes of relocating to Kansas once the new territory was opened for legal settlement. An Ohioan by birth, he had bided his time in Missouri for more than a year, spending several months in the eastern part of the state before coming west to Jackson County in 1853. An acquaintance named Dr. Thornton advised the would-be settler against moving to Kansas, warning that its tense political environment promised trouble for a person of his ideological bent, and instead assured him that excellent land could still be had in the Missouri counties to the south. The newcomer took note and brought his wife and children some fifty miles south to Bates County. Nothing there, whether it was the yet-available land or the presence of slaveholders, seemed to suit them; within a matter of days, James Montgomery gathered his family again and led them across the border toward a new home in Kansas Territory.[1]

He arrived in Kansas during the summer of 1854, at the age of thirty-eight, with an unabashed desire to live in a territory free of slavery. Montgomery had lived most of his adult years in slave states, working as a minister and teacher among people, including his slaveholding in-laws,

1. Franklin B. Sanborn, "Colonel Montgomery and His Letters," 258.

who either owned human property or openly supported the right to do so. Firsthand exposure to chattel bondage and its pernicious effects had sharpened his antislavery convictions. Slavery, in the mind of free-soil critics, not only burdened nonslaveholders with unfair competition but also degraded labor itself by denying slaves both the fruits of their efforts and opportunities for economic advancement. Yet as Montgomery's earliest experiences in Kansas showed, the past fifteen years had not rendered him too inflexible to recognize attractive investment opportunities. In August, he agreed to buy a proslavery man's claim to a fertile piece of land in Linn County. He gave five dollars for the down payment on his new property along Little Sugar Creek, five miles west of Mound City, and thus became one of the first free-soil pioneers to inhabit that part of Kansas.[2]

Two years later, after proslavery bands had harassed and driven dozens of other families from the territory, Montgomery found that few like-minded settlers were left in the county. The situation had grown more ominous during the spring and summer of 1856, when an attack on the antislavery community of Lawrence and the retaliatory killings of five proslavery men along Pottawatomie Creek plunged Kansas into a bloody cycle of tit-for-tat violence. By fall, the prospects for the few free-soil inhabitants who remained in Linn County had grown so dim that they sent Montgomery to appeal for help from John Geary, who just weeks earlier had been appointed governor of Kansas Territory. Geary was a distinguished veteran of the Mexican War and an enormous man for his time, standing six and a half feet tall and weighing more than 250 pounds, yet he seemed powerless to stop the partisan fighting around him. Failing to receive a satisfactory response from the governor, the disappointed settler returned to Linn County and discovered that his home, along with houses and a store in nearby Sugar Mound, had been burned to the ground during his absence.[3]

Although Montgomery had been witness to the feuding between free-soil and proslavery citizens for more than two years, the extent to which he had participated in those early territorial disputes is unclear. What is more certain, however, was the prominent role that he then assumed as an outspoken leader among free-soil partisans. The destruction of his home, which he later replaced with a larger structure that locals dubbed "Fort Montgomery," transformed the Ohio native, galvanizing his attitude

2. Ibid., 258–59; Etcheson, *Bleeding Kansas,* 191. For the free-soil/free-labor critique of slavery, see Foner, *Free Soil,* 47–59.
3. Tommy L. Holman, "James Montgomery in Kansas, 1854–1863," 24; John H. Gihon, *Geary and Kansas: Governor Geary's Administration in Kansas, with a Complete History of the Territory until July 1857,* 105–54.

toward the proslavery faction in Kansas and convincing him that such aggression demanded a forceful response in kind. Unwilling to flee the territory or suffer such abuse quietly, he emerged as a militant partisan warrior, determined to defend the free-soil settlers in his area. Yet in the coming months, the free-soil captain also became increasingly committed to asserting free-soil dominance over rivals, and thus became personally responsible for perpetuating much of the violence and fear that gripped the Kansas-Missouri border.

Montgomery's status as a free-soil leader grew with the 1857 establishment of the "Self-Protective Association," a local outfit that he organized and commanded. Many of the families who had been driven away by proslavery bands over the past two years had started moving back to their old claims during the past winter. Montgomery instructed those who returned that if they hoped to hold their claims with greater success than before, they must be prepared to fight. As a result, he imbued his band of partisan fighters with a mission—ejecting proslavery settlers from the area—that was seemingly less defensive than its name suggested. After identifying the proslavery men living in Linn County, the group warned each one that the time to leave Kansas Territory had come. Threats of violence compelled several proslavery families to retreat into Missouri, and such departures apparently inspired Montgomery and his men to pursue a similar course of action in nearby Bourbon County. When proslavery citizens in Little Osage and surrounding settlements failed to heed these warnings, free-soil partisans moved upon a targeted household, seized the weapons inside, and forcibly removed its members from the property.[4]

Even though federal authorities had dismissed the free-state movement as illegitimate and several of its leaders were jailed or in retreat, a great many Kansans remained firmly committed to the antislavery cause, unmoved by similar threats of proslavery persecution. John Everett expressed such resolve and looked to the near future with hope in an October 1856 letter to his father: "There is still a chance for us to save this territory to freedom and virtue." A month later the son remained ever optimistic. "We have still Justice on our side. Eternal principles are with us. The God of the oppressed is for us. The sympathies and prayers of hundreds of thousands in the free North are ours still." Breathless accounts of proslavery intimidation had indeed broadened free-soil support among the northern public, but Everett had another reason to feel confident. Free-soil families, in his estimation, composed a majority of the

4. Sanborn, "Colonel Montgomery," 260; Holman, "Montgomery in Kansas," 31–36; J. Johnson, *History of Vernon County,* 226.

settlers in his Linn County neighborhood. His spirits were further buoyed in late November, when he noted, "We stand better numerically now than in July."[5] Everett's perceptions proved correct, for a major demographic change was taking place in Kansas. In addition to the return of free-soil exiles, the stream of free-state emigrants, which had been steadily rising since 1854, was set to burst forth into a full-blown torrent and thereby shift the tide of the territorial struggle in favor of the free-state movement.

By 1857, the rate of free-soil immigration clearly began to outpace the influx of settlers from Missouri and other slave states, as an analysis of federal census data reveals.[6] Table 3 (Nativity of Households with Parents of Kansas-Born Children, 1854–1860) outlines the shifting sources of immigration by using a sample of the 1860 federal population census from three counties in southeastern Kansas. The sample consists of households that included a child who was born in Kansas between 1854 and 1860. It first uses the age and nativity data of each household's children to approximate the year when a family settled in the territory. Looking at the family of George and Ada Hobson, for example, one sees that their daughters, four-year-old Julia and two-year-old Rebecca, were born in Illinois and Kansas, respectively, thus indicating that the family had settled in Bourbon County sometime between 1856 and 1858. After identifying the approximate date of arrival for each family, households were organized according to the birthplace of the parents and were then separated into three groups: households with parents born in slave states, households with parents born in free states, and households of mixed nativity. Households were also divided into those with children born in Kansas in the early territorial period (1854 to 1856) and those with children born in the late territorial period (1857 to 1860).[7]

An important demographic change was in fact taking place by 1857. During the early territorial period, most of the children born in southeastern Kansas came from families in which both parents were born in a slave state. If one includes households of mixed nativity (in which one parent was born in a slave state and the other a free state), the proportion of at least partial southern ancestry rises to nearly 75 percent. Almost all

5. Everett and Everett, "Letters of John and Sarah Everett," 150–52 (John Everett to Father, October 29, November 13, 20, 1856).

6. Later correspondence from Kansas settlers provided anecdotal evidence that 1857 was the major regional turning point in the settlement of territorial Kansas. See Augustus Wattles to Thaddeus Hyatt, December 3, 1860, Hyatt Collection, KSHS.

7. Author's sample, U.S. Census Bureau, Manuscript Census, Kansas, Bourbon, Linn, and Miami Counties, Schedule I (Population), 1860, hereinafter cited as Census-Pop. In the cases where two or more children were born in Kansas, the age of the oldest Kansas-born child is used to approximate the date of arrival.

of these southern parents had come directly from Missouri or the Upper South slave states of Kentucky or Tennessee. Only one in four Kansas-born children came from families in which both parents had been born in free states. In the late territorial period a strikingly different pattern emerged. More than half of the children born then came from free-state parents, while the ratio of children with southern-born parents slipped to 28 percent. The balance of power in Kansas Territory, as these figures reveal, was steadily shifting from proslavery to free-soil settlers.

Some informed generalizations can be drawn about the several thousand settlers who descended upon the Kansas Territory during the late 1850s. The typical immigrants, as suggested above, tended to come as families. They were young, though not much younger than Missouri settlers across the border; they were westerners by birth, coming principally from Illinois, Ohio, or Indiana (see table 4, Nativity of Settlers, Kansas Border Counties, 1860), western states where the populations had descended from a mixture of northern and southern stock; and they were slightly better educated than the average Missourian.[8] Unlike the early antislavery colonists whose travels had been assisted by northern emigrant societies, the majority of these settlers came on their own. Many Kansas City businessmen had recently feared that the territory's deserved reputation for lawlessness would cripple their own commercial prospects and stem the tide of northern immigration, but the aggressive actions of proslavery partisans may have actually inspired some free-soil observers to emigrate.[9] The people who were coming to Kansas seemed prepared to stay for the long haul, or at least had arrived undeterred by sensational accounts of partisan violence. Some potential migrants found reassurance from kinfolk already living in Kansas. Bourbon County settlers Thomas and Nancy Hamilton, for example, encouraged their friends and family back in Indiana to come west. They admitted, "We have some trouble here on account of politicks [sic]," but were hopeful "there shall be no slavery here. This is too good a country to be cursed with slavery."[10] The fight for a free Kansas, the Hamiltons hoped, could be won through greater strength in numbers, rather than arms.

8. More than 75 percent of settlers in southeastern Kansas were younger than thirty, and the average age for heads of households was around thirty-six (ibid.).

9. For the impact of the border troubles on business interests in Kansas City, see Everett and Everett, "Letters of John and Sarah Everett," 154 (John Everett to Father, December 4, 1856); Charles N. Glaab, *Kansas City and the Railroads: Community Policy in the Growth of a Regional Metropolis*, 46–52; and Al Theodore Brown, "Business 'Neutralism' on the Kansas Border: Kansas City, 1854–1857."

10. Thomas and Nancy Hamilton to "Brother and Sister," June 22, 1858, Nancy McCrum Hamilton Papers, KSHS.

The rapid growth of the free-state population endangered the proslavery regime's claims to legitimacy in Kansas, for with each passing month the prospects for antislavery candidates, as well as the antislavery constitution they would inevitably draft, grew ever brighter. Seeking to capitalize on political support in Washington, the Lecompton government moved expeditiously to secure entry as a slave state. In early 1857, territorial officials announced that an election to be held in June would decide the delegates for that fall's constitutional convention. Barely one-fourth of the territory's registered voters turned out to select the convention delegates. Many proslavery citizens simply neglected to vote, and most free-soil settlers, considering the contest a farce, simply refused to participate. Not surprisingly, a large majority of proslavery candidates, several of whom ran unopposed, were elected. Meeting at Lecompton in September, the delegates of the constitutional convention framed a charter that would be submitted for the approval of Kansas citizens three months later.[11]

By the time the proslavery Lecompton constitution had been drafted, the population of free-soil settlers in Kansas had grown to the point that free-state candidates could realistically look toward gaining control of the territorial legislature in the forthcoming October election. When the results of that contest were announced, the proslavery faction appeared to have narrowly retained control of the legislature, thanks in large part to extraordinary support in two counties located along the Missouri border. Territorial governor Robert Walker soon learned that most of the proslavery votes in these counties were fraudulent, with the names of would-be voters there having been copied directly from the *Cincinnati Directory*. The governor promptly dismissed the returns from those districts and thereby shifted control of the territorial legislature to the free-state party. One settler marveled at the vote totals in Lykins County (which would be renamed Miami County in 1861), where the free-soil slate won 85 percent of the vote, and noted that its triumph would have been even greater had that summer's immigrants been eligible to vote.[12]

The vote on the Lecompton constitution that had been scheduled by the proslavery legislature took place in early December 1857. Kansans faced a choice between two proslavery constitutions: the first choice, known as the "constitution with slavery," placed no legal restrictions upon slavery; the second choice, curiously described as the "constitution without slavery," protected slavery where it already existed but prohibited the further

11. Potter, *Impending Crisis*, 300–305.
12. Ibid., 306; Everett and Everett, "Letters of John and Sarah Everett," 185–86 (John Everett to Cynthia Everett, October 5, 1857; to Robert Everett, October 6, 1857).

introduction of slaves into Kansas. With the protection of slaveholders' interests a fait accompli, the vote offered little more than a rubber-stamp endorsement of the Lecompton government. In a vote that was not close, the "constitution with slavery" won by a margin of 6,226 to 569. Free-soil voters, however, refused to participate, and the results were once more mired in controversy. On January 4, 1858, the newly elected free-state legislature called Kansans back to the polls to vote on the Lecompton constitution yet again; with proslavery voters now abstaining, the charter lost by a resounding margin. Eight months later, the U.S. Congress asked Kansas voters to vote on the Lecompton constitution for a third and final time, seeking to entice their approval with the offer of a large land grant. Settlers flatly rejected this so-called English bill, named for congressional sponsor John English of Ohio, by a count of 11,300 to 1,788. In the meantime, antislavery citizens had assembled in Leavenworth to draft a constitution that would secure Kansas's entrance as a free state. Even though a majority of voters ratified the Leavenworth constitution, it faced strong opposition from both President Buchanan and southern interests in the U.S. Congress. The prospect that Kansas would soon become a state, free or slave, remained slight.[13]

Northern immigration into Kansas from 1857 forward ensured the triumph of the free-state movement and essentially resolved the political debate over slavery in the territory. Throughout much of Kansas, this turnabout also spelled an end to the fighting between free-soil and proslavery partisans.[14] In southeastern Kansas, however, bitter guerrilla violence raged on, burning with even greater intensity along the Missouri border. The fighting there helped to give a divisive new meaning to the state line, as it became an openly violent boundary between free and slave societies. An experiment in political geography, popular sovereignty produced a political outcome that was markedly different from what many observers had expected barely a year earlier. Through 1857, both proslavery and free-soil settlers had been guilty of violently harassing their political rivals, but the latter group, notwithstanding John Brown's raid, had generally borne the brunt of the persecution. With the arrival of thousands of new free-state emigrants and the return of many families who had been driven away by ruffian gangs, this dynamic changed, as the proslavery minority faced increasing persecution from James Montgomery, Charles Jennison, and other free-soil partisans.

13. Morrison, *Slavery and the West*, 197; Potter, *Impending Crisis*, 306–25; Holder and Rothman, *Post on the Marmaton*, 89.
14. Cecil-Fronsman, "'Death to All Yankees,'" 152–53.

The return of exiled free-soil settlers by early 1857 had fueled much of the guerrilla warfare in the upper Osage valley. In many cases, economic disputes were again a convenient pretense for violence. Pennsylvania native Joseph Trego, who had settled north of the Little Osage River, related the nature of the fighting in his neighborhood, where free-state families returned to find that their claims and livestock had been seized by Missourians. "In short, there was continual bra[wls?] among them," Trego noted. "The pro-slaves being the most numerous in this locality they could enforce the bogus laws and have things pre[tty] much their own way. The free-state men 'would'nt give it up' and some of them are not the most peaceable kind of fellows either, and the disturbances encreased until there was open war between them [sic]." A similar scenario played out in nearby Bourbon County when the Stone family, who had been driven from the country by marauding ruffians, returned to find their claim jumped by a proslavery Methodist minister named Southwood. Unwilling to withdraw yet again, the Stones built another cabin on their claim, and with the assistance of the neighborhood's growing free-soil majority, they succeeded in driving their rival tenant from the premises.[15]

Reverend Southwood may have joined the significant number of proslavery sympathizers who fled following the free-state ascendancy of the late 1850s. According to one Miami County settler, southern men had become "universally discouraged" by the end of 1856. Jefferson Buford's colonization scheme, the most prominent attempt to attract southern immigrants to the territory, proved to be a complete failure. The expedition disbanded only months after its arrival; some of its members supposedly remained in Kansas, having enlisted in the United States Army, but most either retreated to Missouri or headed back home to Alabama.[16] Census returns from several Missouri counties reveal that some of the proslavery settlers who left Kansas found refuge across the state line. Wiley Patterson, a thirty-five-year-old slave-owning farmer from Georgia, lived in Arkansas with his wife and three children until they emigrated to Bourbon County, Kansas, in the mid-1850s. The Pattersons stayed for a few years, long enough to see their two youngest children born in the territory. In the summer of 1857, they paid another Kansas settler five hundred dollars for a young slave woman named Lucinda in what was likely one of the few recorded instances of the slave trade in

15. Trego, "Letters of Trego," 122 (to Alice Trego, December 21, 1857); Cutler, *History of Kansas*, 2:1066–67.

16. Everett and Everett, "Letters of John and Sarah Everett," 158 (John Everett to Father, December 26, 1856); Fleming, "Buford Expedition," 46–48.

Kansas. In 1860 the family moved just across the border to Deerfield Township in western Vernon County.[17]

The campaign of intimidation waged by free-soil partisans, including those who belonged to the self-styled Self-Protective Association, undoubtedly spurred the flight of many proslavery emigrants. Several antislavery guerrillas roamed the border counties with weapons furnished by the Kansas State Central Committee, an organization that coordinated the activities of the Free State Party and distributed the food, clothing, and donations sent from northern benefactors. Montgomery, for example, carried a Sharps rifle and a Colt revolver that were donated "to be used in defense of Kansas."[18] As with their proslavery foes, some free-soil guerrillas were sometimes motivated less by ideological scruples than by a thirst for personal vengeance. "The country is filled with armed men," wrote John Vansickle. "The worst . . . is thieves and robers on boath sides" who "claim politics when it soots them and when it does not [suit] thare notion they go in with out any excuse [sic]." The targets of plundering raids, which extended into western Missouri, included partisan enemies and innocents alike, and even some free-soil settlers came to fear Montgomery. William Smith claimed that the guerrilla captain's aggressive tactics had reshaped the basic social divisions of southeastern Kansas. "Formerly it was Pro-Slavery and Free-State," Smith wrote. "Now it is Free-State men against a gang of thieves and murderers headed by Jim Lane and Montgomery." A great many antislavery settlers, however, continued to condone the free-state guerrillas. "He is one of the nobelist [sic] men that I ever saw," claimed Frank Walker. "He can command 5000 men if he wants to. He is said to be one of the likedest men in Kansas."[19]

The cycle of retaliatory violence reached its brutal nadir on the morning of May 19, 1858, when a group of twenty to thirty proslavery men, many of whom had taken refuge in Missouri, rode back into Kansas under the command of Charles Hamilton, a Georgia native who, according to one Fort Scott resident, had been driven from his Kansas claim.[20]

17. Census-Pop, Missouri, Vernon County, 1860; Cutler, *History of Kansas,* 2:1066.

18. Kansas State Central Committee, circular, *To the Friends of Free Kansas in the States,* October 20, 1856; and "Record of Arms Disbursed by the Kansas State Central Committee," 1, September 24, 1858, James Blood Papers, KSHS.

19. Vansickle to Father and Mother, March 3, 1858, Vansickle Collection, University of Kansas, Kenneth Spencer Research Library; Smith to Samuel McKitrick, February 2, 1859, Smith Papers, KSHS; Miner, *Kansas,* 74–75; Walker to M. B. Walker, March 4, 1859, Walker Correspondence, University of Kansas, Kenneth Spencer Research Library.

20. Hamilton (or Hambelton) apparently was driven from his Kansas claim, but there is no clear proof. See Holder and Rothman, *Post on the Marmaton,* 84.

Passing through the town of Trading Post, Hamilton's band seized eleven free-soil settlers from their cabins and fields and marched them to a wooded ravine outside of town, just north of the Marais des Cygnes River. The proslavery guerrillas then ordered their captives into line and fired upon them. All eleven men fell, and five died instantly. Hamilton's gang, believing all the captives to be dead or fatally wounded, fled into Missouri. Four of the free-soil settlers were seriously wounded but survived, and the other two somehow escaped injury.

Within hours of the crime, a militia unit of outraged Kansans had been formed to arrest the murderers, and it raced to the border town of West Point, Missouri. Montgomery demanded that the Kansans surround the town and wait until every local man could be produced. The posse's other members, however, overruled this proposal and elected to send a delegation ahead to speak with the town's leading citizens. The village's inhabitants disavowed any connection to Hamilton or his men—one local condemned them as dishonorable "imps of purgatory"—and offered to assist with the search, but none of the killers was immediately found.[21] Some militia members later claimed that during the lengthy exchange between the two delegations a few fugitives managed to escape unnoticed. Nearly all of the murderers eluded arrest; only William Griffith, a native of Bates County, Missouri, who was caught and executed five years later, was ever punished.[22]

Letters written by settlers on opposite sides of the Missouri-Kansas border in the days immediately after the murders belied the likely unease that gripped the region. Two specific pieces of correspondence, a letter from Al Burchard of Missouri and another by John Everett, played down the danger faced by the area's inhabitants. Both authors made reference to the massacre but only after sharing the mundane details of their everyday lives. Burchard began by updating his sister, Aggy, on the progress of his farm, informing her that they had completed that spring's planting and had commenced building a house and fences. The first half of Everett's letter focused on the principal news of the day, which, in his opinion, concerned the forthcoming land sales and the mounting political opposition to the Lecompton government. When the two men eventually mentioned the killings, they took pains to emphasize their distance

21. Al Burchard to Sister Aggy, May 30, 1858 (reprint), Special History Collection, Fort Scott National Historic Site.
22. J. T. Botkin, "Justice Was Swift and Sure in Early Kansas," 488–91; Welch, *Border Warfare*, 87–104; William A. Mitchell, *Linn County, Kansas: A History*, 211–14.

from the crime and to underscore their families' safety. Living barely five miles from the murder, Burchard provided a much more detailed account, yet he nonetheless claimed to be "in no danger whatever." He concluded the letter by assessing the prospects of his peaches and strawberries; Everett closed by noting that his and Sarah's baby was nearly walking.[23] Carefully crafted to assuage the fears of distant relatives, these letters suggested a determination to carry on even in the face of a mounting guerrilla threat that was driving war-weary settlers from the area.

Other accounts from the border counties underscored the dangers that potential immigrants might expect to face in territorial Kansas. In an effort to dissuade eastern relatives from migrating to Kansas, John Vansickle relayed news of violent depredations by "armed desperados" such as Brown and Montgomery, and confessed to his father, "I cannot only give you a faint idea of the brutality that is practised in this county." The Bourbon County resident confessed a small measure of doubt about passing along such fearful news. "This is the first time I have ever said a word to you about it and should not have dunso this time if you had not bin tawking of coming out here [*sic*]." Vansickle noted that fears of partisan retaliation had made many correspondents, himself included, reluctant to report the difficult circumstances in Kansas as they presently existed. "The people here," he wrote, were "afraid to write the facts in the case to their friends for fear it might find its way to the public press."[24]

In public, Montgomery was careful to point out that his free-soil partisans would not treat all proslavery citizens alike. At a speech in Raysville, he announced, "The quiet, peaceable Pro-Slavery man has nothing to fear from us; he may remain among us, and enjoy his political opinions in his rights." After he alluded to the unoffending examples of proslavery neighbors near his own farm, the guerrilla leader focused his partisan wrath: "Those proslavery men who continued to harass peaceful settlers, on the other hand, had no future in the territory." The free-soil captain, convinced by the numerical strength of his own side, declared that the conquest of Kansas was now complete and informed his rivals, "This country is ours; you and I have fought which shall have it, and we have fairly conquered you, and mean to have it. In so many days you must leave it." To help accelerate this forced exodus, Montgomery also announced his intention to forage upon proslavery enemies. "As the idea

23. Burchard to Aggy, Sister May 30, 1858 (reprint), Special History Collection, Fort Scott National Historic Site; Everett and Everett, "Letters of John and Sarah Everett," 299 (John Everett to Father and Mother, June 22, 1858).

24. Vansickle to Father, December 28, 1858, Vansickle Collection, University of Kansas, Kenneth Spencer Research Library.

of 'guerrilla' is self-sustaining," he said, "if you have any money, we must have some of it, and if you have any horses, we must have them for service."[25] In time, the practice of such plunder and theft became commonly known as "jayhawking," its free-soil practitioners "jayhawkers."[26]

After the Marais des Cygnes massacre and the failed search at West Point, several free-soil guerrillas clamored for a general invasion of Missouri to punish the murderers and other proslavery sympathizers. Montgomery, on the other hand, focused his attention on southeastern Kansas, where a number of personal and political scores remained unsettled. He had been reluctant to conduct raids upon Fort Scott, fearful of provoking the federal troops stationed there, and thus directed the attacks at the proslavery settlers scattered throughout the Bourbon County countryside. Although political loyalties in Fort Scott had generally been divided, an increase in raids across the outlying settlements made the town a greater refuge for proslavery families seeking protection from free-state harassment. On the morning of June 7, Montgomery and his men cast aside their prior inhibitions and carried out a predawn assault upon the town. They inflicted few casualties and caused relatively little damage in their failed attempt to burn down the proslavery Western Hotel, but the attack demonstrated that not even the presence of U.S. soldiers would deter the guerrilla fighting.[27]

Territorial governor James Denver, the seventh man to hold that office in barely four years, traveled to Fort Scott a week later to negotiate a truce that would forestall retaliatory attacks and check the growing outmigration. Two weeks earlier, army captain Nathaniel Lyon had passed through the area and reported that many of the houses north of the Little Osage River had indeed been abandoned. Certain that additional violence would also interrupt farming well to the south of Fort Scott, Lyon recommended that federal troops be permanently stationed in the area, but the Montgomery raid had exposed the inadequacy of such an option. When Governor Denver met with local free-state and proslavery leaders at Fort Scott, he maintained that each faction was to blame for the violence of the past two years. In order to break the cycle of retribution, he introduced a proposal that would grant amnesty from prosecution to

25. Holman, "Montgomery in Kansas," 52. For Montgomery's peaceful relationship with nearby proslavery neighbors, see Robert Gould Shaw to Mother, June 29, 1863, in Shaw, *Blue-Eyed Child of Fortune: The Civil War Letters of Colonel Robert Gould Shaw*, 364.

26. Mitchell, *Linn County*, 22; Miner, *Kansas*, 74–75.

27. Welch, *Border Warfare*, 125–26; Holder and Rothman, *Post on the Marmaton*, 85–86.

partisans from both sides, and in return each faction would cease its armed attacks.[28] Both sides agreed to the governor's compromise; Montgomery returned to his farm along Little Sugar Creek, and for a promising moment it appeared that peace had at last come to southeastern Kansas. However, in spite of Denver's best efforts, he could not fully soothe the antipathies hardened by years of factional bitterness, and the terms of his accord, particularly its provision of amnesty, quickly became a source of further dissension. Settlers on each side were eager to see justice served and thus were reluctant to let the crimes of the past go unpunished.[29] More than ever, the border itself became a battle line in the war over the future of slavery.

Promises of peace did not sway the defensive preparations of Missourians across the state line, where many communities braced themselves for seemingly inevitable partisan reprisals. Within days of the Marais des Cygnes murders, local settlers established militias in the Missouri towns of Pleasant Hill, Harrisonville, Austin, and Butler. Other citizens petitioned Missouri governor Robert M. Stewart for additional assistance. Several residents of Bates County gathered at West Point on June 5—two days before Montgomery raided Fort Scott—to express their fears and grievances in an anxious plea for military protection. Describing the abuses suffered at the hands of Kansas guerrillas, the Missourians wrote, "They have threatened us. They have invaded our state, they have marched into one of our towns and insulted its citizens. They robbed, plundered, destroyed the property and insulted peaceable citizens. They have chased and shot at men who were tending to their own business. . . . They have disregarded the dignity of our state [and] have forced us to stand guard day and night, to go armed about our daily avocations." Jayhawker persecution, they claimed, had also forced a large number of families living near the Kansas border to abandon their homes.[30] Traveling through the border region, Adjutant General Gustavus Parsons heard similar claims from other citizens. "A large strip of country within our

28. Homer E. Socolofsky, *Kansas Governors,* 66; Christopher Phillips, *Damned Yankee: The Life of General Nathaniel Lyon,* 115. For another reference to the depopulation of Little Osage, see Augustus Wattles to William Hutchinson, April 28, 1858, Hutchinson Papers, KSHS.

29. Cutler, *History of Kansas,* 2:1069, 1106; Holder and Rothman, *Post on the Marmaton,* 87.

30. Joseph Clymer, "Statement of Citizens of Bates County Concerning Border Troubles," June 1858; S. G. Allen to Robert M. Stewart, Harrisonville, May 30, 1858; James S. Hackney to Stewart, Independence, June 6, 1858, Missouri-Kansas Border War Collection, Missouri State Archives, hereinafter cited as MKBWC.

state," he noted, "is almost entirely depopulated, our citizens driven from their homes and . . . threatened with death should they return."[31]

Observers who had been dispatched to western Missouri by Governor Stewart agreed with the contention that the safety of local settlers warranted some degree of military intervention. Parsons reported that local militias would not provide sufficient protection to the communities situated along the Kansas border. J. F. Snyder, an inspector with the Missouri Militia, visited the Osage River town of Papinsville and reached a similar conclusion about the necessity of military force in restoring order to the region. Snyder noted that the breakdown of civil authority had been exacerbated by the arrival of proslavery partisans seeking safety from the "unhappy difficulties" in Kansas. "Some of those refugees," he wrote, "actuated by a spirit of retaliation or revenge, have gone back into the territory and committed depredations, and in turn, they have been pursued by citizens of that territory into this State." He also stressed the necessity of relying on soldiers without personal ties to the inflamed border region. The local militias, he concluded, "would be too much influenced by self interest, prejudice, or revenge to act impartially."[32]

Although the governor was inclined to follow the recommendations of advisers and cries for help from agitated settlers, he hesitated to pursue an aggressive course that might ignite open war between Missouri and Kansas Territory. Stewart believed that the presence of Missouri soldiers could invite further free-soil aggression and therefore ordered the limited force under General Parsons's command to assume a strictly defensive posture. The governor informed James Denver of his intention to station a militia detachment along the western border and expressed his hope that the Kansas governor would help "prevent any occurrence calculated to mar the cordial feeling generally existing between the citizens of Missouri and Kansas." Denver, for his part, feared that a military mobilization would undermine the fragile peace in the southeastern counties. Though he pledged to cooperate in bringing order to the region, the Kansas governor remained skeptical about the usefulness of additional troops. The marauders, he asserted, were merely horse thieves who "can be exterminated only by the active and energetic exertions of the people themselves. In fact it is better at all times that the people should be taught to rely on themselves for protection." Determined to keep the guerrilla conflict from devolving into open war between Missouri and Kansas,

31. Parsons to Stewart, Harrisonville, June 16, 1858, MKBWC.
32. Snyder to Stewart, Papinsville, August 7, 1858; Stewart to Parsons, Jefferson City, May 31, 1858; Parsons to Stewart, Harrisonville, June 16, 1858, MKBWC.

both governors forbade their respective troops from crossing the state line.[33] Even though the border was no impediment to the violent forays of irregular partisans, it remained an extremely sensitive boundary to formal authorities, who were loath to inflame the most explosive intersection of free and slave soil in the United States.

The tenuous peace along the border lasted only through the fall of 1858. In late October, a proslavery gang fired a volley of shots into the home of James Montgomery as he entertained guests J. H. Kagi and George Gill. The nighttime attack failed to injure the guerrilla leader, but it effectively destroyed the June truce. Montgomery returned to Fort Scott in mid-December with a force of nearly a hundred men and the intention to free Benjamin Rice, an ally who had been jailed for robbery. As the free-state raiders passed through the town's main plaza, having freed Rice from jail, they were fired upon by John Little, a proslavery shopkeeper and former marshal. Little missed his target and was quickly gunned down. Distraught at the death of her fiancé, Gene Campbell addressed a furious letter to Montgomery and his men. "O, the anguish you have caused," she wrote. "He was the noblest man ever created, brave and true to his country and word." She closed with a sharp warning: "But remember this, I am a girl but I can fire a pistol and if ever the time comes I will send some of you to the place where theirs 'weeping and knashing of teeth [*sic*].'"[34]

Campbell's impassioned letter sheds uncommon light on the emotional costs of the guerrilla struggle. Her missive also showed that women were not passive participants in this conflict. Most young women probably did not dare to threaten or kill such notorious guerrillas, but many made valuable contributions as spies, smugglers, and informants. Among the contributions that grew from women's traditional responsibilities as domestic caretakers was a noteworthy example near the Little Osage River. A group of free-soil women there presented Montgomery with a new suit of clothes, to replace the old apparel that had been worn out in their defense.[35] Taking up arms against women, even among the moral dislocation and social disorder of guerrilla war, remained beyond the pale of masculine civility and honor, but Campbell's angry missive

---

33. Stewart to Denver, August 7, 1858; Denver to Stewart, August 18, 1858, MKBWC.

34. *Fort Scott Democrat,* December 16, 1858; Vansickle to Father, December 28, 1858, Vansickle Collection, University of Kansas, Kenneth Spencer Research Library; Holman, "Montgomery in Kansas," 66; Campbell to Montgomery, January 4, 1859 (reprint), Fort Scott National Historic Site.

35. Nicole Etcheson, "'Labouring for the Freedom of This Territory': Free-State Women in the 1850s," 73–86.

demonstrates the extent to which the conflict inevitably affected men and women alike.[36]

The firing on the Montgomery home and the subsequent assault on Fort Scott triggered yet another outbreak of guerrilla violence. The fighting, as always, stemmed from the factional conflict between free-soil and proslavery settlers, but it also increasingly took the form of simple banditry and harassment against innocent families. Not long after the Fort Scott raid, for instance, a group of armed men ransacked the Bourbon County home of an elderly settler named Boydston, robbed him of his horse and nearly every other item of value, and threatened to kill the old man, going so far as to fasten a noose around his neck.[37] Such widespread lawlessness, as much as the personalized feuding between political enemies, was responsible for driving many settlers from the border region.

The winter of 1858–1859 also witnessed a fierce offensive against Missouri slaveholders. John Brown returned to Kansas from an eastern sojourn in which he had solicited aid for his ongoing war against slavery. The leader of the Pottawatomie massacre conducted several raids on Missouri farms located in the western townships of Vernon and Bates Counties. On the night of December 20, Brown led a party to the farms of James Lawrence and Isaac Larue, located less than three miles from the Kansas border, and there seized a total of ten slaves, as well as horses, guns, and other household goods.[38] One slaveholder was killed during the raid. Ten days later, an armed posse of Linn County settlers seized a similar number of slaves from the farm of Jerry Jackson. Many of the freed slaves fled to Osawatomie, where the Underground Railroad helped to deliver them further to safety; others took refuge near the army garrison at Fort Scott. The proposed exclusion of black emigrants, though widely supported by free-state and proslavery settlers, had never been implemented, and these former slaves, along with a small number of free black immigrants, formed the early nucleus of Kansas's African American population.[39]

36. Fellman, *Inside War,* 197–207.

37. *Fort Scott Democrat,* December 23, 1858. The outraged newspaper article indicates that the thieves even went so far as to steal the shoes from the feet of the family's children.

38. Harvey Hicklin, "Sworn Statement," Lawrence Papers, VCHS. For Brown's requests for eastern aid, see Brown to George L. Stearns, April 28, 1857; and Stearns to Brown, May 6, 1857, Brown Papers, Library of Congress, Manuscript Division.

39. James E. Mooney to Stewart, January 4, 1859, MKBWC; J. Johnson, *History of Vernon County,* 222–28; Vansickle to Father, December 28, 1858, Vansickle Collection, University of Kansas, Kenneth Spencer Research Library; Monaghan, *Civil War,* 110–11. The exact number of slaves taken from the Jackson farm is unclear. Mooney's letter to Stewart estimates their total value at somewhere above six thousand dollars. For an example of free black immigrants in Fort Scott, see Charles W. Goodlander, *Memoirs and Recollections of Charles W. Goodlander of the Early Days of Fort Scott,* 34.

For Missouri slaveholders, the war that John Brown had brought across the border represented the very kind of abolitionist invasion they had feared for years. Since the 1854 organization of the Massachusetts Emigrant Aid Company, a state-chartered organization committed to building a free Kansas, masters along the border had railed against the fanatical intentions of antislavery radicals. Yet during the intervening years, antislavery settlers had refrained from waging the anticipated crusade against slavery in Missouri. When the long-awaited invasion finally occurred, outraged slaveholders condemned the winter slave-stealing raids as an unjustifiable assault on local communities' "most peaceable and worthy citizens" and their vulnerable wives, children, and homes.[40]

The final will and testament that Cecil Ball drafted in early 1859 illuminated the defensive wariness of many Missouri masters. According to this instrument, Ball sought to distribute several thousand dollars among organizations such as the Southern Aid Society, the Missouri Colonization Society, and the Missouri Bible Society, as well as to local churches. Only his bequest of five thousand dollars to the Presbyterian Church and Society of Little Osage came attached with a carefully drawn political stipulation. In order to receive its gift, the church must "never hire nor employ or keep any preacher . . . who shall teach or preach in public or private any abolition or anti-slavery doctrine or principles." Failure to do so, the benefactor insisted, would result in a forfeiture of the money. The Massachusetts native need not have worried about maintaining conformity among the local congregation. Most members, whether they owned slaves or not, accepted chattel bondage as it existed and likely favored its westward extension, and were thus as unwilling to hire or support such a minister. Yet with the creeping threat of abolitionism finally upon their doorsteps, slaveholders left nothing to chance and circled their ideological wagons against its intrusion in any form.[41]

Some settlers, such as the hundred men who joined the local militia captained by James Mooney, took more aggressive action to defend their households and honor from the harassment of Kansas raiders. Other Missourians again turned to their state government for protection. Vernon County residents issued multiple pleas for assistance, claiming that Montgomery's forces were amassing along the state line and "threaten-

---

40. For descriptions of cross-border "invasions," see Mooney to Stewart, West Point, January 4, 1859, MKBWC.

41. Ball, Last Will and Testament, April 16, 1859, Ball Papers, VCHS.

ing to lay waste to the whole country on the Little Osage."[42] The Missouri General Assembly responded to such appeals with an appropriation of thirty thousand dollars to protect the "persons and property on the western border of this state." In addition, Governor Stewart redirected troops under Adjutant General Parsons back to the counties principally affected by the winter raids. By April, however, Captain William Doak of the Missouri Militia found little to substantiate the rumors of an imminent jayhawker invasion, and his reconnaissance of western Bates County revealed "nothing of an exciting nature."[43]

At the very moment when Missourians were bracing for imminent conflict, partisan foes in Kansas were actually preparing to put down their arms. On January 15, Montgomery told a Lawrence newspaper, "We desire peace, and no man will do more than I to obtain it on honorable terms." Days later the guerrilla leader surrendered to authorities for an attack on a Willow Grove shopkeeper. Citizens in the Bourbon County town of Dayton, meanwhile, organized a peace convention and issued a series of resolutions to Samuel Medary, the new Kansas governor, calling for an end to the guerrilla lawlessness. The territorial legislature took action to alleviate the troubles in southeastern Kansas by passing an amnesty act that absolved citizens in six counties for the commission of past "political" offenses. This measure, like the Denver compromise before it, led to a remarkable decline in feuding. The *Lawrence Republican* marveled at the restoration of order in southeastern Kansas. "The amnesty bill has worked a miracle in Linn County," observed the paper. "The Jayhawkers have returned to their farms, and are once more in safety pursuing the business of the season."[44] The departure of many notorious guerrillas helped make such an extraordinary change possible. "The violent proslavery men," one settler observed, "are all driven out, except for perhaps a very few in Fort Scott who promise to be peaceable." Perhaps the most significant exodus took place sometime in the spring, when John Brown quietly left Kansas for the final time.[45] By July 1859,

42. Petition of Vernon County Residents, Vernon County, March 28, 1859, MKBWC. For similar pleas, see Petitions of Vernon County Residents from August 25, 1859, and November 21, 1860, ibid.

43. Doak to Stewart, April 21, 1859; Stewart to Parsons, April 5, 1859; Stewart to Samuel Medary, April 8, 1859, MKBWC.

44. Quotes from Holman, "Montgomery in Kansas," 78, 82; Holder and Rothman, *Post on the Marmaton*, 92.

45. Everett and Everett, "Letters of John and Sarah Everett," 302 (John Everett to Father and Mother, January 29, 1859). The counties affected by the Amnesty Act included Allen, Anderson, Bourbon, Linn, Lykins, and McGee (Cutler, *History of*

things had become so peaceful that Kansans and Missourians came together at an extraordinary Independence Day celebration held at the Custard farm south of Fort Scott.[46]

As a new era of peace seemed to be descending upon the borderland, its inhabitants began to notice that another kind of threat was slowly developing around them. At some point during the summer of 1859 the rain stopped and simply refused to fall again. The danger was imperceptible at first, as a few days and then a week passed without rain, but as the weeks of dry weather dragged on for months, streambeds dried up, crops withered, and settlers in Missouri and Kansas found themselves trapped in a crippling drought. For settlers who had suffered through bitter warfare and the two-year economic depression that followed the panic of 1857, the timing of the crisis seemed especially cruel.[47] Area farmers responded to crop failures with desperate experimentation. When wheat failed, families plowed up their fields and planted corn; if the corn faltered, then they tried buckwheat, or even turnips. Reuben Lamb, a minister from Linn County, noted that only sorghum seemed to produce even half a normal crop. As hay and grain crops suffered, so did livestock production. Rather than see their animals starve, many farmers slaughtered their hogs and cattle or sold them for a pittance. Others turned to the area's abundant prairie grasses for forage, as bluestem, grama, and other indigenous species proved to be nutritious and remarkably drought tolerant. Purchasing surplus hay was hardly an option for most livestock owners, given the reduced local supply and the fact that most settlers had little cash on hand. In order to feed their families and their stock, some farmers put themselves into debt, taking out mortgages on their already uncertain claims.[48]

Farm families considered the hardships forced upon them by the drought more awful than the terrible years of civil strife. David Reese, a self-described "old settler," believed that he was worse off than before the

---

Kansas, 1:179). The decline of guerrilla fighting in 1859 is noted in several Kansas histories but can also be inferred from the noticeable drop-off in correspondence from settlers in western Missouri to Governor Stewart.

46. Goodlander, *Memoirs and Recollections,* 47.

47. George Edwin McFadin, "Kansas in Early Times," McFadin Papers, KSHS; Joseph G. Gambone, "Economic Relief in Territorial Kansas, 1860–1861," 149–50.

48. Gambone, "Economic Relief," 150–52; Lamb, "The Destitution of Kansas," in *The Prayer of Thaddeus Hyatt to James Buchanan, President of the United States, in Behalf of Kansas, Asking for a Postponement of All the Land Sales in That Territory, and for Other Relief,* by Hyatt, 32–42; Samuel L. Adair to Florella Brown Adair, Osawatomie, March 26, 1861, box 1, folder 3, Samuel L. Adair Family Papers, KSHS; J. Johnson, *History of Vernon County,* 199.

border troubles had erupted. "Then we had money; now we have none. I believe that if all the money in Linn was distributed out even, it would not count three dollars to a man," he wrote. "I have been here since early in '56 and gone through the troubles then; was taken prisoner and dragged away from my family; saw my neighbors' houses burnt and robbed—but, sir, this hour is a darker one for Kansas than even that!" Florella Adair, the half sister of John Brown, echoed Reese's disenchantment with the state of affairs along the border. Adair had traveled back to their former home in Ohio, and, writing to her husband and daughter who remained in Osawatomie, she expressed a deep reluctance to return to Kansas. "It seems to me that the Territory is cursed of the Lord, and that it is fighting against him to try to live there and do any thing but barely to exist," she wrote. "I cannot help feeling a perfect disgust for Kansas life, and most of Kansas people."[49] A great many other individuals may have shared such frustration and joined the swelling exodus from the border region. "A full half the settlers that was here last summer has left and more will leave," wrote one Bourbon County farmer.[50]

The unfortunate timing of the initial public land sale in southeast Kansas made this dire situation even worse. Surveys of the New York and Miami Indian tracts were completed in the summer of 1859, five years after the territory had been officially opened. The lands along the Missouri border were scheduled to hit the market late the following year, at the exact moment when hundreds of settlers no longer had the money necessary to pay for their claims. Many would-be buyers, impoverished by the crop failures that followed the drought, feared their lands could be bought from under them by speculators, railroad developers, and moneyed outsiders.[51] Troubled by the prospect of widespread dispossession in the midst of a worsening famine, Thaddeus Hyatt, an antislavery philanthropist from New York, prevailed upon President Buchanan to postpone the sale of the Kansas lands. Buchanan assured Hyatt that after a fact-finding commission had investigated the situation in Kansas, he would provide whatever relief was necessary, even contributing one hundred dollars of his own money. The president's promises, however, went unfulfilled, and the land sales were carried out as scheduled. Some

49. Testimony of Reese, in *Prayer of Thaddeus Hyatt*, 32; Adair to Samuel and Emma Adair, November 21, 1860, Adair Family Papers, KSHS. Hyatt estimated the size of the total exodus from Kansas in 1859–1860 to be somewhere near one hundred thousand people (*Prayer of Thaddeus Hyatt*, 7).

50. Vansickle to Father, August 17, 1860; to Sir, November 27, 1860, Vansickle Collection, University of Kansas, Kenneth Spencer Research Library.

51. *Fort Scott Democrat*, September 1, 1860; Gambone, "Economic Relief," 162.

two hundred troops mobilized to prevent an outbreak of hostilities, but the proceedings were remarkably uneventful. Sympathizing with the vulnerable plight of the area's cash-poor settlers, officials in the Fort Scott land office conducted the sales quickly and thereby prevented extensive bidding by speculators. Only a small number of claims, fourteen 80-acre tracts in all, were actually sold, going for a price of between $1.25 and $5.50 per acre, and most preemption claims remained in the hands of bona fide settlers.[52]

Although Hyatt had been unable to stop the southeast Kansas land sales, he succeeded in alleviating the suffering of the territory's inhabitants through his work with the large-scale relief program that took shape by the fall of 1860. Hyatt's ties to Kansas stretched back to 1856, when he served as the president of the National Kansas Relief Committee, an organization that provided financial assistance to antislavery colonists. Building upon long-standing ties to eastern benefactors, he also appealed directly to state legislatures and local governments, asking them to contribute to the relief of settlers affected by the drought in Kansas, regardless of their political leanings. His entreaties produced striking results. By the spring of 1861, contributors had donated more than eight million pounds of food, clothing, and grain, in addition to sending more than $80,000 in cash. A surprised Samuel Adair expressed great delight when a complete stranger forwarded him $25 through the mail, and he rejoiced, "The money has come at a time when it was much needed." Eastern charity helped to ease hardship among settlers during the famine of 1859–1860, but lasting relief and a return to self-sufficiency would come only with a change in the weather.[53]

The illusory peace established in 1859 suggested that the worst of Bleeding Kansas was finally over. Ratification of the free-state Wyandotte constitution signaled the final defeat of the Lecompton regime and squelched any lingering hopes for the extension of slavery into Kansas. The goal of statehood, meanwhile, continued to elude Kansans. Both the *Dred Scott* case, in which the U.S. Supreme Court declared that slaves were not U.S. citizens and that Congress could not prohibit slavery in the territories, and John Brown's failed assault on the federal garrison at Harpers Ferry had further widened the nation's sectional schism and made Kansas's admission to the Union even more unlikely. It soon became apparent that the guerrilla conflict, although temporarily stilled, had not

52. Hyatt, *Prayer of Thaddeus Hyatt*, 7; Gambone, "Economic Relief," 162–63.
53. Adair, diary, March 4, 1861, 22, Adair Family Papers, KSHS; *Fort Scott Democrat*, November 10, 1860; Cutler, *History of Kansas*, 1:178; Gambone, "Economic Relief," 152–75.

yet burned itself out. While free-soil Kansans like Montgomery were still fiercely opposed to human bondage and the whites who sought to preserve it, slaveholding Missourians stayed ever distrustful of their antislavery neighbors. Ideological hostility, the ingredient that had fueled the struggle over Kansas, now coupled with raw memories of violence and harassment to make additional fighting a persistent and likely danger.

The emergence of a free Kansas resolved the fate of liberty in the West—the freedom to settle apart from slaves, not with them, had prevailed—but it had also sharpened the divisive meaning of the border with Missouri, making it a violent front line in the battle between defenders and opponents of slavery. By the end of 1860, as sectional tensions finally ripped the United States asunder, no other place illustrated the nation's ideological fissure as starkly as the boundary between Missouri and Kansas. The rolling prairies that stretched southward from the confluence of the Missouri and Kaw (or Kansas) Rivers were one of the few areas in the United States where no clear natural boundaries separated slave territory from free. This country was not, of course, the only place where an artificial boundary marked the limits of slavery. The survey line established by English astronomers Charles Mason and Jeremiah Dixon, which cut across the Allegheny Mountains of Pennsylvania and Maryland, had become the popular shorthand for the boundary between North and South. Within just a few years, however, the Kansas-Missouri border rivaled the Mason-Dixon line as a telling regional marker, having emerged as the most explosive intersection of free and slave societies in the United States.

The open border that separated Kansas and Missouri ran almost imperceptibly for some 150 miles, a distance that offered few reflections of the abrupt ideological divide that it had become. Fierce rhetoric aside, the differences between Kansans and Missourians manifested themselves in varied and subtle ways. Data gathered from the federal census of 1860, for example, exposed similarities as well as contrasts between the two border populations. Most of Kansas had been settled initially by Missourians, and a significant number of Missouri-born settlers continued to live in the eastern tier of counties even after the surge in free-soil violence during the late 1850s.[54] As table 5 (Nativity of Total Population, Kansas and Missouri Border Counties, 1860) illustrates, one of every eight settlers in Bourbon, Linn, and Miami Counties had been born in Missouri.

54. James R. Shortridge confirms the widespread distribution of Missouri-born settlers throughout other counties in eastern Kansas (*Peopling the Plains: Who Settled Where in Frontier Kansas*, 19–21). Shortridge, it should be noted, relies upon the state census conducted in 1865.

There was an obvious generational dimension to this group, as more than three-fourths of the Missouri natives were younger than eighteen. More than a quarter of the adult population in southeastern Kansas, like most settlers in western Missouri, had been born in the slaveholding states of the Upper South. Lingering imprints left by Missourians and other southerners included the Kentucky namesake of Bourbon County and the success of one of its leading newspapers, the proslavery *Fort Scott Democrat*.[55]

Settlers on both sides of the border also seemed to share a common western heritage and to occupy a similar place within the developing frontier economy. More than four out of every five persons living in southeastern Kansas, and an even higher proportion in Missouri, had been born in states west of the Appalachians.[56] Tables 6 and 7 (Distribution of Occupations, Missouri Border Counties, 1850–1880, and Distribution of Occupations, Kansas Border Counties, 1860–1880) outline the distribution of the occupations claimed by household heads in the 1860 census. Families on both sides of the border did indeed share similar economic skills and interests. Through the second half of the nineteenth century, the western United States remained a place where small independent farmers predominated, and the borderland clearly typified this agrarian character. More than 60 percent of the household heads in the six sample counties worked as farmers, whether as independent proprietors, tenants, or laborers.[57] The percentages of merchants, artisans, professionals, and those in other nonagricultural occupations were also consistent across the border. Familiar with the rigorous demands of migration and settlement, the people who settled the border counties had staked their futures to that of the new West, and they maintained a shared interest in the conditions, such as the availability of good land and access to market opportunities, that they saw as necessary to its growth.

Mutual economic interests had the potential to defuse ideological divisions along the border during the territorial period. After the triumph of the free-state movement had resolved the debate over slavery in Kansas,

55. There are apparently no extant newspapers from the adjacent Missouri counties in the antebellum and wartime periods.

56. Calculating the proportion of settlers born west of the Appalachians required that settlers born in Pennsylvania or New Jersey be removed from the Lower Midwest sample and that those born in Virginia, Maryland, and Delaware be removed from the Upper South cohort. The proportion of western-born settlers in Missouri was 87 percent.

57. The extraordinarily low proportion of farmers listed in Bourbon County for 1860 (along with the concomitant spike in the ratio of tenant farmers and farm laborers) likely says more about the peculiar record keeping of that district's enumerator than the importance of farming to the local economy.

free-soil and proslavery elites in many communities made common cause of advancing the territory's commercial development. By the late 1850s, boosters in Lawrence and other Kansas towns had forged commercial ties with mercantile interests in Missouri, and the issue of railroad expansion had helped to facilitate the rapprochement between former political adversaries.[58] Such reconciliation was limited largely to northeastern Kansas, where the guerrilla war had effectively subsided by 1858. In southeastern Kansas, where the border war raged on and spilled into western Missouri, economic concerns, such as the contested question of land claims, continued to serve as a frequent pretense for feuding. The prospect that shared economic interests could override sectional and ideological division would not be tested there until the postwar period.

Despite suggestive demographic comparisons, the seething border conflict exposed fundamental differences between the inhabitants of eastern Kansas and western Missouri. Although the population of territorial Kansas may have closely resembled that of western Missouri in 1855, the contrasts along the border were more obvious five years later. In 1860 three of every four inhabitants of western Missouri hailed from a slave state; two out of three settlers in southeastern Kansas, meanwhile, had been born in free territory. Both populations had indeed sprung from the trans-Appalachian West, but they had plainly come to the border from opposite sides of the slavery divide. Nearly half of the Kansas settlers were born in the states located north of the Ohio River, but barely one out of five Missourians came from the same region. This trend is particularly clear if one looks solely at the heads of household, rather than the entire population, of Kansas (see table 8, Nativity of Southern Heads of Household, Kansas Border Counties, 1860). The majority of household heads in Missouri had come from the Upper South, with almost all of these people having been born in Kentucky, Tennessee, or Virginia.[59]

The more balanced distribution of northern- and southern-born household heads in Kansas merits comment. Within the Missouri border counties, the proportion of household heads who had been born in Missouri or other slave states (75 percent) far exceeded the percentage (21) of those born in a free state. In Kansas, on the other hand, these ratios—33 percent were from slave states and 57 percent from free states—were significantly closer. In some respects, this combustible mélange of free- and slave-state

---

58. SenGupta, *For God and Mammon*, 5–6, 139–57.

59. In the 1860 census sample, 505 household heads in Missouri were born in the Upper South; of this group, 496, or 98 percent, were from Kentucky, Tennessee, or Virginia.

emigrants resembled the more peaceful mixing of northern and southern populations that had taken place a generation or two earlier in the Ohio valley states of Illinois, Indiana, and Ohio.[60] Given their location along the Missouri border, it is not surprising that the eastern tier of counties had a higher concentration of Upper South natives than any other Kansas counties.[61] The southerners who remained after the free-state triumph may have included lingering proslavery partisans, such as the scattered members of Jefferson Buford's failed colonization expedition, but the failure of that effort and the expulsion of many Missouri natives suggest that relatively few stayed.[62]

According to the territorial census of 1855—taken amid the proslavery dominance of the territory—which showed only 200 slaves living in Kansas, relatively few southerners were willing to bring slaves into a territory where human bondage faced an uncertain legal future.[63] Most southerners in the three eastern Kansas counties either had been born in Missouri or had migrated directly from there. Almost all of the southerners who were not from Missouri had been born in other border states of the Upper South. A large number of these settlers, such as Jacob Washburne of Bourbon County, a Tennessee-born farmer who had migrated from Illinois with his wife, Anna, and four children, were born in slave states but spent much of their adult lives in a free state. Within the 1860 census sample, the migration routes of 193 southern heads of households can be traced by looking at the nativity of their children. Like Washburne, more than one-third of this group (36 percent) had been born in a slave state and then moved to free states before immigrating to Kansas.[64]

Most Kansans, therefore, were not the invading Yankee abolitionists that anxious Missourians imagined or portrayed them to be, though there were in fact enough of those to justify such fears. The 1860 census returns from the open border reveal that the proportion of household heads born in the North (New York and New England) was more than four times

60. Nicole Etcheson, *The Emerging Midwest: Upland Southerners and the Political Culture of the Old Northwest, 1787–1861*, 1–14.

61. Shortridge, *Peopling the Plains*, 20–23.

62. Fleming, "Buford Expedition," 48; J. Johnson, *History of Vernon County*, 227.

63. For southerners' migration to the Old Northwest, see Richard Lyle Power, *Planting Corn Belt Culture: The Impress of the Upland Southerner and Yankee in the Old Northwest*, 38; and Etcheson, *Emerging Midwest*. Kansas slaveholding figures come from Gary L. Cheatham, "Divided Loyalties in Civil War Kansas," 93.

64. The sixty-eight southern natives excluded from this calculation either had no children or had only infant children recently born in the Kansas Territory. For anecdotal evidence of other southern-born Kansans who were opposed to slavery, see Everett and Everett, "Letters of John and Sarah Everett," 286 (John Everett to Father, October 26, 1857).

higher in Kansas (17.5 percent) than in Missouri (4.3 percent). This northern population did not dominate any of the three counties in southeastern Kansas, but a survey of its geographic distribution shows an extraordinary concentration of northerners in the Osawatomie township of Miami County, where Yankees, most of them New Yorkers, composed half of the adult population. The several self-described abolitionists who lived in the immediate vicinity of Osawatomie included Florella Brown Adair, half sister of the executed John Brown, and her husband, Samuel, an Oberlin-educated Congregational minister, as well as John and Sarah Everett, dairy farmers who had migrated to Kansas with the expressed purpose of making it a free territory.

Nativity data is but one means of assessing the antagonistic societies that had taken shape along the Missouri-Kansas border. Simply knowing where individuals were born offers an imperfect measure of their attitudes toward slavery. The debate over extending bondage into the western territories had framed basic divisions along the border, but that issue did not fully explain the cultural and political distance that lay between Kansans and Missourians in 1860. The cause of that distance also lay with the tumultuous events of the past five years, which had been responsible for driving people already separated by birth and divided over slavery even further apart. The recent territorial struggle had profoundly influenced the way that settlers along the border saw themselves and their neighbors across the state line. Bleeding Kansas had reinforced each side's worst stereotypes of the other and had fostered the rise of the nation's most explosive political fault line. Both the presidential election of 1860 and local reactions to the secession of southern states in the months that followed would provide a fuller measure of these divisions.

The presidential election of 1860 exposed the extent to which the slavery debate had split America's major political parties. Many of the sectional fractures exposed in that contest could be traced back to the Kansas crisis. When the Kansas-Nebraska Act was passed by Congress in 1854, it had torn the Democratic Party along sectional lines, gaining nearly unanimous support from southerners while dividing northern Democrats. The controversial submission of the proslavery Lecompton constitution widened the North-South schism, and shortly after April 23, 1860, when Democratic delegates gathered at the nominating convention in Charleston, South Carolina, the party split into two regional factions, each of which would nominate its own presidential candidate. The Kansas-Nebraska Act also spelled the demise of the Whig Party, whose members were equally unable to reconcile their differences over slavery. In the South, many former Whigs aligned themselves with the Democratic

Party; northern ex-Whigs gravitated toward the Know-Nothing, Liberty, and Free-Soil Parties, which had emerged in the wake of the collapsed two-party system. In the North, many former Whigs who opposed slavery would eventually rally behind the candidacy of Abraham Lincoln, the presidential nominee of the recently formed Republican Party.[65]

The Kansas-Missouri line reflected the political cleavages that had reshaped the American political system. Within five years of its organization, Kansas had become a clear Republican stronghold. Loyal identification with a regionally based, antislavery party was predictable in parts of the territory, such as the town of Lawrence, where social, cultural, and political ties to northeastern abolitionists had always been strong. Elsewhere, support for the Republicans was less widespread. In addition to the proslavery immigrants who were bound to the Democratic Party by ties of family and tradition, most of the free-state candidates elected to the extralegal Topeka legislature in January 1856 had also identified with the party of Andrew Jackson. Charles Goodlander recalled that when he arrived in southeastern Kansas in April 1858, the local population could be classified politically into three groups: proslavery Democrats, free-soil Democrats, and politically indifferent border ruffians. He supposed that Tom Roberts and a man known locally as "Old Roach" were the only two Republicans in the area.[66] By the late 1850s, however, the territorial dominance of Kansas Democrats had passed, leaving stalwarts like the hidebound publisher of the *Fort Scott Democrat*, a proslavery partisan and steadfast defender of James Buchanan, in the political minority.[67]

The declining fortunes of the Democratic Party in Kansas reflected a sea change in the partisan loyalties of the territory's voters. The influx of free-soil settlers from the Old Northwest, where the Republican Party drew much of its gaining strength, facilitated this transformation.[68] Opposition to the expansion of slavery was the central issue for this new party and proved a ready ideological fit for the thousands of settlers working to make Kansas a free state. The territorial crisis transformed a great many other Kansans into new Republicans. For many free-state settlers, the Democrats had become hopelessly identified as the party of proslavery Missourians, ruffians, and the abusive Lecompton regime. What's more, actions pursued by successive Democratic presidents, Pierce and Buchanan—the

65. James McPherson, *Battle Cry of Freedom: The Civil War Era*, 213–33; Etcheson, *Bleeding Kansas*, 19–20.
66. Goodlander, *Memoirs and Recollections*, 13; Monaghan, *Civil War*, 46.
67. *Fort Scott Democrat*, May 20, 1858.
68. Foner, *Free Soil*, 109; Paul Kleppner, *The Cross of Culture: A Social Analysis of Midwestern Politics, 1850–1900*, 8–12.

appointment of ineffective territorial governors, the endorsement of the Lecompton constitution, and the mismanagement of federal land sales— drove many Kansans from the party's ranks.[69]

The formal organization of the Kansas Republican Party took place in May 1859 at Osawatomie, a town that had been burned by Missouri raiders three years earlier. Among the gathering of nearly seventy delegates and five hundred onlookers assembled to hear Horace Greeley speak that day was Frank Walker, a Mound City farmhand who viewed the meeting as a sign of Kansas's certain admission as a free state.[70] The magnitude of the political shift in southeastern Kansas became apparent by the fall of 1859, when local Republican candidates in Bourbon, Linn, and Miami Counties all won with substantial majorities. The entire slate of Republican candidates was again elected in 1860.[71]

If the territorial period had indeed been the crucible of Kansas Republicanism, it also served to strengthen the established Democratic allegiances of settlers in western Missouri. The outcome of the gubernatorial race held in 1857, in which Democrat Robert Stewart faced James Rollins, a former Whig from Columbia, reflected the border counties' partisan leanings. Stewart won the election by a slim margin of 337 votes (out of 95,616 ballots cast), but in the three counties on the open western border he trounced Rollins by more than twenty percentage points. Democratic candidates in this area would enjoy an even stronger showing in the regular gubernatorial election in August 1860. Mirroring the earlier fracture at the national convention in Charleston, Democrats in Missouri split into two factions: one, the so-called Douglas Democrats, endorsed the more moderate northern wing, while the other supported the Ultra, or states' rights, platform. The Douglas wing chose Claiborne Fox Jackson of Saline County, and the Ultras (or Breckinridge Democrats) selected Hancock Jackson from Randolph County. Two other candidates, Republican James Gardenhire and Constitutional Unionist Sample Orr, rounded out the crowded gubernatorial ballot.[72]

The August election (see table 9, Results of Missouri Gubernatorial Election, 1860) revealed that although Missouri voters were still politically divided from their Kansas neighbors, they nevertheless favored

69. Castel, *Frontier State*, 17; Miner, *Kansas*, 56.

70. Walker to Brother, May 23, 1859, box 91, Walker Papers, KSHS; Cutler, *History of Kansas*, 2:879; Etcheson, *Bleeding Kansas*, 201.

71. *Fort Scott Democrat*, November 10, 1859, November 17, 1859; *Mound City Report*, November 16, 1860.

72. March, *The History of Missouri*, 2:856–58. The special election of 1857 was organized to fill the vacancy left by the resignation of Trusten Polk (Missouri Gubernatorial Election Results, Bates, Cass, and Vernon Counties, 1857, Missouri State Archives).

candidates who promoted compromise over sectional extremism. The winner of the election, Claiborne Fox Jackson, was barely five years removed from participating in one of the infamous cross-border raids in which citizens from western Missouri marched into Kansas to vote in territorial elections.[73] Jackson owed his triumph to a perceptive awareness of Missourians' preference for political moderation. A protégé of Senator David Rice Atchison, he privately sympathized with southern Democrats but recognized that rumblings of secession could alienate many potential supporters. He thus held his ground as a Douglas Democrat in title, if not spirit. This shrewd calculation paid off, as Jackson claimed 47 percent of the statewide vote. He and Sample Orr, the other middle-of-the-road candidate, together won almost 90 percent of the ballots. Neither Hancock Jackson, the third-place finisher, nor Gardenhire, who received most of his votes from parts of Missouri with large German American populations, played a significant role in the overall race.

Slight differences distinguished the results along the open border from the broader statewide tally. There, as elsewhere, the two most moderate choices, Claiborne Fox Jackson and Samuel Orr, received strong support. Democrats fared even better in the border counties than they had in the gubernatorial election of 1857, with the Jacksons polling more than 80 percent of the votes in Bates and Vernon Counties. The Unionist candidate, Orr, ran well in Cass County, winning nearly half the votes, but he struggled in the two counties to the south. Gardenhire, the lone antislavery candidate, received zero votes in the three border counties.[74] Missouri voters, it seemed, had no taste for politicians who would stand for the restriction or elimination of slavery in the western territories.

The most striking feature of the gubernatorial election along the border was the unusually strong showing by Hancock Jackson in all three border counties. Although the Ultra candidate failed to win any of these counties, he received a significantly higher proportion of the votes there (16 percent in Bates, 21 in Cass, and 38 in Vernon) than he did statewide (7 percent). His greatest success came in the county most directly affected by the violence of the jayhawker raids and slave-stealing expeditions of the past two years. The effect of these events on local citizens, more than any other factor, explained Hancock Jackson's popularity in Vernon County. Neither he nor any of the other three candidates benefited from

73. Phillips, *Missouri's Confederate*, 201.

74. Missouri Gubernatorial Election Results, Bates, Cass, and Vernon Counties, 1860, Missouri State Archives; March, *The History of Missouri*, 2:858–59; William E. Parrish, *A History of Missouri*, 1–3.

any geographic advantage. In fact, the two candidates from western Missouri, Orr (from Buchanan County) and Gardenhire (Greene County), received the fewest votes.[75]

Any number of factors clearly defined Vernon County as part of the American West in 1860. Yet in spite of its isolation, sparse population, and brief history—the county had been formally organized only four years earlier—the voting preferences of local citizens revealed that they had come to see themselves as southerners as much as westerners. Even though Hancock Jackson was the most ardently proslavery candidate, slaveholding statistics do not by themselves explain his appeal on the border, for Vernon had the lowest incidence of slave ownership (less than 5 percent of households) and the smallest average slaveholding (2.2 slaves per master) among the three counties sampled.[76] Although most citizens did not own slaves, Vernon County voters—defensive, fearful, and politically galvanized by the continued danger of guerrilla attacks—embraced the criticisms that Hancock Jackson and other proslavery leaders leveled against abolitionists, Republicans, and the exclusion of slavery from the western territories. These Missourians' ardently proslavery politics were thus an expression of their newfound oppositional identity. That is, Vernon County voters' support for the Ultra candidate was not simply an affirmation of Hancock Jackson's political platform; rather, it was an explicit rejection of what their free-state foes in Kansas represented.[77]

The August election foreshadowed the outcome of the presidential contest that was held three months later. Statewide, Missouri voters continued to support moderate candidates who stood, above all else, for the preservation of the Union and the protection of southerners' right to own slaves. Stephen A. Douglas, the standard-bearer of the northern Democrats, saw his only electoral triumph come from Missouri. He received 58,801 votes, barely more than the 58,372 ballots cast for John Bell, the nominee of the Constitutional Union Party and winner of the Upper South states of Kentucky, Tennessee, and Virginia. John C. Breckinridge

75. Missouri Gubernatorial Election Results, Bates, Cass, and Vernon Counties, 1860, Missouri State Archives. For details surrounding the slave-liberating expeditions of John Brown and others, see J. Johnson, *History of Vernon County*, 222–30, 264; and Reynolds, *John Brown, Abolitionist*, 278–80.

76. Census-Slave, Missouri, Bates, Cass, and Vernon Counties, 1860; Phillips, *Missouri's Confederate*, 181–205. The proportion of slaveholding households was 8 percent in Bates County and 18 percent in Cass County; the median slaveholdings there were 5.7 and 3.5, respectively.

77. For oppositional identity, see James C. Cobb, *Away Down South: A History of Southern Identity*, 4–6; and Anne Sarah Rubin, *A Shattered Nation: The Rise and Fall of the Confederacy*, 86.

swept the states of the Deep South but placed third in Missouri, winning 31,317 votes. The Republican candidate, Abraham Lincoln, won just over 17,000 votes, or almost three times the total Gardenhire had received in August, but finished a distant fourth. Lincoln's decisive triumph throughout the North, however, gave him enough electoral votes to become the nation's sixteenth president.[78]

Results from the presidential election are hard to come by in the border counties, but limited evidence from western Missouri shows an area that was politically at odds with the new president-elect. In Vernon County the election again proved to be a three-person contest and resembled the vote from the Deep South more closely than it did the statewide race. Improving upon Hancock Jackson's strong showing, Breckinridge claimed a majority (51 percent) of the county's votes, while Bell and Douglas finished second and third, respectively. Yet again the Republican candidate failed to record a single vote.[79] Nativity patterns also do not explain the greater support that secessionist candidates received in Vernon County, as the percentage of southern-born adults was actually lower there in 1860 than in the other two border counties.[80]

Election-day accounts recorded in a pair of local histories reveal the depth of Missourians' hostility toward the antislavery party. When one older citizen attempted to cast his ballot for the Republican ticket, an election official laughed and turned him away, explaining there was no Lincoln poll book available. Cowed by the threats of local Democrats, other settlers who might have voted Republican—a group estimated at perhaps twenty men—simply chose to stay home, unwilling to risk their safety through a public voice vote.[81] The few Republicans who lived in Bates County also faced widespread harassment but were nonetheless allowed to vote. After the election, however, they no doubt recoiled to find that their ballots had been posted in public alongside notices encouraging those voters to "make themselves scarce."[82] Election fraud and

78. March, *The History of Missouri,* 2:859; McPherson, *Battle Cry of Freedom,* 232.

79. Results for the November election in Missouri were available only in Vernon County. Contemporary newspapers from Linn and Bourbon Counties in Kansas provided the election results for local offices, all of which were apparent Republican victories, but not the presidential race. See *Mound City Report,* November 16, 1860; and *Fort Scott Democrat,* November 10, 17, 1860.

80. The percentages of household heads born in the Upper South or Lower South were 56.6 percent in Vernon County, 61.7 percent in Bates County, and 70.6 percent in Cass County.

81. J. Johnson, *History of Vernon County,* 264–65, which provides the estimate of potential Republican voters, indicates that viva voce voting remained the norm in most districts.

82. Bates County Old Settlers Society, *Old Settlers' History,* 38.

political violence, both threatened and real, had plagued the state line for years, but until now it had mostly taken place on the Kansas side of the line. Missouri Republicans, no longer welcome in communities where the bounds of political dissent had been forcefully circumscribed, may have joined the growing exodus of settlers that had begun in the western townships years earlier.

The presidential election fueled anxieties about disunion and war for citizens living along both sides of the border. Recognizing the momentous significance of the contest at hand, the parishioners of a Methodist church in Kansas dedicated November 2, the Friday before the election, as a day of fasting and prayer "for the preservation of the Union, in the coming crisis." These settlers understood that with the election of Abraham Lincoln, indignant slaveholders who had long raised the possibility of secession were now more likely to act upon those threats. "Can we regard it [Lincoln's election] as anything less than a declaration of war upon the whole slave property of all the Southern States?" exclaimed Missouri's governor-elect, Claiborne Fox Jackson. "Is it not a moral dissolution of the Union?" As the election results filtered into a Fort Scott newspaper office, the editor offered his pessimistic assessment of the situation. "We will await with extreme anxiety the operations of the next sixty days," he wrote. "We feel that the Union of the States is hanging by a brittle thread which may now, at any moment, be snapped. A spark has been kindled, and the *breath of Disunion* will endeavor to kindle it into a flame. The signs of the times indicate a fearful catastrophe, which nothing but the protecting hand of an overruling Providence can overt."[83]

While the potential fallout from Lincoln's election in the South captured the attention of observers throughout the nation, the renewal of civil war along the Kansas-Missouri line came quickly. During the drought of the past two summers, a decline in guerrilla violence had nurtured a false sense of security among many people living in Kansas. "The summer of 1860 passed undisturbed by the Jayhawk troubles, and we felt that we were through with them," recalled one Kansan.[84] Many of the conflict's worst antagonists had in fact fled the scene. John Brown, the most mythologized warrior of Bleeding Kansas, was gone, executed for treason by the Commonwealth of Virginia, and Charles Hamilton, mastermind of the Marais des Cygnes massacre, had escaped to Georgia. Nevertheless, the most notorious jayhawker chieftains of recent years, James Montgomery

83. *Fort Scott Democrat*, November 3, 1860; Jackson quoted in March, *The History of Missouri*, 2:859; *Fort Scott Democrat*, November 10, 1860.
84. Goodlander, *Memoirs and Recollections*, 61.

and Charles Jennison, were still in the country, and hostilities between jay-hawkers and Missouri slaveholders continued to fester. As a result, the threats, rumors, and suspicions of an impending jayhawker invasion remained fresh in the minds of Missourians.

Montgomery's maneuverings over the past year, had they been widely known in Missouri, certainly would have warranted such anxiety among proslavery citizens. During the late summer, as a second year of drought continued to cripple agriculture in Kansas, he had traveled to Boston and New York to solicit the aid of wealthy eastern donors. After Montgomery met with George Stearns, the chairman of the Massachusetts State Kansas Aid Committee and the person who had helped furnish arms to John Brown, he returned home in September to await shipment of the peculiar assistance he had sought. That assistance—a cache of Sharps rifles—arrived within a month, and although some of the weapons had been damaged in transit, their recipient gladly declared the goods serviceable.[85]

Weeks later, in the days that followed Lincoln's election, free-soil Kansans renewed their attacks against slavery along the Missouri border. This campaign began with the harassment of prominent proslavery settlers still living in Kansas. Less than a week after the election, a gang organized by Jennison lynched Samuel Scott, a wealthy Bourbon County resident and former sheriff of Bates County, Missouri. A few nights later, a large number of armed riders surrounded the home of Lester Moore, who had helped a local vigilance committee hang a free-state man, who had himself been accused of horse stealing months earlier. After Moore refused the bandits' demands to be admitted, Jennison kicked down the door and shot the man as he sat in bed.[86] The jayhawker bands also targeted individuals who were suspected of seizing freed blacks and returning them to slavery in Missouri. The execution of Russell Hinds, who had received a twenty-five-dollar bounty for returning an escaped slave to his Missouri master, represented the most prominent example of the free-soil effort to deter the recovery of fugitive slaves. After hanging Hinds in the timbered bottoms along Mine Creek, just west of the state line, the lynch mob abandoned his body, leaving a note in his pocket to affirm that he was executed for "kidnapping negroes."[87]

85. Montgomery to Stearns, October 6, 1860, Stearns Papers, KSHS; Holman, "Montgomery in Kansas," 91–93.

86. *Fort Scott Democrat*, November 17, 1860; Gustavus A. Parsons to Robert M. Stewart, December 8, 1860, MKBWC; Cutler, *History of Kansas*, 2:1070.

87. Jennison to Stearns, November 28, 1860, Stearns Papers, KSHS; *Fort Scott Democrat*, December 1, 1860; Cutler, *History of Kansas*, 2:1106; Etcheson, *Bleeding Kansas*, 221.

Kansans' reactions to the Hinds murder revealed their ambivalence about whether fugitive slaves should be returned to bondage. The *Fort Scott Democrat* condemned the recent killings and the brazen willingness of Montgomery and his banditti to steal slaves from Missouri farms in direct contravention of the Fugitive Slave Act. From the *Democrat*'s perspective, free-soil vigilantes, rather than slave catchers, posed a greater threat to the security of local communities. "These men must be got rid of. They must be killed, driven out of the country, or intimidated," the paper concluded. "The Montgomery gang must be put down, or every honest man must leave the country." Many other Kansans, however, supported the jayhawkers' actions. A convention held in Mound City on December 8 passed a series of resolutions justifying the murders of Scott, Moore, and Hinds. The editorials issued by the Republican publisher of the *Mound City Report* embodied such sentiments. The "barbarous, and sinful, degrading, inhuman and unnatural" practice of "man hunting" demanded forceful action. "It has become a settled principle here, that every person who engages in man hunting, forfeits his life," asserted the editor. "The time had come when our people had either to submit to man hunting, or they had to deal promptly with the man hunter. There was no longer opportunity to evade the issue."[88]

James Montgomery, for his part, denied any involvement in the Hinds lynching but found no fault in the execution of the proslavery partisan. He and other free-state guerrillas scoffed at the moral legitimacy of the Fugitive Slave Act and the ability of federal troops to enforce it. Montgomery had been assisting and sheltering fugitive slaves from Missouri and Arkansas since at least October. "In regard to slaves, our position is this: If any State wishes to keep slaves let her keep them at home. If they allow them to come here, they must be free," he concluded. "Fugitives," the guerrilla leader added, "are as safe here as they would be in Canada." The jayhawkers found sanction for their punishment of slave catchers in Old Testament scripture, quoting Exodus 21:16: "He that stealeth a man, and selleth him, or if he be found in his hand, he shall surely be put to death." The killings of proslavery men represented an aggressive turn in the jayhawkers' ideological war on slavery in the West. According to the *Fort Scott Democrat*, Montgomery reportedly delivered a speech in the town of Mapleton in which he declared, "We are neither Democrats nor Republicans, but ABOLITIONISTS. We are determined that slaves shall never be retaken in Kansas. We intend to operate against South-west Missouri as soon as we clear out all opposition in the Territory. We have been

88. *Fort Scott Democrat*, December 1, 1860; *Mound City Report*, November 16, 1860.

preparing for this a year, and have now arrived at that point when concealment is no longer desirable."[89]

News of recent killings and rumors of a general jayhawker invasion alarmed Missouri settlers across the border. On November 21, citizens of Vernon County wrote lame-duck governor Robert Stewart, asking for protection from invading Kansans; two days later, Bates County residents sent word to the capital, echoing the call for assistance. Similar pleas had led Stewart to station soldiers along the border twice during the past two years, in the summer of 1858 and the spring that followed. Hearing of the potential crisis along the state line, a host of local militias throughout Missouri now volunteered their services to the governor. Eager companies from Hannibal, St. Joseph, Cape Girardeau, Fredericktown, Louisiana, and Cedar County all offered to take up arms against Montgomery and company. Moving quickly to defend the western boundary yet again, Stewart dispatched a brigade of state militia under General Daniel Frost to the open border.[90]

The commencement of the Southwest Expedition, as the mission to the border became known, occasioned considerable fanfare as Frost's men departed from St. Louis on November 25. Governor Stewart had charged the Missouri troops with a strictly defensive purpose—the protection of the western counties—and although he had cautioned them against crossing into Kansas, at least one soldier looked forward to taking the battle across the state line: "There is every prospect of our marching . . . and possibly entering Kansas in pursuit of Montgomery."[91] The brigade traveled by rail as far west as the yet uncompleted Missouri Pacific could take them, reaching the town of Smithton, and then prepared to hike the remaining seventy miles across the rolling, snow-covered prairies. At Windsor, in northeastern Henry County, a large crowd of local settlers saluted the volunteers with boisterous applause, but as the troops moved closer to the border the reception was less than enthusiastic. "Many along our route have failed to treat us with ordinary civility for fear of incurring the displeasure of these Kansas outlaws and marauders," Frost noted. John Dryden resented the presence of any troops, saying, "I think it is a pretty pass when we have to have an army quartered on us. Ought not such a government be ashamed of itself."[92]

89. Montgomery to Stearns, November 27, December 12, 1860, Stearns Papers, KSHS; Cutler, *History of Kansas*, 2:1106; *Fort Scott Democrat*, January 5, 1861.

90. Vernon County Residents to Stewart, petition, November 21, 1860; Frost to Stewart, November 22, 1860, MKBWC.

91. Phillip T. Tucker, "'Ho, for Kansas': The Southwest Expedition of 1860," 30.

92. Frost to Stewart, December 5, 1860, MKBWC; Dryden, December 25, 1860, *With Plow and Pen: The Diary of John G. Dryden, 1856–1883*, 9.

When the expedition set up camp at Balltown, near the deserted mill that had belonged to Cecil Ball, its leaders were struck by the desolation they encountered.[93] Much of the countryside, Frost observed, was rapidly becoming depopulated as farmers abandoned their homes out of fear of guerrilla harassment. Describing the economic impact of the border war to the governor, he wrote, "The pecuniary losses are incalculable. Lands which were, and should be worth from fifteen to twenty dollars an acre are now offered at five dollars and find no purchasers." Gustavus Parsons found that the population decline was offset by an influx of proslavery Kansans seeking temporary refuge in Missouri. Although both men agreed that local anxieties and the unsettled state of affairs justified the troops' presence along the border, the rumored guerrilla invasion never materialized. On December 8, barely a week after the expedition had established Camp Daniel Boone by the banks of the Little Osage River, Frost concluded that Montgomery and his marauders had disbanded. Stewart, sensing that a crisis had again been averted, ordered most of Frost's men back east but left a small force, dubbed the Southwest Battalion, to protect the state line. The soldiers who returned to St. Louis, having repelled the jayhawker threat, were greeted as heroes.[94]

News of the military presence across the border sparked great excitement among Kansans, who girded themselves for a seemingly inevitable confrontation with their Missouri neighbors. One editor described the wary tension that pervaded Fort Scott and concluded, "The people are now on the alert." Montgomery, whose free-state guerrillas had not in fact disbanded, deemed the militia's latest mobilization a prelude to open warfare. "I am not in favor of invading the slave state," he wrote to an ally. "But if they cross the line to interfere with us as Missouri is now threatening to do, then I would consider the war begun."[95] Over the past four years, Kansas emerged as the first battlefield in the nation's fight over slavery; the boundary between free Kansas and slaveholding Missouri was now the front line of that conflict. With that, the guerrilla captain joined thousands of Kansans and Missourians in casting his eyes across the border, convinced of his neighbors' hostile intentions and expecting the worst to follow.

93. Ball had died just days earlier, on November 24. See J. Johnson, *History of Vernon County*, 388.

94. Frost to Stewart, December 5, 1860; Parsons to Stewart, December 2, 1860; Frost to Stewart, December 8, 1860; Stewart to Frost, December 10, 1860, MKBWC; Tucker, "'Ho, for Kansas,'" 33.

95. *Fort Scott Democrat*, December 1, 1860; Montgomery to F. B. Sanborn, January 14, 1861, Stearns Papers, KSHS.

FOUR

" 'REVENGE' WAS THE WATCHWORD"

*I*n April 1861, John Dryden recorded two significant occurrences in his journal. He greeted the first development, the arrival of spring rains, with relief. Consecutive years of unusually dry weather had crippled agriculture along the Kansas-Missouri border, causing successive crop failures and, with the onset of winter, raising the unsettling prospect of starvation. Many families had fled the country, but the Drydens stayed put, surviving on a limited diet of cornmeal and wild game. Their perseverance was rewarded in late March, when a steady rain began to fall and continued unabated for nearly a fortnight. Reed's Creek had been dried out by two rainless summers, but now swollen by the springtime deluge, it spilled over its banks and inundated much of the family's farm. Drought had ruined the previous season's wheat and left the corn stalks withered and twisted, but as the precipitation softened the soil of their cracked fields, it brightened the Drydens' hopes for the planting that was at hand.[1]

John Dryden had experienced enough excitement over the past decade to appreciate the simple promise of April showers. At the age of seventeen, he had left his parents' farm in Buchanan County, Missouri, to join the surge of emigrants seeking wealth and adventure in California. Young Dryden, like most would-be miners, found little gold. But his western

1. Dryden, diary, April 7, 1861, Dryden Papers, VCHS. For another ebullient reaction to the rainfall, see *Fort Scott Democrat*, April 6, 1861.

excursion did not leave him empty-handed, and he returned with enough wealth to acquire a modest farm at the relatively young age of twenty-one. Having indulged his youthful wanderlust, John settled down in western Missouri on a promising tract of land near the Little Osage River. This claim offered access to water and timber, plus close proximity to the trading post at Fort Scott. There was a serious drawback to the farm's location, however, as it lay in the middle of the bloody feud being waged by proslavery Missourians and free-soil Kansas settlers. Dryden arrived in Vernon County during the summer of 1856, just months after the murder of five men along Pottawatomie Creek; the Marais des Cygnes massacre would take place two years later and barely twenty miles away. His closest brush with Bleeding Kansas came in December 1858, when John Brown brought his holy crusade against slavery within five miles of Dryden's home.[2]

Unlike many neighbors who were harassed, robbed, or murdered by jayhawker bands, Dryden apparently suffered few abuses. He professed to hold little personal interest in whether Kansas became a free or slave state. The majority of Missourians, himself included, did not own slaves, but most whites accepted the presence of slavery within their own state. A few, like Dryden, quietly criticized the institution as a "relic of barbarism." As a newcomer to the open western border, he was also unburdened by the grudges and personal enmity that fueled much of the guerrilla fighting. Although the threat of violence had driven away more than a thousand settlers on both sides of the border, Dryden stubbornly held to his 120-acre claim. He managed to stay out of the border war for almost five years and amid unnerving circumstances went about an ordinary life of raising crops and starting a family, as he had married Louisa Meek, a native of southern Indiana, on August 6, 1857.[3]

While springtime thunderstorms refreshed Dryden's hopes for the coming year, the second major event that he recorded in April 1861 threatened to upset any prospects for a peaceful future. The event had taken place more than a thousand miles to the east, but its importance was as evident as the rain falling outside John and Louisa's door. "Sumpter [sic] is bombarded!" he noted on the evening of April 15, referring to the Confederate attack on the federal garrison in Charleston

2. Dryden, 1856–1860, *With Plow and Pen*, 1–10.
3. Dryden, diary, November 13, 1865, Dryden Papers, VCHS. Dryden's views on slavery and race were expressed in other diary entries. See Dryden, May 22, 1863, *With Plow and Pen*, 17. Brophy's notes indicate that Louisa and John were born in adjacent Indiana counties. It is unclear whether they knew each other before moving to Missouri.

harbor three days earlier. He immediately surmised that the bombardment of Fort Sumter marked the commencement of war between the United States and the newly formed Confederate States of America. The attack was a concussive effect of the nation's inability to mend its divisions through compromise, and in Dryden's angry estimation it also signaled the failure of America's republican experiment. "Is it possible that man is not capable of self-government?" he wondered. The Union had begun to unravel months earlier with the secession of South Carolina and six other southern states. This sectional rupture distressed but did not surprise Dryden, for he had feared such an outcome as far back as 1856, during the tense period that followed the Pottawatomie murders. The weeks following the Confederate attack on Fort Sumter, which saw the secession of four more southern states and the mobilization of the Union war machine, affirmed Dryden's fears: a national civil war had come at last.[4]

By the spring of 1861, the open border between Missouri and Kansas had been engulfed in internecine strife for nearly five years. In fact, local newspapers would recall a hundred years later that the American Civil War had started in their own backyards.[5] The bitter guerrilla fighting that began in territorial Kansas and extended into western Missouri had indeed served as both a prelude and a catalyst for an even more ruinous war. In some respects this confrontation was a continuation of an ongoing guerrilla struggle waged by familiar foes, border ruffians and jayhawkers, who continued to pursue a strategy of terror to punish partisan enemies. At the same time, however, the fighting that took place from 1861 to 1865 was part of a unique and altogether more devastating crisis. Bleeding Kansas, the most murderous chapter of the antebellum sectional struggle, had claimed only a fraction of the lives that would be lost over the next four years.[6] A more complex, all-encompassing crisis than the Kansas struggle, the Civil War reinforced the existing hostility between Missourians and Kansans, slaveholders and abolitionists. Yet this conflict also hardened the ideological divisions from the territorial conflict by invoking fundamental questions of loyalty and patriotism and thus revealed new divisions on each side of the border. The onset of war had dramatically different effects on opposite sides of the state line. To the west, the attack on Fort Sumter and Lincoln's call for troops galvanized support for the Union among Kansas citizens and eroded old

4. Dryden, April 15, 1861, *With Plow and Pen,* 10–11.
5. *Butler (Mo.) newsXpress,* May 2000.
6. For an assessment of casualties during Bleeding Kansas, see Dale E. Watts, "How Bloody Was Bleeding Kansas? Political Killings in Kansas Territory, 1854–1861."

partisan divisions; to the east, Missourians greeted these events with ambivalence, torn between a hope to preserve both the Union and slavery, and latent sympathies toward southerners and secession.

The presence and policy of the United States Army, charged with the difficult task of subduing the guerrilla threat, also changed the dynamic of the border war. This was particularly true in Missouri, where most of the fighting between guerrillas and soldiers would take place. Restrained by a Buchanan administration reluctant to intervene in territorial Kansas, federal troops had played only a minor role during the troubles of the late 1850s. With the fall of Fort Sumter, securing the loyalty of Missouri and other border states became a top priority for President Lincoln. The Union army established control in most of Missouri during the early years of the war but struggled to contain the violent guerrillas who infested much of the rural western border.

The army's efforts were complicated by the widespread support that pro-Confederate guerrillas enjoyed among Missourians, whose own latent southern loyalties had been aroused by the Kansas crisis and would be inflamed by an unwelcome military occupation. A frustrated Union command therefore developed a two-pronged strategy that aimed not only to eliminate these guerrillas but also to undermine the popular support they received from local citizens. As the conflict shifted primarily to Missouri, it pitted federal soldiers against guerrillas and the society that supported them and thus became a total war in which the lines between combatants and civilians were often blurred.[7]

John Dryden understood well the implications of disunion. Though he may not have foreseen the terror and destruction that would soon be visited upon the Missouri-Kansas border, he likely comprehended his own precarious position in the coming war. He had survived the Kansas crisis with his home and health intact, but it would be much more difficult for him to remain disengaged from the impending conflict. The centrifugal momentum of recent events—the unending traumas of Bleeding Kansas, the *Dred Scott* decision, John Brown's failed takeover at Harpers Ferry, the fractured presidential election and Southwest Expedition of 1860, and, finally, the assault on Fort Sumter—made neutrality practically untenable and dissent increasingly dangerous. An outspoken Union man in an area dominated by secessionists, Dryden clung to unpopular views that would make him a repeated target of guerrilla harassment. Eventually, he would

7. Fellman, *Inside War*, is the most outstanding history of the border war from 1861 to 1865. For the emergence of southern identity in Missouri, see Phillips, *Missouri's Confederate*.

take refuge on the Kansas side of the political divide, finding shelter among Unionists and opponents of slavery like himself.

Like Dryden, citizens in Kansas Territory, regardless of their partisan loyalties, were shaken by news of South Carolina's secession from the Union. A proslavery Democrat in Fort Scott condemned the act as the mark of a "rash and fanatical set of a few ambitious and misguided men."[8] Free-state men in Linn County regarded the withdrawal of South Carolina and six other southern states as a sign that war was nearly inevitable, and soon mustered themselves into a local militia, the Mound City Rifle Guards.[9] Many Kansans feared that the dissolution of the Union might trigger additional violence closer to home and thus resolved to lay aside their prior differences for the greater good of the nation. "We believe it to be the first duty of every citizen, in view of the present disintegrated condition of the Union, to ignore all minor considerations, until the Union is restored or reconstructed," insisted a Bourbon County editor. Speaking to a large gathering in Fort Scott, Senator James Lane, who had hardly been a unifying figure in territorial politics, encouraged residents of Kansas and Missouri to cultivate friendly relations.[10]

The question of secession engendered less unanimity among a divided Missouri citizenry. The possibility of withdrawing from the Union attracted an influential group of advocates in the state. In the legislative election held just two months earlier, the secessionist Breckinridge Democrats had claimed 47 of the 132 seats in the Missouri House and 15 of the 33 senate seats; among the Missourians who were most sympathetic to the idea of secession was the state's recently inaugurated governor, Claiborne Fox Jackson. The roots of an ardently southern political identity that bound Jackson and other would-be secessionists could be traced back to the recent Kansas crisis.[11] Yet even after the bitter feuding of the past decade, most of the state's citizens were nevertheless reluctant to withdraw from the Union, hopeful that national unity could be preserved at any cost. John Dryden echoed the sentiments of many Missouri Unionists, both conditional and unconditional, when he exclaimed, "Secession! Thou art a demon." The Missouri General Assembly, acting

8. *Fort Scott Democrat,* January 5, 1861.

9. Cutler suggests that when Governor Charles Robinson commissioned the Linn County group into service on February 19, it became the first military company in the Union organized to support the Lincoln administration (*History of Kansas,* 2:1106).

10. *Fort Scott Democrat,* March 9, 1861. For Lane's controversial role in territorial affairs, see Castel, *Frontier State,* 19–22.

11. Phillips, *Missouri's Confederate,* 230, 293; Phillips, "'Crime against Missouri.'" For the reluctance of other border states to secede, see McPherson, *Battle Cry of Freedom,* 254–55.

upon the advice of Governor Jackson, called for a statewide convention to consider the issue of secession. Missourians returned to the polls on February 18, 1861, to choose the delegates for this convention, which was scheduled to meet ten days later. Of the 99 delegates selected, 88 were slaveholders, but none were avowed secessionists. The delegates who gathered in St. Louis refused to dissolve the state's ties with the Union.[12]

Word of the Confederate attack upon Fort Sumter, as well as President Lincoln's call for 75,000 federal troops to suppress the rebellion, soon tested Missourians' loyalties again. Jackson dismissed Lincoln's request as "illegal, unconstitutional, and revolutionary in its object, inhuman and diabolical."[13] Many citizens in rural Missouri were likewise unwilling to take up arms to serve the federal government. As in many communities across the South, some settlers organized themselves into local militias and began preparing for a possible fight against, not for, the United States. At Nevada City, where a majority of voters had recently backed states' rights candidate John C. Breckinridge's bid for president, a militia company began drilling regularly with arms acquired from nearby Camp Daniel Boone.[14] Simmering anger and fear animated antifederal sentiment along the western border. Lincoln's election and the withdrawal of most southern legislators from Congress put control of the U.S. government squarely in the hands of leaders who opposed slavery, but the border's recent history had offered Missouri settlers an alarming glimpse of what such antislavery men were capable of doing.[15]

The unfortunate events that followed the federal capture of Camp Jackson in St. Louis drove many more Missourians, whose Unionism had outweighed latent Southern sympathies, into the pro-Confederate ranks. Governor Jackson had sent troops under Daniel Frost, commander of the late border expedition, to seize the large cache of federal arms housed at the arsenal just west of St. Louis. Before Frost's men could move upon the arsenal, however, U.S. Army captain Nathaniel Lyon had taken the initiative and removed the arms to Illinois. Lyon's troops then captured the militiamen, and as they marched their prisoners through the city streets, violence broke out when a growing crowd began to harass the federal soldiers. In the melee that followed, more than twenty people were killed

12. Dryden, January 15, 1861, *With Plow and Pen*, 10; March, *The History of Missouri*, 2:860–67; Phillips, *Missouri's Confederate*, 230–39.

13. Bonnie Murphy, "Missouri: A State Asunder," 107.

14. J. Johnson, *History of Vernon County*, 264. A native of Bates County, Atkeson recalled that most locals were "overwhelmingly . . . for secession, disunion, and the formation of the Southern Confederacy" (*History of Bates County*, 136).

15. Rubin, *Shattered Nation*, 11–42; Phillips, *Missouri's Confederate*, 293.

or injured. Although the unruly onlookers and federal soldiers were both to blame, the incident provoked broad condemnation of the federal government throughout the Missouri countryside, where many people saw it as yet another example of heavy-handed federal authority.[16]

Distressed by the turn of events in St. Louis, Governor Jackson redoubled his efforts to maneuver Missouri into the Confederacy. He convinced the general assembly to pass an emergency militia act giving him sweeping executive powers and providing for the organization of the Missouri State Guard. Skeptical of Jackson's intentions, Lyon's forces moved quickly up the Missouri River, but as they advanced upon Jefferson City, the governor and several secessionist legislators fled the state capital. The U.S. Army pursued them to Boonville and in a brief skirmish routed Jackson's militia, driving the Confederate sympathizers to the southwestern corner of the state. With many of Missouri's elected leaders now exiled in the Ozarks, members of the secession convention organized a provisional state government with a Unionist, Hamilton Gamble, as the governor.[17] The onset of the Civil War thus found Missouri in a situation not unlike that of territorial Kansas years before, with two competing governments, neither fully legitimate, laying claim to authority.

Meanwhile, across the state line, the weeks that followed the assault on Fort Sumter brought Kansans together as never before. Aside from a scattered number of Southern sympathizers, who were dismissed by their enemies as "desperate characters," most of the citizens in southeastern Kansas, an area recently wracked by partisan bloodshed, rallied around the Union cause. On April 24, the largest public gathering in the history of Fort Scott—a town that had previously been known as a proslavery stronghold—produced an outpouring of Unionist songs and speeches. "The sentiment in Kansas is very strongly patriotic," wrote one Miami County couple. "There is little apprehension of home trouble since we heard the glad news of the uprising of the North."[18] In Washington, D.C., Senator James Lane, who had fast become an outspoken ally of President Lincoln, arranged for fifty-one Frontier Guards from Kansas to be stationed in the East Room of the White House. Responding to Governor Charles Robinson's call for the mobilization of local militias, settlers in Bourbon County formed two volunteer companies. Although partisan differences had not been entirely forgotten, they

---

16. March, *The History of Missouri*, 2:869–73.
17. Ibid., 873–81; Phillips, *Missouri's Confederate*, 248–68.
18. Gary L. Cheatham, "'Desperate Characters': The Development and Impact of the Confederate Guerrillas in Kansas"; Everett and Everett, "Letters of John and Sarah Everett," 371 (John and Sarah Everett to "Folks at Home," May 7, 1861); Cutler, *History of Kansas*, 2:1070–71.

were now subsumed within more pressing considerations of loyalty and Union. Charles Jennison, who had been commissioned by Robinson as a lieutenant colonel and commander of the military forces of southern Kansas, issued a proclamation that framed the terms of the impending crisis. "We do not care about your past political opinions," he wrote. "No man will be persecuted because he differs from us, but neutrality is ended. If you are patriots, you must fight. If you are traitors you will be punished. The time for fighting has come. Every man who feeds, harbors, protects, or in any way gives aid and comfort to the enemies of the Union will be held responsible for his treason, with his life and property."[19]

Not surprisingly, the moment also found James Montgomery prepared for battle. Free-state partisans had maintained a relatively low profile during the spring, but spent much of that time awaiting arms that had been promised to them by George Stearns and other eastern donors. John S. Bowen, Missouri commander of the "Southwest Battalion" that had been positioned along the border months earlier, attributed this lull to the presence of his soldiers and their artillery. "The 'Jayhawkers' of Kansas are completely intimidated and temporarily broken up," wrote Bowen. "They have *utterly failed* for the present and I believe will never have courage to make another attempt unless reinforced by Eastern Abolitionists." This failure, he concluded, "is due to no change of sentiment or to any kind of friendly feelings for Missourians, but result[s] from fear." Montgomery, however, was in fact actively mobilizing his fellow Kansans, who were indeed equipped with guns that Stearns had sent. He organized a militia regiment on May 8 and soon thereafter accepted a formal position on the governor's staff. The newly minted colonel finally marched upon Missouri in late June, when he led a force of nearly two hundred men to the encampment of Missourians, which was located near the mill once owned by Cecil Ball. That brief skirmish along the Little Osage River saw just one man wounded and a horse killed, although Kansans claimed to have routed their foes. Montgomery's unit reportedly killed several men during separate skirmishes the next day, suffering few losses themselves, before returning across the state line. The raid produced relatively few casualties, but by blowing the lid off tensions that had mounted but never exploded over the past two years, it proved that open warfare now riddled the state line yet again.[20]

19. William Elsey Connelly, Correspondence, box 13, KSHS; Cutler, *History of Kansas*, 2:1071; Paul W. Burch, "Kansas: Bushwhackers vs. Jayhawkers," 86.

20. Bowen to Claiborne F. Jackson, March 10, 1861, Missouri Volunteer Militia Papers, Rare Book, Manuscript, and Special Collections Library, Duke University; Montgomery to Stearns, October 6, 1860, Collection 507, Stearns Papers, KSHS; Holman, "Montgomery in Kansas," 101–4.

More than a month later, on August 10, 1861, Union and Confederate soldiers clashed at Wilson's Creek in the first significant battle in the trans-Mississippi West. Yet this battle in southwest Missouri, some hundred miles away from John Dryden's farm, was hardly typical of the conflict that would engulf the Missouri-Kansas border in the years to follow. Now entering its second phase, the guerrilla war along the state line would not be fought by organized armies using conventional tactics, as frustrated Union commanders would quickly learn. The border war would be waged by many of the same antagonists as before, although several old partisans, such as Colonels Montgomery and Jennison, now assumed the guise of regular soldiers, and in this sense it essentially remained a war of vengeance. "'Revenge' was the watchword," wrote one Kansas soldier. "Old scores from the early Kansas troubles had to be settled. The war was not commenced at Fort Sumter; it started in Kansas in 1856, and the fires had been kept bright until the Fort Sumter breeze had fanned the entire border counties into a flame."[21] Given the thirst for retribution shared by settlers on each side of the border, the conflict would quickly devolve into a bitter, total war in which individuals' loyalties and associations made them targets for harassment and murder.

Kansans received word in late August that the Missouri State Guard under Sterling Price was moving north through the border counties across the state line.[22] By the first of September, Fort Scott buzzed with nearly three thousand troops, many of them under the command of James Lane, whose sudden presence along the Missouri border caused considerable unease for Kansas governor Robinson. Concerned that the firebrand senator-general might unnecessarily provoke violence along the border, Robinson wrote to John C. Frémont, Union commander of the Western Department, and asked that Lane's unit be removed.[23] The governor's fears were soon realized. After an anticipated invasion by the Missourians never materialized, a group of Lane's soldiers moved east to thwart Price's forward movement. They engaged the advance guard of

21. H. E. Palmer, "The Border War—When—Where," 3, KSHS. For the Battle of Wilson's Creek, see Phillips, *Damned Yankee*, 252–57.

22. For a local settler's reaction to the rebel victory at Wilson's Creek, see Everett and Everett, "Letters of John and Sarah Everett," 373 (Sarah Everett to Cynthia and Jennie, September 4, 1861).

23. Castel, *Frontier State*, 51; Richard S. Brownlee, *Gray Ghosts of the Confederacy*, 44. It is unclear whether Frémont ignored the request or simply never received it. Monaghan, *Civil War*, suggests that Lane disregarded an order to march north and overtake Price.

the Missouri militia near Drywood Creek but were driven back into Kansas, suffering four casualties and the loss of eighty-four mules.[24]

Although the Battle of the Mules barely slowed Price's march to the Missouri River town of Lexington, it stiffened Lane's resolve to punish the Southern sympathizers living in western Missouri. Lane set out with a force of some two thousand men (twelve hundred infantry and eight hundred cavalry) and pushed across the state line on September 10 with the stated intention of "clearing out the valley of the Osage." Lane's men tore through the towns of Butler, Papinsville, Harrisonville, and Clinton, plundering, burning, and killing as they went. The community of Osceola suffered worse than any other. Standing at the head of navigation on the Osage River, it was an important trade center for settlers across southwest Missouri and the suspected site of a Confederate arsenal. The Kansans reached Osceola on September 22 and after overwhelming a small rebel force set themselves to the task of destroying the town. Before doing so, however, they helped themselves to whatever they could find: horses, mules, bank deposits, brandy, coffee, flour, sugar, and more. Among the plunder, which reportedly filled thirty wagons, were a piano and several silk dresses for the general's own home. Other wagons were used to haul the "dangerously thirsty" soldiers too drunk to march back to Kansas. When Lane departed, his men had reportedly killed fifty rebels and burned nearly every building in Osceola, including the St. Clair County Courthouse.[25]

Although Robinson and Major W. E. Prince, commander of federal troops at Fort Leavenworth, condemned Lane's actions as excessive, many of the soldiers who carried out the invasion were free-state settlers who now relished the opportunity to exact violent justice upon Southern sympathizers. As one such volunteer, Joseph Trego, rode back toward Mound City on a horse seized near Butler, he regretted the hardships that fell upon women and children but still looked upon the plundering of Missouri farms with approval. "It does me good," Trego wrote, "to use the luxuries of these fellows that have always been the enemies of Anti-slavery men." General Lane, he continued, was determined to make

24. Goodlander, *Memoirs and Recollections,* 65; Holder and Rothman, *Post on the Marmaton,* 108. For fears of an invasion by Price, see Montgomery to Lane, August 23, 1861, in U.S. War Department, *The War of the Rebellion: A Compilation of the Official Records of the Union and Confederate Armies,* ser. 1, 3:453, hereinafter cited *O.R.;* and Trego, "Letters of Trego," 290 (to Alice Trego, September 5, 1861).

25. Lane to W. E. Prince, September 10, 1861, *O.R.,* ser. 1, 3:485; Palmer, "Border War—When—Where," 3, KSHS; John Speer, "The Burning of Osceola, Mo., by Lane, and the Quantrill Massacre Contrasted," 306–7; Castel, *Frontier State,* 54. Casualty figures come from B. Rush Plumly to Thomas A. Scott, October 3, 1861, *O.R.,* ser. 1, 3:517.

"secessionists in Missouri *feel* the difference between being loyal and disloyal citizens. . . . We have camped where there was secession farms on one side and Union farms on the other, when we would leave the secession farms were stripped of every thing like crops & fencing while the others remained untouched." Few firsthand accounts survive to substantiate the leniency of Lane's troops toward Missouri Unionists, but at least a few settlers were compensated for the property appropriated by plundering troops. Trego and others believed this "traitorous" policy was tantamount to "giving aid to the enemy."[26]

Perhaps the most striking feature of Lane's brigade was the growing contingent of former slaves who followed the troops as they swept across western Missouri. Traveling as far east as Springfield, the soldiers freed hundreds of African Americans; by November, the "Black Brigade" led by chaplains H. H. Moore and H. D. Fisher contained enough freed slaves to fill 160 wagons. With the barrier between bondage and freedom thrown open, many African Americans fled to safety across the state line, but others remained with the troops through the duration of the expedition, finding work as cooks, teamsters, and servants. Lane himself claimed to be uncomfortable wearing the mantle of liberator. His troops, he explained, "shall not become negro thieves, nor shall they be prostituted into negro catchers." The general nonetheless recognized that the seizure of such contraband could prove to be a boon for his own troops and an obvious hardship for their enemies. As a result, the "confiscation of slaves and other property which can be made useful to the Army should follow treason as the thunder peal follows the lightning flash." Lane thus unleashed a uniquely vengeful form of total war: a strategy that not only liberated—or stole, as Missouri masters saw it—hundreds of slaves and triggered major social upheaval in rural Missouri but also entailed the destruction of homes, farms, and property belonging to potentially disloyal settlers. It proved to be a strategy that prominent generals elsewhere would adopt following years of bloody fighting, long after the border war's antagonists had demonstrated its ruthless effectiveness.[27]

26. Brownlee, *Gray Ghosts,* 39; Castel, *Frontier State,* 60–61; Trego, "Letters of Trego," 293–98 (to Alice Trego, September 5, October 28, 1861).

27. Allen Ward to parents, October 27, 1861, Ward Papers, Collection 528, KSHS; Trego, "Letters of Trego," 298–99 (to Alice Trego, October 28, November 12, 1861); Castel, *Frontier State,* 55–56; Richard B. Sheridan, "From Slavery in Missouri to Freedom in Kansas: The Influx of Black Fugitives and Contrabands into Kansas, 1854–1865," 162–63; Lane to S. D. Sturgis, October 3, 1861, *O.R.,* ser. 1, 3:516. For the role of revenge in Kansans' slave-liberating expeditions, see Fellman, *Inside War,* 212. For the implementation of total war by William Tecumseh Sherman and Philip Sheridan in Georgia and the Shenandoah Valley, respectively, see McPherson, *Battle Cry of Freedom,* 778–80.

The actions of Lane and his troops brought withering criticism from their superiors in the Union army. General Henry Halleck, commander of the Department of Missouri (which included the Department of Kansas), believed that the Kansans' attacks aggravated anti-Union sentiments among rural settlers and thus served to intensify the resistance to federal authority in the state. "The course pursued by those under Lane and Jennison," Halleck contended, "has turned against us many thousands who were formerly Union men. A few more such raids . . . will make this State as unanimous against us as in Eastern Virginia." Jennison's men "are no better than a band of robbers; they cross the line, rob, steal, plunder, and burn whatever they can lay their hands upon." Despite such protests and a strong personal reluctance to provoke civil unrest in the border states, Abraham Lincoln was unwilling to take action against his loyal political ally, writing, "I am sorry General Halleck is so unfavorably impressed with General Lane."[28] Faced with pressing military concerns in the eastern theater, President Lincoln, much like his immediate predecessor, was unwilling to use federal authority to check violent abuses taking place on the western frontier.

Halleck's frustration was understandable, for Lane's invasion made a difficult situation even worse. By attempting to settle old feuds, the raid had given new intensity to the border war and threatened to complicate the federal army's task of maintaining peace among the unsympathetic citizens of Missouri. Although the jayhawking troops tried to spare self-professed Unionists, settlers of all political stripes undoubtedly suffered, including many innocents who were guilty of nothing more than living in Missouri. The outbreak of open war also aggravated the already deep political divisions that plagued rural society in that state. One federal officer urgently maintained that murder, rapine, and robbery threatened to consume every county between the Missouri and Osage Rivers. "The rebels have declaired [sic] that no Union man shall remain in this part of the state," wrote James Eads in November 1861. "And *you may rest assured that they mean to do just what they say.*" Three weeks later scouts in the Cass County home guards issued a report that reinforced Eads's dark warning. Rebels, they testified, "are committing all manner of outrages upon the loyal citizens of Bates, Cass, and other border counties." Such intimidation accelerated the Unionist exodus that had begun a year earlier, when fearful settlers fled the border counties for safer surroundings. A

28. Halleck to George McClellan, December 10, 1861; Halleck to Lorenzo Thomas, January 18, 1862, *O.R.*, ser. 1, 8:819, 507–8. Lincoln quote from ibid., 450, in Holder and Rothman, *Post on the Marmaton*, 114.

large number of exiles arrived in eastern Kansas with nothing save a few personal possessions. Struck by the poignant situation of Missouri Unionists filtering into the town of Paola, one correspondent noted, "Our town is full to overflowing of poor miserable wretches begging for food to keep them alive."[29]

The terrorizing raids that took place in the fall of 1861 eroded Missourians' faith in the U.S. Army as they also enhanced popular support for the pro-Southern guerrillas, or bushwhackers, who emerged as symbols of resistance to the aggression of Kansans or federals. *Bushwhacker* was a term, like *jayhawker* or *border ruffian*, that was used pejoratively by critics but was ultimately embraced by the guerrillas themselves. Like partisan irregulars during the Kansas struggle, these men fought for a variety of reasons. Some pro-Confederate guerrillas, hopeful of seeing the Southern states gain their independence, were galvanized by questions of politics and ideology. Others took up arms to avenge unsettled personal grievances that dated back to the Kansas conflict. A large number of young men from western Missouri volunteered to fight in the Confederate army or for the Missouri State Guard; several others chose to remain closer to home and take to the woods as guerrilla fighters. As the war dragged on, and especially after the rebel defeat at Pea Ridge, Arkansas, in March 1862, Confederate deserters and other former soldiers, such as Frank James, who had been captured at Wilson's Creek and later paroled, continued to fight as irregular partisans. "About half of the farmers in the border tier," one Union officer estimated, "at different times since the war began entered the rebel service. One half of them are dead, or still in the service. The other half—having quit the rebel army— have gone to bushwhacking."[30]

The case of Coleman Younger reveals how personal and political motivations were often intertwined for Missouri guerrillas. Younger's father, Henry, was a wealthy Unionist stock raiser and livery owner who had lost more than four thousand dollars in June 1861 when marauding federal troops, many of them Kansans, passed through Harrisonville and

29. Eads to Halleck, November 23, 1861; A. G. Newgent to Halleck, December 17, 1861, Letters Received, 1861–1867, Record Group 393, Records of the U.S. Army Continental Commands, 1821–1920, Department of the Missouri, National Archives Building, hereinafter cited RG 393, NAB; Ward to parents, October 27, 1861, Ward Papers, Collection 528, KSHS.

30. Thomas Ewing to C. W. Marsh, August 3, 1863, Letters Received, 1861–1867, RG 393, NAB. For rebel soldiers who later fought as guerrillas, see John McCorkle, *Three Years with Quantrill: A True Story Told by His Scout*, 7–21; and Brownlee, *Gray Ghosts*, 29. For analysis of Union and Confederate desertion rates, see Maris A. Vinovskis, *Toward a Social History of the American Civil War: Exploratory Essays*, 10.

seized carriages, wagons, and forty horses from his stable there. A profession of loyalty apparently offered insufficient protection for one's family or property, as a series of subsequent tragedies seemed to demonstrate. After attending a cattle sale at Independence, the elder Younger was robbed and murdered by a Union captain; months later, soldiers burned the family's home, driving away his ill widow, who was sick with consumption. Not long thereafter, eighteen-year-old Cole Younger joined Quantrill's raiders to take vengeance for his family's mistreatment; in time, his brother, Jim, also became a noted guerrilla.[31]

Like Cole Younger, a great many bushwhackers had not previously shown a penchant for bloodthirsty criminality. Many bushwhackers were young men born to families of southern heritage who were generally wealthier and more likely to own slaves than the typical Missouri farmer. As the eldest sons of families that had experienced some degree of upward mobility, these guerrillas were not the backward savages described in contemporary northern newspapers but were instead the progeny of respectable southern families, committed to the defense of economic status and privilege. The Gabberts of Montevallo demonstrated that bushwhacking could indeed be a family affair. A well-off Kentucky-born farmer in his midforties, William Gabbert joined his sons, John and Peter, in conducting raids into nearby Cedar County. His eldest daughter, Elisa, was an effective bushwhacker spy and informant. Many such bushwhackers saw themselves as defenders of family and community, and regarded their guerrilla warfare as necessary resistance against the invasion carried out by Unionist Kansans and the federal troops who now occupied their neighborhoods.[32]

Some Missouri guerrillas did not readily fit this social profile. A few unscrupulous figures were little more than opportunistic criminals and brigands who seized upon the chance to indulge in adventure, robbery, and nihilistic violence. For many Kansans, such descriptions seemed to fit all bushwhackers. A member of the Eleventh Kansas Cavalry, for example, characterized the bushwhackers as demons roused by a thirst for plunder and "dare devil notoriety." Guerrilla captain William C.

31. Younger, *The Story of Cole Younger by Himself: Being an Autobiography of the Missouri Guerrilla Captain and Outlaw*, 9–31; Brownlee, *Gray Ghosts*, 43–61; Etcheson, *Bleeding Kansas*, 234.

32. Don R. Bowen, "Guerrilla War in Western Missouri, 1862–65: Historical Extensions of the Relative Deprivation Hypothesis," 30–51; Census-Pop, Missouri, Vernon County, 1860; J. Johnson, *History of Vernon County*, 318–38. For the defensive mind-set of Missouri guerrillas and their supporters, see John Edwards, *Noted Guerrillas; or, The Warfare of the Border*, 19–20.

Quantrill was at once the most revered and reviled bushwhacker in Missouri and came to embody the dichotomous perceptions of bushwhackers along the border. For many Missourians, Quantrill and his fellow guerrillas were heroes who took a stand against jayhawker harassment and Union occupation; for Kansans, he was the epitome of lawless cruelty. A native of Ohio, he had moved to Miami County, Kansas, in 1857 at the age of nineteen. Quantrill worked as a schoolteacher until charges of horse stealing threatened to drive him from the territory in late 1860. The nature of his departure from Kansas in early December shaped his reputation on both sides of the border. Presenting himself as a faithful abolitionist, he had joined five young Quakers from Lawrence on an expedition to liberate the twenty-six slaves held on the Blue Springs, Missouri, farm of Morgan Walker. As the young men neared the Walker place, Quantrill went ahead under the ostensible purpose of surveying the farm's layout but instead exposed the group's plan to Walker's son, Andrew. When Quantrill and the five abolitionists moved upon the farm, Andrew and his neighbors ambushed them, killing three of the Quakers and injuring the other two, who managed to escape across the state line. Quantrill was unhurt. The Kansas City newspapers noted the incident with approval, helping to make him a folk hero among wary Missouri slaveholders; across the border, the reports of his deceit cemented his status as a treacherous villain.[33]

The attacks on Osceola, Butler, and other western Missouri towns fueled reprisal raids into Kansas the following year. The sheriff of Bates County led an attack on the villages of Potosi and Humboldt, where the guerrillas looted stores and homes and killed at least three people.[34] More common than these coordinated assaults were the countless raids carried out against individual farms on both sides of the state line. The abuses suffered by the McFadin family in Kansas were typical of the harrowing experiences that many rural settlers faced during the guerrilla war. The McFadins were well acquainted with frontier violence, having joined the exodus of free-state Kansas settlers who fled proslavery harassment in 1855 before returning a year later. With the border war's renewal, the family's southern heritage again rendered them suspect in the eyes of many neighbors, and by 1862 jayhawkers raided their home on at least three different occasions, determined to kill Mr. McFadin and take what-

---

33. Palmer, "The Border War—When—Where," 3, KSHS; Brownlee, *Gray Ghosts,* 54–57.

34. Cutler, *History of Kansas,* 2:1106; Castel, *Frontier State,* 63. For other examples of reprisal attacks, see Brownlee, *Gray Ghosts,* 64.

ever valuables they could find. Safety, the family discovered, could be elusive on both sides of the state line.[35]

The McFadins' experiences illuminate several important characteristics of the guerrilla threat on both sides of the border. First, the harassment inflicted upon noncombatants was usually personal in nature, as bushwhackers and jayhawkers typically knew their victims, and vice versa. John Dryden noted that he was well acquainted with the bushwhackers who attacked his home, but he held his tormentors in such abhorrence that he refused to besmirch his journal with their names. Second, stealthy guerrilla bands utilized the element of surprise to intimidate and terrorize rural families. One rarely knew when or where raiders would strike, and the seeming randomness of guerrilla violence amplified the fear that permeated the rural border. In addition, most attackers operated at night, moving under the cover of darkness like the "midnight minions" who nearly burned Dryden out of his home. Violence could come at any time, of course, as proved by the daytime murders of seven Unionist farmers, shot by bushwhackers while working in their fields. Finally, guerrilla raids served both practical and political purposes for bushwhackers who foraged upon the local population, demanding food, guns, money, and horses wherever they went. One Vernon County diarist indicated that they even resorted to stealing the shoes off a widowed grandmother's feet.[36]

Many of the families who were determined to remain in Missouri or Kansas came to accept extraordinary circumstances as part of their daily lives. For some, preparations for an expected nighttime raid became a daily routine. "Every night before I go to bed," wrote one Kansan, "I hide all valuable articles that I conveniently can, expecting to have a visit from the jayhawkers before morning, and every morning feel surprised that we have passed another night without being robbed." Hundreds of other families were less willing to endure such constant anxiety and instead joined the continued out-migration that was taking place on both sides of the state line. A large number of these fearful exiles never figured to return. B. L. Riggins, a merchant who fled southeastern Kansas in the fall of 1861, offered his apologies and encouragement to a business partner who chose to remain, writing, "I never expect to moove [sic] back to Fort Scott."[37]

35. George Edwin McFadin, "Kansas in Early Times," box 55, McFadin Papers, KSHS.

36. Dryden, April 1863, November 13, 1865, *With Plow and Pen*, 12–13, 20–22; *Fort Scott Western Volunteer*, May 24, 1862. For an erudite analysis of guerrilla tactics, see Fellman, *Inside War*, 23–48; and T. J. Stiles, *Jesse James: Last Rebel of the Civil War*, 110.

37. Ward to parents, October 27, 1861, Ward Papers, Collection 528, KSHS; Riggins to Augustus Baker, September 23, 1861, Baker Papers, VCHS.

Union officers had taken forceful steps to impose order in rural Missouri soon after the Civil War began. On August 30, 1861, General John C. Frémont had issued a sweeping proclamation that declared martial law throughout the state; ordered the property, including slaves, of known rebels to be confiscated; and authorized the execution of those who took up arms against the United States. Although Lincoln had quickly overruled Frémont's order and its controversial emancipation clause, its punitive tone had set a precedent that subsequent Union officers would follow.[38] On December 17 of that same year, Lincoln authorized Halleck to suspend the writ of habeas corpus within his district; the general announced days later that anyone caught destroying bridges, railroads, or telegraph wires would face military trial and, if found guilty, would be shot. Other orders issued in the following weeks held that all guerrillas and "predatory partisans" captured behind federal lines would be subject to the same punishment. Although these measures resulted in the execution of several bushwhackers, they also emboldened many other guerrillas, who were now resolved to fight to the death. One Kansas soldier would later describe this kind of take-no-prisoners fighting: "Quarter was neither asked nor given; in fact was never thought of in this warfare; and when we met each other only death or flight of all the parties on one side or the other put an end to the barbarous conflict."[39]

By the middle of 1862, the Union army had gained control of Missouri's major rivers and northern counties, but the unsettled condition of the western borderland remained an intractable problem. Subduing the bands of guerrillas who operated there demanded tactics that were dramatically different from those needed to defeat conventional Confederate armies. Because bushwhackers operated on horseback and in small groups, large troop concentrations were generally ineffective. It was impossible to capture bushwhackers, one federal soldier would later recall. "They never stood to fight, or held together in retreat," and instead escaped into the brush, only to regroup at a different time and place. The Union army therefore established posts at Balltown, Harrisonville, Pleasant Hill, and other points along the Kansas border from which antiguerrilla sorties could be launched.[40] Even this approach proved ineffective

38. March, *The History of Missouri*, 2:899–900; Monaghan, *Civil War*, 185.

39. Brownlee, *Gray Ghosts*, 25–26, 64–65; Charles Blair, speech, Cincinnati, September 30, 1879, in Thomas Ewing Family Papers, box 212, folder A, Manuscript Division, Library of Congress, hereinafter cited as TE-LOC. See also Ewing to C. W. Marsh, August 3, 1863, RG 393, NAB.

40. Blair, speech, September 30, 1879, box 212, folder A, TE-LOC; Fellman, *Inside War*, 93–94. For details of the Union encampment at Balltown, see Charles W. Porter, *In the Devil's Dominions: A Union Soldier's Adventures in "Bushwhacker Country,"* 79–176.

against an elusive foe who could easily blend into local society and the surroundings of the frontier landscape. The shelter and assistance that pro-Confederate bushwhackers received from sympathetic settlers further hindered the army's efforts.

As Union leaders devised increasingly stringent policies to undermine such support, the very nature of the conflict had changed on the Missouri side of the border: it became a battle against both the guerrillas and the predominantly southern population that sustained them. Authorities implemented a special tax assessment that was designed to punish disloyal Missourians, to compensate the victims of guerrilla depredations, and to pay for federal military expenses. A board of loyal citizens in each county determined the size of the assessment by surveying the wealth of disloyal residents and property owners therein. An assessment of ten thousand dollars was levied against the citizens of Cass County in the fall of 1862. Plagued by widespread abuses, however, this system often encouraged the confiscation of unoffending citizens' property. In Vernon County, for example, federal soldiers seized nearly one hundred dollars and one hundred pounds of honey from Dryden, a devoted Unionist.[41]

The difficulty of distinguishing loyal citizens from rebel sympathizers compounded the abuses associated with the assessment system. In late 1861, the state's provisional government had offered protection to all Missourians who were prepared to take a loyalty oath and put up a bond securing their continued allegiance to the United States. Many innocent citizens, such as Henry Toppin, willingly pledged an oath in support of the Union. Toppin was arrested in March 1862 while trying to rent a farm in Henry County but was released upon swearing that he had never served in the Confederate army or supported the rebel cause. Other settlers saw their claims of loyalty affirmed or challenged by the testimony of their neighbors. Four people came forward in June 1863 to declare that they knew Hamilton Finney to be a secessionist at the start of the war. Two local Unionists, John Christian and William Jack, claimed that Finney, who had served as clerk of Cass County for fourteen years, fought for the rebels at the Battles of Lexington and Wilson Creek; John Coughenour, meanwhile, tempered his claim by noting that he had never heard the man threaten Union supporters.[42]

41. March, *The History of Missouri*, 2:925–26; Dryden, November 13, 1865, *With Plow and Pen*, 24; Brownlee, *Gray Ghosts*, 166; Murphy, "Missouri: A State Asunder," 115.
42. Statement of Toppin, March 26, 1862; statements of Christian, Jack, Coughenour, and Hugh G. Glenn, June 3, 1863; and letter from George W. Weber, June 3, 1863, Cass County, Union Provost Marshal Papers, Missouri State Archives, hereinafter cited as UPMP; O. Williams, *Cass and Bates Counties*, 387, 442.

The willingness of pro-Confederate Missourians to swear such oaths demonstrated how remarkably malleable political identities could be in times of crisis. Many people offered loyalty oaths that were fueled less by patriotism than by a desire to secure the protection and good favor of federal troops. Some ersatz loyalists simply lied while giving such statements. One noteworthy example came from a proud and fierce secessionist mother named Zerelda Samuels, who was being held in custody by federal troops north of the Missouri River. Samuels's decision to sign a loyalty oath on June 5, 1863, helped secure her release, but it would do nothing to stop her, once she returned to her Clay County home, from continuing to provide food, shelter, and assistance to her teenage bushwhacker sons, Frank and Jesse James.[43]

Unionist John Dryden questioned the oath's ability to compel the loyalty of any single person and noted, "It did not render me one whit more loyal toward the government." Thousands of other Missourians were unable or unwilling to take the loyalty oath. Isaiah Jackson was a sixty-nine-year-old farmer who had worked as a teamster for the rebel militias until his capture at the Battle of Lone Jack. Giving his reasons for not taking the oath, Jackson explained, "I am not in favor of the present abolition administration. I am an old constitutional subject, against the abolition of slavery and in favor of Rebellion. What I have . . . I am willing to contribute it to the cause of the South and if obliged would fight for her."[44] Such hardened resistance, even in the face of federal interrogation, was the lifeblood of bushwhacker activity.

General John Schofield called upon the population of loyal Missourians in July 1862 and ordered that able-bodied men who had not already enlisted in the Missouri State Militia or the Union army report for service in the Enrolled Missouri Militia (EMM). The EMM was organized with the consent of provisional governor Gamble and created "for the purpose of exterminating the guerrillas" that infested Missouri. Like the militia units and home guards established in many communities, the EMM served essentially as an adjunct of the federal army already fighting bushwhackers throughout the state. Although more than fifty thousand citizens joined the EMM by the end of the year, Schofield's order was poorly received by many Missourians. Thousands of men apparently fled to escape enrollment, and a good many others decided to join the guerrillas rather than fight them. Officers charged with leading EMM regiments

---

43. Stiles, *Jesse James*, 90; Fellman, *Inside War*, 49–52; Rubin, *Shattered Nation*, 248.
44. Dryden, November 13, 1865, *With Plow and Pen*, 23; statement of Jackson, October 14, 1862, UPMP.

in the western counties sometimes struggled to root out suspected rebel sympathizers from their ranks; at least a few suspicious recruits were mustered into service but not furnished with arms.[45]

The unfriendly attitudes that many Missouri settlers had developed toward the federal troops who occupied their communities undoubtedly served as one of the unspoken inspirations behind the creation of the EMM. Missouri troops, it was thought, might be more welcomed and more effective guerrilla fighters. After the Lane invasion, residents of the border counties maintained a wary apprehension of—and in many cases an outright hostility toward—Union soldiers, even though many of the troops stationed there were from Wisconsin, Iowa, and Ohio, and not just Kansas.[46] The real hardships imposed by the federal soldiers' presence often justified such resentment, as they often took food from the tables and forage from the livestock of local families. "Federal soldiers," one woman recalled, "were thieves . . . [who] took poor people's stock." A Vernon County farmer believed that the foraging members of the First Ohio Cavalry preyed upon settlers near Balltown to "gratify their thievish propensities" and to "steal themselves rich in the name of liberty." Union troops on the state line, wrote one Kansas lieutenant, were better fed, better clothed, and generally healthier than the civilians they encountered—a fact that the Missourians rarely failed to notice.[47]

The Union army sought to appease settlers in western Missouri by reining in the rancorous excesses of Kansas troops. Not long after George McClellan had received word that soldiers serving under Jennison and Lane had ignored orders to cease the unnecessary harassment of Missouri civilians, some Kansas units were removed to military theaters outside of Missouri. In April 1862, Jennison was arrested and sent to a military prison under charges that he had tried to recruit members of the Seventh Kansas Cavalry into guerrilla bands. He was later transferred to Louisiana upon being paroled but soon returned to Kansas and his old jayhawking ways, thanks largely to his friendship with the politically

45. March, *The History of Missouri,* 2:922–23, 1593–94. For disloyalty among EMM soldiers, see Kersey Coates to Gamble, March 5, 1863, Missouri Volunteer Militia Papers.

46. For specific military units stationed along the border, see Bates County Old Settlers Society, *Old Settlers' History,* 41; and Porter, *In the Devil's Dominions,* viii–xiii.

47. Addie Aldridge Gordon Papers, 1881–1973, "Entry into Missouri," Collection KC 068, folder 1, Western Historical Manuscripts Collection, Columbia; Dryden, November 13, 1865, *With Plow and Pen,* 24; Trego, "Letters of Trego," 297 (to Alice Trego, October 28, 1861). For reactions and responses of southern households to foraging troops during Sherman's march, see Jacqueline Campbell Glass, *When Sherman Marched North from the Sea: Resistance on the Confederate Home Front,* 14–50.

powerful Lane. Not all Kansas volunteers embraced the reinstatement. Jennison, one soldier asserted, was "a coward and a murderer . . . [who] brought only disgrace to Kansas soldiery." Rumors that the former guerrilla might be installed as a Union officer at Fort Scott worried many of the town's residents. "This people, loyal and patriotic to the core," wrote one federal, "will abandon their property and flee for their lives if Jennison takes command, their terror is so great, and they know his hatred so well." Union commanders took note of such alarm and withheld the controversial commission.[48]

Federal soldiers who fought in the Civil War's eastern theater entertained mixed opinions of James Montgomery, who had left Kansas to lead a regiment of black soldiers in South Carolina. His commanding officer, Robert Gould Shaw, lauded the Kansan as a conscientious man of extraordinary energy and piety who never drank, smoke, or swore. "He is not what one would call a 'Kansas Ruffian'—being very quiet and reserved, & rather consumptive-looking," wrote Shaw. "You would think at first sight that he was a school-master or parson. The only thing that shows the man, is that very queer roll or glare in his eye—and a contraction of the eyebrows every now & then, which gives him rather a fierce expression." Montgomery's fellow officers were particularly struck by the kind of fighting he had mastered along the Missouri border. The former guerrilla, one man observed, believed "praying, shooting, burning, and hanging were the true means to put down the Rebellion." Shaw and others occasionally recoiled at Montgomery's style of leadership, particularly his execution of a deserter without a court-martial and the ruthless tactics he used against southern civilians. The Kansan defended his actions, saying that southerners must be made to feel the suffering of "real war," as "they were to be swept away by the hand of God, like the Jews of old."[49]

A thousand miles to the east, Confederate authorities in Richmond maintained an ambivalent distance from Missouri bushwhackers and their brutal irregular warfare. On one hand, the few thousand irregular partisans in Missouri served a useful military purpose by tying down more than fifty thousand federals who might otherwise be employed in the major campaigns of the East.[50] The guerrillas benefited the Confeder-

---

48. Brownlee, *Gray Ghosts,* 48; Fellman, *Inside War,* 116; Etcheson, *Bleeding Kansas,* 228. Quotes from Palmer, "The Border War—When—Where," 3, KSHS; and Charles Blair to Ewing, Nov. 19, 1863, TE-LOC.

49. Shaw to Brother, June 1863; to Father, June 22, 1863; to Mother, June 28, 1863; to Annie, June 9, 1863, in Shaw, *Blue-Eyed Child of Fortune,* 356–63, 341–45; Holman, "Montgomery in Kansas," 110–12.

50. Brownlee, *Gray Ghosts,* 109.

ate cause by functioning as detached cavalry, harassing Union lines of supply and communication. Many bushwhackers, seeking to formalize their relationship with the rebel army, lobbied for and received independent military commissions. Quantrill, for instance, spent several weeks in Richmond trying to obtain a formal endorsement for his band of guerrillas, but Jefferson Davis only belatedly granted him a captain's commission for independent partisan service. The vaguely worded Partisan Ranger Act, which the Confederate government passed in 1862, gave official sanction to existing guerrilla bands but belied larger misgivings about the nature of the bushwhackers' tactics. Although the guerrillas' refusal to abide by conventional rules of war proved useful, it also posed a serious threat, in the eyes of many southern gentlemen, to Christian civilization and standards of masculine honor.[51]

Back in Missouri, many Union soldiers hardly concealed their disdain for the people who lived in the Osage valley. According to Webster Moses, a sergeant from Maine, the town of Clinton bore the depressing scars of a slaveholding society. "The inhabitants here are most all very ignorant and consequently Secesh," he wrote. "The curse of slavery is visible. Business has been neglected and houses are going to decay. They need a little Yankee enterprise here."[52] Soldiers who were charged with keeping peace in the area likewise felt little pity for the Southern sympathizers affected by the ongoing border troubles. Since these settlers' support for the guerrilla insurgency undermined the army's efforts to pacify Missouri, they were thus to blame for their own hardships. Others held Missourians in considerably higher regard. The members of the Third Wisconsin who were stationed at Balltown appreciated the services of Dr. Leonard Dodge, an ardent Unionist who tended to both sick federal soldiers and the secessionists in his own neighborhood. In addition, the Wisconsin natives frequently socialized with the young women living in Vernon County. In fact, five of the soldiers from that unit would marry Missouri women, including four from the Josiah Austin household alone.[53]

Army leaders came to embrace the use of African American soldiers to help quell the guerrilla insurgency along the border. James Lane had pushed for the enlistment of African Americans not long after his destructive raid through western Missouri had liberated hundreds of slaves, a move that Kansas abolitionists welcomed and that other officers

51. March, *The History of Missouri*, 2:937; Fellman, *Inside War*, 97–112.
52. Fellman, *Inside War*, 160.
53. Porter, *In the Devil's Dominions*, vii–xii, 78–79; J. Johnson, *History of Vernon County*, 393.

later embraced.[54] General John Schofield endorsed the use of black soldiers but feared alienating any Unionist masters who remained in Missouri. "I am quite willing to enlist into the service," he wrote, "all the able bodied negroes in MO. if that be declared the policy of the Government." The black volunteers who joined Kansas regiments proved to be effective fighters. In October 1862, a unit of the First Kansas (Colored) Regiment ventured into Missouri on a foraging expedition and defeated a guerrilla force twice its size southwest of Butler in a skirmish that would become known as the Battle of Island Mound. When these troops were later mustered into federal service in 1863, they became the fourth black regiment in the Union army. Their triumph at Island Mound, however, had earned them an important historical distinction, as they were the first African American regiment to experience combat in the entire Civil War.[55] Some white citizens would later celebrate the courage of such volunteers, proudly noting Kansas's distinction as the first state to enlist black troops, but many civilians and soldiers had initially been uncomfortable with the idea. "There is an evident antipathy among our soldiers against arming the negroes," claimed one Fort Scott newspaper, which favored freeing "every rebel's slave; not for the sake of the Negro, but to punish treason." The writer then offered a backhanded endorsement of the enlistment of former slaves from his town, noting caustically, "We are heartily glad to be rid of them."[56]

Whereas the war brought liberating opportunity to former slaves, John Dryden lamented the devastated condition of his Little Osage neighborhood. "O, that we had peace!" Dryden wrote. "This unfortunate war has produced a great deal of misery, wretchedness & destitution." Like other Missouri Unionists, he had found that political loyalty carried a steep price, bringing bushwhacker abuses upon his farm household. The border war had dragged on for almost seven years—almost as long as Dryden's tenure along the state line—yet he nevertheless looked to the future with hope: "As [war] cannot last always it is to be hoped that it will be productive of some good. Those who survive it, will certainly know how to appreciate peace when it does come, with all its attending blessing."[57]

54. Lane's own advocacy for greater racial equality reflected a significant shift in his own attitudes toward black Americans. See Etcheson, *Bleeding Kansas*, 245.

55. Schofield, Diary of Events in Department of the Missouri, 1863, Schofield Papers, Manuscript Division, Library of Congress; Holder and Rothman, *Post on the Marmaton*, 167. For a detailed history of the engagement at Island Mound, see Chris Tabor, "The Skirmish at Island Mound, Mo."

56. *Fort Scott Western Volunteer*, August 16, 1862. For changing attitudes toward black volunteers in the postwar period, see *Fort Scott Monitor*, June 12, 1867.

57. Dryden, May 2, 1863, *With Plow and Pen*, 13.

The events of the summer months that followed would severely test such guarded optimism.

By the middle of 1863, the U.S. Army had failed to check the guerrilla violence that continued to rage along the Missouri-Kansas border. Quantrill and other bushwhackers were still active throughout western Missouri, burning towns, murdering Unionist settlers in their homes, and overwhelming the ordinary functions of civil government. The army's struggles resulted in part from insufficient resources and inefficient technology. Federal soldiers who each carried a single-shot musket were routinely outmaneuvered by mounted guerrillas using rapid-fire Colt pistols. The army's greatest problem remained an inability to compel the loyalty and cooperation of the local population that supported the bushwhackers and supplied them with food, shelter, guns, and horses. Another federal soldier later estimated that a full three-fourths of Missourians opposed the federal troops in their midst, with the remaining quarter too intimidated to voice their Unionist loyalties.[58] Unable to defeat the guerrillas through force of arms, the Union leadership intensified its efforts to eliminate the sources of their popular support in the late summer of 1863.

Unlike many of the Union commanders who had been stationed in St. Louis, Thomas Ewing Jr., the general now charged with subduing the guerrilla threat, was personally familiar with the ongoing border troubles. The son of an influential Ohio family and brother-in-law to William Tecumseh Sherman, he had come to Leavenworth, Kansas, to practice law in the late 1850s and had served as chief justice of the Kansas Supreme Court until resigning in 1861. Ewing's experiences along the border convinced him that the guerrilla insurgency could not be quelled unless the army took more direct action against both the Missouri guerrillas and their relatives. Some two-thirds of Missouri families, he wrote, "are of kin to the guerrillas, and are actively and heartily engaged in feeding, clothing, and sustaining them. The presence of these families is the cause of the presence there of the guerrillas. I can see no prospect of an early and complete end to the war on the border . . . so long as those families remain there." Ewing and his commanding officer, Schofield, each believed this situation left the Union army with two choices: either dramatically increase the number of troops stationed along the border or

---

58. Fellman, *Inside War*, xviii; J. Johnson, *History of Vernon County*, 296; Dryden, May 27, 1863, *With Plow and Pen*, 17–18; Bates County Court, Minutes, February 3, 1863, 1:425–26; Brownlee, *Gray Ghosts*, 69–70, 104–15; W. C. Ransom to Ewing, May 30, 1871, box 212, folder D, TE-LOC.

remove the bushwhackers' families, the source of the guerrillas' subsistence, far from western Missouri. "The country is rich and supplies them well," wrote Ewing. "But it is so rugged, heavily timbered, and full of places of concealment and ambuscade, that these bands could not possibly be expelled from it with forces in the field less than three times our own." Neither commander expected to receive additional regiments that summer, when more pressing campaigns, such as Ulysses Grant's siege at Vicksburg and the pursuit of Robert E. Lee's forces into Pennsylvania, made it difficult to spare even small forces for the District of the Border.[59]

The expulsion of guerrilla sympathizers in Missouri became the Union army's primary focus by late summer 1863. Ewing outlined his intentions on August 3, writing, "I think that the families of several hundred of the worst of the men should be sent, with their clothes and bedding, to some rebel district south, and would recommend the establishment of a colony of them somewhere on the St. Francis or White River in Arkansas, to which a steamboat could carry them direct from Kansas City." To initiate the removal of these families, Union soldiers began arresting the female kinfolk of known bushwhackers and holding them in buildings throughout Kansas City. By targeting the wives, mothers, and sisters of noted or suspected guerrillas, the army hoped to strike at the nexus of the guerrilla's social and economic support system. The assistance offered by many Missouri women had allowed the bushwhackers to thrive across the rural landscape. Such protective assistance was a striking inversion of traditional gender roles. The Civil War had threatened white male southerners' roles as the defenders of their families and homes; when men departed to fight in the war or failed to carry out that role, women stepped forward to protect southern households in their absence.[60] For Union leaders, eliminating the vital economic contributions of pro-Confederate women seemed the most obvious means of weakening the bushwhackers' local support.

On August 13, one of the army's makeshift jails, a three-story brick building, collapsed, trapping almost a dozen prisoners in the rubble. The accident killed five women; among them were the sisters of guerrillas Bill

59. March, *The History of Missouri*, 2:938–39; Etcheson, *Bleeding Kansas*, 235; Ewing to Schofield, *O.R.*, ser. 1, vol. 22, pt. 2, 428; Ewing to C. W. Marsh, August 3, 1863, RG 393, NAB. For the impact that the siege of Vicksburg and other campaigns had on troop levels in western Missouri, see Schofield to Ewing, January 25, 1877, box 212, folder D, TE-LOC.

60. For the wartime protection offered by women in rural western Missouri, see Rebekah Weber Bowen, "The Changing Role of Protection on the Border: Gender and the Civil War in Saline County," in *Women in Missouri History: In Search of Power and Influence*, ed. LeeAnn Whites, Mary C. Neth, and Gary P. Kremer, 119–33.

Anderson and John McCorkle. The tragedy immediately fueled accusations that direct responsibility lay with Union officers, who had only recently transferred the women to the dilapidated structure. For enraged guerrillas, the soldiers' guilt was a settled point. There was no clear evidence, however, to show that Ewing or his subordinates actively sought to bring about the deaths of their prisoners, although they were likely negligent of the women's safety. The jail collapse alone may have been enough to incite a violent reprisal by Quantrill's men, but the army's publication a few days later of Order No. 10, which essentially codified Ewing's removal policy, was the catalyst that spurred the bushwhackers to act.[61]

The brutal denouement of the decadelong border war between Missourians and Kansans came three days after Ewing released Order No. 10. On August 19, Quantrill led a band of more than 400 guerrillas across the state line on a westward gallop toward Lawrence, the home of James Lane and a notorious antislavery stronghold. Eluding the detection of military authorities as they passed through Cass County, the bushwhackers thundered across eastern Kansas, killing more than a dozen people as they passed. The guerrillas descended upon the sleeping town of Lawrence at dawn on the morning of Friday, August 21, and set themselves to killing every male resident they could find. Kit Dalton, a Kentucky guerrilla who had arrived in Missouri just weeks earlier, described the scene as he and other bushwhackers ravaged the town: "It was a battle no longer, but the slaughter of men too terror stricken to surrender and too wild with the fright that possessed them to offer any effective resistance. For three hours the terrible slaughter went on." Dalton, Quantrill, and company killed 182 men and boys, burned 185 buildings, and caused an estimated two million dollars in damage before fleeing sometime around ten o'clock. The guerrillas raced hurriedly back to Cass County, Missouri, where they scattered in the timber along Big Creek, just ahead of pursuing federal cavalry.[62]

News of the Lawrence massacre spread quickly, sparking outrage and horror among alarmed Kansans. Reverend Samuel Adair, an army chaplain stationed at Fort Scott, received word of the attack early that afternoon. "Excitement here," he reported, "has been great. Arguments were made for organizing for defense and for going into the field if necessary. Very great blame (and probably justly) is attached to gen. Ewing." The

61. Charles F. Harris, "Catalyst for Terror: The Collapse of the Women's Prison in Kansas City"; McCorkle, *Three Years with Quantrill*, 77–79. Brownlee puts the date of the collapse at August 14 (*Gray Ghosts*, 118–21).

62. Dalton, *Under the Black Flag*, 101–2; E. D. Thompson, statement, August 5, 1895, box 212, folder A, TE-LOC; McCorkle, *Three Years with Quantrill*, 80–84; Edwards, *Noted Guerrillas*, 188–204.

general was himself keenly aware of such sentiments. "My political enemies are fanning the flames, and wish me for a burnt offering to satisfy the just passions of the people," he wrote to Schofield. With the clamor for revenge rippling throughout the state, Lane, who had narrowly escaped harm by taking refuge in a cornfield behind his Lawrence home, warned President Lincoln that further bloodshed appeared likely. Correspondents of the *New York Herald* shared similar worries: "The massacre of Lawrence, we fear, will be the preface to a border warfare, more terrible and relentless than any that history records.'" Anxieties about additional invasions gripped some uneasy Kansans. Adair's wife, Florella, believed that Osawatomie was a likely target: "I have no doubt in my own mind, but the same thing will be repeated here, as soon as the excitement of this wears away & the people are off their guard."[63]

Condemned for his failure to stop Quantrill, Ewing initiated a sweeping policy to discourage a retaliatory attack by incensed Kansans and to prevent further bushwhacker incursions. "The excitement in Kansas is great," he explained to Schofield, "and there is . . . great danger of a raid of citizens for the purpose of destroying the towns along the border." A week after the slaughter in Lawrence, Ewing issued General Order No. 11, which called for all Missourians living in the four counties that composed the army's District of the Border "to remove from their present places of residence." Its first provision held that every person in Jackson, Cass, Bates, and northern Vernon Counties (except for the residents of Kansas City) who could not prove their loyalty to the satisfaction of local commanders was required to leave the district within fifteen days. Unionist citizens who could establish their loyalty were allowed either to relocate within one mile of the military stations at Independence, Hickman Mills, Pleasant Hill, and Harrisonville or to settle in any part of Kansas beyond the eastern tier of border counties. All other settlers—and given the unpopularity of loyalty oaths along the border, this meant thousands of people—would be banished within a fortnight. The order's second provision, which called for the confiscation of settlers' grain and hay, was designed to undercut the guerrillas' ability to forage off the small farms that dotted the prairies. This measure dealt a costly blow to the border's predominantly agrarian society, for only loyal citizens would be reimbursed for the forage they surrendered. A final stipulation revoked the amnesty clause that had been recently extended in Order No.

63. Adair, diary, August 21, 1863, Adair Family Papers, KSHS; Ewing to Schofield, August 25, 1863; *New York Herald* (n.d., reprint), box 212, folder A, TE-LOC; F. Adair to S. Adair, August 24, 1863, Adair Family Papers, KSHS.

10, which had allowed for professed guerrillas to lay down their arms and join exiled family members without fear of recrimination. Avowed bushwhackers and the disloyal families who supported them now stood beyond the pale of the Union army's mercy.[64]

The devastating impact of Order No. 11 was unevenly felt throughout the border counties. Although the proclamation held that disloyal settlers had two weeks to prepare for their removal, most were forced to leave within days of its circulation, or whenever federal troops showed up at their door. As a result, a great many refugees were driven away carrying what few personal possessions could be gathered at a moment's notice. Plundering troops set fire to much of the countryside and destroyed buildings, fences, and other improvements, transforming much of the borderland into a smoldering wilderness that would soon become known as the "Burnt District." Ewing was himself struck by the desolation he encountered while touring the district and noted that only one house between Kansas City and Independence was inhabited. None of the military posts where loyalists could take refuge was situated in Bates County; as the only county to be completely depopulated, it essentially ceased to exist for the next eighteen months. In Vernon County, the order affected only the townships north of the county seat, which Union militiamen had burned to the ground months earlier. The journal of John Dryden was filled with notes about the unusually hot and dry weather but failed to mention the depopulation that was taking place just miles to the north.[65]

For the old-stock inhabitants affected by Order No. 11, dispossession was a bitter reversal of fortune. A defensive, independent-minded class of settlers, they had driven away a succession of groups—the Osages, Mormons, Republicans, and Unionists—but now found themselves cast away from the upper Osage valley. Many observers were shaken by the sight of refugees streaming out of the border counties. "Never can I forget the many scenes of misery and distress I saw," wrote Francis Fristoe Twyman. "The road from Independence to Lexington was crowded with women and children, women walking with their babies in their arms,

64. *O.R.*, ser. 1, vol. 22, pt. 2, 473. Since the southern boundary of the District of the Border (the thirty-eighth parallel) cut across Vernon County, only its northern townships were affected by Order No. 11.

65. Bates County Old Settlers Society, *Old Settlers' History*, 198–99; Albert E. Castel, "Order Number 11 and the Civil War on the Border," 357–68; Ann Davis Niepman, "General Orders No. 11 and Border Warfare during the Civil War," 185–210; Fellman, *Inside War*, 95–96; Ewing, statement, Kansas City, January 1890, box 212, folder A, TE-LOC; Dryden, August 24, 1863, *With Plow and Pen*, 18. For the burning of Nevada City, see Patrick Brophy, *Bushwhackers of the Border: The Civil War Period in Western Missouri*, 65–66.

packs on their backs, and four or five children following after them—some crying for bread, some crying to be taken back to their homes."[66]

Some Union soldiers nonetheless challenged the veracity of such poignant descriptions. Charles Blair suggested that because years of guerrilla warfare had already driven most settlers from rural western Missouri, the evacuation policy affected relatively few Southern sympathizers. "It simply ordered what had been done," concluded Blair. "There was not a family living any where in these border counties except in the immediate vicinity of the posts." Another officer from Kansas, R. H. Hunt, offered a similarly skeptical assessment: "There was very little suffering because of this order. The loyal poor were provided with food and maintained by the government, while those who were of pronounced Southern tendencies were carried beyond the line of interdiction." Hunt acknowledged, however, that confiscation and destruction of disloyal settlers' grain, hay, and provisions were common.[67] It is nearly impossible to calculate how many people were removed under Order No. 11. In 1860 there had been almost forty thousand people living in the three counties that were principally affected by the order. Although that number had no doubt declined amid the violence of the following three years, it is likewise difficult to believe that the order caused hardships for so few Missourians.

Refugees from the Missouri border counties scattered across a broad area, but most stayed relatively close to their former homes. Many families relocated to nearby counties in western and central Missouri. A group of settlers from Bates County slipped across the Henry County line to Germantown, where they attempted to maintain a county government-in-exile for the next two years.[68] Some exiles, such as the family of Thomas Shortridge, who went to Illinois, returned east to stay with relatives or friends. Others headed west, relocating to central Kansas, California, or Colorado, where lingering excitement over the Pikes Peak gold discovery attracted many immigrants. Many exiles, of course, never returned to the western border. One such couple, Stephen and Ann Old-

66. United Daughters of the Confederacy, Missouri Division, *Reminiscences of the Women of Missouri during the Sixties*, 263.

67. Blair to Ewing, May 23, 1871, TE-LOC; Hunt, Fifteenth Kansas Cavalry, "General Orders No. 11," Kansas Commandery of the Military Order of the Loyal Legion of the United States, 4, Feb. 1908, TE-LOC.

68. Those counties included Boone, Buchanan, Clay, Cooper, Henry, Howard, Johnson, Lafayette, Miller, Pettis, Ray, St. Clair, and Saline. See settler biographies in O. Williams, *Cass and Bates Counties;* and United Daughters of the Confederacy, Missouri Division, *Reminiscences*, 42–43, 249. See also Joanne Chiles Eakin, *Tears and Turmoil: Order #11*, 38–65, 86–92; and Bates County Court, Minutes, 1863–1865.

ham, fled to Chariton County, Missouri, where they lived in a tobacco barn during the unusually cold winter of 1863–1864 and then migrated to Fannin County, Texas, shortly thereafter.[69]

Observers across Missouri howled in protest at Ewing's far-reaching policy and denounced it as the callous work of vindictive Kansans. Among the measure's fiercest critics was George Caleb Bingham, a Union officer and Missouri artist, who sought to underscore the repressive brutality of the depopulation edict in his famous though overdrawn painting *Order No. 11* (also known as *Martial Law* or *The War of Desolation*), which portrayed federal soldiers forcibly ejecting a slaveholding family. One settler from western Missouri, Richard Vaughn, complained about the military's misguided sense of political geography. Writing to Edward Bates, the attorney general of the United States, who was himself a Missourian, Vaughn exclaimed, "The great mistake was annexing part of our state to the military district of Kansas, and the next great error was in placing a Kansas politician in command of it." Schofield understood such anger yet was reluctant to change commanders. "A man entirely disconnected with Kansas would be better in some respects," he wrote, "but such a man would lack the knowledge to avoid the shoals and quicksands which would surround him." Ewing made no apologies for the fact that a large number of Kansans, including some former jayhawkers, were among the federal soldiers charged with executing the order. Upon assuming control of the district, he had specifically requested that Kansas regiments be stationed under his command because their recruits were intimately familiar with the countryside and its inhabitants, as well as the habits and haunts of Missouri guerrillas. For the exiled Missourians, this circumstance added insult to injury.[70]

Privately, Ewing defended the order as a reasoned extension of the army's existing policy toward the family members of guerrillas. He insisted that the army did not depopulate rural western Missouri in retaliation for the Lawrence massacre and instead maintained that his actions kept Kansans from exacting violent revenge on both innocent and guilty Missourians. The general's correspondence also suggested that Order

69. I am indebted to James Shortridge for sharing with me his wealth of genealogical information about the Shortridges, Oldhams, and other ancestors from western Missouri.

70. Vaughn quote, August 28, 1863, in *O.R.*, ser. 1, vol. 22, pt. 2, 485, as quoted in Niepman, "General Orders No. 11," 198; Schofield, diary, September 3, 1863, 81; Ewing to Schofield, June 23, 1863, RG 393, NAB. For well-reasoned analyses of Bingham's painting, see Etcheson, *Bleeding Kansas*, 241; and Castel, "Order Number 11," 360–63. For Unionist criticisms of the painting, see Hunt, "General Orders No. 11," 5.

No. 11 was a policy of last resort. "Every expedition I sent out to overtake the guerrillas failed to achieve the object sought," wrote Ewing many years later. "We could not overtake them. On every side of us were living people who not only befriended and sympathized with the guerrillas, but furnished them with advantageous information as to the movement of the army or any detachment."[71]

Schofield endorsed the depopulation order, having drafted a nearly identical proposal just before its issue, and thus found himself beset by criticisms from all corners. Many Kansans called for the removal of Ewing, whom they held responsible for the Lawrence massacre. Radical Unionists in Missouri criticized the general's "conservative policy" in the state; others, such as Lieutenant Governor Willard Hall, demanded that he transfer command of the district to General E. B. Brown, a Missourian who was himself critical of Ewing's inability to keep out Kansas guerrillas, or "red-legs," and put down the bushwhackers. Hamilton Gamble, the Unionist governor of Missouri, believed that the federal army should take greater pains to secure the protection of loyal citizens within the state. Schofield received word in early September that Lane had assumed control of a movement in Paola, Kansas, that was planning to invade Missouri. Determined to thwart such cross-border retaliation, the general published an order holding that the militias of Kansas and Missouri must be used only for the defense of their respective states and therefore could not cross the state line without the approval of the district commander.[72]

The Unionist settlers who had been spared by Order No. 11 were apparently among Ewing and Schofield's few supporters. After visiting Westport on September 6, Schofield reported that loyal men there regarded the measure as a wise and necessary policy. "I have yet to find the first loyal man in the border counties who condemns it," he wrote in his diary. The general then met citizens of "all shades of loyalty" in Independence, where the order enjoyed less unanimous support. "All seem willing to submit to it," Schofield observed, "if it could produce the desired result. The chief objection was the great loss of property that must result from a rigid enforcement of the order." The general agreed that the destruction of property was largely unnecessary and useless; he believed that the information and food passed along by family members were the real keys to the bushwhackers' survival. Later that evening he resolved to modify Ewing's order so that property of known rebels

71. Ewing, statement, January 1890.
72. Schofield, diary, August 26, 31, September 3, 1863, 68–78.

would be appropriated for use by federal troops or destitute Unionists, rather than be destroyed.[73]

Although Order No. 11 reduced the bushwhackers' presence in the tier of border counties, it failed to eliminate the guerrilla threat entirely. Brown observed that the adjacent western counties that had not been depopulated were "in a very bad state" by late September. The problem, he explained, came "not from the evils arising from the depredations of rebel bushwhackers so much as that of men stealing in the name of the Union and from the spirit of intolerance that pervades all classes." The general breakdown in order likewise threatened the military posts that were located within the depopulated counties. Bandits from Kansas raided the station at Harrisonville in October and seized forty cattle that belonged to Unionist farmers. The post's commander, C. S. Clark, stated that the thieving "patriotic citizens" were caught and the cattle returned, but complained that the capture required several soldiers, which meant that he had "15 men less to hunt Bushwhackers." Ewing publicly condemned such raids in a speech he delivered in the Kansas town of Olathe, which was later published in the *Kansas City Journal of Commerce*. "There are very many men in Kansas who are stealing themselves rich in the name of Liberty. These men must find some other mode of giving effect to their patriotic zeal. As they want to kill rebels, let them join any old regiment," he declared. "I mean to stop with a rough hand all forays for plunder from Kansas into Missouri." Whether this announcement had any salutary effect, Ewing believed that guerrillas in each state took notice of the army's intentions, writing, "My Olathe speech has made a sensation and greatly distressed the red-legs and ultras generally."[74]

Over the coming weeks, conditions along the border improved enough that one Union officer could claim, "For all present practical purposes it will be safe to say next first of March or April that the 'Border Question' is 'settled.'" Many exiled Missourians began petitioning the army for permission to return home, but Ewing was himself reluctant to welcome back the recently banished Southern sympathizers. The general suggested that displaced persons might be allowed into the district of the

---

73. Ibid., September 6, 8, 1863, 80, 82–83.
74. Brown to Schofield, September 29, 1863, RG 393, NAB; Clark to Ewing, October 5, 1863, box 212, folder C; Ewing, speech at Olathe (reprint), *Kansas City Journal of Commerce*, October 27, 1863, box 212, folder B, TE-LOC; Ewing to Father, n.d. Men stationed at Pleasant Hill reported weeks later that ten to twelve guerrillas were seen just east of town. See Consolidated Report of Stations, October 12, 1863, box 212, folder C, TE-LOC.

border if they received the approval of the local post's commander. Individuals would not be allowed to resettle in homes that were located in the timber, unless they were also situated near a military station, and absolutely no settler could return to areas that were watered by the Sni-A-Bar Creek, a heavily wooded stream that ran through Jackson and Lafayette Counties and was deemed the "great lair of the bushwhackers." (Ewing later conceded that Order No. 11 should have been applied to Lafayette County as well.) Any settler's return, the general maintained, would be conditional, and if disloyal acts were committed by any member of that person's family, "the whole of them" should be ousted yet again.[75]

Although Schofield took note of these recommendations, he soon transferred the depopulated counties into Brown's central Missouri command, a move that appeased longtime Missouri critics. In January 1864, Brown declared that all persons not "disloyal or unworthy" could return to their homes, though many had already been reduced to ashes. He also loosened the qualifications by which individuals could prove their loyalty to return home. Brown's actions exasperated Ewing, who thought that such clemency would undo the army's efforts in Missouri. Such fears, however, never materialized because only a small portion of families took advantage of the policy shift and returned to the district. Many guerrillas, however, continued to lurk along the desolate border for the duration of the war. One observer attributed the bushwhackers' lingering presence to the lenient turn in military policy. "At least one third of the men who had obtained permits to return under the orders issued last Spring by General Brown are now 'in the bush,'" argued a Union colonel named Ford. After visiting the homes of now-returned families in June, Ford wrote, "The men could not be found. Sometimes the women would tell three or four different stories as to their whereabouts. Sometimes they would pretend that they were dead, or that there were no man belonging to the family, or any of a number of different stories." Weeks earlier Quantrill and several other guerrillas had returned from Texas and assaulted a Union garrison in the Missouri town of Lamar.[76]

Guerrillas had attempted to drive John Dryden from his Vernon County farm in early 1863, and a year later he again faced the perilous

75. P. B. Plumb to Ewing, November 24, 1863, box 212, folder B, TE-LOC; Ewing to Schofield, November 9, 1863, RG 393, NAB.

76. Bates County Old Settlers Society, *Old Settlers' History,* 45; Castel, "Order Number 11," 357, 366–68; Paul B. Hatley and Noor Ampssler, "Army General Orders Number 11: Final Valid Option or Wanton Act of Brutality? The Missouri Question in the American Civil War," 77–87; Colonel Ford, *Daily Journal* (reprint), June 28, 1864, box 212, folder B, TE-LOC; March, *The History of Missouri,* 2:987.

consequences of loyalty to the Union. On the night of May 27, a band of five bushwhackers attacked the Drydens' home and set it ablaze before retreating when he fired upon them with his shotgun. "Why is it that I am troubled so much with these villains!" Dryden exclaimed. "Merely because I am loyal to the government." Louisa Dryden managed to extinguish the fire, but after three fearful weeks the family, which now included an infant daughter, abandoned its home and sought safety across the state line. They spent the next several months "vagabonding" though eight Kansas counties, where John worked as an itinerant farm laborer for the duration of the war.[77]

Eastern Kansas was to be an incomparably more hospitable environment for the Drydens. After nearly a decade of guerrilla violence and the particularly difficult summer of 1863, which Sarah Everett had considered the most hateful she had ever known, the counties of southeastern Kansas found themselves at the cusp of relative peace and prosperity. "As regards *danger* from Rebel or more properly Guerrilla raids we . . . never *feel* any," wrote Everett. "We are never afraid. . . . The border is now thoroughly protected."[78]

Kansans had certainly endured privation during the early years of the civil war, but several factors stimulated economic development as the war dragged on. First, the Union army's control of the Missouri River and the telegraph and railroad lines that linked Kansas to eastern markets lessened the state's relative isolation. The U.S. Army also fueled the continued development of Fort Scott, which had become an important southwestern supply depot, and more than a million dollars in military commissions absorbed agricultural surpluses and provided work to hundreds of citizens. Such investment attracted thousands of new immigrants, including a large number of Missouri Unionists and hundreds of former slaves. At least one Missourian believed that property plundered from secessionist households helped stimulate the wartime growth of southeastern Kansas. As Mrs. R. K. Johnson recalled, "Daily wagons were seen loaded with pianos and other furniture, carpets, etc., for the purpose of furnishing Union homes and camps. Kansas settlers were well supplied from Missouri homes."[79]

77. Dryden, November 13, 1865, *With Plow and Pen*, 20–21. The eight counties were Allen, Anderson, Bourbon, Douglas, Franklin, Johnson, Linn, and Miami.

78. Everett and Everett, "Letters of John and Sarah Everett," 381 (letter from Sarah Everett, "Late in 1863").

79. *Fort Scott Democrat*, June 29, 1861; *Fort Scott Western Volunteer*, June 21, 1862; Holder and Rothman, *Post on the Marmaton*, 102; United Daughters of the Confederacy, Missouri Division, *Reminiscences*, 254.

Lasting peace did not come to the Kansas side of the border until the fall of 1864. In September, Sterling Price led a Confederate invasion into south-central Missouri in a last-ditch effort to retake the state. Union forces under Ewing thwarted Price's troops at Pilot Knob, forcing them to abandon any plans of capturing St. Louis. The Confederates instead moved to western Missouri, hoping that Southern sympathizers would rise up en masse and defeat the occupying federal army. The anticipated insurrection, however, never materialized, and after being soundly defeated at the Battle of Westport, the Confederate invaders retreated southward through eastern Kansas ahead of pursuing Union troops. In late October, the federal army caught up with the rebels in Linn County and in a major cavalry engagement near Mine Creek routed Price's men and drove them into Arkansas.[80]

Although the defeat of Price's army also marked the end of major combat in Missouri, the peaceful resettlement of the Burnt District was not soon forthcoming. Kansas City newspapers could accurately declare by March 1865 that "bushwhacking" was "played out" in Jackson County, but the situation to the south remained unstable. On April 27, John Atkinson, sheriff of Bates County, described his dire situation to Governor Thomas Fletcher: "The Bushwhackers are numerous in this County. They are passing almost every day in bands of from six to thirty, robbing as they go." One band that swept through the area that spring stopped briefly near the Osage River, where they captured a lone militiaman. The group's leader, Archie Clement, slit the man's throat and scalped him while Jesse James and two other bushwhackers pinned the victim to the ground. Such bands, however brutal their behavior, were still not the most feared men in rural western Missouri, as the conclusion of Atkinson's letter showed. "I wish to call your attention to another class of the human species more to be dreaded here than the bushwhackers. I refer to the 'Kansas troops.' They have been here three or four times in the last months and have taken more or less stock each time . . . [and] threaten the life of any man who reports them." He closed the report with plaintive exasperation: "How long, Governor, is this state of things to exist in our County? Is there no help for us?"[81]

The plundering of western Missouri would ultimately cease by year's end, but there would be no clear moment of finality for the border war akin

---

80. Holder and Rothman, *Post on the Marmaton,* 207–12; March, *The History of Missouri,* 2:990–94.

81. Brownlee, *Gray Ghosts,* 233; Atkinson to Fletcher, April 27, 1865, UPMP; Stiles, *Jesse James,* 150.

to Robert E. Lee's April 9 surrender at Appomattox Courthouse in Virginia. When John Dryden returned to Missouri in November 1865, he likely shared the feelings of many other disillusioned, war-weary settlers on both sides of the border. "Have we gained anything for all our sacrifice of blood and treasure?" he asked. "If we have I can't see it." Given the ignominious losses of recent years, many white Missourians probably would have agreed. Yet even amid the devastation that confronted him, Dryden found redeeming purpose in the war just concluded. "We have freed the slaves," he noted. "No more forever will that 'relic of barbarism' stain the fair name of our country. I have looked on slavery as being an evil for several years, yet," like many other Missourians, "was willing for it to work out its own destiny. It was an institution regulated by law and recognized in the Constitution of our country and as a Christian citizen I was called on to submit whether I liked it or not.—Now that the slaves are free, what next?"[82]

Dryden's question captured both the promise and the uncertainty of the start of the Reconstruction era. Inhabitants of the borderland apprehended how profoundly the war had changed their lives. For African Americans, this transformation brought the many blessings of freedom, including the opportunity to raise their families and build communities as they saw fit. Yet as black settlers began their new lives in unfamiliar places—for most, it was the nearby counties in Kansas—they still found opportunities circumscribed by persistent racism. The social upheavals caused by the war also had major consequences for whites, especially in Missouri. Thousands of dispossessed southerners and Confederate sympathizers had been driven far from their homes; a great many of these people would return, often to find homes and property that had been destroyed in their absence. Guerrilla violence likewise had scattered Dryden and other Unionists, many of whom escaped to Kansas or other parts of Missouri. In addition to rebuilding their homes and communities, the settlers who returned would also face an extraordinary opportunity to reshape the boundaries of political identity. Former Unionists would engage in an active debate about what rights and privileges African Americans, defeated Confederate sympathizers, and women should enjoy in the new postwar world. Yet although this debate anticipated the future of U.S. citizenship, its participants put forth arguments that were informed by familiar prejudices, tensions, and fears, as the long shadow cast by the border war loomed over its survivors for years to come.

82. Dryden, November 13, 1865, *With Plow and Pen*, 27–28.

A BORDER RECONSTRUCTED

C lear proof that the Civil War had finally burned itself out came with the return of several thousand settlers who had been exiled from the borderland during a near decade of fighting. A great many people, particularly in the depopulated counties of western Missouri, faced a gloomy homecoming. Bates and Cass Counties, which had been depopulated by the Union army in 1863, were so devastated that observers described the desolate countryside there, simply, as the Burnt District. Many homes had been reduced to ashes, victims of the unchecked fires set by plundering guerrillas or soldiers. The few landmarks that survived—perhaps a naked chimney and foundation here, a garden rank with weeds there—offered sullen reminders of the destruction that had visited much of the Osage valley. Families who had been driven out left carrying what few items could be gathered at a moment's notice, and those who came back returned with little more, often to find their farms ruined and livestock gone. For Southern sympathizers, incalculable losses were both tangible and emotional, as grief and the bitter sting of defeat cast shadows over the necessary tasks of starting anew. In spite of such widespread hardship, or perhaps because of it, the physical reconstruction of the Kansas-Missouri border proceeded quickly in the years immediately after the war. There was more rebuilding to be done east of the state line; Kansans certainly had suffered greatly during their own territorial struggle but generally had avoided the devastation and dispossession that the Civil War brought to Missouri.

Rebuilding, wherever it occurred, was hard work, but it represented only one element of the broader reconstruction of the borderland, which included institutional, social, and legal changes that promised to transform life in other obvious ways. The declaration of martial law had diminished the power of local governments, and by 1865 many basic services had been neglected for years. As taxes went unpaid and then uncollected, schools were neither taught nor attended, and area roads were not maintained, thus making the restoration of civil authority a major priority. The rapid demobilization of federal troops had at least two other important consequences. First, it meant that Missouri, unlike the states of the defeated Confederacy, would not be occupied by the U.S. Army for years to come; second, the responsibility for preserving law and order fell upon local officials, or, as many people still believed, private citizens.

Neither the war's conclusion nor the army's departure could quickly heal the social divisions that had hardened over the past decade. By the end of the Civil War, the Kansas-Missouri border held a peculiarly divisive distinction in a country torn asunder. In perhaps no other American place had such hard feelings divided neighbors of such close proximity for so long. How, given this history of hostility, would free-soil and proslavery partisans, jayhawkers and bushwhackers, or Unionists and rebels live together in peace? Settlers who were inclined to forgive asserted the need to move forward from the violent past, not to indulge in vengeance and anger. Other citizens, however, found it more difficult to heal, much less ignore, old divisions. Thrown into the tense mix of old-stock settlers were several thousand postwar immigrants, people for whom the savage cruelty of the border war was not raw and personal, and recently emancipated African Americans, most of whom had fled from Missouri to Kansas.

The twisting social dynamics between these groups found clear expression in spirited debates about civil rights and the dimensions of postwar citizenship. The five years after the war witnessed an extraordinary moment of political self-examination, in which white male Unionists paused to consider whether former Confederates, freedmen, and women should enjoy the full benefits of U.S. citizenship, especially the right to vote. With respect to the unsettled status of former Confederates and rebel sympathizers, wartime governments in many states, such as the provisional authority in Missouri, had stripped disloyal citizens of the right to vote. After the war, state governments asked whether erstwhile rebels should be fully restored to their antebellum rights and privileges for the sake of sectional reconciliation and national unity. Many

Radical Republicans argued that disfranchisement was an appropriate punishment for those who had taken up arms against the Union. The status of emancipated slaves was likewise a contentious issue. Many citizens in Kansas and Missouri believed that African Americans, particularly Union veterans, deserved the right to vote, but dissenting voices, including many Republicans, feared that the expansion of civil rights for free blacks might soon bring about the social equality of the races. In Kansas, the question of black suffrage also set off an impassioned public debate about the political rights of women, who theretofore had been denied the vote, and revealed the many ways that gender, as well as race and patriotism, shaped conceptions of political identity.

Taken together, these various elements of reconstruction—physical, social, political, and, as later chapters will argue, economic—had the combined potential to reshape the meaning of the Kansas-Missouri border. Just years earlier the border had been an explosive symbol of the ideological divide between freedom and slavery, but it now offered a telling example of the unexpected alliances and tensions that would erode old divisions. The political fault line between former Unionists and Confederates was not easily bridged, however, because enduring memories of war would often complicate the process of reconciliation. In addition, the persistence of racism on both sides of the state line thwarted efforts by African Americans to realize the full extent of their newfound freedom.

By 1865, the wartime devastation of the depopulated counties in western Missouri rivaled or exceeded that anywhere in the South, including the broad swath of territory destroyed in Sherman's infamous March to the Sea.[1] A Kansas businessman traveled southeast from Kansas City to Pleasant Hill and noted the desolate condition of the country between the two towns. "Now and then you could see a lone house that had escaped the hands of the Jayhawkers," he wrote, "but as far as the eye could reach in every direction you could see lone chimneys standing singly and in pairs, all that was left at that time of what was called good homesteads. The grass had grown over the foundations and left no sign of there ever having been a house where the chimneys stood." The war's destructive imprint on the rural landscape was also keenly felt in the places where prospering towns had once stood. West Point had been an active trading center, due in large part to its location on the western border and along a major Texas cattle trail. By the end of the war the village had been oblit-

---

1. For recent treatments of Sherman's march, see Anne J. Bailey, *War and Ruin: William T. Sherman and the Savannah Campaign*; and Campbell, *When Sherman Marched North*.

erated, never to be rebuilt. With the destruction of local stores and farms, hungry refugees relied on wild game for food or paid the inflated post-war prices charged at trading posts across the border in Kansas.[2]

A need to reestablish the basic functions of civil government impelled the swift rebuilding of Missouri county seats such as Harrisonville, Butler, Nevada City, Lamar, and Osceola, each of which had been plundered and burned during the war. Although local authorities had surrendered much of their power early in the war, when the Union army declared martial law throughout Missouri, many county governments had continued to function in a limited capacity. The members of the Bates County Court had managed to convene in regular session through the spring of 1863, well after the courthouse and much of Butler had been torched. When Order No. 11 drove the judges from the county, several officials had reassembled in a neighboring county. For all practical purposes, though, most local governments were forced to start anew in the postwar period. Many of the officials who had been elected before the war were either dead, permanently removed from the country, or disqualified from service under wartime loyalty oaths. Courthouses, schools, jails, and bridges had been destroyed, as had many administrative, judicial, and financial records. Most counties lacked the financial resources to make immediate improvements. The government of Vernon County faced thousands of dollars in outstanding warrants and unsettled accounts, but given the scarcity of cash among local citizens, its empty treasury would not be quickly replenished. The few greenbacks that appeared in local circulation were often depreciated, bringing barely seventy-five cents for every dollar in gold.[3]

In this moment of massive rebuilding, opportunistic citizens in Cass County saw a chance to redraw the political boundaries of western Missouri to their own advantage. Business leaders from Pleasant Hill advocated the creation of a new county, Richland, from parts of Jackson, Cass, Johnson, and Bates Counties. Pleasant Hill, from the perspective of local promoters, was an especially deserving location for the seat of this new county. As one of the four military posts designated in Order No. 11, the town had been spared from much of the destruction inflicted upon the

2. Goodlander, *Memoirs and Recollections*, 107; O. Williams, *Cass and Bates Counties*, 960–62. One settler recalled paying eighteen dollars for a barrel of salted pork at Trading Post, Kansas, in the winter of 1866 (Bates County Old Settlers Society, *Old Settlers' History*, 152).

3. Bates County Court, Minutes, February 3, 1863, 1:425–28; J. Johnson, *History of Vernon County*, 312–20. For the campaign to fund a new courthouse in Bates County, see *Bates County Record*, October 10, 1868.

surrounding countryside. In addition, Pleasant Hill had become the western terminus of the Missouri Pacific Railroad in October 1865. Local reaction to the Richland County proposal foreshadowed the spirited town rivalries that would take shape over the next decade. The scheme drew vehement opposition from the residents of Jackson County; Harrisonville, the existing seat of Cass County, which had also served as a Union post; and Butler, where one editor dismissed the county-division movement as a gigantic fraud. The bill that would establish the new county passed through the Missouri House of Representatives by a vote of seventy-eight to thirty-nine, but staunch opposition from the Burnt District helped to stall the measure in the senate, where it ultimately died.[4]

Popular resistance or indifference toward the Richland County proposal stemmed from the pressing economic concerns that lay before the citizens of the western counties. Thousands of dollars in school and property taxes, which had been levied against landowners through 1863, remained unpaid. Old-stock settlers who returned to the border, especially those who had fled the area during the violence of the late 1850s, were undoubtedly distressed when they discovered the substantial tax burden that had been assessed during their absence. Forced exile had rendered several families utterly destitute, and, with most of their chattel either stolen or destroyed, large numbers of families lacked the means to satisfy their mounting tax debt. Whereas Union veterans were at times exempted from paying the property taxes that had accumulated during the war, secessionist civilians were left to sell timber or whatever else they could find to raise the cash needed to pay their taxes. Lacking any other alternatives, a great many old-stock settlers were forced to sell their land at public auction.[5]

The forced disposal of tax-delinquent lands raised the possibility of an extraordinary redistribution of wealth along the Kansas border. One source suggests that during the late 1860s, as much as half of the land in Bates County was advertised for sale to pay back taxes.[6] Although this estimate may be exaggerated, the sale of tax-delinquent lands was clearly a major problem on both sides of the Missouri-Kansas border. Newspa-

4. *Pleasant Hill Leader,* February 4, 11, 18, 1870; *Bates County Record,* January 29, February 26, 1870.

5. A. Thompson to Albert Badger, 1865, and O. C. Badger to Albert Badger, June 21, 1867, Badger Papers, VCHS. Acting as auditor for public accounts, Thompson explained that Badger's military service in the Naval Ordnance Department exempted him from paying local property taxes through 1865.

6. Mann, Higgins, and Kolbe, *Soil Survey,* 9. Bates County Old Settlers Society, *Old Settlers' History,* 45, notes that "much of the land" in the county was sold for taxes.

pers in Vernon County, for example, listed hundreds of Missouri farms, which together totaled tens of thousands of acres, that were to be sold at public auction, and similar notices about Kansas tracts, which had presumably been abandoned during the war, covered entire broadsheets in the weekly papers of Linn County.

In the Burnt District, the public auctions that sheriffs carried out on the steps of county courthouses had the makings of a serious upheaval in the local economic order. Sheriffs' sales threatened to dispossess many antebellum families who had been financially ruined by the war, including some of the area's earliest pioneers. Those individuals who lost their property could expect to see it ignominiously purchased out from under them by longtime neighbors, wealthy speculators, northern immigrants, or old rivals. Neither age, birthplace, nor antebellum wealth determined which families were likely to lose their land. Before the war, Ohio natives Gibson and Eliza Garwood had been farmers of modest means, owning real estate worth sixteen hundred dollars, but in early 1866 they were unable to pay the taxes that had been assessed on several lots in Butler. As a result, these parcels were snapped up at a sheriff's sale by George Lowe, an English farmer who had originally settled in southeastern Kansas, and Calvin Boxley, a twenty-six-year-old attorney and recent emigrant from Indiana.[7] The availability of such tracts at relatively low prices proved to be an obvious boon for newcomers like Lowe and Boxley, but for the Garwoods and other locals, it was a hard reminder of the war's crippling economic impact.

For all the pathos and radical possibilities that surrounded the sales of tax-delinquent lands, they apparently produced modest changes in property ownership. Turnover was limited in large part by the ability of many settlers to retain ownership and possession of their respective properties. Local court records from the western counties indicate that many sheriffs' sales were not conducted until the spring of 1867, thus giving former exiles several months to raise the funds needed to satisfy outstanding debts. The account book of John and Louisa Dryden, who had fled their Missouri home in the summer of 1864, offers an instructive example of how some families pieced together enough money to pay their taxes. John's services as a justice of the peace, officiating weddings and executing deeds for as much as two dollars each, produced a respectable income, but the cash he and Louisa earned from both his occasional work

---

7. Cass County Circuit Court Records, vol. E, 177, April 6, 1867, 271, April 9, 1867; Bates County Circuit Court Records, vol. C, 173, 247, April 1867, Missouri State Archives.

as a day laborer and the local exchange of farm products, such as honey, eggs, butter, bacon, and corn, was usually sufficient to pay their annual tax bill of approximately twenty-five dollars.[8] The Drydens' experience suggests that after returning for a full growing season, settlers engaged in livestock production could often generate enough revenue to eliminate much, if not all, of their accumulated tax burden (provided, of course, that their livestock had not been lost during the war).

A survey of newspaper accounts and sheriffs' deeds from the western border reveals that most of the land sold at public auction fell into the hands of old-stock settlers, rather than immigrants or nonresident investors. Commenting on the annual sale of tax-delinquent lands, one Butler editor confirmed this fact: "The purchasers consisted entirely of citizens of our own county, and the land thus sold, belonged mostly to non-residents."[9] In Cass County, more than half of the individuals who purchased tax-delinquent land in the late 1860s can be positively identified in a census sample of border residents from 1850 and 1860. Although the persistence of property ownership among old-stock neighbors quieted fears about the encroachment of carpetbaggers and other outsiders, an important change was nonetheless taking place in Missouri, one that redounded to the benefit of one class of locals much more than others.

After all, not every Missourian who came back after the war was mired in poverty, and several natives, such as farmer Robert Brown, returned with enough wealth to indulge in extensive land speculation. Heralded as one of the area's earliest pioneers, Brown had settled in Van Buren (later renamed Cass) County in 1842 and had been elected as a delegate to the 1861 state convention that had voted against secession. Although the Democrat's Unionist principles had repeatedly incurred the wrath of pro-Confederate guerrillas, he survived the war with most of his considerable wealth intact, thanks in no small part to his farm's close proximity to the army post at Harrisonville. Starting in the spring of 1867, Brown began purchasing several of the tracts of land that were auctioned off by the county sheriff. Joining him in this flurry of postwar speculation were four other men who had been born in slave states: J. M. Armstrong, a merchandiser from Pleasant Hill; Frank Chilton and Robert Foster, Harrisonville merchants; and Fleming Hollaway, who operated a grocery in

---

8. John Dryden, "Memoranda for 1863," "Memoranda for 1865," and "Memoranda for 1867," Dryden Papers, VCHS. For examples of Dryden's annual tax bill, see Dryden, December 18, 1875, and December 24, 1878, *With Plow and Pen*, 90, 111.

9. *Bates County Record*, October 17, 1868.

Prairie City.[10] The prosperity of these five merchants illustrates the uneven financial impact of the war on the old-stock southern natives. Though many locals—particularly the exiled Confederate sympathizers who would never return to the area—had suffered unmistakable ruin, many middle-class Unionists who had been spared by Order No. 11 managed to maintain their place atop the postwar social structure by consolidating much of the wealth that had been lost by southern neighbors.

The sale of tax-delinquent lands eventually helped local governments return to solvency, but persistent lawlessness proved to be a more intractable problem. Primary evidence indicates that violent crime remained widespread in the border counties for at least a decade after the war. This violence and the men who perpetrated it were relics of the recent guerrilla war, and much of the crime that took place assumed familiar forms. Horse thieves flourished on both sides of the border, as did plundering highway bandits who preyed upon innocent travelers. To give but one example of several audacious murders, four men on horseback ambushed an immigrant on his way to Bates County, robbed him of nineteen hundred dollars, and escaped unharmed, leaving their victim's dead body along a nearby creek.[11] Some former guerrillas settled into a life of quiet respectability; John McCorkle, a scout in William Quantrill's band, retired to Howard County and took up farming. Others, such as Thomas Sabine, carried on as belligerent public nuisances. One Saturday evening, Sabine came into Harrisonville, "got crazy drunk," and began firing his pistols wildly as he staggered about the streets. After the "ruffian" was shot by a local man, "all were relieved and gratified," according to one newspaper account.[12]

The 1867 murder of Sheriff Joseph Bailey in Vernon County demonstrated the vulnerability of civil authorities who struggled to contain lawlessness in the postwar West. In late March, Bailey had apprehended former guerrillas Perry and Lewis Pixley. As he was transferring the brothers to the county jail, the captives broke free, killed the sheriff, and escaped with the help of at least one accomplice. Although many details surrounding the Pixleys' escape remain unclear, the incident illustrates

10. Cass County Circuit Court Records, vol. E, 350–60, April 1867; O. Williams, *Cass and Bates Counties*, 217–19, 441, 451, 482, 622–23. For guerrilla harassment of the Brown family, see statement of J. T. Blake, July 1863, Union Provost Marshal Papers, Missouri State Archives, hereinafter cited as UPMP.

11. *Miami County Republican*, July 5, 1873; *Bates County Record*, July 11, August 1, 1868; Bates County Old Settlers Society, *Old Settlers' History*, 46; J. Johnson, *History of Vernon County*, 315; Fellman, *Inside War*, 231–33.

12. *Pleasant Hill Leader*, August 25, 1871; McCorkle, *Three Years with Quantrill*, 156.

local officials' inability to carry out the most basic functions of law enforcement. Prosecutions for violent crime were exceedingly rare in the early postwar period, especially when one considers the frequency with which reports of murders and robberies appeared in area newspapers. From 1865 to 1867, grand juries in Cass County issued forty-two indictments for gambling or public intoxication but only one indictment for murder, which, like many of the vice prosecutions, was subsequently dismissed. To the south, Bates County juries issued four times as many indictments for morality crimes (gambling, drunkenness, Sabbath breaking, and so on) as for murder, assault, and robbery. Courts in Vernon County saw relatively few prosecutions for crimes of any kind. When criminal prosecutions were actually adjudicated, default convictions were usually rendered, as most defendants failed to appear in court.[13]

Given the ineffectiveness of institutional authorities in limiting postwar lawlessness, people along the Kansas-Missouri line turned to extralegal violence as a means of restoring order to the countryside. Citizens in Vernon County established a vigilante organization, dubbed the Marmaton League, which reportedly "became the terror of criminals." Within a week of Sheriff Bailey's murder, a lynch mob captured and killed Tom Ingram, who had been suspected of aiding the Pixleys' escape. A day after a pair of horse thieves in Butler had posted bail to free themselves from jail, a posse of twenty-five men, convinced that local courts would not mete out a just punishment, apprehended the duo and hanged them. Vigilantes across the border in Kansas murdered John Chrisman for stealing mules later that same year. The roots of such vigilantism and extralegal violence reached back to the struggle to control territorial Kansas, not to mention the earlier campaigns to rid Missouri of the Osages and Mormons. Like the Sons of the South, claims clubs, and secret societies of the previous decade, postwar settlers sanctioned vigilante action as an appropriate exercise of community authority and a legitimate means of protecting life and property, especially when lawful authorities failed to take action. After a tumultuous decade in which the government had often failed to contain guerrilla violence, many citizens no longer saw the courts and formal institutions of law enforcement as the most effective means of securing justice.[14]

---

13. Cass County Circuit Court Records, vol. C, 530, vol. D, 128, 1865–1867; Bates County Circuit Court Records, vol. C, 71, 1866; Vernon County Circuit Court Records, vols. A and B, 1865–1867, Missouri State Archives.

14. *Bates County Record*, March 6, 1869. For the "crisis of authority" that fueled vigilantism in Missouri, see David Thelen, *Paths of Resistance: Tradition and Democracy in Industrializing Missouri*, 59–60; and J. Johnson, *History of Vernon County*, 315–37.

Although the rash of lawlessness and vigilantism that afflicted western Missouri seemed to have fewer parallels across the state line, Kansans shared a history of frontier violence that fostered a popular acceptance of summary justice. During the war, Unionist settlers had shown little compunction about hanging suspected horse thieves.[15] One instance of postwar mob violence in Kansas actually resulted from an unexpected instance of cross-border cooperation. In the fall of 1865, Elias Foster and Scott Holderman had committed a series of highway robberies and had murdered a Linn County man near the Marais des Cygnes River. After the bandits fled, Foster was subsequently caught while hiding across the Missouri line in Butler. A decade earlier, fugitive outlaws and proslavery settlers had found refuge on the far side of the border, but Missourians were now readily disposed to hand over suspected criminals and let Kansans deal with their own offenders. Foster was delivered to authorities in Mound City and put under close guard. Within weeks of his arrest, a mob of up to thirty men overwhelmed county officials, seized the prisoner, and lynched him. Not long thereafter, Holderman was likewise hunted down and summarily executed.[16]

Fresh memories of the border war continued to darken some settlers' perceptions of the antagonists in their midst and across the state line. A Republican editor from Miami County, Kansas, was disturbed by reports that Union and Confederate veterans in Missouri might reunite at a barbecue to be held in the summer of 1867. "We do not believe," he wrote, "the Union men of Missouri will forget the bloody sights that blacken the pages of crime, and deafen their ears to the horrid shrieks of murdered friends, by giving countenance to any such thing. They cannot be deceived by any such attempt to wipe out the blood stains that glitter on the garments of the rebels of that State. It would be an insult to loyalty." Thomas Brockman, an itinerant Kansas minister, refused to preach to the "secesh" of Vernon County, as he believed that they had not been sufficiently subjugated during the recent conflict. Within sharply divided Missouri communities, postwar reputations were intimately linked to past associations. On June 6, 1865, Thomas Collins declared that his honor had been impugned by a bushwhacker named James Curry. Hearing of this accusation, Curry sued Collins for slander. When the charge eventually reached the Missouri Supreme Court, the judges ruled that calling someone a bushwhacker in that particular case was not by itself a slanderous charge, as the plaintiff had failed to prove that the claim had

15. *Paola Union Crusader,* June 17, 1864.
16. Botkin, "Justice Was Swift," 491–92.

caused any real damage.[17] The fact that Collins's charge ever became a matter of such legal importance reveals the extent to which wartime allegiances shaped postwar reputations and conceptions of respectability.

Unfortunately, the fresh memories and attitudes that most Kansans and Missourians maintained about the border war and their former enemies remain unknown. A dearth of primary evidence obscures the perspectives of this largely silent majority. Most people simply never took the time to record the details of their everyday lives, much less their thoughts, feelings, and memories of the recent conflagration. Settlers, in their defense, were instead immersed in the urgent tasks of planting crops and rebuilding their homes. Dryden, for instance, was an otherwise faithful diarist but made only three journal entries for all of 1866 and 1867. The diaries, letters, and manuscripts that do survive offer only passing glimpses into the war's significance. That existing documents are relatively silent on the subject of war may itself be a meaningful reflection of local attitudes. Rather than dwelling on the hardships and losses of the past decade, many old-stock settlers may have been more inclined to focus on the challenges of the present and to look forward to the opportunities that lay ahead. Historians, at the same time, must also beware the positivist fallacy, which holds that an absence of evidence can be taken as evidence of absence. The fact that in the postwar borderland some men and women did not make note of lingering ill will surely does not mean that such feelings did not exist. To the contrary, hard feelings were for some people among the most enduring legacies of the war, but the elusiveness of undocumented sentiments obliges historians to use caution when describing or explaining postwar perspectives.[18]

In spite of the persistent hard feelings among some, mutual forgiveness became an indispensable element in the reconstruction of a self-governing society in late-nineteenth-century America. Many people on both sides of the border, hoping to stop the long-running cycle of violent retribution, indeed proved willing to pardon old foes. John Dryden, who had been repeatedly abused by bushwhackers and federals alike, articulated the sentiments of men and women who preferred to let bygone grievances remain in the past. Charged with settling a wartime feud between

17. *Miami County Republican*, July 20, 1867; Dryden, August 19, 1866, *With Plow and Pen*, 29–30; *Curry v. Collins*, 37 Missouri 324.
18. See Dryden, August 19, 1866, *With Plow and Pen*, 29–30. Dryden's rare entries from these two years are a marked contrast to the more regular entries of prior and subsequent years. For the challenges of studying elusive and ephemeral historical memories, see W. Fitzhugh Brundage, *Where These Memories Grow: History, Memory, and Southern Identity*, 3–5.

two neighbors, he concluded, "I will not hold citizens responsible for what southern Confederate, bushwhackers, or federal done."[19] Dryden's brief note in his diary offered few clues to the sources of his apparent magnanimity. Overlooking bygone offenses may have been good sense, as the adjudication of seemingly endless grievances probably would have yielded as many headaches. At the same time, a spirit of Christian forgiveness may have guided this ruling. Like many settlers along the border, Dryden considered himself a devout Christian and filled much of his diary with observations about religion, local church happenings, and the spiritual well-being of his neighborhood, himself included. Biblical teachings about grace, forgiveness, and loving one's enemies no doubt informed many people's attitudes toward old foes and almost certainly helped to make peacetime reconciliation more likely.

The religious beliefs of most postwar settlers were not well documented and thus remain another elusive subject for historical study. Census enumerators, however, did study church membership along the border, with varying degrees of success. Even though church affiliations were often fluid—Dryden himself attended the services of many denominations, preferring Methodist sermons over the "disorderly" worship of Baptist revivals—they nonetheless illustrate an important cultural similarity between Kansans and Missourians: a common Christian faith and remarkably similar memberships in Protestant denominations. As table 10 (Religions Affiliation along the Kansas-Missouri Border, 1870) illustrates, the religious communities in both states were dominated by Methodist, Baptist, and Presbyterian denominations, which together comprised three-fourths of local churches. Methodist churches were the most popular denominations in both states, with Baptist organizations coming in a close second.[20] Shared church memberships suggest that postwar settlers held many mutual values and beliefs; perhaps more important, these religious affiliations represented one thread among the many that were shaping a growing sense of common identity.

Even clearer proof of this developing regional identity came in that same 1870 census, which illuminates a wave of immigration that was making populations along the border even more alike. Nationally, the Civil War had temporarily curbed the pace and extent of westward expansion, and on the Kansas-Missouri border, years of irregular warfare

19. Fellman, *Inside War*, 264; Dryden, May 23, 1868, *With Plow and Pen*, 44.

20. A few subtle differences distinguished the churches in each state; for example, there were only one Catholic church and one Congregational church in all three Missouri counties, but in Kansas there were five of each kind.

had earned the area a national reputation for violence and disorder. Nevertheless, a remarkable influx of immigrants flocked to the area in the late 1860s, undeterred by sensational accounts of Bleeding Kansas or ruthless guerrillas. Most immigrants came from northern states and arrived in such large numbers that they reshaped the population of the Burnt District and reinforced the dominance of free-soil natives in Kansas. Two other developments also helped to remake rural society along the border. First, many of the old-stock southerners who had been exiled during the war never came back; second, communities of African Americans, composed largely of former Missouri slaves, sprang up in several Kansas towns. Taken together, all of these changes served to make the racial and regional composition of the counties on both sides of the border much more alike. After the ratification of the Thirteenth Amendment, the Kansas-Missouri border no longer remained the western boundary between freedom and slavery, and changing migration patterns would soon call into question whether it remained a significant social divide at all.

Like other postwar changes in western Missouri, the decline in old-stock southern influence had been made possible by the Union army's depopulation of the border counties. After the war, a great many southerners who had left the area—some fleeing jayhawkers early in the war, some forced out by Order No. 11—never returned. The population of the Missouri border counties had been in flux since the opening of Kansas Territory, making it difficult to determine, with the use of decennial census figures, exactly how many settlers were displaced. Having been burned out of their homes, some of the wartime refugees undoubtedly found it easier to start over elsewhere. The fate of N. R. Marchbanks resembled that of some exiled southern pioneers. In 1860, Marchbanks had been one of Vernon County's most prosperous farmers and stock raisers. Such wealth had made him an attractive target to jayhawking Kansans, who stole all of his livestock in repeated raids. Even greater personal losses had come with the deaths of the family's two eldest sons, a Confederate captain and a noted bushwhacker. In 1863, N. R. Marchbanks had led the rest of the family to Nebraska, where they stayed for the duration of the war. Eventually, the family came back to southwest Missouri, but not to their old homes; the elder Marchbanks died in Lawrence County, more than seventy miles from his former homestead.[21]

21. J. Johnson, *History of Vernon County*, 413; Census-Ag, Missouri, Vernon County, 1860. My analysis of agricultural census data indicates that the cash value of Marchbanks's farm put him in the top quartile of local farmers. Moreover, his diversified livestock holdings were generally larger than the local average.

The old-stock settlers who did come back to the Burnt District returned from a variety of locations. A few exiled natives had spent the last years of the war hundreds of miles from the border. When Solomon and Sarah Yoder were driven from Harrisonville, the Mennonite couple and their two children escaped to their former home in Ohio, but they promptly returned to western Missouri in 1865. Many Confederate veterans filtered back to the area from Virginia and western theaters of combat. William Brown had served under General Sterling Price and was among the last rebel troops to have surrendered at Shreveport, Louisiana, in May 1865; he eventually wandered back to his Cass County farm after spending several months drifting through eastern Texas. Anecdotal evidence suggests that more than half of the people driven away by Order No. 11 had found refuge closer to home, staying with other relatives in Missouri. John Daniel, for example, returned to the site of his former home in 1866 after spending two years with his family in nearby Pettis County. Jeremiah Sloan, meanwhile, slipped across the state line and took shelter in Paola, Kansas. Tennessee native Allen Blunt regarded that option as far too dangerous. "The state line was only sixteen miles distant, but every road and cow path leading to Kansas was guarded by the bushwhackers," he wrote. "Every man that was caught trying to get to Kansas was supposed to be a Union man, and he was robbed or killed, sometimes both."[22]

The end of the war also brought about the return of old-stock Missourians who had spent much of the past decade in Kansas. Beginning with the guerrilla fighting of the late 1850s, extensive cross-border migrations had reshuffled the populations of both states. Proslavery and freesoil partisans had taken turns trying to force one another from territorial Kansas, and Southern sympathizers in Missouri had driven out many of the Unionists in their midst, only to be later evicted themselves. An examination of census data from 1870 indicates that more than 40 percent of the postwar settlers in Missouri border counties who had come from Kansas had previously lived in Missouri. Of the forty-two households that had children listing a Kansas birthplace, eighteen also had a child, usually older, listing a Missouri birthplace.[23] The homecoming of George Requa marked the return of one of west-central Missouri's oldest families. Requa's father was a New York–born physician who had tended to

22. O. Williams, *Cass and Bates Counties*, 678, 471–72, 624, 1293–94, 1304–5; Bates County Old Settlers Society, *Old Settlers' History*, 152.

23. Census-Pop, Missouri, Bates, Cass, and Vernon Counties, 1870; Census-Pop, Kansas, Bourbon, Linn, and Miami Counties, 1870.

the white evangelists and Osage charges at Harmony Mission. The family had fled to Kansas with the outbreak of war, and George Jr. had soon joined the Fifteenth Kansas Cavalry, led by Colonel Charles Jennison. Shortly after the war, Requa purchased a farm and settled down in Bates County, the same country that had only recently been plundered by many of his fellow soldiers. Other members of the Requa family chose to remain in Kansas, thus stretching their bonds of kinship across the state line.[24]

The old-stock natives who rebuilt the Burnt District were joined and would soon be outnumbered by an extraordinary surge of immigrants from the Lower Midwest, particularly the states of Illinois, Indiana, and Ohio. Several newcomers were Union veterans eager to establish their claims to unsettled lands in the developing West. Some, like George Hardy, were already familiar with the Kansas-Missouri border from their service in the military. A member of the Second Ohio Cavalry, Hardy had been stationed at Fort Scott for only a few months in early 1862 but had been sufficiently impressed by the country during his patrols through Vernon County that he returned shortly after the war to farm and teach school.[25]

Within five short years, the population of the Missouri border counties, which had been emptied within weeks and depopulated for more than a year, assumed a strikingly different appearance. The return of old-stock settlers and the oncoming wave of new immigrants doubled the prewar populations of Bates, Cass, and Vernon Counties.[26] As significant as this remarkable population growth was the conspicuous change in the regional backgrounds of local residents, which is illustrated in tables 11 and 12 (Nativity of Missouri and Kansas Border Populations, 1870–1880, respectively). Before the Civil War, the great majority of household heads in these three counties had been born in the South, with the proportion of those from the Upper South states of Kentucky, Tennessee, and Virginia often exceeding 60 percent (see tables 1 and 8). After the Civil War, southern-born households still accounted for a substantial proportion (38 percent) of the rural Missouri population, but their influence had been diminished by

24. O. Williams, *Cass and Bates Counties*, 914–21; Census-Pop, Kansas, Miami County, 1880. For an example of other Missouri natives who had fought in Kansas militias and then returned home to the Burnt District, see O. Williams, *Cass and Bates Counties*, 1180–81, 1353; and Cheatham, "Divided Loyalties."

25. J. Johnson, *History of Vernon County*, 799–800.

26. The aggregate population figures from the three counties were: Bates, 7,215 in 1860 and 15,960 in 1870; Cass, 9,794 in 1860 and 19,296 in 1870; and Vernon, 4,850 in 1860 and 11,247 in 1870. U.S. Bureau of the Census, *Eighth Census: Population of the United States, Compiled from the Original Returns*, 162–65, 286–98; *Ninth Census: The Statistics of the Population of the United States*, 29–30, 43–45, 143–45, 187–95.

the steady immigration from states where slavery had been illegal. In 1860, only one out of every five household heads (21 percent) had been born north of the Ohio River; ten years later, that proportion had nearly doubled (to 40.1 percent). The expansion of northern influence becomes just as clear when one looks at the entire population, as the Lower Midwest claimed a higher percentage than any other nativity group.

The demographic transformation in western Missouri also included the changing distribution of people from the Northeast, Lower South, and abroad. Although the number of Yankee household heads was still small in 1870, accounting for less than 10 percent of the population in all three sample counties, the proportion of settlers who were born in the northeastern United States had nearly doubled since the last census enumeration. During the same period, immigration from many states of the Lower South had essentially dried up, causing a considerable decline in the proportion of the settlers from that area. The population of the western border remained predominantly American born, though there was also a remarkable increase in the number of immigrants from Ireland, England, Germany, and Canada. In Bates and Cass Counties, for example, the proportion of foreign immigrants had tripled since 1860.[27]

The most sweeping demographic shifts occurred in Bates County, the only jurisdiction within the District of the Border to have been completely depopulated during the war. Aggregate census figures from three of the county's townships reveal the extent to which immigration altered the area's postwar regional identity. In 1860, more than two-thirds of Bates County's residents had been born in Missouri or other states within the Upper South. A decade later, settlers from those states accounted for less than half the county's residents. As suggested above, the emigration of old-stock southerners cannot explain this change, for the number of Upper South and Missouri natives in Mingo Township and elsewhere continued to grow. The answer instead lies with the extraordinary influx of northern immigrants throughout the county. Mount Pleasant Township, which contains the county seat of Butler, illustrates this change most clearly. People from the Lower Midwest had constituted 20 percent of the township's antebellum population, but after the war their numbers tripled, thus making southerners and native Missourians a shrinking minority.[28]

27. Census-Pop, Missouri, Bates County, 1860.
28. From 1860 to 1870, the aggregate number of native Missourians went up, but their proportion declined, slipping from 42 percent to 34 percent of the local population. The ratio of Missouri-born household heads remained relatively unchanged, at just over 11 percent (Jeremy Neely, "Bates County, Missouri: The Transformation of a Middle Western Frontier, 1855–1895," 25–57).

The reasons behind the shifting sources of immigration lay with the disparate impacts of the Civil War on the South and the North. The stark contrast between the regions in the spring of 1865 was analogous to the situation on opposite sides of the Missouri-Kansas state line; although each side had suffered terrible losses, a disproportionate toll fell upon the states of the former Confederacy. Like Missouri, many southern states had been ravaged by a long war fought largely on their own soil. In addition to the extensive damage to the region's infrastructure and economy, the high casualty rates sustained by the Confederate army had claimed a significant proportion of the South's adult male population, further compounding the difficult plight of many southern families. Given the widespread destruction, poverty, and personal losses they faced, southerners may have been less likely to emigrate than their northern counterparts.

A greater proportion of northerners, in contrast, had survived the war in relatively sound condition, as had most Kansans. The demands of the Union war effort had stimulated northern agriculture and industry, and the region entered the postwar period with a large pool of potential migrants who possessed the means to finance westward migration and settlement. The restoration of peace and changes in federal land policy also served as ample inducements for would-be immigrants. The Homestead Act of 1862 had put the goal of obtaining free title to western lands within the reach of those individuals who were prepared to endure the hardships of frontier life. With much of Kansas yet unsettled, thousands of northern emigrants soon poured into the state.

Postwar immigration into southeastern Kansas did not produce the same kind of dramatic regional transformation that occurred in the adjacent Missouri counties but rather served to reinforce the dominance of northern settlers who had given the territory a free-soil majority in the late 1850s. An analysis of federal census manuscripts for 1870 (see table 12) indicates that more than 56 percent of household heads in the three Kansas counties had been born in the free states of the Old Northwest, the mid-Atlantic region, or New England. As in Missouri, a large number of Union veterans fueled this postwar northern influx. One Kansas historian estimates that by 1870, as many as seventy-five thousand former soldiers had entered the state. Eager to promote such immigration, boosters along the border appealed to the patriotic sentiments of emigrating veterans. "The border counties, south of the Missouri River, of Kansas and Missouri are the ones for loyal men to settle in," affirmed the editor of the *Fort Scott Monitor.* "They have been purified by war, and have no half-way patriots—but men who fought for the Union, because they believed it to be a sacred compact, and should be preserved. To all such, we say, if you want good homes, cheap and fertile lands, and desire to live in a loyal community, come to Bourbon county, Kansas."[29]

Among the inhabitants "purified by war" were a significant number of Kansans who had been born in the Upper South. Many of these individuals were Missouri settlers who had crossed over shortly after the territory had been opened; others, like James Requa, were Unionists who had been driven away by bushwhacker harassment. Taken together, southerners—that is, people born in Missouri or the states of the Upper South and Lower South—still accounted for more than 30 percent of the adult population in Bourbon, Linn, and Miami Counties in 1870. The concentration of southerners here, in the counties along the Missouri border, was higher than in any other part of Kansas.[30] The proportion of southerners, however, clearly had peaked by the Civil War and thenceforth would continue to decline. In their stead would come increasing numbers of Kansas-born children, a group that by 1870 already constituted one-fifth of the local population.

The counties of southeastern Kansas had a primarily native-born population, despite an increasing proportion of foreign immigrants. From 1860 to 1870 both Bourbon and Miami Counties experienced significant increases in the number of foreign heads of households. By 1870, nearly one out of every eight adult settlers in these counties had been born outside of the United States. Linn County also witnessed a substantial jump in nonnative immigration, but its proportion of foreign settlers was much lower and closer to the levels seen across the Missouri line. More than four-fifths of the foreign immigrants in Kansas came from Germany, Ireland, or Canada.[31] Within the total population, the proportion of foreign-born individuals was considerably lower. In most cases, the children of foreign parents had been born in other U.S. states, a trend indicating that most foreigners did not immigrate directly to Kansas. Welsh farmers Thomas and Sarah Williams, for example, had settled briefly in Indiana in the early 1850s, when their first son was born, and then came to Bourbon County some eight years later.

The overall percentage of adult foreigners was noticeably higher in southeastern Kansas than in adjacent Missouri counties. The differences in the two states' nonnative populations may be attributed to the lingering effects of many Europeans' opposition to slavery, which had limited

29. Castel, *Frontier State*, 227; *Fort Scott Monitor*, December 18, 1867.

30. For an excellent geographic analysis of postwar settlement patterns along the Missouri border, see Shortridge, *Peopling the Plains*, 15–45.

31. Of the 233 foreign-born individuals identified in a sample of the 1870 federal census, 190 (or 82 percent) were listed as natives of Canada, Germany, or Ireland.

antebellum immigration in rural western Missouri, and helped to secure the free-soil faction's triumph in Kansas. Generally speaking, however, the level of foreign immigration along the border would never approximate that witnessed in other parts of each state and elsewhere in the West. Significant concentrations of Germans, Russians, and Scandinavians appeared in ethnic communities in central Kansas, and several German American enclaves dotted the major river valleys in Missouri. The fact that fewer ethnic enclaves appeared along the state line than on the central and northern plains may have been influenced by the comparative lack of available land in the upper Osage valley. A survey of census manuscripts suggests that whereas most foreign immigrants were widely dispersed along the Missouri border, others tended to cluster in small ethnic communities. Examples of such clusters in 1870 included groups of Irish immigrants in both northwestern Miami County and the town of Fort Scott.[32]

In contrast to the subtle differences between foreign-born populations in postwar Kansas and Missouri, the changes witnessed in each state's African American population could hardly have been more striking. The most significant demographic change that occurred in the 1860s involved the migration of hundreds of African Americans from slavery in Missouri to freedom in Kansas. Just prior to statehood, the population of the counties in southeastern Kansas was almost exclusively white. Federal census enumerators in 1860 identified only one African American between Linn and Miami Counties, and the sixty-five blacks in Bourbon County, almost all of them escaped slaves, constituted barely 1 percent of its population. These low figures almost certainly do not provide an accurate reflection of the number of escaped slaves who fled into Kansas and then left the area, traveling north via the Underground Railroad. In the years before emancipation and the ratification of the Thirteenth Amendment, which abolished slavery throughout the United States, the border between Kansas and Missouri held more meaning for African Americans than any other group of people. Among slaves, this invisible boundary between slavery and freedom had gained profound importance within a vivid geography of hope.

The land east of this boundary held almost all of the borderland's antebellum black population. In 1860, only thirteen free blacks could be

<hr />

32. For ethnic enclaves in Kansas and Missouri, see Carl O. Sauer, *The Geography of the Ozark Highland of Missouri;* Shortridge, *Peopling the Plains,* 30–34, 96–108; and Walter A. Schroeder, *Opening the Ozarks: A Historical Geography of Missouri's Ste. Genevieve District, 1760–1830,* 225–66. For the brief personal reflections of one Irish American immigrant and Union veteran in Fort Scott, see Patrick Gorman interview, January 20, 1908, Papers of Sixth Kansas Cavalry, Military History Collection: Civil War, KSHS.

found in the Missouri counties, where slaves made up 3 percent to 10 percent of the local population (a proportion, it should be noted, that decreased as one moved south from the Missouri River). From 1860 to 1870, the black populations in Cass and Vernon Counties were cut nearly in half, whereas that of Bates County retained scarcely one-fourth of its antebellum total. All together, the three counties suffered a net loss of some 900 African Americans. One cannot know with precision where former Missouri slaves emigrated, as the slave censuses conducted in 1850 and 1860 identified the age, gender, and owner of each slave but not their names or birthplaces.

It is safe to suggest that the majority of former slaves in western Missouri took the shortest path to freedom by crossing the state line into southeastern Kansas. Appendix 13 (African American Border Population, 1860–1870) shows that Bourbon, Linn, and Miami Counties experienced an overall increase of 1,825 black residents by 1870, a gain that was more than 50 percent higher than the net loss in the adjacent Missouri counties. The growth in southeastern Kansas's black population may have been even larger than reported, however, because African American settlers were often undercounted in many jurisdictions.[33] Nativity data from the 1870 census support the argument that Kansas became the primary refuge for former Missouri slaves. In the three sample Kansas counties, more black settlers had been born in Missouri than in any other state; most of those who had not been born in Missouri identified their birthplace as another state in the Upper South.

Discussions of African American settlement in postwar Kansas invariably draw to mind the Exodusters, the large number of free blacks who migrated to western Kansas from the South during the late 1870s. The remarkable cross-border resettlement that took place along the Missouri line during and immediately after the Civil War differed from this famous movement in several respects. First, the Exoduster migration would take place on a much broader scale, drawing more than 40,000 African Americans northward from Louisiana, Mississippi, Tennessee, and beyond. In addition, the movement would benefit from the active direction and influence of leaders such as Benjamin "Pap" Singleton, who would organize black settlements at Nicodemus, Dunlap, and the eponymous colony of Singleton.[34] Such colonization efforts would be

33. Arvarh E. Strickland, "Toward the Promised Land: The Exodus to Kansas and Afterward," 403.
34. Ibid., 376–403; Nell Painter, *Exodusters: Black Migration to Kansas after Reconstruction,* 18–35; Robert G. Athearn, *In Search of Canaan: Black Migration to Kansas, 1879–1880,* 71–73.

responsible for attracting the majority of African American settlers to central and southern Kansas in the post-Reconstruction period. Black emigration across the Missouri border during the Civil War era was often a more spontaneous and independent affair. White abolitionists and soldiers, such as John Brown and Jim Lane, were instrumental in bringing hundreds of slaves into Kansas, but an unknown number of African Americans escaped to freedom on their own accord.

Most of the African Americans who migrated to Kansas settled in towns rather than on farms throughout the countryside. Unlike the Exodusters who would settle in predominantly black enclaves, the former slaves who relocated to southeastern Kansas found themselves living in more racially mixed settings. At the end of the Civil War, more than a third of the state's African Americans lived in the towns of Leavenworth, Lawrence, Atchison, and Fort Scott. Like Mound City and Osawatomie, each of which retained a substantial black population, Lawrence had been a station on the Underground Railroad. One historian suggests that in Fort Scott, blacks made up nearly one-third of the town's residents.[35] By contrast, a sample of the 1870 census manuscripts failed to find a single African American in the surrounding rural townships of Bourbon County. A similar distribution emerged in both Linn and Miami Counties, where nearly all of the black population was concentrated in the county seats and other towns such as Paris.

Several possible explanations account for the urban concentration of black Kansans. During the war, Fort Scott had served as a major recruiting center for African American and Native American soldiers, and many black veterans likely returned to the town in peacetime. General Thomas Ewing, who had provided military escorts for former slaves who wanted to reach Kansas, noted that towns in the new state promised ample opportunities for work. Black emigrants, he wrote, "have all had ready employment and earned comfortable livelihoods. . . . I believe there is not a negro pauper in the state."[36] The relative absence of rural black settlers can be attributed in part to the penurious condition of most former slaves upon their entry into Kansas. Because few African Americans possessed the capital necessary to purchase land, implements, or livestock, only a small number of freedmen became landowning farmers. A rare exception was North Carolina native Henry Lacy, who owned a farm worth more

35. Sheridan, "From Slavery in Missouri," 37–38. For another analysis of the 1865 state census, which suggests that the black population in Fort Scott was somewhat smaller, see Shortridge, *Peopling the Plains*, 28–30.
36. Ewing to C. W. Marsh, August 3, 1863, RG 393, NAB.

than a thousand dollars in 1870. The majority of black men found work as unskilled wage laborers in towns along the border. Only a handful, including blacksmith Martin Webster and schoolteacher Samuel Clark, held positions that placed them in the local classes of artisans or professionals. All of the African American women found in the census worked in a service-related job, either as a "washwoman," housekeeper, or cook, occupations that placed them near the bottom of the economic scale.

In addition to the racial prejudice that confronted urban blacks, they also faced inferior and unsanitary living conditions in many Kansas towns. One Paola newspaper complained that the presence of sixteen black families crowded within a single tenement posed an alarming nuisance to the white citizens who frequented the town square.[37] Aside from such impoverished conditions, the clustering of African American settlers within Kansas towns nonetheless facilitated the development of churches, schools, and civic organizations that were critical to the development of nascent African American communities. These public institutions and spaces promoted sociability among men, women, and children whose families had been torn apart by slavery.[38] A sample of twenty-one African American households from the 1870 census found that twelve of them consisted of nuclear (or two-parent) families. Four of the households contained single-parent families. The remaining five households included extended-family members or had an ambiguous structure in which the relationships among members were unclear.[39] According to this limited sample, more than 30 percent of African American families had a female head of household; within white households, that proportion was less than 5 percent.

In spite of its once-powerful meaning for enslaved African Americans, the state line was not a significant marker when it came to distinguishing the postwar status of black citizens. The freed persons who remained in Missouri occupied a similar position within local society. More than 90

37. *Miami County Republican,* July 13, 1867. For difficulties that blacks faced in other Kansas towns, see Athearn, *In Search of Canaan,* 83–88.

38. Conspicuously absent in local histories from southeastern Kansas, African Americans received only passing mention in local newspapers, and it is therefore difficult to track the establishment of black churches, schools, and other institutions with any great detail.

39. Unlike the 1880 federal census manuscripts, the 1870 enumeration did not identify the relationships (father, mother, daughter, grandparent, and so on) of household members and only occasionally noted which members were boarders. For the variety of household structures among African Americans in the Mississippi Delta, see Nancy Bercaw, *Gendered Freedoms: Race, Rights, and the Politics of the Household in the Delta, 1861–1875,* 106–8.

percent of the African Americans identified in the postwar census sample were located in the towns of Butler, Harrisonville, Pleasant Hill, and Nevada. As table 13 indicates, the wartime slave exodus and the postwar influx of northern immigrants had the combined effect of making the freed persons who remained an even smaller fraction of the total population. As in Kansas, most black men and women found work as unskilled laborers or domestic servants, and even fewer black farmers appeared in Missouri than in Kansas.[40] The proportion of African Americans who lived in two-parent or single-parent households was also significantly smaller in Missouri. Nearly half of the black Missourians identified in the 1870 census lived within a household in which most of the members were whites. In some of these cases, these individuals may have been boarders; more typically, however, they were live-in servants and laborers. Nellie Gray, an eighteen-year-old who lived with the family of George Sears, a well-to-do Bates County farmer, was typical of most servants, who were usually young and female. Some of these servants may have been former slaves who still lived with former masters, but there is no clear evidence from the border counties to support such an assertion.[41]

Primary documents offer only limited insights into the nature of postwar social relations between blacks and whites. Although thousands of slaves fled their Missouri masters, some free blacks maintained at least a distant social relationship with their former owners. Sophy Parks, for example, moved away from Vernon County but continued to visit and correspond regularly with the family of Sarah Badger, the daughter of her former master. Many whites on both sides of the border, however, were reluctant to associate with African Americans. A young woman who grew up in Cass County recalled the racial segregation of her hometown, writing, "Our people from the Confederacy did not 'associate' with the free negroes but did not object to them so long as they remained in 'nigger town,' an area at the far end of the town, across the railroad tracks. Whites had no more business there than negroes did in downtown." Fort Scott attorney A. A. Harris spoke for many white Kansans who preferred that African American immigrants not settle within their state. "The people of Kansas," he wrote, "do not want them to come."

40. For the transition from slavery to wage labor in the Deep South, see Julie Saville, *The Work of Reconstruction: From Slave to Wage Labor in South Carolina, 1860–1870*, 6–71.

41. Kimberly Schreck, "Her Will against Theirs: Eda Hickam and the Ambiguity of Freedom in Postbellum Missouri," in *Women in Missouri History*, ed. Whites, Neth, and Kremer, 134–51, details the story of Eda Hickam, a Saline County woman who sued her former masters, arguing they had not informed her she was free until 1889.

Giving voice to a white assumption about black indolence, he continued, "They have as much as they can do to feed themselves, and they are not going to feed a large number of helpless people."[42]

The history of public education along the postwar border illuminated the ambivalence of white settlers toward their African American neighbors. The decade that followed the Civil War saw a remarkable expansion in the number of schools in rural Missouri and Kansas. In 1850, barely one out of every four children in western Missouri had attended school within the past year. Like many others, the school established at Balltown was a private, subscription-driven institution.[43] Educational opportunities thus were limited mainly to children of privilege whose parents could afford to pay tuition. By 1860 close to 40 percent of Missouri children had attended school, a figure that was slightly higher than the enrollment rate of white children across the South. School attendance in Kansas was lower, probably because the territory's recent organization and tumultuous environment had inhibited the construction of schools there. One Bourbon County editor lamented the lack of local schools: "Fort Scott is entirely without even the semblance of an institution of learning. It speaks badly for the city, and its inhabitants."[44] Census enumerators had indicated that no black children, almost all having recently escaped from slavery into Kansas, had gone to school within the past year.

A flurry of postwar school construction improved educational access in Kansas and Missouri for children of both races and genders. Within two decades, settlers in Linn County alone would organize one hundred school districts. Kansas teacher G. S. West regarded such efforts as a critical civic duty, "now that we have emerged from a long and bloody war, during which time our youth have been taught only the art of war." Citizens, he continued, should dedicate themselves to the advancement of free public education, a cause that is "more congenial and better calculated to advance the interest of the present and future inhabitants of our country." In Missouri, the new state constitution of 1865 facilitated the

42. Parks to "Dear Dr. [Albert Badger] and Family," April 22, 1890, Badger Papers, VCHS; Gordon, folder 26 ("Culture"), Gordon Papers, Collection KC068, Western Historical Manuscripts Collection, Kansas City; Harris quote from Athearn, *In Search of Canaan,* 70–71.

43. Little Osage Literary Association Papers, VCHS. For private schools in antebellum Missouri, see Bates County Old Settlers Society, *Old Settlers' History,* 127; and Ralph E. Glauert, "Stereotypes and Clichés: The Pioneer Teacher in Missouri," 136–44.

44. Census-Pop, Kansas, Bourbon, Linn, and Miami Counties, 1860, 1870; Census-Pop, Missouri, Bates, Cass, and Vernon Counties, 1860, 1870; *Fort Scott Western Volunteer,* November 29, 1862. Cobb puts the 1860 enrollment rate of white children in the South at 35 percent (*Away Down South,* 51).

expansion of educational opportunities, as it required the state legislature to establish and maintain free schools for the state's young people. A look at postwar census data (table 14, School Attendance Rates, Kansas and Missouri Children, 1850–1880) uncovers the positive impact of such efforts. Before the Civil War, boys in each state had been slightly more likely than girls to attend school. This trend had been reversed in Kansas by 1870, although it persisted in Missouri; a decade later, attendance rates were nearly equal across the border for both sexes, ranging from 42 percent to 49 percent in all six counties.[45]

Although the 1870 attendance rates among black children in Kansas doubled those in Missouri, such figures were nearly identical in each state ten years later. Standing at 34 percent, the rates for blacks were well below those of white students. Taxpayers in both states claimed to support equal educational opportunities for all children, but most were steadfastly opposed to the "mixed education" of racially integrated schools. "We don't want social equality," wrote one white Kansan, "but we want decent schools." As a result, districts in both states operated separate schools for white and black pupils. Limited evidence suggests that the conditions within these segregated facilities varied considerably. A Pleasant Hill editor, for example, praised the efforts of Mr. Creamer, the teacher at the town's "small and uncomfortable" school for African American children. "Though his task was an unpopular, and to some extent an unpleasant one, he discharged his duties faithfully and well, both as a man and a Christian."[46]

For African Americans, the triumph of the free-state movement had made the Kansas-Missouri border a profoundly important boundary, putting freedom within close reach for slaves living on the Osage plains. The Civil War in turn had triggered the migration of more than a thousand Missouri slaves into adjacent Kansas counties. In spite of the empowering liberty that had come with emancipation, the immediate postwar period also demonstrated that the state line had lost much of its previous symbolic meaning for black Americans, who found themselves in a difficult social and political position whether they lived in Missouri

45. Cutler, *History of Kansas,* 2:881, 1072, 1108; *Linn County Border Sentinel,* July 14, 1865; March, *The History of Missouri,* 2:1081–82. For the history of public schools in Kansas, Missouri, and the broader Midwest, see Wayne E. Fuller, *The Old Country School: The Story of Rural Education in the Middle West,* 26–107. For school construction in Missouri, see Bates County Old Settlers Society, *Old Settlers' History,* 69–70.

46. Quote from James C. Carper, "The Popular Ideology of Segregated Schooling: Attitudes toward the Education of Blacks in Kansas, 1854–1900," 254–65; *Pleasant Hill Leader,* May 5, 1871.

or Kansas. The prospect that black men, even Union veterans, could gain civil rights equal with those of whites remained uncertain.

Like the rest of the nation, the state line's old-stock settlers and recent immigrants struggled to mend profound political and social divisions from the past decade. Common challenges arising out of that conflict—namely, the political status of free blacks and of Confederate sympathizers—confronted citizens in each state. The war had represented a triumph of liberty for African Americans, but the contentious debate that followed it would be distinguished by an uneasy reluctance to grant full citizenship to former rebels, blacks, or women. The punitive strategy that public officials in Missouri pursued in relation to former rebels did little to lessen the enmity of the past decade. The Radical Republicans and Unionists who had gained control of the state's government seized upon the opportunity to punish disloyal citizens. In the spring of 1865, Radical legislators passed an ousting ordinance that vacated the offices of state judges and clerks along with the county offices of sheriff, circuit attorney, and recorder. The authority to fill these newly created vacancies passed to Governor Thomas Fletcher, who used his power to appoint loyal Union men. The ousting ordinance was thus an effective instrument of Radical patronage, as it reduced the likelihood that unsympathetic judges would nullify the party's postwar agenda.[47]

In order to consolidate their own hold on power and to cleanse state government of Confederate sympathizers, Missouri Radicals organized a convention to draft a new state constitution in 1865. The disfranchisement of disloyal Missourians proved to be the most widely discussed issue at this constitutional convention. Rather than curtail the voting rights of rebels through an ordinance, Charles Drake, the Radical leader of the 1865 convention, preferred to incorporate any suffrage restrictions within the new constitution. The proposed disfranchisement article set forth a remarkably broad definition of what amounted to "disloyalty." Among the people who would be disqualified from voting were former Confederate soldiers and officials; bushwhackers and the people who gave them "money, goods, letters, or information"; men who deserted or avoided enrollment in the state militia; and persons who expressed sympathy toward the rebellion against the United States. In addition to having their voting rights stripped, individuals who were unable or unwilling to swear a loyalty oath—the so-called Ironclad Oath—would

47. March, *The History of Missouri*, 2:1009; William E. Parrish, *Missouri under Radical Rule, 1865–1870*, 32–33; Eric Foner, *Reconstruction: America's Unfinished Revolution, 1863–1877*, 42.

also be prohibited from teaching, practicing law, preaching, holding public office, or serving as jurors. People convicted of performing such duties
without first taking the oath would be subject to a five hundred–dollar
fine or a six-month prison sentence. The fact that the loyalty oath and the
biennial voter registration would be locally administered and enforced,
often by officials who were personally familiar with an individual's
wartime sympathies, raised the prospect that vengeful neighbors could
abuse the law with impunity.[48]

Despite widespread support within the Radical faction, the disfranchisement proposal was not uniformly endorsed throughout the state. A
great many Missourians lacked the vindictive zeal of leading Radicals.
Conservative Unionists and German Americans advocated a more
lenient standard of loyalty and argued that political amnesty should be
extended to the large number of Missourians who had briefly sided with
the Confederacy before later rallying behind the Union cause. Furthermore, many loyal Missourians were not themselves predisposed to swear
any public oath, even though they had stood firmly behind the Union
cause. John Dryden, for example, believed that requiring ministers and
church officials to swear an oath marked a step toward the uniting of
church and state. Although the wartime disfranchisement of Southern
sympathizers had helped shape an increasingly Unionist electorate, the
ratification of the new charter was hardly inevitable. Submitted to voters
in the summer of 1865, the constitution faced strong opposition in St.
Louis, the Little Dixie region, and the southeastern part of the state.
When the results of the statewide tally were finally announced in July, the
Radical constitution narrowly passed with 43,670 citizens voting for it
and 41,808 voting against it.[49]

Like Radicals and Unionists in Missouri, Kansas officials were likewise
determined to root out rebel sympathizers from public life. When Governor Samuel Crawford introduced a proposal in 1867 that would disfran-
chise disloyal citizens, it proved to be a much less controversial issue for
Kansas voters. In spite of the violent ideological strife of the territorial
period, Kansas citizens had been remarkably unified at the start of the
Civil War. Several proslavery partisans had already left the territory, and
after the assault on Fort Sumter there remained only a scattered minority

48. Article 2, "Right of Suffrage," Constitution of the State of Missouri, *The General
Statutes of the State of Missouri*, 24–25; March, *The History of Missouri*, 2:1003–6; Parrish,
Missouri under Radical Rule, 26–27.
49. Dryden, August 19, 1866, *With Plow and Pen*, 29–30; March, *The History of Missouri*, 2:1007–8.

of Confederate sympathizers, as most of the settlers who remained rallied behind the Union cause.[50] The wartime depredations of William Quantrill and other Missouri guerrillas had only heightened the widespread hostility toward southern rebels, bushwhackers, and their sympathizers. As a result, the disfranchisement of disloyal citizens passed by a wide margin throughout the state and received the support of almost 70 percent of voters along the Missouri border.[51]

Even with the Union army's mass expulsion of Southern sympathizers, the Radical attempt to fashion a new political order in Missouri produced only an incomplete transformation along the western border. In some cases, the vacancies created by the removal of local officials were filled by Unionist immigrants such as Joseph Bailey, the Vernon County sheriff who was later murdered. Old-stock officials elsewhere continued to occupy the positions they held before the war, and grand juries in all three border counties were replete with longtime residents. The Cass County Court reconvened in the spring of 1865 with the same judge and sheriff as years before, and when it came time to appoint new deputies, county leaders selected George W. Belcher and Joseph Holcomb, two border natives from antebellum southern families.[52]

The Radical test oath also seemed to have a limited effect on the electorate of the border counties, where local officials demonstrated a ready willingness to lift the voting disqualifications levied against rebel sympathizers. The choice for Confederate sympathizers was undoubtedly difficult: swear loyalty to a government whose soldiers had occupied and plundered their communities, and thereby gain the full privileges of U.S. citizenship, or maintain steadfast allegiance to the Southern cause and thus forfeit one's political rights and more. The decision to take the loyalty oath was often an exercise in pragmatism, accommodation, and self-preservation. Court records suggest that men who had fought and surrendered as Confederate soldiers and had then enlisted in the Union army or the state militia were the citizens most likely to have their voting rights restored. Order No. 11 had a peculiar effect in inspiring the patriotic service of many former rebels, as the dates of enlistment for more than half of these men suggest. Elijah Smith, for example, "had been in

50. Cheatham, "Divided Loyalties," 103.
51. *Miami County Republican*, November 9, 1867; *Daily Kansas State Journal*, November 10, 1867; Eugene H. Berwanger, *The West and Reconstruction*, 165.
52. Cass County Circuit Court Records, vol. C, 388, April 5, 1865; vol. D, 3, October 2, 1865. For examples from other border counties, see Bates County Circuit Court Records, vol. B, 390, October 9, 1865; and vol. C, 19, April 1866.

armed hostility to the government of the United States" since August 1861, when Confederate troops had clashed with Union forces at Wilson's Creek. On Thursday, September 10, 1863—the day after which all disloyal settlers were to have been flushed from the District of the Border—Smith had experienced an apparent change of heart and had elected to join the Union army, a decision that no doubt saved himself and his family from expulsion.[53]

Shortly before the election scheduled for the fall of 1868, Thomas Phelan, supervisor of voter registration for the senatorial district that included Jackson, Cass, and Bates Counties, removed the old registering officers. Phelan replaced them with three former Union officers, who in turn jettisoned the old registration guidelines in favor of less restrictive standards. As a result, even more former Confederates were able to cast ballots again, local vote totals exceeded their prewar levels, and the entire Democratic ticket was elected. The Democrats' resurgence was clear proof that old-stock Southern sympathizers had regained a substantial measure of their former influence. More important, this political shift had been made possible by the willingness of Union veterans to welcome former rebels back into the political fold.[54]

Ensuring the loyalty of ministers, attorneys, and teachers was a critical factor in the advancement of the Radical regime. Like the disloyal judges who were ousted throughout Missouri, unsympathetic attorneys posed a potential threat to the legal underpinnings of the Radical agenda. The 1865 constitution also targeted ministers and teachers, the individuals charged with cultivating the hearts and minds of the state's inhabitants, because of the public trust and authority that each position carried at the local level. Judges along the western border, however, were disinclined to prosecute citizens who declined to take the loyalty oath. A survey of postwar court records uncovered only three such prosecutions, all of which were leveled against local ministers. When the three ministers—Abner Dean, a Kentucky-born Baptist, and James B. Harbison and James Lapsley, who had helped to bridge the differences between northern and southern Presbyterians in Pleasant Hill—were brought before the circuit court of Cass County, the prosecutions were dismissed without comment. Less than a year later, a similar prosecution involving a Missouri priest reached the U.S. Supreme Court, and a divided court ruled that the

53. Rubin, *Shattered Nation*, 95, 164–67; Cass County Court Records, vol. E, 50–111, 128, October 6, 1866, April 1, 1867.
54. O. Williams, *Cass and Bates Counties*, 314. Newspapers from the western border counties are a consistent source of election returns, but extant editions are available only from 1868 forward.

loyalty oath as it pertained to clergymen was unconstitutional, as it amounted to a bill of attainder against former rebels in Missouri.[55]

For all the ardor of the Radical campaign against Confederate sympathizers, the architects of the 1865 Missouri constitution were much less committed to the cause of African American suffrage. At first glance, the Drake convention's uneasy support for extending voting rights to African Americans seemed out of step with their swift determination to free Missouri slaves. On January 11, 1865—just five days after delegates had convened in St. Louis and three weeks before the Thirteenth Amendment would be proposed in Congress—the convention had passed an ordinance that provided for the immediate emancipation of slaves in Missouri, with only four of the sixty-six delegates dissenting. Most delegates, however, were not willing to include within the new constitution an article that would give freedmen the right to vote. Convinced that Missouri voters would not ratify a charter that put white and black men on equal political footing, the convention instead tabled the issue for future consideration. When a black suffrage amendment was later put before Missouri voters in 1868, its chances of passing had not improved by much, even with the continued disfranchisement of many former rebels.[56]

Outspoken Radicals still believed that such an amendment was both an indispensable means of abolishing, in one editor's words, the "invidious distinction . . . made on account of color" and a necessary consequence of the war against slavery. John Dryden was a fierce critic of most Radical leaders, but he echoed their endorsement of voting rights for black Missourians. Reflecting on the situation of former slaves years before the introduction of the black suffrage amendment, he wrote, "Seeing that we have sprung from one common stock this thing called prejudice seems to be the essence of folly. . . . Now that the slaves are free, what next? We will admit them to all the rights of citizenship? How can we deny them? We will make them bear their proportion of the burden of taxation yet deny them a voice in the government. Is this simple and evenhanded justice? If it is I for one can't see it." The Vernon County farmer was well aware that few of his neighbors shared similar opinions on race and voting: "What I am penning would be objectional [sic] to the majority of the citizens of Mo." Dryden's assessment was accurate, as the suffrage amendment faltered, losing by nearly nineteen thousand votes. Only with the 1870 ratification of the Fifteenth Amendment to the U.S.

55. Cass County Circuit Court Records, vol. E, 128, April 1866; O. Williams, *Cass and Bates Counties,* 240–42, 366; *Cummings v. Missouri,* 71 U.S. 277.

56. March, *The History of Missouri,* 2:998–1019.

Constitution, which was quickly endorsed by the Radical legislature, did African Americans gain the right to vote in Missouri.[57]

The triumph of black suffrage in turn forced many Radicals to reconsider the franchise restrictions that remained in place against former rebels. Although the Civil War had transformed many Missourians' notions of black liberty, most voters' conceptions of citizenship were still profoundly influenced by long-standing racial attitudes. Voting had long been the exclusive preserve of white men, a fact that the postwar disfranchisement of Confederate sympathizers had modified but not threatened. The enfranchisement of African Americans, however, transformed the racial boundaries of political identity in Missouri and, in the eyes of many observers, called into question the proscription still levied against several thousand white voters. In the wake of the Fifteenth Amendment, most white Missourians were increasingly unwilling to maintain the voting proscriptions set forth in the 1865 constitution. In the fall of 1870, Radical leaders presented Missouri voters with a series of constitutional amendments that would alleviate the restrictions against former rebels. Each of these amendments passed by a large margin and soon hastened the demise of the Radicals, who would be swept from power at the next statewide election, in 1872.[58]

The issue of African American suffrage had faced no certain triumph across the border in Kansas. Despite the state's significant role in checking the westward expansion of slavery, white Kansans had only recently come to support expanded liberties for free blacks. Although the framers of the Wyandotte constitution of 1859 had disregarded calls to block the immigration of free blacks, the free-state territorial charter had nevertheless denied several basic liberties to potential African American settlers, including the rights to vote, bear arms, serve on a jury, and join a militia. In the first few years of statehood, the Kansas legislature had continued to ignore the issue of black suffrage. The Civil War and the military service of African Americans, however, had proved to be an important factor in changing many white citizens' attitudes about black liberty. Kansans ratified the Thirteenth Amendment with remarkable speed, and African American suffrage quickly became the foremost political issue of the postwar era.[59]

---

57. *Bates County Record,* March 6, 1869; Dryden, November 13, 1865, *With Plow and Pen,* 27–28; March, *The History of Missouri,* 2:1019. For the estimated number of rebels disfranchised by the test oath and the biennial voter registration, see the thoughtful analysis in Parrish, *Missouri under Radical Rule,* 272–73, 309.

58. Parrish, *Missouri under Radical Rule,* 280–81, 309.

59. Berwanger, *The West and Reconstruction,* 28; Etcheson, *Bleeding Kansas,* 206–29.

Invoking the service of former slaves who had fought bravely for the cause of liberty in the state where they had found freedom, Kansas editors appealed to the patriotic values of readers in advancing the cause of black suffrage. "The republicans who at the fall of Sumter forsook their fields and workshops, followed the flag of our Fathers to battle, and returned not until they brought peace upon their banners, need no 'lash' to impel them to the performance of duty, and the extension of the franchise to their colored comrades in arms," wrote one Fort Scott editor. Citizens who opposed black suffrage, on the other hand, were dismissed as the same people who had defended slavery, resisted military enrollment, and sympathized with the Confederacy. A fellow Republican in Linn County considered the suffrage issue a matter of democratic fairness: "It is contrary and repugnant to free government, to withhold from a free loyal man the elective franchise." Editors were not alone in promoting greater civil rights for black Kansans, as a large number of African Americans had recently mobilized to advocate equal justice for all of the state's inhabitants. Led by Charles Langston, the Kansas State Colored Convention agitated not only for equal suffrage but also against discriminatory practices in public transportation and accommodations. The effectiveness of such efforts was tested in the fall of 1867, when a constitutional amendment that extended the franchise to African American men was put before Kansas voters.[60]

As in Missouri, Republicans struggled to persuade a majority of white Kansans to endorse equal voting rights for black citizens. The advancement of African American freedom had been a central issue within the Republican platform since the party's inception a decade earlier. Many of the party's members were steadfastly committed to the promotion of black liberty, but Republicans remained sharply divided over African American voting rights.[61] Some members were concerned that differences over the suffrage amendment might split the party, and they therefore minimized the issue's importance as an expression of partisan identity. "The Republican party lacks unanimity on the question of negro suffrage," conceded one Linn County supporter. "It is useless," he continued, "to say a man is not a republican because he opposes negro suffrage." The paternalistic assessment of a Miami County observer, laid out in an essay titled "The Duty of Colored People," illustrated the indifference of many

60. *Fort Scott Monitor*, June 12, 1867; *Linn County Border Sentinel*, October 23, 1867; Berwanger, *The West and Reconstruction*, 129–40; Sheridan, "From Slavery in Missouri," 47.
61. For Republican ambivalence regarding black liberty, see Foner, *Free Soil*, 261–96.

white citizens toward granting political equality to former slaves: "If the proposition is voted down, much of the responsibility will rest upon themselves. They can do more to injure their own cause than all the combined efforts of prejudiced politicians. If they expect the white race to invest them with the privileges of the white freeman, they must show themselves worthy of it. It can not be done by setting the laws at defiance, by indolence, or rendering themselves an evil to the community they live in."[62]

Despite their divisions, Republican leaders in Kansas eventually endorsed the black suffrage amendment, but its prospects were soon complicated by the introduction of a parallel amendment that would enfranchise the state's women. Samuel Newitt Wood proposed the female franchise amendment with the unspoken intention of connecting the two issues within the public debate in order to ensure the defeat of both measures. Upon his arrival in Kansas, Wood had been an active free-state partisan and had even served as a conductor on the Underground Railroad, but after his election to the legislature he had become a vocal opponent of equal suffrage for African Americans.[63] Female suffrage was not a new issue within Kansas politics; several women and men had lobbied strenuously but unsuccessfully for equal voting rights during the constitutional debates of the territorial period.

In spite of these well-known efforts, many of Wood's contemporaries immediately recognized the women's suffrage amendment as a disingenuous ruse. One Kansan reacted to the legislator's feigned support for women's rights by exclaiming, "This whole movement is one of the shabbiest and most disgusting of many tricks and shams for which Sam Wood has always been notorious." The proposal's timing also dismayed African American leaders, who feared that the discussion over female suffrage would indeed draw attention away from their own campaign for black rights. Unfazed by such criticism, Wood organized the statewide Impartial Suffrage Association (ISA), which purportedly endorsed equal voting rights for both blacks and women, and, having appointed himself corresponding secretary, initiated a letter-writing effort and speaking tour to promote the voting-rights amendments.[64]

Kansas Republicans' ambivalence toward Wood's proposal illustrates the complexity of postwar attitudes on race, gender, and politics. Many

---

62. *Linn County Border Sentinel,* October 23, 1867; *Miami County Republican,* August 3, 1867.

63. Frank W. Blackmar, ed., *Kansas: A Cyclopedia of State History, Embracing Events, Institutions, Industries, Counties, Cities, Towns, Prominent Persons, Etc.,* 2:933.

64. Quote in Berwanger, *The West and Reconstruction,* 165; Michael Lewis Goldberg, *An Army of Women: Gender and Politics in Gilded Age Kansas,* 14–15.

Kansans had taken an active interest in promoting female suffrage during the territorial period. Forty-one men and women from Linn County, for example, established the Moneka Women's Rights Society on February 2, 1858, and resolved themselves to securing women's "natural rights" and advancing their educational interests. The society also held that "Kansas cannot be truly free while the words 'white' or 'male' are found within the limits of her constitution."[65] Recent advances in the legal rights of female citizens gave the supporters of Wood's amendment cause for hope. The Wyandotte constitution of 1859 had secured the right of married women to own property "separate and apart" from their husbands, and an 1861 law had granted female settlers the right to vote in school elections.[66] Evidence from the southeastern counties suggests that Kansas women entertained mixed opinions of Wood's organization and perhaps of the suffrage question itself. Nearly all of the women who attended a suffrage rally in Linn County signed a petition in support of the amendment. In Miami County, meanwhile, a New York–born housewife named Harriet Petrie was one of only two women listed among the thirty-four residents who expressed an interest in joining the ISA.

The other woman, Mary Updegraff, had been among the earliest settlers in the abolitionist community of Osawatomie and was one of the ISA's most active correspondents. She found that many women in her neighborhood approved of the franchise amendment but were unwilling to voice their support publicly. Troubled by the prevailing "feeling of indifference," Updegraff believed that the amendment's success depended on the committed action of reformers like herself. "It will require a great effort to carry this county," she concluded. "In my judgment the fight must be made *hot, personal and bitter*. Nothing else will awaken an interest in this matter."[67] Updegraff had been part of the struggle to make Kansas a free territory, and the fervor of her letter, echoing the ideological passion of the previous decade, revealed her conviction that positive change required forceful action.

Updegraff's exasperation resulted in large part from the apathy of border citizens, not to mention the seemingly contradictory notions of equal rights that divided local settlers. One Fort Scott Republican declined an invitation to speak on behalf of suffragists, explaining, "I shall advocate

65. Mitchell, *Linn County*, 331.
66. Wilda M. Smith, "A Half Century of Struggle: Gaining Woman Suffrage in Kansas," 76; Miner, *Kansas*, 77–78.
67. *Linn County Border Sentinel*, August 16, 1867; G. Roberts to Wood, July 22, 1867; Updegraff to Wood, May 27, 28, 1867, Woman's Suffrage Collection, Roll MF 1049, box 1, series A, KSHS.

Negro and not oppose female suffrage, but leave the *advocacy* of the latter to others." R. W. Massey, on the other hand, believed that voting rights should be extended to white females but not African Americans: "I fail to see that the right of our intelligent, moral, high minded patriotic women to vote is the same as the ignorant immoral dirty filthy Negro. The one adds moral strength and power to our political system; the other adds degradation and filth and dirt to a system already degraded and corrupt." Newspaper accounts indicate that many of the noted female suffragists who addressed gatherings throughout Kansas generally refrained from commenting on the subject of African American rights. At least one speaker, Reverend Olympia Brown of Massachusetts, publicly implored her audience not to elevate black voters above the state's white women.[68]

The most vociferous opposition to Sam Wood's female suffrage proposal came from newspaper editors who dismissed it as an attempt to thwart the enfranchisement of African Americans. Like many other Republicans, the publishers of the *Miami County Republican* qualified their opposition, explaining that they rejected the timing of the female suffrage amendment but not the egalitarian principle it represented. They repeatedly criticized Wood as a "shyster" of the worst stripe, a demagogue who promoted an ill-timed effort of "artful intrigue" in order to undermine "manhood suffrage" and to advance his own career. The Paola editors were particularly incensed because Wood had allegedly sprung the issue on Kansas voters without a significant groundswell of public support. "No such legislation," they wrote, "was demanded either by the electors of this State, or by any respectable number of women." From the paper's perspective, the large crowds that flocked to hear ISA speakers in several border communities came out of curiosity more than studied interest.[69] Such a broad turnout, however, suggests that public interest in the suffrage question was in fact quite real.

The *Republican's* construction of feminine respectability, which was spelled out in a series of antisuffrage columns, held little room for politically active women. The paper emphasized the fact that Olivia Brown, Susan B. Anthony, Elizabeth Cady Stanton, Lucy Stone, and other female speakers who toured the state on behalf of the ISA were outsiders who did not adhere to established middle-class gender roles. The "true women"

68. A. Danforth to Wood, May 16, 1867; Massey to Wood, May 17, 1867, Woman's Suffrage Collection, Roll MF 1049, box 1, series A, KSHS; Berwanger, *The West and Reconstruction*, 171.

69. *Miami County Republican*, April 20, 1867. For similar arguments, see issues of February 23, April 6, 1867.

of Kansas, the editors maintained, would neither demand the vote nor take to the stump in such an audacious fashion. "If Lucy Stone will go back to New Jersey, and resume the scrubbing brush and frying pan," they insisted, "she will receive the respect of the women of Kansas, and deserve less of ridicule from her male oppressors." Seeking to underscore the contrast between the "harshly molded," masculine nature of ISA speakers and the gentle domesticity of Kansas women, the *Republican* juxtaposed its withering criticisms alongside a dispatch called "Woman's Sphere" in an adjacent column. The latter feature, which was submitted by Mrs. Sophia Smith, celebrated the "high and holy" domestic duties that allowed women to enlighten and elevate their male kin. In a passing reference to the widening debate about the role of women in public life, Smith concluded, "The sphere of no woman is circumscribed, however much she may vex and agitate herself and the public."[70]

Another contributor, the Reverend I. S. Kalloch, affirmed this point when he contended that equal suffrage would threaten the unique moral superiority of female citizens. "Women are our saviors," he wrote. "They restrain us, they purify us, they exalt us, they make us better men." The minister explained, "The very fact of their different sphere and different pursuits is what gives them their influence and power. It seems to us that in proportion as they lose their womanly ways and habits and approach to masculine methods and pursuits, just in that proportion do they lose that peculiar, potent, though mysterious, influence which God created and intended them to exercise in the world."[71] In the eyes of Rev. Kalloch and others, granting Kansas women the right to vote would transform the political, social, and cultural order of their communities. Full political equality would undermine established gender roles, and, by promising to draw women out of the home and into the unrefined realm of public life, equal suffrage also represented a significant threat to the strict separation of spheres in nineteenth-century America.

What's more, as the Fort Scott newspaper soon pointed out, the potential for political disagreements between husbands and wives posed a dangerous threat to the tranquility of Victorian households. "We all know that among excitable natures, in political discussions, quarrels arise that sometimes become serious. How much more serious will they become when indulged in at home, before the children?" asked the editor. "Jealousies will arise . . . and the peace of the family will be destroyed."[72] The

70. *Miami County Republican*, April 27, May 11, 1867.
71. *Miami County Republican*, August 24, 1867.
72. *Fort Scott Monitor*, October 9, 1867.

home, from this point of view, was a refuge from the tumult of inflamed civic discourse, and good patriarchs need not threaten this domestic peace—and the welfare of vulnerable children, it seemed—by inviting the discussions, quarrels, and jealousies that might come with enfranchised women.

Antisuffrage sentiment among Kansas editors often reflected their anxieties about the potential loss of masculine independence that such a change might bring. Through the late nineteenth century, many white men in the United States continued to ground their political privileges in their race, gender, and authority within their own households. In other words, men's status as free and independent citizens depended on their domestic mastery; that is, control over the property, familial dependents, and servants within a man's household was both an extension and a symbol of a man's political independence.[73] The eruption of political disagreements within Kansas households thus not only would threaten the "peace of the family" but also would challenge the domestic foundations upon which male political privileges had rested.

At the November 1867 election, the suffrage amendments for both women and African Americans lost by wide margins. Barely one-third of Kansas voters approved the black suffrage proposition; an even smaller proportion supported female enfranchisement. In Miami County, some 34 percent of voters favored giving the ballot to black men, but fewer than 20 percent endorsed the same right for women of either race.[74] Rather than unite Kansans, the campaign to extend equal rights to all adult citizens had instead exposed sharp divisions. A large number of Republicans endorsed the broadened conception of liberty that the two amendments represented, but most citizens could not agree that both women and African Americans should enjoy the right to vote. Disappointed by the striking defeat of both propositions, the editor of the *Linn County Border Sentinel* remarked, "Kansas no doubt feels glorious over the result of this election. Not so with us; we feel wounded and sore, yet by no means 'eternally squelched.'" Such sentiments were likely shared by suffragists and sympathetic observers across the Missouri border, where the state legislature remained generally indifferent toward the

73. LeeAnn Whites, *The Civil War as a Crisis in Gender,* 109, 135; Stephanie McCurry, *Masters of Small Worlds: Yeoman Households, Gender Relations, and the Political Culture of the Antebellum South Carolina Low Country,* 6; Bercaw, *Gendered Freedoms,* 3–4.

74. *Fort Scott Monitor,* November 7, 1867; *Daily Kansas State Journal,* November 10, 1867; Berwanger, *The West and Reconstruction,* 172. Statewide, the black suffrage amendment lost by a count of 19,421 to 10,438; for the women's suffrage amendment. the count was 19,857 to 10,070.

issue of female enfranchisement. In 1867 and 1869, the Missouri General Assembly responded to the petitions of suffragists in St. Louis by tabling or dismissing resolutions that would have given the state's women the right to vote.[75] In contrast to the active debate over women's suffrage in Kansas newspapers, editors and readers in western Missouri rarely commented on the issue, perhaps because most did not feel a need to address a reform that remained yet unpopular.

The defeat of the suffrage amendment in Kansas was but one of many early setbacks faced by advocates of female enfranchisement. By explicitly protecting the voting rights of "male inhabitants" and "male citizens," the Fourteenth Amendment had become the first amendment to interject gender into the U.S. Constitution. The ratification of the Fifteenth Amendment two years later further reinforced the gendered dimensions of postwar citizenship. The Fifteenth Amendment held that American citizens' voting rights could not be abridged on the basis of race, color, or "previous condition of servitude." Protections against disfranchisement on the basis of sex, however, were conspicuously absent. Kansas women would nevertheless gain the right to vote in municipal elections in 1887, thanks largely to the organizational efforts of the Kansas Women's Christian Temperance Union (WCTU) and the Kansas Equal Suffrage Association (KESA). That triumph, wrote Elizabeth Cady Stanton, was the "legitimate fruit" of seeds that had been sown twenty years earlier.[76] The full enfranchisement of women in Missouri would not take place for almost another fifty years. Until the ballot was won, however, women along the border would continue to exert their influence on public life in myriad ways, most notably in the temperance struggles discussed in the concluding chapter.

The suffrage referenda of the late 1860s showed that most Unionists in Kansas and Missouri held a view of citizenship that privileged loyal white men, and eventually Confederate sympathizers, over African Americans and women. When it came to discussions about the intersections of race, gender, and politics, the line between Kansas and Missouri was hardly a boundary at all. Over the coming decades, a common construction of patriotic manhood that emphasized the bravery of veterans on both sides while minimizing slavery, secession, and the origins of old divisions would play a critical part in eroding the political divisiveness of

75. *Linn County Border Sentinel,* November 15, 1867; Parrish, *Missouri under Radical Rule,* 274–75.

76. Stanton, "Kansas Train the Revolution," 1–4, Stanton Papers, Manuscript Division, Library of Congress. For the emergence of the WCTU and the KESA, see Goldberg, *Army of Women,* 9–86.

the state line. Within this reconciliation, the commercial and ideological bonds that linked community boosters in each state proved to be equally important. Eager to advance the economic development of the border region, these individuals feared that the area's violent reputation could scare away potential investors and immigrants. Determined to lead their communities beyond the violent past and toward a bright commercial future, like-minded boosters would embrace cross-border railroad schemes as a means of both economic development and sectional reconciliation. The railroad debate, especially the question of whether local taxpayers would pay for costly transportation projects, would expose new divisions and partnerships that ran along lines of economic self-interest, but not the once-inflamed state boundary.

Six

"THAT THE DISPUTE HAS TWO SIDES IS EVIDENT"

*A*t the same time that settlers along the Kansas-Missouri border wrestled with the changing boundaries of U.S. citizenship, they also engaged in an active public debate about their communities' economic futures. Although a decade of guerrilla warfare had wrecked the economy of the state line, especially on the Missouri side, the continued settlement and development of the trans-Mississippi West had resumed apace by late 1865 and gave renewed hope to local boosters on both sides of the border. Optimistic by nature, this class of promoters, merchants, newspaper editors, and other self-styled visionaries drew inspiration from the fact that their communities stood near the westernmost reaches of the nation's advancing railroad network. Railroad expansion, as growth-minded settlers well understood, was the central development of the post-war West. In the estimation of most promoters, acquiring a rail connection was a likely and necessary achievement. Railroads were a transportation revolution that transcended the existing limits of time and space and promised to reduce the isolation of the borderland by integrating its communities within the nation's industrializing market economy. According to the boosters, the improvements that would accompany market integration were also plain to see: people and products could be transported more quickly, farmers could ship their goods more cheaply, and all settlers would enjoy greater access to consumer goods manufactured in the East.

Although many westerners shared the boosters' confidence, not all people regarded railroad expansion as an unquestionably good change.

Many of the old-stock pioneers who had survived the war received the promoters' promises with doubtful skepticism and were instead content to preserve the antebellum status quo. According to these critics, the myriad railroad schemes introduced in the late 1860s raised a number of troubling questions. Foremost among them was who exactly would pay for these projects. In the capital-starved West, the burden of financing such ambitious transportation initiatives fell largely upon local governments, which would subsidize rail expansion through the purchase of bond subscriptions to the capital stocks of the various railroad companies. Heirs to a fiscally conservative political culture that valued limited government, many citizens were strongly opposed to the higher taxes that would be imposed to pay for these bonds. Rural critics also questioned which segment of society was most likely to benefit from expensive railroad schemes, as many taxpayers feared that local merchants, speculators, and other commercial interests stood to profit at the expense of property-owning farmers.[1]

Derided by their booster contemporaries as hidebound and hopelessly backward mossbacks, such critics were also skeptical of the broader changes that would come with railroads and market development. Many citizens resisted these changes because they threatened a traditional way of life in several important respects. Transportation improvements would surely erode the relative isolation of the upper Osage valley, but some settlers had long accepted the area's remoteness, which had insulated them against interference from speculators and powerful outsiders. Integration within regional and national markets would also likely erode the localism and person-to-person character that had long shaped everyday commercial exchanges. Settlers entertained mixed feelings about participating in these developing markets; most were not averse toward realizing a small profit, but many shared a general reluctance to assume risks that would jeopardize the security and independence of their own households. Citizen resistance against railroad development took many urgent forms—electoral, rhetorical, and violent—yet such expressions would hardly be limited to the Missouri side of the border.[2]

1. Charles Sellers, *The Market Revolution: Jacksonian America, 1815–1846*, 392–95; Etcheson, *Emerging Midwest*, 54–74. Although published nearly seventy years ago, Edwin Lopata's *Local Aid to Railroads in Missouri* remains the most detailed treatment of public railroad promotion in Missouri.

2. Michael Cassity, *Defending a Way of Life: An American Community in the Nineteenth Century*, 55–60. Thelen employs the rubric of an "Old Order" to describe the traditional values, attitudes, and folkways threatened by industrialization in Missouri (*Paths of Resistance*, 29–35, 59–70).

In Kansas and Missouri communities, postwar divisions over railroad expansion would not follow predictable lines of regional or partisan identity, nor would they mirror old ideological differences over slavery. Although railroad promotion became part and parcel of the Radical economic program, the ranks of community boosters, as well as those of their critics, were filled with both Republicans and Democrats. Northern immigrants played a central role in promoting several rail initiatives, particularly in Missouri. As a group, however, there was no clear ideological consensus among recent settlers, who, like old-stock natives, drew upon past experiences to craft competing visions of the region's economic future. Many immigrants had come west hoping to spur the kind of development recently witnessed in their former states; many other newcomers relocated to the frontier in order to escape those very changes. Attitudes toward economic development instead seem to have been influenced more heavily by settlers' economic circumstances. Generally speaking, merchants, government officials, and other residents of border towns were more likely to support railroad expansion than the farming population that predominated in the outlying rural townships.

Given the bitterness of recent history, the most significant consequence of the campaign for postwar development was the degree of cross-border cooperation fostered between Missouri and Kansas railroad promoters. In the years immediately after the Civil War, boosters from each state introduced a series of east-west routes that promised to bind together their communities' economic fates. Showing that economic interests could trump old political animosities, such proposals reflected a new willingness to move past the sectional divisions of the past decade.[3] Like the contemporaneous suffrage debates, which illuminated an ideological common ground for white male Unionists in each state, cross-border railroad promotions made reconciliation between development-minded Kansans and Missourians a conceivable, if not more likely, development. The rapprochement between commercial elites would indeed signify a momentous departure from the rancor and violence of the previous decade. Yet as local boosters cultivated optimistic visions and alliances that were unmoored from the border's violent past, they struggled to persuade skeptical voters within their own communities. The economic reconstruction of the Missouri-Kansas border could soothe many of the tensions caused by the border war, but the push for railroad expansion would simultaneously expose new divisions that cut across wartime loyalties.

3. SenGupta, *For God and Mammon*, 140–57.

In Missouri, the origins of the controversies and taxpayer outrage that often attended railroad promotions could be traced to the policies implemented by the state's Radical regime shortly after the war. During the 1850s, well before the Radicals had ascended to power, the Missouri legislature had loaned private railroad companies several million dollars to finance the construction of major trunk lines radiating west from St. Louis toward the Iowa, Kansas, and Arkansas borders. Many of these railroad companies had fallen into financial disrepair by the end of the Civil War, and although 912 miles of track had been laid, most of the trunk lines were yet unfinished. Desperate to expedite the completion of these routes, Radical authorities surrendered the state's financial interests in these roads in exchange for token payments and the companies' promises to complete each project. By 1868, when the Missouri legislature released the railroads from their indebtedness to the state, the corporations had repaid barely one-fifth of the money they owed. As a result of this concession, Missouri taxpayers were saddled with the burden of retiring the twenty-five million dollars in bonds and interest that the railroads had left unpaid. Previously, citizen concerns about corporate malfeasance had been tempered by widespread eagerness to see the roads completed, but the suspicion that many legislators had been bribed by railroad officials now produced broad taxpayer outrage.[4]

The Missouri legislature's railroad giveaway in 1868 marked a noteworthy departure from the fiscal restraint that Radicals had exercised in drafting the new state constitution three years earlier. Certain articles within the 1865 constitution had been passed in reaction to the arguably overzealous state subsidies for railroads during the late antebellum period. Article 11 of the postwar Radical constitution, for example, had forbidden the state legislature from extending the state's credit to any private individual, association, or corporation. With state funding no longer available, railroad promoters would be forced to rely on county and local governments to subsidize further construction. The constitution had apparently anticipated such a development, for although it placed no ceiling on the credit that local governments could lend to railroads, any extension of public aid now required the approval of a simple majority of local voters.[5]

Kansas lawmakers shared a similar disposition toward promoting railroad development, notwithstanding the Wyandotte constitution's prohi-

4. Parrish, *Missouri under Radical Rule*, 191–210; March, *The History of Missouri*, 2:1030–38; Thelen, *Paths of Resistance*, 61–62.

5. Lopata, *Local Aid*, 7; Parrish, *Missouri under Radical Rule*, 198; March, *The History of Missouri*, 2:1037.

bition against direct state investment in railroads and other internal improvements (a measure that was no doubt influenced by the overextension of state credit in Missouri). Despite this proscription, the state found other ways to offer substantial assistance to railroad corporations. Upon Kansas's entry into the Union, the state had received a grant of five hundred thousand acres from the federal government. In 1866, the Kansas legislature in turn divided this generous grant among four major railroads. As in Missouri, however, railroad companies in Kansas depended on the stock subscriptions of local governments to raise the money necessary for construction.[6]

Long on promises but short on capital, railroad promoters forged a symbiotic relationship with local officials and boosters and relied on the fierce competition between rival towns to squeeze the largest possible contributions from winning bidders. In exchange for the construction of the rail lines that they coveted, boosters promised to drum up local support for the bond subscriptions that would help finance road construction and thus lighten the costs that railroad corporations would face. If it appeared that local companies could amass the revenue needed to survey and level the prospective roads, they presented their proposals to the officials of the county court, an administrative body akin to a present-day board of commissioners, which would then decide whether to call a special election to settle the issue. County courts exercised inordinate control over the fate of local railroad initiatives, and their disapproval sealed the doom of many schemes. In instances where railroad plans managed to reach the ballot, county courts decided whether bond subscriptions would be issued, and if so, how much support taxpayers would have to provide.[7]

Attempts by community boosters to generate public enthusiasm for a given railroad proposal were enhanced by the influence that such individuals wielded within local society. Boosters typically held positions of considerable power; in many instances, the judges of the county courts and other officials were themselves keen advocates of railroad expansion. In addition, the merchants, traders, land speculators, and other commercial-minded settlers who endorsed railroad development were usually some of the area's wealthiest citizens. Perhaps the most significant advantage that the boosters enjoyed was their control of local newspapers, which enabled them to shape and dominate the public discourse

6. Miner, *Kansas,* 100–102.
7. James Willard Hurst, *Law and the Conditions of Freedom in the Nineteenth-Century United States,* 64; Thelen, *Paths of Resistance,* 62–70.

about internal improvements. Newspaper editors were the most vocal and articulate proponents of the unabashedly optimistic booster ideology. The weekly newspapers in towns like Butler and Fort Scott were each fiercely partisan instruments of competing political parties, but rival editors were nonetheless united by a common faith that railroads were a necessary component of their communities' growth.[8]

The booster-editor message was invariably confident, although its substance often fluctuated between grandiloquent promises of spectacular growth and plainspoken assessments of the benefits that would accrue to railroad communities. Editors pointed to the dramatic growth of Chicago to illustrate the far-reaching impact of a single rail connection, which, in their estimation, could transform even the most isolated village into a grand and booming city. Encouraged by the surge of postwar immigration, they also argued that the area's manifold "natural advantages"—fertile soils, rich pastures, salubrious climate, abundant resources, and an enterprising population—were proof enough that their communities were destined for greatness. Some journalists drew upon their previous experiences in the eastern United States to illuminate the tangible benefits produced by internal improvements. O. D. Austin, the Republican editor of the *Bates County Record,* had migrated to the western border from Washington, D.C., in the spring of 1866. Austin steadfastly promoted the many benefits that a railroad would bring to inhabitants of Butler and surrounding townships: "It will reduce the price of everything we eat, drink or wear. It will reduce the rate of travel. It will expedite the movement of freight, passengers and mails. It will bring in immigration and money. It will increase the value of real estate. It will increase the amount of personal property and reduce the ratio of taxation. It will give an outlet for grain, fruit, stock and coal."[9]

Austin's assurances were undoubtedly well received by settlers frustrated by their communities' relative isolation and the difficulty and expense of overland transportation. Prior to the advent of the railroad, rivers had offered the most efficient means of moving goods and people. Although several meandering tributaries of the upper Osage River sliced through the Kansas-Missouri border counties, their shallow channels

8. For thoughtful treatments of the booster ideology, see Cronon, *Nature's Metropolis: Chicago and the Great West,* 31–41, 63–81; and Daniel Dupre, *Transforming the Cotton Frontier: Madison County, Alabama, 1800–1840,* 98–133.

9. Cronon, *Nature's Metropolis,* 35–38. Austin's autobiography indicates that he was a spectator in Ford's Theater on the night that Abraham Lincoln was assassinated. See O. Williams, *Cass and Bates Counties,* 1087–88, 1115; and *Bates County Record,* June 4, 1870.

rendered them practically inaccessible to steamboats. Most of the settlers in the six border counties lived more than forty miles, or a daylong horseback ride, from Westport and Osceola, the nearest ports on the Missouri and Osage Rivers. River travel also suffered from the seasonal inconveniences brought on by drought and cold weather, as "freight and fare," one pioneer had found, usually became "enormous" during the winter months.[10] The alternative to river transport was hauling goods overland, but that option, as most border settlers had learned, was slower and more cumbersome, even with the establishment of passable routes such as the Frontier Military Road that ran from Fort Leavenworth to Fort Scott.

Postwar enthusiasm for railroad expansion was hardly limited to the Osage valley and instead raged across Missouri, Kansas, and most of the West. The majority of railroad proposals put forth during this period involved the construction of short feeder routes that would connect border communities to the east-west trunk lines that now traversed the states. The dozens of such proposals that sprouted throughout the border counties reflected a growing faith that such a route might transform even the smallest village into the state's next important city. In Harrisonville, a large throng of citizens gathered around the Cass County Courthouse in support of a liberal railroad subscription, leading one observer to conclude that the town "caught the railroad contagion; has it fearfully." Expressions of spontaneous enthusiasm appeared elsewhere along the border. When the Vernon County Court subscribed an additional two hundred thousand dollars to its existing railroad debt, seemingly all of Nevada City's residents turned out to serenade both the politicians and the railroad officers who had made the generous subscription possible. The acute urgency that fueled such public fervor was itself a product of the railroad competition between rival towns. Local boosters moved with a haste endemic to the rapidly developing West and were convinced that a failure to attract a railroad connection would surely doom their towns to insignificance. Furthermore, though it would be bad enough to see their community's support waver and thus fail to attract a railroad, it would be even worse to lose out to a rival town. Describing the competition to attract the proposed Chillicothe, Lexington, and Fort Scott Railroad, the *Pleasant Hill Leader* wrote, "There are other towns competing for it, and unless there is a goodly quantity of energy manifested here, there is a probability of loosing [sic] it. The road will be built *somewhere*." Lest

10. G. Schultz, "Steamboat Navigation"; Trego, "Letters of Trego," 119 (to Alice Trego, December 11, 1857).

the town suffer the ignominious loss of the Chillicothe road, the paper threw itself behind that project and many others.[11]

For all the feverish competition among border towns, however, a considerable amount of collaboration among communities paradoxically remained necessary. Railroad proposals were, by their very nature, cooperative efforts that linked separate towns in common cause, and the names of the proposed routes, such as the Pleasant Hill, Butler, and Fort Scott or the Sedalia, Butler, and Emporia, testified to this fact.[12] The most significant examples of translocal cooperation came from the Kansas and Missouri towns that joined together to promote mutually beneficial railroad initiatives. These efforts reflected the boosters' grasp of a simple geographic reality: the nation's rail network was generally spreading from east to west, and border towns consequently needed to work with, rather than against, the towns that lay across the once-inflamed state line. Such cooperation also depended on no small measure of forgiveness, yet should the alliance forged between railroad supporters in each state produce concrete results, it would mark an important step toward the reconciliation of the border war's survivors.

In spite of its contentious past, the open border between Missouri and Kansas had never posed a firm barrier to interstate commerce, as settlers on each side had long participated in an active market exchange. Just as Missourians had made frequent trips to buy and sell goods in Fort Scott, pioneers in Kansas had likewise ventured across the state line to do their trading. Even the most ardent abolitionists, including some of Jennison's jayhawkers, had been able to set aside their political prejudices long enough to buy vegetables, fruits, and other items in the slave state that they otherwise loathed. After the war, Allen Blunt and many of the other refugees who had returned to the Burnt District looked to Kansas to find work and provisions.[13] Even at the peak of the guerrilla violence, merchants along the open border provided a commercial nexus where the peaceful engagement of otherwise hostile populations became possible.

Once the slavery question had been settled in territorial Kansas, shared commercial interests began to help facilitate the reconciliation of partisan antagonists. During the short period between the submission of the Wyandotte constitution and the start of the Civil War, enterprising

11. Lopata, *Local Aid*, 62–63; *Pleasant Hill Leader*, July 9, 1869.
12. For a detailed list and discussion of the border's many postwar rail proposals, see O. Williams, *Cass and Bates Counties*, 1084–93.
13. Trego, "Letters of Trego," 125 (to Alice Trego, January 9, 1858); 125; Bates County Old Settlers Society, *Old Settlers' History*, 152. For other anecdotal examples of cross-border trade, see Dryden, August 21, 27, 28, 1868, *With Plow and Pen*, 50.

leaders of the proslavery and free-soil factions submerged their differences over slavery for the sake of promoting railroad development in the northeastern Kansas towns of Atchison, Leavenworth, and Lawrence. The circumstances in that part of the territory, where the ratification of the antislavery constitution had marked an effective end to guerrilla fighting, were quite different from those in southeastern Kansas, where the Marais des Cygnes massacre and John Brown's slave raids were part of an unending cycle of violent retaliations. Yet other events in the upper Osage valley lend support to the argument that the seeds of sectional reunion were sown by development-minded elites. As in northeastern Kansas, popular support for railroad development had persisted through the territorial crisis. In the winter of 1858, one Linn County settler believed that the area would boast a railroad connection to St. Louis within a couple of years, declaring, "The prospects for Mound City are indeed very flattering."[14]

Antebellum Missouri boosters had also been also eager to establish an interstate route. In August 1860, railroad promoters put a $150,000 subscription to the Osage Valley and Southern Kansas route before the voters of Bates County, but the measure was defeated by a large margin. That same month, the Cass County voters authorized the formation of a contract with the Missouri Pacific Railroad and a subscription of $100,000.[15] The Civil War halted construction on the Pacific road, and further railroad promotion ceased for the next four years, as sectional tensions and marauding guerrillas, who had set themselves to destroying Union transport lines, made cross-border cooperation nearly unthinkable.

By 1870, however, settlers in Missouri and Kansas had introduced nearly a dozen cross-border railroad measures. The individuals who proposed these initiatives came from a variety of regional backgrounds but shared the common characteristic of possessing at least a modest amount of wealth. A great many were recent northern immigrants who fitted the typical booster profile as merchants, editors, speculators, and commercial farmers who stood to profit from market access and increased land values. Several boosters were old-stock settlers. Missouri native Frank Anderson, for example, had held a variety of jobs, working as a teacher, clerk, teamster, county treasurer, speculator, horse trader, and merchant, before he eventually became a self-described "railroad contractor." Some

---

14. SenGupta, *For God and Mammon*, 139–58; Trego, "Letters of Trego," 128 (to Alice Trego, January 24, 1858).

15. O. Williams, *Cass and Bates Counties*, 391–93.

local promoters, including Richard DeJarnett, a Kentucky-born farmer who had come to the border in the 1840s, had also been slave owners.[16]

Like most boosters, James D. Snoddy of Mound City assumed a prominent role in the civic affairs of his community. The editor of the *Border Sentinel* newspaper, Snoddy was an active free-soil Republican, and in the summer of 1867 he was appointed as Linn County's representative to the State Committee of the Kansas Anti-Suffrage Movement. That fall local voters also elected him to the Kansas state legislature, turning back a challenge from African American candidate T. J. Baskerville. Snoddy's staunch abolitionism and wartime sympathies seemed to make him an unlikely ally of DeJarnett and other old-stock Missourians. In 1860, the Kansas editor had written a sharply worded editorial in which he openly condoned the lynching of a Missouri ruffian suspected of kidnapping fugitive slaves. Yet on December 21, 1868, Snoddy and several other Kansas associates traveled across the border to Butler, one of the villages that Jim Lane's jayhawkers had burned seven years earlier. The Kansas delegation hoped to build support among Butler's residents for its Jefferson City, Osage, and Neosho Valley rail project, as well as a potential connection to the Tebo and Neosho railroad. All accounts of the boosters' meeting at the Pickett Hotel indicate that the Kansans' entreaties were warmly received, as many of the Missourians in attendance had recently failed to persuade the residents of Fort Scott to support a different bistate project. The meeting concluded with pledges of cooperation from the citizens of both states, a result that may have been fostered by the Snoddy delegation's willingness to elect two Missouri boosters, D. S. Fairchild and M. S. Cowles, as chairman and secretary of the new organization.[17]

The Mound City–Butler convention illustrated the extent to which commercial interests could transcend old partisan rivalries, but like most of the other initial bistate proposals, it struggled to produce the kind of tangible results its promoters anticipated. In many cases, boosters completed extensive surveys of potential routes and even began the process of grading and preparing the roadbed until waning support thwarted further construction. The lack of progress may be attributed to the variety of competing roads that served to dilute the popular interest in any given scheme. While Snoddy's party was selling the Mound City route to Fairchild and Cowles, another prominent resident of Butler, John R.

16. *History of Vernon County*, 613; Census-Slave, Missouri, Bates County, 1860; O. Williams, *Cass and Bates Counties*, 1087–88.

17. *Linn County Border Sentinel*, September 13, November 15, 1867; *Mound City Report*, November 16, 1860; *Bates County Record*, January 2, 1869; O. Williams, *Cass and Bates Counties*, 1086–88.

Walker, a successful livestock dealer and founder of the Bates County Agricultural and Mechanical Society, was aggressively promoting a rival project that would create a feeder route between Pleasant Hill, Butler, and Fort Scott. In addition, a separate group of boosters simultaneously threw themselves behind a road to Wichita, while yet another labored to build a link to the Chicago and Alton railroad through Warrensburg.[18] Given the multitude of proposed railroads, each seemingly brimming with promise, it was not altogether surprising that residents of Butler did not rally behind a single project.

The ambivalence of local taxpayers accounted for the slow and uneven pace of early railroad construction. The initial burst of enthusiasm for railroads soon faded with the growing recognition that most boosters, in spite of their grand visions and lofty promises, were unable to deliver immediate results. Several local railroad companies, as the public would find out, existed only on paper or in their promoters' imaginations. Although a large proportion of border citizens could agree on the general principle that railroads would be a positive development, many other settlers still were not swayed by the boosters' promises. The apparent lack of consensus became even more obvious in the heated debate about taxpayer support for private railroads.

In the years immediately after the war, county court judges were complicit in the taxpayer effort to control the booster agitation for railroad development. An 1861 Missouri law had made it illegal for county courts to subscribe to the capital stock of a railroad company without first putting the issue to a vote by local residents. Even though many judges shared the booster faith in internal improvements, most took seriously their legal obligation to uphold the democratic safeguards against unchecked speculative excesses. In the late 1860s, the Bates County Court seemed immune to the growth fever that had nurtured the peculiar alliances between Kansans and Missourians. The court's judges dismissed many railroad proposals out of hand, deeming them unrealistic, too expensive, or otherwise unfit for voter consideration. Local officials occasionally regarded the railroad-bond elections as matters of such public importance that they even allowed disfranchised former secessionists to vote on—and presumably against—proposed subscriptions.[19]

In the early instances when county courts submitted railroad bonds to the voters, citizens proved stubbornly reluctant to embrace an increased tax burden. From 1867 to 1869, the Bates County Court put nearly a

18. O. Williams, *Cass and Bates Counties*, 1086–88, 1087–94.
19. Lopata, *Local Aid*, 34, 78.

dozen railroad subscriptions on the ballot, and voters rejected every single one of them. Some of these proposals were expensive; in July 1867, for example, citizens rebuffed a $450,000 subscription by a four-to-one margin. Other subscriptions were much smaller but nonetheless faced strong resistance. Citizens in Hudson Township, for example, rejected a $20,000 bond issue by a count of eighty-four to two. Few records survive to illuminate the motivations that led voters to reject these railroad subscriptions, but extant sources can provide suggestive clues about possible influences. According to census data, for example, such thorough opposition did not result from the dominance of any particular regional group, for households of northern and southern origins were almost evenly divided in the county.[20]

A survey of postwar election results likewise complicates the argument that early antirailroad sentiment reflected the continued influence of former secessionists or amounted to an outright rejection of the Radical Republican agenda. Even after the reinstatement of disfranchised rebels, which had helped to restore Democratic politicians to most local offices, the Republican Party continued to poll well throughout the county, and it would continue to enjoy a narrow majority in Hudson Township through the early 1880s. Rather than regional or partisan differences, the opposition to these initial railroad subscriptions most likely grew from broadly shared antitax sentiments. Whereas voters tended to be more accepting of public expenditures for bridges and roads—low-cost projects that yielded immediate, tangible benefits—more expensive projects enjoyed less support. In 1868, voters defeated a $20,000 bond issue that was introduced to finance a new courthouse, and proposals to build a new county jail failed in twelve straight elections.[21]

The story of the Tebo and Neosho proposal illustrates how local boosters were unbowed by early opposition to bond subscriptions. Named for the river valleys that it sought to link in west-central Missouri and southeastern Kansas, the Tebo and Neosho emerged as one of many southwestern routes that sought to link settlers in the lower Missouri valley with the developing cattle country in Texas. Having failed in their initial attempt to draw a countywide subscription, the road's promoters focused their attention on townships located in southeastern Bates County. In the

20. Bates County Old Settlers Society, *Old Settlers' History*, 50; Atkeson, *History of Bates County*, 187–93; O. Williams, *Cass and Bates Counties*, 1089. In 1870, the residents of Hudson Township were most likely counted within the enumeration district of Pleasant Gap Township.

21. O. Williams, *Cass and Bates Counties*, 1047–68; *Bates County Record*, September 19, 1868, November 6, 1880.

fall of 1868, voters in Prairie City Township, which was situated in the far corner of the county, narrowly defeated a $50,000 subscription. By the following spring, they had experienced an apparent change of heart, approving a subscription that was only half as large—a proposal that must have struck some voters as a real bargain—by a nearly unanimous vote. Key elements of the Tebo and Neosho proposal, not least of which was the renegotiated price, lent themselves to greater public support. Like most other rail proposals, the terms of the subscription held that the bonds would be delivered only after the cars were running through the township. Perhaps more important, control of the road's affairs would rest in local hands, as nearly all of the railroad's directors came from towns in western Missouri. Despite this shift in Prairie City, the residents of nearby Pleasant Gap and Lone Oak Townships remained steadfast in their resistance and voted down separate, and smaller, bond proposals.[22]

In spite of the opposition the Tebo and Neosho project faced in Bates County—or perhaps because of it—the proposal attracted greater support within neighboring counties. In 1869, Vernon County citizens approved a $200,000 proposal, but soon canceled that subscription and replaced it with a $300,000 contribution the following summer. Not all residents, it should be noted, supported this project. After replanting his corn on the morning of May 17, farmer John Dryden noted in his journal, "I go to the election to vote on the railroad question—No!"[23] As in Prairie City Township, the extension of Vernon County's assistance was tied to the road's progress: one-third of the subscription was to be paid once the track had been laid to Nevada City, another third would be paid once the cars actually ran to the town, and the final third would come after the road was completed through the western edge of the county.

Railroad enthusiasm in Vernon County may have been influenced by the Tebo and Neosho's support across the state line. In May 1867, Bourbon County citizens had endorsed a $150,000 subscription by a slim margin of 468 to 442. That contest was quickly ensnared in controversy, as the results from Franklin and Walnut Townships had not been included in the countywide totals. A U.S. district court thus had declared the 1867 subscription void, finding that the ballots from Franklin Township alone would have swung the overall vote against the subscription. At a subsequent election in 1869, however, Bourbon County residents affirmed their interest in the Tebo and Neosho proposal and approved another $150,000 subscription

22. O. Williams, *Cass and Bates Counties*, 1087; Lopata, *Local Aid*, 64.
23. Dryden, May 17, 1869, *With Plow and Pen*, 63.

by a two-to-one margin. By the fall of 1870, the Missouri, Kansas, and Texas (MKT) Railroad, as the Tebo and Neosho had been renamed, had been completed as far west as the town of Fort Scott, linking the eastern Kansas border with the Missouri River town of Boonville.[24]

The MKT was one of two important east-west railroads constructed through the border counties in the years immediately after the war. The other road, the Missouri Pacific, ran through northeastern Cass County and linked the town of Pleasant Hill with St. Louis and the neighboring City of Kansas. For the inhabitants of western Missouri, St. Louis had long been the major market center where they traveled to make important purchases in the spring and fall.[25] The expansion of the nation's rail network, however, brought about a dramatic restructuring of the market hinterland of the trans-Mississippi West. No longer dependent on river transport, towns that welcomed a new railroad connection were now being swept into the market economy that centered around rail hubs such as Chicago. Such changes were not lost on boosters along the Kansas-Missouri line, as they increasingly realized that the economic fate of their communities lay less with the distant city of St. Louis than with the bustling rail center taking shape just to the north.[26]

The City of Kansas, the municipality's official title until 1889, had been the site of active railroad promotion since the late 1850s. Although the town benefited from important natural advantages, such as a durable rock riverbank and an opportune setting on the southern banks of the Missouri and Kaw (or Kansas) Rivers, its emergence as a regional metropolis was hardly foreordained. The city's decisive triumph over Leavenworth and other competitors would come only with the completion of the Hannibal railroad bridge across the Missouri, which would link the city to the Hannibal and St. Joseph Railroad and thus the northern half of the state. More important, the Hannibal and St. Joseph would also draw Kansas City and communities of the upper Osage valley into the vast rail network that was radiating from Chicago.[27] Well before the Hannibal Bridge was completed, Kansas City boosters had dedicated themselves to improving ties of transportation and commerce with the grain- and livestock-producing country that lay to the south and west. These individu-

24. Cutler, *History of Kansas*, 2:1072; J. Johnson, *History of Vernon County*, 322.

25. For examples of settlers who traveled to St. Louis for major purchases, see Dryden, March 28, 1868, *With Plow and Pen*, 41; Trego, "Letters of Trego," 119 (to Alice Trego, December 5, 1857); and Goodlander, *Memoirs and Recollections*, 30.

26. Glaab, *Kansas City and the Railroads*, 38. For the competition among Chicago, St. Louis, and other aspiring rail centers, see Cronon, *Nature's Metropolis*, 55–93.

27. Glaab, *Kansas City and the Railroads*, 2–17.

als recognized that the city's growth was inextricably linked to the future of this rapidly developing region, which they dubbed the "New West." Rail access to the Gulf of Mexico, the boosters believed, would someday provide western farmers and ranchers with a more direct and economical outlet for their surplus products, which could then be more readily absorbed by international markets. Convinced that Kansas City could become the railroad hub for this vast plains region, local promoters worked tirelessly to establish a north-south rail corridor that would link the city with Galveston or other Gulf ports.[28]

Shortly after the conclusion of the Civil War, Miami, Linn, and Bourbon Counties and Fort Scott each subscribed $150,000 to a Kansas and Neosho Valley project. Set to run from Kansas City along the eastern border of Kansas and through the Indian Territory before entering Texas, this railroad had been incorporated by Kansas City merchants in 1865. It had soon become evident, however, that the initiative's success depended upon the cooperation of urban developers and rural interests farther south. The distribution of corporate authority and stock ownership within the company reflected the extent of this urban-rural interaction. Four of the railroad's directors came from Kansas City, while Bourbon County and Miami County each provided three. The City of Kansas was the road's largest stockholder, owning 2,026 shares, and the Bourbon County commissioners were close behind, with 1,500.[29] Although the support of the border-county boosters was a promising sign for the Kansas and Neosho Valley initiative, the project's progress soon slowed due to sharp divisions that pitted local settlers against the railroad's management.

When deciding where to locate their route, railroad officials had preferred eastern Kansas over western Missouri because much of the land in Kansas had until recently been under Indian ownership and thus, in the promoters' estimation, could be bought at a cheap price and resold for a handsome profit. Located in the southeastern corner of Kansas and encompassing a large part of Bourbon County, the eight hundred thousand–acre Cherokee Neutral Tract had been ceded by treaty to the U.S. government in 1866 and became the subject of intense interest by railroad developers and speculators as quickly as its indigenous tenants had been removed. Rather than treat the Cherokee cession as part of the public domain, which had been governed by laws such as the Pre-Emption and

28. H. Craig Miner, "The Kansas and Neosho Valley Railroad: Kansas City's Drive for the Gulf," 75–77; Cutler, *History of Kansas*, 2:881, 1072, 1108; Glaab, *Kansas City and the Railroads*, 189–91.

29. Miner, "Kansas and Neosho Valley Railroad," 81.

Homestead Acts, Secretary of the Interior Orville Browning instead sold the lands to James F. Joy on October 19, 1867, a Detroit-based speculator and president of the Chicago, Burlington, and Quincy railroad system.[30]

Having recently taken over management of the Kansas and Neosho Valley road, Joy planned to consolidate that route within his regional rail system, but his designs were complicated by the presence of thousands of white squatters already living on the Neutral Tract. Many of these people had been squatting on the Cherokee lands for up to a decade. The 1860 federal census, which had indicated that only 13 percent of Bourbon County farmers owned any appreciable real estate, reflected the fact that a substantial proportion of southeastern Kansas's residents were living on lands that had not yet come up for public sale. By contrast, in the two counties to the north, where Indian titles had been extinguished much sooner, more than 70 percent of farm households had owned some appreciable real estate.[31]

These squatters expected that once the Cherokee reserve had been surrendered by its indigenous owners, most of whom had moved farther south to Indian Territory by the start of the Civil War, it would be disposed of by the federal government under the favorable terms of either the Preemption or Homestead Acts. Most of these residents adhered to the conventional squatter defense that occupancy and improvement of the land justified their claims. A great many of the tract's postwar inhabitants were also former Union soldiers who had come west hoping to use their military land warrants. Joy's purchase of the Cherokee lands, however, meant that the current tenants would be forced to purchase their claims from a speculator whom they believed had taken the land out from under them, rather than from the federal government. The squatters therefore organized themselves into the Cherokee Land League and declared that Joy would not be able to build his railroad unless they were allowed to purchase their claims for $1.25 per acre, the same price at which lawful tenants had been able to purchase public lands under the Preemption Act of 1841.[32]

By early 1869, ownership of the Kansas and Neosho Valley passed into the hands of Boston financiers Nathaniel Thayer, William F. Wells, and

30. H. Craig Miner, *The End of Indian Kansas,* 117; Miner, "Border Frontier: The Missouri River, Fort Scott and Gulf Railroad in the Cherokee Neutral Lands, 1868–1870," 105–6; Holder and Rothman, *Post on the Marmaton,* 234–39.

31. Census-Pop, Kansas Territory, Bourbon, Linn, and Miami Counties, 1860.

32. Eugene F. Ware, "The Neutral Lands"; Miner, "Border Frontier," 105–10; Cutler, *History of Kansas,* 2:1072; John Opie, *The Law of the Land: Two Hundred Years of American Farmland Policy,* 56.

Sidney Bartlett, who renamed it the Missouri River, Fort Scott, and Gulf Railroad. This new title reflected the investors' broader regional aspirations as well as an obligatory concession to the line's Fort Scott supporters. Not long thereafter, the Gulf railroad purchased the Cherokee lands from Joy but retained him as the agent responsible for negotiating the sale of the various claims. The change in ownership did little to break the stalemate over the neutral lands, where the growing number of squatters now exceeded ten thousand. Unwilling to accept the initial demands of the land league, the Gulf railroad instead offered to sell the former Cherokee lands at a price of two to five dollars per acre, a cost that most of the tenants immediately dismissed as too expensive. Because the tenants' continued presence posed a significant obstacle to the route's construction, Joy tried to expedite the land sales by presenting a modified offer that distinguished between classes of settlers according to their length of tenure. He maintained that the railroad held no quarrel with the first class of settlers, who had resided on their claims prior to the Cherokee cession and thus enjoyed clear title to the land. The second class of settlers included those who had squatted during the one-year period between the cession treaty and Joy's purchase. Joy intimated that he was willing to give these squatters perhaps four months to "prove up" their claims. The final group of settlers—those who had arrived after the 1867 purchase—would receive no special treatment and as a result would have to pay the regular market price of six to twelve dollars per acre.[33]

Most squatters, regardless of their tenure, were not mollified by Joy's revised offer, and in the spring of 1869 the members of the land league and other paramilitary squatter organizations unleashed a campaign of intimidation and violence against the railroad. Many of these efforts targeted the economic interests of the railroad and its local boosters. In Girard, a band of squatters destroyed the offices of a prorailroad newspaper. League members imposed a boycott on the stores in the Cherokee County town of Baxter Springs and discouraged many of their neighbors from providing timber, limestone, or other building materials to the Gulf project. To further hamper the road's construction, the league burned railroad ties as quickly as they were laid. Vigilante squatters also harassed and threatened to assault the railroad's construction crews and surveying teams. Such warnings sometimes amounted to more than idle bullying. On April 29, for example, an impromptu "squatter's court" of more than a dozen armed men seized a Fort Scott engineer named John Runk, who

33. Holder and Rothman, *Post on the Marmaton,* 240; Miner, "Kansas and Neosho Valley Railroad," 84.

had recently conducted the railroad's survey of the neutral lands. The mob robbed Runk and sentenced him to fifteen lashes. A month later, league members executed another railroad employee, hanging him from a tree on Cow Creek.[34]

The violent actions of Kansas squatters were among many instances in which western settlers would revolt against railroad expansion in the post–Civil War era. The government's handling of the Cherokee lands fostered widespread anger and disillusionment among squatters who believed that politicians had sold out bona fide settlers for the sake of promoting rapid railroad expansion. The leaguers' opposition to railroad construction was a rejection of both this policy and the inordinate power that nonresident speculators like Joy seemed to wield within local affairs. The sale of the Cherokee tract to railroad developers also sparked fears that the squatters were losing control of their everyday affairs. According to the widely accepted principles of nineteenth-century republicanism, landownership was a safeguard of personal independence and welfare, but the impending sale of the Neutral Tract, which put these lands within the grasp of the wealthy bidders, posed a serious threat to squatter households.[35]

Political leaders in Kansas, however, concluded that the league itself was a greater threat to the security of the Gulf railroad and surrounding communities. Four companies of the Sixth U.S. Infantry Regiment were mobilized in the summer of 1869 to restore order and protect the commercial interests of southeastern Kansas. Most of these troops, which would later include a group from the Seventh U.S. Cavalry, were stationed in temporary barracks that had been constructed along the railroad. Rather than provoke or engage their fellow Civil War veterans, league members ceased their insurgency almost immediately. Although the army's presence marked an effective end to political violence on the Cherokee tract, the legal disposition of the land dispute came from no less an authority than the U.S. Supreme Court, which upheld the railroad's title to the land. Most of the settlers agreed to the railroad's terms of sale and chose to remain on their claims. A large number of squatters, believing they could find other good lands more cheaply elsewhere, refused Joy's asking price and simply migrated farther west.[36]

34. Miner, "Border Frontier," 111–14; Holder and Rothman, *Post on the Marmaton,* 241–42.

35. Thelen, *Paths of Resistance,* 44–75; Etcheson, *Emerging Midwest,* 64.

36. Miner, *End of Indian Kansas,* 117–19; Miner, "Border Frontier," 116–22; Holder and Rothman, *Post on the Marmaton,* 233–42. For a monthly broadsheet that extolled the advantages of the Neutral Lands, see C. Rollin Camp, *Camp's Emigrants' Guide to Kansas.*

Looking upon the neutral-land fuss, newspaper editors in Missouri were reluctant to take sides. "That the dispute has two sides is evident," concluded the *Pleasant Hill Leader,* "but precisely where the blame lies is not so clear." The majority of the settlers apparently were not at fault, having arrived "with no intention of wronging any one." In addition, Joy's speculative interests, which the paper described as "not unnatural," and the "fair and reasonable" sale terms he had proposed also seemed beyond reproach. The paper's Republican editor concluded that the responsibility for the land fiasco ultimately rested with both the league's unprincipled leaders and the shortsighted government officials who failed to anticipate the depth of squatter outrage.[37]

Such muted criticisms of the railroad company were perhaps influenced by the eagerness of Missouri boosters both to keep pace with the development taking place across the state line and to forge their own rail connections to Kansas City. In early 1870, the city council of Kansas City had furnished $2,000 to conduct a preliminary survey of a route that would sweep through the counties of western Missouri on its way to Memphis. To help make this Memphis road a reality, St. Clair and Bates Counties provided subscriptions of $250,000 and $400,000, respectively. The Bates County subscription enjoyed particularly strong support, having been approved by a four-to-one majority on May 3, 1870. Within a month, however, a large number of citizens became suspicious of the Memphis organization's dubious legality, and they asked the county court to rescind the $400,000 appropriation. The court refused to withdraw its support but later agreed to reduce the subscription to $125,000, half of which would be payable once the cars were running through Butler.[38]

The Memphis project soon faltered, like so many of the initiatives introduced shortly after the Civil War, and the road was never built. The failure of this railroad and others confirmed their critics' suspicions about the emptiness of booster promises and the corruption of rail promoters. Unwilling to impugn private developers, frustrated boosters attributed the sluggish pace of railroad expansion to the complacency and conservatism of Missouri taxpayers. One editor castigated local citizens for their lack of enthusiasm, writing, "Bates County could be transformed into something better than she is today. Would that some one of unyielding determination would take hold of the helm and dare to do right, brave all risks of losing popularity, and succeed in throwing the

37. *Pleasant Hill Leader,* June 4, 1869.
38. *Bates County Record,* April 9, May 7, 1870; O. Williams, *Cass and Bates Counties,* 1090; Glaab, *Kansas City and the Railroads,* 198.

careless apathy of our people to the dogs." Skeptical citizens had repeatedly thwarted railroad development, and even though boosters sharply disagreed with antitax sentiments, they nevertheless had accepted such opposition as a legitimate expression of majority rule. With taxpayer support waning by the early 1870s, the era of postwar rail construction seemed at an end in eastern Kansas and Western Missouri.[39] Rather than see their railroad visions extinguished, however, a small group of boosters and local officials concluded that not even the will of the people should remain an obstacle to continued development.

Voters in Bates County had repeatedly proved themselves unwilling to support railroad expansion. Within five years of the Civil War, citizens in neighboring counties had approved railroad subscriptions totaling $761,500 and $317,000, but Bates County taxpayers, on the other hand, had subscribed only $155,000. Because most of this funding had gone to a project that was never built—the Lexington, Lake, and Gulf Railroad— only a few miles of the MKT road had been laid through the county's southeastern corner. The county seat, Butler, sat more than a dozen miles from the MKT, a fact that convinced local merchants and officials that they had been outmaneuvered by other border communities. In January 1872, the members of the county court, desperate to attract a railroad and exasperated by stubborn taxpayer opposition, issued a $250,000 county-wide bond subscription without first submitting it to a public vote. This subscription would fund the construction of a branch line that would connect Butler with the MKT road to the southeast. Whereas the greatest benefits of the proposed route would redound to the residents of the county seat, taxpayers throughout the county would be saddled with the new line's high cost.[40]

The actions of the Bates County Court demonstrated local officials' readiness to defy their constituents' wishes. Not surprisingly, the court's brazen defiance of public will ignited widespread outrage among rural citizens. Seeking to enjoin the county government from honoring the subscription, voters quickly organized meetings in several townships to express their outrage. In early February, settlers gathered in Altona to demand that the court members resign. A resentful farmer in Mingo Township refused to subsidize the Butler line, concluding that the court "seems to be . . . in the hands of speculating men who aim to fleece the

39. *Bates County Democrat,* January 18, 1872. Paul Wallace Gates describes how the federal support for railroad expansion likewise waned with the economic downturn in the early 1870s (*History of Public Land Law Development,* 369–86).

40. Atkeson, *History of Bates County,* 191–93; O. Williams, *Cass and Bates Counties,* 1091–92.

working classes." The citizens who assembled in Pleasant Gap Township agreed to sever all commercial ties with the city of Butler, the perceived source of railroad manipulation, unless the bonds were rescinded. One of the court's judges responded to these criticisms by portraying the MKT subscription as a shrewd and timely maneuver. In an unsigned letter to the *Bates County Record,* he wrote, "This was our last, our only chance to take advantage of a legal method of equalizing and perhaps excelling our neighboring counties." In spite of the judge's devious suggestion that the subscription had somehow been licit, it had in fact circumvented a state law passed in 1861 and the state constitution of 1865, as well other subsequent laws. The court quickly rescinded the subscription once it realized the extent of widespread voter outrage.[41]

This hostility toward boosters was undoubtedly informed by settlers' awareness that postwar immigration and development had heightened the differences between the inhabitants within the county seat and those in the surrounding countryside. The county seat, by its very function and central location, had always served as the locus of political influence. In addition to being the administrative center where citizens gathered to vote and pay taxes, it was typically the county's cultural and commercial nexus, containing the cluster of shops, saloons, and churches that brought together settlers from miles around. In the years leading up to the Civil War, the population around the county seats along the state line was hardly different from that of the predominantly agrarian outlying townships. According to a sample of the 1860 federal census, the distribution of settlers' occupations was remarkably similar in most townships, including those that contained each county's seat. Within every township, even in Pleasant Hill, which was set to become the western terminus of the Missouri Pacific Railroad, the largest class of settlers—more than 80 percent in most places—worked as farmers or farm laborers. The proportions of skilled laborers, merchants, and professionals, whose ranks included physicians, attorneys, and editors, were usually higher in the county-seat townships—Pleasant Hill was an obvious exception—but generally remained much smaller than the proportion of farmers. Ten years later the differences between populations of the county seat and the surrounding countryside became even sharper. Although farming was still by far the most common way to make a living in the outlying townships, the situation had changed in county-seat townships, which saw a rising number of merchants, professionals, and skilled laborers. This shift was especially apparent in the townships that contained major towns situated along the

41. *Bates County Record,* January 27, February 3, 24, March 16, 1872.

railroads—Pleasant Hill and Center in Missouri and Scott, Potosi, and Paola in Kansas.[42]

The sharp criticisms that rural settlers leveled against boosters in urban areas (if the census bureau's liberal designation of "urban" may be borrowed) belied the common interests that linked these groups. The prosperity of farmers and merchants was often closely linked. Individuals in both groups were typically members of the middle class—small entrepreneurs who possessed a limited amount of wealth, faced a significant risk of economic failure, and, though they cherished the ideal of self-sufficiency, welcomed the opportunity to make a small profit from their work. Farmers and merchants, however, were divided by a critical difference; members of the former group earned their living as producers, whereas the latter group, commonly dismissed as "middlemen," often profited from the work of others.[43]

Agrarian opposition to public railroad financing and their resentment of local commercial interests was hardly a knee-jerk rejection of the spread of rural capitalism. Among producers who had recently witnessed the many sheriffs' sales held on nearby courthouse lawns, these opinions were not borne of vague anxieties but were the result of lived experience. Postwar farms operated on slim financial margins, and in many cases the difference between success and failure seemed less than a family's yearly tax bill. This situation, coupled with increased levels of mortgaged indebtedness, meant that dispossession was neither an abstract nor a distant possibility, but something that could and did happen to producers like themselves.

The enmity of rural citizens toward the commercial interests within the county seat had other sources as well. Many settlers invoked basic conceptions of fairness to justify their opposition to the MKT branch to Butler, arguing that although the railroad's benefits would accrue disproportionately to the town's residents, the costs would be shouldered by taxpayers throughout the countryside. One citizen observed that the railroad boosters in Butler "constitute but a small minority of the people, and yet the Government has been conducted almost exclusively in their interests." It was clear, according to railroad opponents, that the town's promoters wielded inordinate influence over local politicians. Reflecting on

---

42. Census-Pop, Kansas, Bourbon, Linn, and Miami Counties, 1860, 1870; Census-Pop, Missouri, Bates, Cass, and Vernon Counties, 1860, 1870.

43. Scott McNall, *The Road to Rebellion: Class Formation and Kansas Populism, 1865–1900*, 107. For the relationship between farmers and the inhabitants of small towns, see Lewis Atherton, *Main Street on the Middle Border*. Rugh makes a similar point about the nature of antirailroad sentiment (*Our Common Country*, 138).

the canceled MKT subscription, one settler wrote, "A ring of all the merchants of Butler and their invited lobbyists, from the fact of the feindish [*sic*] secrecy in the matter during the leisure hours for several years past discussed the best propriety of taxing and legally defrauding the farmers of Bates County out of their property and their homes."[44]

These antirailroad criticisms bespoke anxieties that would become hallmarks of late-nineteenth-century agrarian radicalism. The denunciation of a secretive "ring" of merchants was a common feature of farmers' complaints that would be repeated elsewhere in the months to come. Years before the leaders of the Farmers' Alliance and the Populist Party formulated indictments against powerful eastern interests and financiers, border citizens articulated their own impassioned critique of conspiratorial developers. Drawing on the agrarian conviction that they were bound together by common interests, farmers grounded their criticisms in the belief that conspiracy subverted the democratic process by shrouding in secrecy the discourse over economic development. Yet unlike the Populist criticism of "the money power," settlers along the border did not level their criticisms against distant and shadowy figures but, rather, targeted figures with whom they were personally acquainted.[45]

The anxieties that Missouri settlers harbored about corruption of local railroad promoters reached violent proportions in early 1872. The state's most explosive example of railroad violence came just a few short weeks after the Bates County Court fiasco of early 1872, but its causes can be traced to the late antebellum period. In 1857 Cass County voters had approved a $150,000 subscription to the Missouri Pacific Railroad but had soon reduced that amount, with the railroad's approval, to $100,000. All of the county's bonds had been printed, but only three of them, each valued at $500, had actually been delivered to the railroad. During a Union army raid on the county seat of Harrisonville, a federal officer had seized the remaining $98,500 in bonds and had delivered them to Fort Leavenworth for safekeeping. Once these bonds had been returned to Cass County after the war, local officials and the railroad's officers soon agreed to cancel the subscription. Although the three-member county court had voted to destroy the Pacific railroad bonds, two of the judges, J. C. Stevenson and Robert W. Forsythe, had disregarded the order.[46]

44. *Bates County Advocate*, September 25, 1878; *Bates County Record*, February 24, 1872.

45. For a critical assessment of the significance of conspiracies within "the Populist imagination," see Richard Hofstadter, *The Age of Reform: From Bryan to F.D.R.*, 70–93.

46. George H. Preston, *A History of the Cass County, Missouri, Bond Swindle*, 7–20; Lopata, *Local Aid*, 105–7.

Both Stevenson and Forsythe were postwar immigrants from the North who had quickly made names for themselves. Stevenson, one cynical settler would later recall, had come to the border with barely $1,000 but had accumulated $15,000 in five years, even though "he was no better farmer, no more industrious than his neighbors." (By contrast, the third judge, J. C. Copeland, who had been excluded from the ring, was an old-stock settler and native of Tennessee.) Acting in collusion with several local boosters, Stevenson and Forsythe had secretly refunded the existing bonds and in August 1869 had transferred the subscription, which with accrued interest was worth $229,000, to the St. Louis and Santa Fe Railroad, which would be constructed through Harrisonville. When the judges' actions were later uncovered, local citizens were infuriated. "BOND ROBBERY!" shrieked the *Pleasant Hill Leader*. "While the court and its satellites discriminated in every possible way against this and other sections of the county, and in favor of the county seat, they secretly labored for the furtherance of selfish ends." The paper demanded that all "bribe-takers and robbers" be purged from their offices and that they, along with their accomplices, be punished accordingly. Responding to the hue and cry, Sheriff A. C. Briant arrested both judges, attorneys J. D. Hines and James Cline, and at least two other boosters implicated in the bond transfer. Another suspect committed suicide shortly after he was apprehended by authorities in Kansas City.[47]

Most of the suspects posted bail, but their actions upon being released from jail served only to heighten the public's indignation. On the morning of April 24, 1872—twelve days before their scheduled trial—Stevenson, Cline, and a Harrisonville city councilman named T. E. Dutroe strolled through the county seat, reportedly bragging about their exploits and loudly predicting their certain acquittal. When the suspects received word that their brash actions had spurred the formation of an angry vigilance committee, the trio hastily boarded a train for Kansas City. By the time the train approached Gunn City—a hamlet that consisted of little more than a store, a blacksmith shop, and three homes—an armed mob of fifty to sixty men gathered along the tracks. Throwing an old plow and several other objects across the rails, the vigilantes stopped the train's progress, dragged the three suspects from their car, and shot each one to death. Before dispersing, the mob reportedly threatened to murder the

---

47. Preston, *Cass County Bond Swindle*, 6–7; Census-Pop, Missouri, Cass County, 1850; *Pleasant Hill Leader*, March 8, 1872. For the order that purported to cancel the Pacific bonds, see ibid., September 23, 1870, August 11, 1871; O. Williams, *Cass and Bates Counties*, 391–429; Preston, *Cass County Bond Swindle*, 75–77; and Lopata, *Local Aid*, 105–6.

ring's other associates and any passenger who dared to testify against the vigilantes, as well as Governor B. Gratz Brown or any state militiamen who might try to intervene in the county's affairs.[48]

Wire services splashed news of the Gunn City killings across papers in New York, Chicago, and beyond, garnering western Missouri even more widespread notoriety. Locally, a Paola newspaper condemned the "reign of terror" that had descended upon its neighboring county and reported that many Harrisonville residents had fled into Kansas to escape further mob violence. Deeming the incident "disgraceful alike to the fair name of Missouri and to our common civilization," Governor Brown ordered the guilty parties to disarm and disband, and he encouraged local officials to bring the mob to justice. To enforce this order, the governor sent troops under Albert Sigel and more than two thousand pounds of ammunition to Harrisonville. Despite the mob's previous threats, the militia apparently restored order to the area without a shot being fired. Seven months later a Cass County grand jury indicted forty-four men for the April murders. These men were an extraordinary cross section of local society, as their ranks included old-stock natives, postwar immigrants, successful merchants, poor farmers, Republicans, and Democrats. One local editor regarded the desultory indictments as a sign that law and justice reigned supreme within the county. Each of the men pleaded not guilty, but none was ever convicted. Officials eventually recovered most of the controversial bonds. The majority of the bonds were immediately destroyed, but two were saved and were posted on the wall of the county clerk's office as a reminder of the court's actions.[49]

The Gunn City affair elicited mixed reactions from observers along the Kansas-Missouri border. Boosters living in the neighboring Kansas counties roundly condemned the mob's actions. The editor of the *Miami County Republican,* for example, concluded, "The indignation of the people of Cass county against the men who cheated them was just, but there are none who will uphold or excuse the horrid crime which the misguided passions of men engaged in this murderous outrage." The *Mound City Border Sentinel* echoed these sentiments: "There is no justification. . . . The murder was not only bloody, foul and premeditated, but it was *cowardly* in the extreme." Editors in western Missouri, ever defensive about the area's lawless reputation, were likewise dismayed by the likelihood

48. Preston, *Cass County Bond Swindle,* 85–88; Lopata, *Local Aid,* 106.
49. *Miami County Republican,* May 3, 1872; *Pleasant Hill Leader,* May 3, November 22, 1872; O. Williams, *Cass and Bates Counties,* 427; Allen Glenn, *History of Cass County, Missouri,* 203–11. Lopata indicates that some of the bonds had been sold to a Kansas City investor but were later declared void by a Missouri court (*Local Aid,* 106).

that the murders would further tarnish their communities. O. D. Austin, a Butler Republican, spoke for many local boosters when he wrote, "We very greatly regret the occurrence for many reasons. The people of Cass County could better afford to pay the $229,000 than to have the county stigmatized as containing a large body of lawless, deliberate murderers; beside, the whole State suffers in a degree from such lawlessness. Immigrants are detered [*sic*] from settlement where lawlessness is tolerated, and investment of capital and public improvements are deferred."[50]

The proprietors of the *Fort Scott Daily Monitor* refused to condone the Gunn City murders but correctly observed that the murders were a dire warning to public officials who would dare to defy their constituents' wishes. Mindful of their vested interest in the economic development of local communities, progress-minded Cass County editors were particularly reluctant to criticize the vigilantes. A Pleasant Hill resident, stunned by the news of the "terrible tragedy," assured Kansas City correspondents that anarchy did not prevail within the county. "The people of Cass county, considering the circumstances, deserve to be commended for their forbearance," one settler asserted. "The parties accused of these bond robberies . . . brought this calamity upon themselves. They knew their duty but they did it not. They tested the forbearance of their fellow citizens beyond endurance, and as the natural and *universal* result, the short-cut to justice was taken. The same may occur in any community." Defending the citizens' reliance on mob action, he continued: "The voice of the people is the supreme law. That voice may not always be lawfully expressed, yet this does not render it less potent or worthy of respect." Another local resident, George Preston, also reckoned that the Gunn City victims had received a just punishment, given their insolent behavior on the streets of Harrisonville. "Day after day," Preston wrote, "they added insult to injury by boasting of their achievements, and taunting the poor, bankrupt citizen by reminding him of his poverty. Was all this not enough to heat the blood of the most law-abiding people in the land, and prompt them to deeds of violence?"[51]

The Gunn City vigilantes were not the only Missourians who employed violence against public officials suspected of fiduciary malfeasance. A mob in the northeastern part of the state threatened to lynch the court of Knox County if it broke with voters' wishes by subscribing to the stock of a certain railroad company. In nearby St. Clair County, where the county court had approved railroad subscriptions in defiance of bond

50. *Miami County Republican*, April 27, 1872; *Bates County Record*, April 27, 1872.
51. *Pleasant Hill Leader*, April 26, May 17, 1872; Preston, *Cass County Bond Swindle*, 90.

elections, a group of citizens broke into the courthouse, seized the county's tax assessments, and burned them, thereby complicating the job of local officials who might try to collect further railroad taxes.[52] The Gunn City murders, like the actions of the Cherokee Land League, were part of a much larger phenomenon of postwar western violence. In Missouri and Kansas, these incidents must also be understood within the context of both the recent guerrilla war, in which vigilantism and summary justice had repeatedly found popular sanction, and the culture of violence that had long prevailed across much of the American frontier. Within this culture, the use of violence against corrupt or unlawful targets could be deemed an acceptable and legitimate exercise of authority so long as it upheld the traditional values of most citizens.

Missouri was also home to Jesse James, the most widely mythologized railroad antagonist in the United States. According to an astute recent biography, much of the bandit's appeal in his home state grew from his powerful political symbolism as much as the devil-may-care fearlessness of his robberies. James styled himself not merely as a Robin Hood figure who robbed the rich and gave to the poor but also as an avenger who resisted the Radical economic agenda and all its corrupt excesses. Several years after the Civil War ended, old allegiances and resentments still resonated throughout much of Missouri, continuing to divide neighbor from neighbor, and the lingering pull of wartime loyalties thus made support for James, himself a former bushwhacker, especially strong among fellow ex-rebels. Many former Confederates, however, refused to condone such violent behavior and instead emphasized the need to maintain law and order in Missouri.[53]

The Gunn City murders revealed how the politics of economic protest could transcend the politics of war along the state line. Angry opposition to railroad corruption was not limited to Confederate sympathizers, and it instead linked citizens of different political, regional, and economic backgrounds. Such opposition, meanwhile, did not always translate into support for all antirailroad outlaws. The editors who feverishly denounced the conspirators killed by the Cass County vigilantes, for example, were just as quick to wring their hands about the lawless behavior of Jesse James. The Gunn City affair also marked an unsettling end to the era of railroad expansion that had begun after the Civil War. Wearied by the dizzying barrage of rail proposals, voters throughout Missouri

52. Thelen, *Paths of Resistance*, 65–68.
53. Stiles, *Jesse James*, 225–38, 386. See ibid., 260–74, for how the debate over law and order divided Missouri Democrats.

struggled to pay high railroad taxes. The annual per capita railroad debt in Cass County was nearly forty dollars, or almost 10 percent of the value of an average household's real estate. Even with substantial tax increases, however, the governments of many border counties remained unable to pay for all of the railroad subscriptions approved after the war. Bates, Cass, and Vernon Counties were among several Missouri counties that were sued in April 1873 for defaulting on railroad bonds, and the counties almost always failed to win such suits. Local governments that were unwilling or unable to pay their bondholders usually appealed such decisions. Rather than wait for these appeals to reach their final adjudication, parties typically settled these legal controversies by renegotiating the terms of the agreement. In many instances, counties would not retire their railroad debts until the early twentieth century.[54]

In the wake of this antirailroad violence, Missourians implemented a host of institutional reforms to curb the speculative excesses of the early postwar period. In 1871, the Missouri legislature tried to limit overspending by local governments when it imposed a ceiling on railroad bond subscriptions, holding that officials could no longer introduce subscriptions that would cost more than 10 percent of a county's most recent assessed valuation. Within a year of the Gunn City murders, state lawmakers made it a felony for county court officials to approve railroad subscriptions without first submitting such packages to a vote by local taxpayers. The legal reaction against postwar railroad development reached its climax with the ratification of a new state constitution in 1875. Elevating the 1872 statute to a matter of constitutional import, this charter revoked the authority of municipal, city, or county officials to subscribe public funds without the approval of local voters. More important, the 1875 constitution imposed a higher threshold for taxpayer-funded projects, as local governments could no longer assume any debt without first receiving the approval of two-thirds of voters. For citizens determined to assert fiscal discipline and local over the course of economic development, this particular measure was an important achievement; for boosters and growth-minded officials, the supermajority threshold would pose a difficult obstacle for decades to come.[55]

Aside from the unfavorable political climate that helped produce these reforms, railroad expansion also faltered as a result of the panic of 1873. By

---

54. Thelen, *Paths of Resistance,* 66; Census-Pop, Missouri, Cass County, 1870; Lopata, *Local Aid,* 107.

55. Lopata, *Local Aid,* 37–38; March, *The History of Missouri,* 2:1135–36; Cassity, *Defending a Way of Life,* 60.

that summer's harvest, the prices that border farmers received for their corn, potatoes, and butter plunged almost to wartime lows. Property values suffered a precipitous decline, and money quickly became scarce, leaving settlers with little cash to pay their mounting tax burdens.[56] Describing the depression's impact, an old-stock Kansas settler would later recall, "Banks failed, business was paralyzed, everybody in debt and financial ruin seemed inevitable." Other unfortunate events compounded the dire economic situation. A disastrous fire ripped through central Fort Scott in 1873, destroying or damaging more than twenty-five businesses. One year later a plague of grasshoppers descended upon the central plains and cast many farmers into even greater destitution.[57]

Years after the effects of this severe economic downturn had abated, railroad promotion would resume yet again, but such efforts would proceed under markedly different terms. Since taxpayers had asserted their reluctance to subsidize speculative railroad development, the costs of further expansion would fall to wealthy private investors. Aside from James Joy and the Missouri River, Fort Scott, and Gulf Railroad, an enterprise that was made attractive by the explosive growth of Kansas City and the cheapness of the former Cherokee lands in Kansas, eastern financiers shied away from funding transportation projects through the Osage plains. By the late 1870s, however, the extensive coal reserves that underlay the state line gave foreign developers a new reason to invest in the region. Although local boosters had long believed that the area's abundant coal resources would support a profitable industry, such potential was not realized until developer E. B. Brown and Jay Gould, the owner of the Missouri Pacific Railroad, established a coal-mining operation in the Bates County town of Rich Hill.

In 1880, Gould quickly built a feeder road, the Lexington and Southern, to transport the coal needed to power his expanding rail empire. Running from Kansas City toward the southwestern Missouri town of Joplin, which had become an important lead and zinc mining center, the Lexington and Southern stimulated yet another burst of immigration and economic growth along the border. Within a year of its construction, the Gulf railroad completed its own feeder route to the bustling coal mines of western Missouri. "Rich Hill boomed as no other town ever did," crowed local editor F. J. Wiseman, one of many local boosters who supposed that

56. J. Johnson, *History of Vernon County*, 447; Lopata, *Local Aid*, 73; *Bates County Record*, August 16, 1873. For a comparison of the eventual rebound in the prices of farm products, see ibid., May 15, 1875.
57. Botkin, "Sixty Years in Kansas," 4, Botkin Papers, KSHS; McNall, *Road to Rebellion*, 106.

the aspiring metropolis might soon rival Kansas City in wealth and influence. "She is without a parallel except Virginia City, Nevada, and Leadville, Colorado. But their wealth—elements of greatness—is ephemeral." The success of the Rich Hill mines briefly made Bates County the leading coal producer in Missouri, rewarded Gould's investment, and confirmed the loftiest predictions of local boosters. Industrialization also brought about new institutions of corporate authority, such as the company town and store, which many settlers did not embrace. Furthermore, the area's sudden prosperity would ultimately last only as long as the coal held out, for once the mines gave out, the mining companies and their foreign owners would surely pull out of the area as well.[58]

An examination of the fight over railroad expansion on the Missouri-Kansas border does not readily produce a clear set of winners or losers. After decades of tirelessly promoting the benefits of railroads and market integration, boosters celebrated the many goals that had been fulfilled. The web of trunk and feeder railroads that stretched across the state line had helped to triple the border counties' antebellum population and had linked settlers with producers and consumers living in distant cities. In particular, these routes reinforced the border counties' place within Kansas City's expanding economic orbit. Local critics, however, resented the higher taxes and corruption that accompanied railroad promotion, as well as the expensive freight rates that they believed discriminated against western farmers. Opponents nonetheless could find some consolation in the series of postwar reforms that reasserted taxpayer controls and fiscal discipline over the course of future development.

The most significant feature of the struggle over railroad expansion was the fact that the divisions it engendered did not follow predictably neat lines of sectional or political identity. The debate instead produced new alliances born of mutual economic and ideological interests. Boosters in Kansas and Missouri agreed that their common economic future impelled them to move past previous differences over slavery and secession. "Our political hope for the future," wrote John Rice of Paola in 1865, "is in the restoration of the old fraternal feelings which ought to grow year by year stronger since the cause of estrangement is removed." Speaking of the former Confederates who lived across the state line, the editor of the *Miami County Republican* continued, "The political fomentations of the past ten years have resulted in nothing but loss to them and to us, and any future attempts in this direction should be resisted as inim-

---

58. *Rich Hill Western Enterprise,* September 10, 1886. For more on the mining boom in Rich Hill, see J. Neely, "Bates County, Missouri," 78–112.

ical to the best interests of the whole people. If either of the old parties has no future before it except that based upon a revival of old issues and of old differences, that party may as well retire from the field."[59] Yet even as railroad promotion fostered the reconciliation of former antagonists, it revealed new fractures within rural society, pitting town boosters against farmers from the surrounding countryside. Although border farmers shared a common distaste for railroad taxes, most producers embraced the commercial opportunities that new routes presented. The next chapter shows how settlers in Kansas and Missouri responded to market integration in a similar fashion, adopting a mixed-farming strategy that would come to be known as Corn Belt agriculture.

59. *Miami County Republican*, July 3, 1875.

SEVEN

THE BORDER OF THE CORN BELT

The month of February 1875 had been unusually difficult for John Dryden. A debilitating illness characterized by "sick headaches" and "lung fever" had swept over the Little Osage valley, claiming the lives of three neighbors and leaving his wife, Louisa, bedridden for weeks. The Indiana native also had experienced disappointment as a teacher at the local schoolhouse. Frustrated with a school board that had failed to pay his wages, he had concluded that resigning in the middle of the term was his only option. "I can't afford to work for nothing," he wrote, "and submissively take all the abuse which the 'dear people' in the plenitude of their generosity see fit to heap on me." Although the family's farm would continue to provide for most of their needs, the operation faced its own unique challenges. Dryden had found that birds were gobbling up the grass seed sown in his newly harrowed pasture; determined to eliminate the foraging offenders, he had killed 285 birds on a single Saturday. Four weeks later, however, the farmer noted in his journal that an even graver threat—an infestation of grasshopper eggs, set to hatch at any moment—jeopardized the coming season's prospects. "I am afraid they will, with the help of the chinch bugs, destroy the crops."[1]

Recent history no doubt fueled Dryden's fear. He had already endured one fearful grasshopper invasion during his twenty years along the

1. Dryden, January 30, February 1, 3, 13, 16, 20, 25, March 1, 1875, *With Plow and Pen*, 83–84.

Missouri-Kansas border. In September 1866, the insects, which entomologists would later identify as *Melanopolus spretus,* or the Rocky Mountain locust, had invaded the Osage plains, where they had proceeded to eat "every green thing in the country and much that was not green, even the clothing and carpets that were put out to be aired." Locusts had reappeared late in the summer of 1874, inflicting tremendous devastation as they swept across the Great Plains. Barely a year after the panic of 1873, the migrating swarm descended on the border in the early fall but seemed to spare farms and orchards from the kind of destruction inflicted farther west. In fact, the locusts had deposited millions of eggs throughout the area before departing from Kansas and Missouri. The following spring, Dryden and other anxious farmers concluded that the best way to prevent the locusts from hatching was to cover the eggs, which had been buried just beneath the ground, and then to burn a layer of straw placed atop them. Such efforts were unfortunately not effective, and by early April a great swarm of locusts enveloped the country that stretched between Topeka, Kansas, and Sedalia, Missouri.[2]

Settlers likened the 1875 grasshopper invasion to a cruel meteorological event. According to old-stock residents of Bates County, locusts covered the entire ground like a blanket of damp snow. The insects that took flight formed a hazy cloud, dimming the afternoon sun and giving the western sky a "strange and wildly weird appearance." Other observers compared the insects that pelted the roofs of their homes to a violent hailstorm. "It literally rained grasshoppers," one Missourian would later exclaim. "It is simply impossible to convey to those who were not here at the time any conception of the innumerable throng of these hungry pests which dropped down upon us." For seven weeks the locusts feasted upon the border counties, stripping trees of their leaves and devouring whatever vegetation they could find among the woods, fields, and tallgrass prairies. "The grasshoppers have eaten everything," noted Dryden on May 25. "There is not a blade of grass between here and the river."[3]

Inhabitants of the denuded borderland devised a number of desperate tactics to cope with the locust problem. Some settlers dug trenches around their fields and tried to crush the insects that fell into them, while others built large fires, hoping that the flames and smoke would drive

---

2. Botkin, "Sixty Years in Kansas," 3, Botkin Papers, KSHS; Dryden, March 24, 1875, *With Plow and Pen,* 84; Bates County Old Settlers Society, *Old Settlers' History,* 200; March, *The History of Missouri,* 2:1056; Joanna L. Stratton, *Pioneer Women: Voices from the Kansas Frontier,* 102.

3. Bates County Old Settlers Society, *Old Settlers' History,* 80, 193; March, *The History of Missouri,* 2:1056; Dryden, May 25, 1875, *With Plow and Pen,* 85.

away the pests. A number of farmers tried to gather the locusts and feed them to their hogs. In time, Charles Riley, the state entomologist of Missouri, openly wondered whether the insects might be fit for human consumption. As each of these approaches failed to bring relief from the plague of locusts, believers looked to divine intervention as a final option. Missouri governor Charles Henry Hardin declared that Thursday, June 3, would be a statewide day of prayer and fasting. When the designated date came to pass, the western part of the state still teemed with locusts, and many citizens faithfully observed the governor's proclamation, gathering in churches and homes to pray for deliverance. Dryden was himself a Christian but quietly doubted the efficacy of such an observance, writing, "I have but little faith in such exercises." Whether through divine mercy or perhaps because there was simply little vegetation left to eat, the locusts finally abandoned the Missouri-Kansas border and headed north in the middle of June. One person jokingly suggested that Hardin "had prayed the grasshoppers clear out of Missouri and up into Iowa."[4] In the locusts' wake, however, there remained a dire crisis.

Unlike the grasshopper invasion nine years earlier, which had occurred in the fall after most of the corn and oats had been harvested, this infestation struck after farmers had planted their crops and thus threatened to ruin the rest of the growing season. With the coming harvest imperiled, Dryden captured the desolation that gripped much of the countryside. "What is to become of us, God only knows. There is bound to be much suffering if some means of relief is not devised, and that too, immediately." Although replanted crops could still be harvested successfully, many households, barely two years removed from the panic of 1873, lacked the money to purchase additional seed or forage for the hungry livestock that might soon face starvation. To reduce the tax burden of afflicted farmers, the Missouri State Board of Equalization reduced the assessment on land and horses by 10 percent.[5] Settlers could receive limited relief from local and state authorities but usually did so with considerable reluctance. Vernon County farmers, for example, grudgingly applied for assistance from township boards, which would provide fifty pounds of "very indifferent seed corn," as one recipient described the handout. Some settlers were as disgusted by the situation as they were by

4. Dryden, June 3, 1875, *With Plow and Pen,* 86; March, *The History of Missouri,* 2:1056. For the grasshoppers' destructive impact in Minnesota, see Annette Atkins, *Harvest of Grief: Grasshopper Plagues and Public Assistance in Minnesota, 1873–1878,* 13–57.

5. Dryden, May 25, 1875, *With Plow and Pen,* 85; *Bates County Record,* June 5, 1875. For examples of other governmental responses to postgrasshopper devastation, see Atkins, *Harvest of Grief,* 58–127.

the individuals who "think the state or general government should provide us with clothes and rations." Like most of his neighbors, Dryden preferred to pay cash for his goods; yet, given the present circumstances, he
agreed to buy additional foodstuffs and seed on credit, even though taking on debt often brought its own peculiar discomfiture. Entomologist
Riley estimated that the locusts inflicted losses of more than two million
dollars on the farms along the border, but by early July, when most families had finished replanting their crops and it had become clear that most
of their livestock would survive, local anxieties slowly began to diminish.[6]

The immediate response to the grasshopper infestation revealed a great
deal about the family farm culture that had taken root along the state line
and elsewhere in rural America. Like other producers, John Dryden took
pride in the self-reliance and independence of his farm, which he maintained with cherished values of hard work, thrift, and piety. Accepting
public charity, even when faced with the threat of starvation, seemed
to undermine those principles. Many individuals were reluctant to
seek direct aid from the government at any level because they had long
believed that the success of their households instead depended on the
vital contributions of the men, women, and children in each family. Experience had taught them that assistance, whenever it became necessary,
could be sought and given without question by cooperative kinfolk
and neighbors. In the darkest moment of the crisis, Dryden fumed, "This
country never was designed for civilized man. It was an outrage on the
part of the Government that the Indians were ever divested of their title to
it. Here . . . the buffalo should have been permitted to remain forever."[7]
Such anguish was certainly common, but he and most other farmers
exhibited an unspoken determination to remain on the land. For settlers in
the Osage valley, rural life quickly resumed its familiar seasonal rhythms,
and the family farm would long remain the central social and economic
institution of the rural Kansas-Missouri border.

Local historians and longtime settlers would in time look back upon
the grasshopper plague as the most serious crisis that confronted farmers
in the post–Civil War era. Most would regard it as an enduring lesson
about perseverance and the triumph of agrarian values. J. T. Botkin, who
had arrived in Kansas as a young boy, celebrated the tenacity of local
farmers by comparing the invasion of locusts with the drought of

6. Dryden, June 14, 15, 19, 1875, *With Plow and Pen*, 86; J. Johnson, *History of Vernon County*, 325; *Bates County Record*, May 15, June 19, 1875. For agrarian anxieties about debt, see Dryden's diary entry ("O, dear! but I am in debt!") from June 29, 1875 (*With Plow and Pen*, 87).

7. Dryden, June 23, 1875, *With Plow and Pen*, 87.

1859–1860 and the border war, which together had driven off thousands of settlers. "The sturdy pioneers," he would later explain, "had not braved the dangers of civil war and faced drouth [sic], famine, and pestilence, to be driven from their homes by one more plague, and so they stayed on and in staying, won."[8] When put within the larger story of postwar agricultural progress, the grasshoppers became a temporary foil that was overcome during the onward march of agrarian capitalism. By withstanding the crises of drought, war, and plague, tenacious producers like Dryden became latter-day embodiments of the free-soil ideology that had triumphed in Kansas Territory decades earlier.

The development of market agriculture was the most significant economic development of the quarter century that followed the war. The origins of commercial agriculture—that is, surplus production dedicated to making a profit, rather than production primarily for use—can be traced to the antebellum period, but ultimately it was the railroads that turned farming into a business. The profound impact that new railroads had on local agriculture was easily measured, as border producers, who were now linked to millions of potential customers, improved an increasing proportion of their farm acreage and raised crops and livestock in ever greater numbers. For all their widespread ambivalence toward high railroad taxes and freight charges, farmers on both sides of the border more often than not were willing to embrace the commercial opportunities that the new railroads created.

In addition, the mixed-farming strategy that came to prevail along the rural Missouri-Kansas border further blurred the differences between settlers living on opposite sides of the state line. Corn Belt agriculture, as historians and geographers have described this farming strategy, emphasized the surplus production of grain crops, especially corn but also oats and wheat, and feeder livestock, such as beef cattle and hogs. Although the Corn Belt eventually stretched across much of the Lower Midwest that had once been dominated by tallgrass prairie (the so-called Prairie Peninsula), it had first taken shape throughout the Ohio valley, the great regional mixing ground where the dispersal of northern and southern immigrants had helped give rise to a self-conscious western identity generations earlier.[9] The border settlers who had emigrated from the Ohio valley brought many of its livestock-feeding practices with them. The

8. Botkin, "Sixty Years in Kansas," 5, Botkin Papers, KSHS.
9. For the historical origins of the Corn Belt, see Power, *Planting Corn Belt Culture;* and Hudson, *Making the Corn Belt.* For analyses of northern and southern regional cultures in the Ohio Valley, see Etcheson, *Emerging Midwest;* and Rugh, *Our Common Country.*

families who settled in the Osage plains, in spite of their different regional backgrounds, responded to market integration in a consistently similar fashion, choosing to produce more corn, hogs, and cattle for faraway consumers rather than maintain the subsistence-level agriculture of the area's first pioneers.

This response, Corn Belt agriculture, was both an economic strategy and an emerging regional culture, a way of working and living in which the entire family—men, women, and children—took part in the survival of the household and success of the farm operation. The state line between Missourians and Kansans had never been a meaningful environmental boundary—neither drought nor locust, after all, had adhered to clean lines of political geography—and in the twenty years after the Civil War, it would become an even less significant marker of distinctive farm cultures. People along the border lived in a common watershed, worked similar soils, and cursed the same fickle weather, but this shared environment was only part of the common cultural landscape that was being created by farmers in Kansas and Missouri. Just as important were the decisions they made: what kinds of crops to grow, how many acres to plant or animals to sell, which kinds of fencing or labor to use, and how much debt to assume. In the decade after the Civil War, these decisions and the actions gave rise to a Corn Belt landscape, a patchwork quilt of farms and ranches that rendered the border between them practically invisible.

Looking at the antebellum origins of commercial agriculture, one sees that partisans on both sides of the slavery debate shared a common disposition toward market production.[10] Missouri slave owners, as Chapter Two showed, were among the most profit-minded settlers along either side of the border. One of the richest individuals living in the three Missouri border counties, slave owner George Douglass, added to the modest fortune he had amassed as a land speculator by becoming a successful trader in hay and livestock. In 1860, when the average farmer in Bates County owned a few dozen animals that were worth around seventeen hundred dollars, Douglass owned several hundred cattle, hogs, and sheep,

10. For a helpful overview of the historiographical debate regarding the market transition, see Allan Kulikoff, "The Transition to Capitalism in Rural America," 120–44. Important works that deal with this issue include Christopher Clark, *The Roots of Rural Capitalism: Western Massachusetts, 1780–1860*; Faragher, *Sugar Creek*; Steven Hahn, *The Roots of Southern Populism: Yeoman Farmers and the Transformation of the Georgia Upcountry, 1850–1890*; Christopher Morris, *Becoming Southern: The Evolution of a Way of Life, Warren County and Vicksburg, Mississippi, 1770–1860*; and Rugh, *Our Common Country*.

as well as dozens of horses and asses, that were together valued at more than eighty thousand dollars. The Virginia native was almost certainly the most successful livestock dealer on the border, but he was hardly the only Missouri pioneer to profit from selling cattle and draft animals to westering migrants. Frank Chilton, a Cass County slave owner, was one of several settlers who sold cattle to California-bound immigrants "to good advantage."[11]

In addition to surplus livestock production, free-soil migrants in territorial Kansas produced cheese and butter on a commercial scale that was theretofore unknown in the adjacent counties of western Missouri. The most successful antebellum dairy in southeastern Kansas belonged to John and Sarah Everett, Miami County abolitionists who had come west to help thwart the expansion of slavery. The Everetts quickly recognized the economic opportunity that lay before enterprising immigrants such as themselves. After only a few months in the territory, John wrote to his father in New York that the family's dairy prospects seemed nearly unlimited. Two more years in Kansas only strengthened his faith, and in early 1857 he asserted, "Any one who could come out with means enough to go right to making cheese with 20 to 40 cows could almost make their fortune in one season. . . . The pasture is unlimited and most excellent. Milch cows and all stock get as fat as butter in the summer." As the turmoil of Bleeding Kansas roiled around them, the Everetts managed to achieve a steady cash income from the sale of milk, butter, and cheese. Their success depended in large part on the assistance of distant relatives, who provided the couple with a necessary supply of rennets, the lined membranes taken from the stomachs of young calves that were used to curdle milk. The Everetts believed that it made good economic sense to purchase rennets from family and friends who lived hundreds of miles away rather than sacrifice their own calves. "The reason we dont [sic] kill calves," they explained, "is because all it costs to keep one here is the fodder in the winter which is a mere trifle, and when they are three or four years old they are worth from forty to a hundred dollars a yoke. We can better pay $1.00 for every rennet we use and the postage besides than kill the calves."[12]

11. Census-Pop and Census-Ag, Missouri, Bates County, 1860; O. Williams, *Cass and Bates Counties*, 441.

12. Everett and Everett, "Letters of John and Sarah Everett," 159, 350 (John Everett to Robert Everett, January 1, 1857; John and Sarah Everett to Jennie, September 1, 1859). For dairy production in New York during this time period, see Nancy Grey Osterud, *Bonds of Community: The Lives of Farm Women in Nineteenth-Century New York*.

Although the family's dairy benefited from the lack of competition from other farmers, John believed that many westerners failed to appreciate the economic potential of the abundant prairie grasses. "Thousands of tons of hay (uncut) are burnt right under our nose," he noted. "All that is wanting to make this valuable is cows to eat it and turn it into milk." Everett's mindful assessment revealed more about his own commercial ambitions than the supposedly desultory grazing practices of farmers in the surrounding countryside. Few of these settlers had migrated from areas where dairy expertise was widespread. Farmers in western Missouri and eastern Kansas had grazed their cattle on the open prairies ever since the area's earliest settlements, but the cultivation of hay and other domestic grasses had steadily become more common in the years leading up to the Civil War. In 1850, more than a quarter of Missouri producers harvested hay on their farms, averaging at least twelve tons apiece during the droughty summer and fall of 1859.[13]

Primary evidence indicates that even amid the border troubles, settlers living on both sides of the state line participated in an active market exchange. Achieving a basic measure of self-sufficiency was a foremost goal for even the most commercially oriented frontier households. In the winter of 1860, Sarah Everett wrote with great satisfaction to her eastern relatives, "We are growing almost everything we need for the table." Yet most households were also able to augment their subsistence with a modest surplus, which was usually sold locally. Such exchanges were conducted on a barter or cash basis. Buyers typically paid cash for the cheese, eggs, and butter sold by the Everetts. On at least one occasion, however, when the family traded butter to satisfy store debts, such readily salable commodities served as the medium of exchange. John Dryden's diary reveals what a wide variety of surplus items—bacon, butter, apples, cider, honey, eggs, soap, cucumbers, corn, wheat, hogs, and steers—were traded locally.[14]

The success of the Everetts' dairying operation depended on the joint contributions of husband and wife, yet in many other households female settlers played an especially prominent role in the production, processing, and sale of goods, such as cheese, butter, eggs, and poultry, which were at the heart of the local market economy. An account of a Missouri

13. Everett and Everett, "Letters of John and Sarah Everett," 292 (John Everett to Robert Everett, March 8, 1858); Bates County Old Settlers Society, *Old Settlers' History*, 48–49; Census-Ag, Missouri, Bates, Cass, and Vernon Counties, 1850, 1860.

14. Everett and Everett, "Letters of John and Sarah Everett," 145 (Sarah Everett to Cynthia, July 22, 1856); Dryden, Memoranda for 1863, 1865, and 1867, Dryden Papers, VCHS.

farmwife's "big work," which her husband had proudly related to a local newspaper, suggested that butter making was the special domain of rural women. The paper noted that in addition to the butter churned for her own family's consumption, Mrs. W. O. Smith had produced and sold more than seven hundred pounds of butter to a local grocer in the past year. "The entire work of milking, churning, etc., was performed by Mrs. Smith with the exception of a little assistance rendered by Mr. Smith. It might be well to add," the paper continued, marveling at her domestic talents, "that [she] also did all of her own household work—without assistance—in addition to this work."[15]

Butter was a staple product in most frontier farm households, regardless of regional background. Antebellum production figures from western Missouri reveal that families from the Lower Midwest and the Upper South were just as likely to make their own butter. Settlers from these two regions usually produced roughly equivalent quantities of butter each year, making between 80 and 100 pounds in 1850. Border households made even more butter in subsequent decades. In 1870, when agricultural census data became available for both states, Kansas households were more likely to produce butter, and to do so in greater quantities, than their Missouri counterparts. It is unclear whether such differences reflected a significant divergence in regional farm ways or disparate impacts from the border war. Within each state, settlers from the Upper South were somewhat more likely to make butter than their neighbors who were born north of the Ohio River. A decade later, however, a consistent regional pattern was no longer discernible with respect to the prevalence of butter production, although Kansas farms continued to produce butter in significantly higher quantities. Settlers in Bourbon County, for example, produced an average of 250 pounds in 1880, or more than twice as much as the Vernon County households across the state line.[16]

There were no clear regional differences between the domestic production of farm women in Missouri and Kansas counties. Before the Civil War, cheese making seemed to have been more common in the households of transplanted northerners, such as the Everetts, who were often struck by the absence of specialized dairying in their new country. A daughter of former Alabama slaveholders, Addie Aldridge Gordon was born and raised along the Kansas border, and looking back upon her

15. *Nevada Daily Mail*, February 9, 1885; Osterud, *Bonds of Community*, 12, 142–60.

16. Census-Ag, Missouri, Bates, Cass, and Vernon Counties, 1850–1880; author's sample, U.S. Census Bureau, Manuscript Census, Kansas, Bourbon, Linn, and Miami Counties, Schedule II (Agriculture), 1870, 1880, hereinafter cited as Census-Ag.

youth, she recalled the foods that were prepared within her predominantly southern community. "No one in our neighborhood knew how to make cured cheese," she remembered. After the Civil War, however, the incidence of cheese making seemed to decline in households of all regional backgrounds and became relatively uncommon among the northern and southern immigrants in both states, a change that likely resulted from an increase in cheese marketing and specialization elsewhere. In 1870, none of the households in the sample of Missouri farms made any cheese, and the proportion among Kansas farms was only 1 percent to 2 percent. The contrasts between domestic production in each state were even less conclusive when one considers egg-production data. In 1880, when such data first became available, approximately 40 percent of households produced eggs in both states; although the incidence of egg production was slightly higher in Kansas, Missouri farms tended to produce slightly more eggs that year.[17]

Census manuscripts and government reports confirm that butter and eggs were produced for both home consumption and local exchange. According to the 1873 report of the Kansas State Board of Agriculture, most of the butter produced in the counties along the Missouri border was consumed within the home, as the rate of home consumption ranged from 53 percent to 78 percent in every township. The 1873 report suggests that an awareness of local prices informed but did not determine one's decision to consume or sell butter. In Linn County's Liberty Township, for example, farmers sold butter for the low average price of 12 cents per pound; perhaps not surprisingly, the proportion of family consumption in this township (78 percent) was remarkably high. In Wea Township of Miami County, on the other hand, butter brought 15.5 cents per pound—the highest price in two counties—but the rate of family consumption (71 percent) was higher there than all but one of the county's townships.[18] The somewhat unpredictable relationship between local prices and home consumption may be attributed to the idiosyncratic choices of individual households; an ability to produce more or expand, due to the number of cows, kind of equipment, and labor at a household's disposal; and the interplay of structural factors such as uneven access to markets and transportation inequalities.

17. Gordon, folder 4 ("Food: Preparation and Types"), Gordon Papers, Collection KC068, Western Historical Manuscripts Collection, Kansas City; Census-Ag, Kansas, Bourbon, Linn, and Miami Counties, 1870, 1880; Census-Ag, Missouri, Bates, Cass, and Vernon Counties, 1870, 1880.

18. Kansas State Board of Agriculture, *Records of the Kansas State Board of Agriculture: Abstracts of Statistical Rolls, 1873*, vol. 3 (A47A24 26-14-05-02).

Addie Gordon would later recall that domestic products typically sold for low prices, but she maintained that local producers nonetheless took satisfaction from participating in commercial exchanges. "Food was cheap but we were on the selling end," she noted. "People prided themselves on selling freshly laid eggs and freshly churned butter. The latter was ten cents a pound if molded with a pretty design (acorn, sheaf of wheat, etc.) on top, only eight cents if in a plain pat." Forty miles to the south, John and Louisa Dryden received between 12 and 13 cents for every dozen eggs they sold. In difficult times, such as the grasshopper invasion of 1875, the modest income garnered from domestic products was invaluable for border households. One young woman explained that after cinch bugs ravaged the corn crop for many Kansas farms, "Dairying and poultry saved the day. Butter and eggs, what would people have done without them?"[19]

The expansion of the nation's railroad network and increased investment in agricultural implements facilitated unprecedented levels of crop and livestock production among nineteenth-century farmers.[20] Table 15 (Average Annual Investment in Implements, 1850–1880) shows that the average investment in farm implements among western Missouri households doubled during the 1850s. Most of this money was spent on implements such as steel plows, reapers, drills, mowers, and threshers used in the fields, where most men's labors were traditionally concentrated. Technological advances had a less profound impact on the dairy production of rural women. Like Mrs. Smith of Vernon County, who relied on five common cows and an old-fashioned churn, most female settlers continued to produce butter in the same laborious fashion as had their mothers and grandmothers. Recalling her personal distaste for the time-consuming duties that awaited girls of a certain age, Gordon would later exclaim, "But oh! the misery of the churning!"[21]

New railroads also had an undeniable impact by linking rural producers with urban consumers of meat and grain. At the same time, railroad expansion sparked a noticeable decline in the incidence of home manufactures by making newly available manufactured goods an attractive

19. Gordon Papers, folder 6 ("Farmers: Our Woods"), Western Historical Manuscripts Collection, Kansas City; Dryden, May 8, 1868, *With Plow and Pen*, 43; Stratton, *Pioneer Women*, 60.

20. Census-Ag, Missouri, Bates, Cass, and Vernon Counties, 1850–1880. Two prominent examples of the instrumentalist interpretation are Cronon, *Nature's Metropolis*; and Bogue, *From Prairie to Corn Belt*.

21. Glenda Riley, *The Female Frontier: A Comparative View of Women on the Prairie and the Plains*, 59; *Nevada Daily Mail*, February 9, 1885; Gordon Papers, folder 1 ("Entry into Missouri"), Western Historical Manuscripts Collection, Kansas City.

and realistic alternative to homespun cloth and other locally produced goods. More than half of antebellum Missouri households had produced household manufactures, a trend that may have been influenced by the presence of slave women. By 1870, fewer than one-quarter of the farm families along the border continued to do so. Home manufactures were even less common across the Kansas border, where only one in ten households produced such goods. Eager to stimulate domestic industry within area communities, one Kansas editor condemned the "shallowness" of this trend, writing, "A mania for imported goods from the East, possesses the people; they seem to wholly ignore home manufactures, if equally as good, if their purse is only long enough to reach Eastern markets. . . . Why not encourage home industry with your patronage, instead of 'going East' with your money?" The railroads' impact on butter production was more ambiguous, for although new routes brought more consumers and producers to the area, the Drydens and most other families still transported their surplus goods by wagon, usually going only as far as just across the county line.[22]

The railroads' most significant impact on the economy of the rural border involved the emergence of Corn Belt agriculture, a practice of diversified commercial farming that was devoted primarily to the production of corn, beef cattle, and hogs. By the last quarter of the nineteenth century, this farming strategy prevailed across much of the former Prairie Peninsula, a roughly triangular physiographic region that stretched from eastern Kansas through Ohio and as far north as Minnesota. This broad area's rich prairie soils and humid continental climate, which provided both sufficient precipitation and an ample growing season, were well suited to the production of small-grain crops and forage grasses. The commercial production of both corn and livestock also represented an extension of the corn-and-hog frontier strategy that had spread from the Upper South and Ohio valley throughout the rest of the developing West.[23] As such, the emergence of market agriculture entailed a shift in scale and emphasis, rather than simply a change in the kind of diversified farming that settlers in this region adopted.

Geographer John C. Hudson provides perhaps the most thorough study of the Corn Belt as a regional cultural type. Hudson uses a pair of quantitative guidelines to map the extent of Corn Belt agriculture, relying

22. *Miami County Republican,* February 16, 1867. For examples of the Drydens' trips to Nevada, Rich Hill, and Fort Scott, see August 6, 31, 1875, March 24, 1881, *With Plow and Pen,* 88, 140.
23. Hudson, *Making the Corn Belt,* 3–7, traces the origins of intensive Corn Belt agriculture to five "islands" in Ohio, Kentucky, and Tennessee.

on a values of 7.5 bushels of corn per acre of improved farmland and 18.5 bushels of corn per head of livestock. Noting both the predominately southern antebellum population of western Missouri and the significant postwar immigration from the corn-producing states of Illinois and Indiana, he contends that the Osage plains had joined the Corn Belt by the 1850s. An analysis of agricultural census data, however, indicates that most farmers in the counties along the Missouri-Kansas border did not meet both definitions of Corn Belt agriculture until 1880, after railroads had linked the area with the national market economy. Fewer than one in six Missouri border farms had satisfied these thresholds in 1850. In contrast to the specialization of postwar agriculture, the corn and hogs that antebellum farmers raised were part of a general mix of crops and stock. By 1860, however, per capita corn production had nearly quadrupled in Bates and Cass Counties, rising from 330 to 1,198 bushels per farm, and almost half of the border counties' farms now met Hudson's Corn Belt criteria. Over the next ten years, the proportion of Corn Belt farms actually declined, as farmers on both sides of the state line, especially in Missouri, struggled to recover from wartime devastation. The 1870 agricultural census indicates that the average corn harvest in all six counties had dropped well below antebellum levels, sinking to a low of 369 bushels in Vernon County. Only one-third of the farmers in either state could be described as Corn Belt producers.[24]

By 1880, all six border counties had clearly joined the Corn Belt. The production of maize increased on both sides of the border; Kansas farmers harvested an average of 1,175 bushels that year, while their counterparts in Missouri brought in more than 1,400 bushels. The majority of farms in each county met both statistical thresholds. As usual, a larger proportion of farmers fulfilled the requirement based on the corn–improved acreage ratio, though an increased number also qualified as livestock-feeding operations. Perhaps the most striking feature of the Corn Belt statistics was the remarkable similarity of the figures from each state. Although the percentages uncovered for each county did vary somewhat, the averages for the three border counties in each state were nearly identical.[25]

Several factors helped to facilitate this convergence of regional farm cultures. First, the extensive postwar immigration of settlers from the Old Northwest, where commercial corn and livestock production had taken

24. Hudson, *Making the Corn Belt,* 7, 141; Census-Ag, Kansas, Bourbon, Linn, and Miami Counties, 1860, 1870; Census-Ag, Missouri, Bates, Cass, and Vernon Counties, 1850–1870.
25. Census-Ag, Kansas, Bourbon, Linn, and Miami Counties, 1880; Census-Ag, Missouri, Bates, Cass, and Vernon Counties, 1880.

hold a generation earlier, served to accelerate the spread of intensive farming. Railroad expansion also played a critical part by integrating the farms across the borderland into a larger regional market economy. In the early nineteenth century, transporting corn over long distances was both expensive and cumbersome, and most of the corn that was not consumed locally was either exported as distilled whiskey or fed to hogs that would later be driven to market.[26] Rail transportation, on the other hand, not only reduced the long-distance shipping costs for corn and other agricultural goods but also linked settlers with a new host of buyers and thus gave farmers another means of disposing of their harvest. Most of the corn, cattle, and hogs that farmers shipped from the rural border arrived in Kansas City, the nearest urban center and a place whose own spectacular growth outstripped even the wildest booster dreams. From 1860 to 1880 the city experienced a tenfold explosion in population and quickly emerged as both a major grain and livestock trading center and an important railroad hub for the central plains and lower Missouri valley. Although railroads transported many farm commodities to Chicago and other eastern markets, the growth of the rural economy that was taking root along the state line was tied most directly and symbiotically to the bustling City of Kansas.[27]

Private manuscripts and government documents illuminate the close economic relationship that border farmers maintained with Kansas City purchasers. Elias Falor was a wealthy grain farmer who had migrated to the western border from Hopewell, Illinois, not long after the war, and he eventually established farms near the towns of Rich Hill, Sprague, Metz, and Little Osage. Farm receipts show that he shipped his hay and winter wheat to Kansas City via the Gulf railroad, but that same route occasionally conveyed the wheat to an elevator in Hillsboro, Kansas. The cattle, hogs, and hay raised on the farm of Falor's son, Charles, were likewise sent to Kansas City, although many of the animals were later transported to Chicago for processing. An 1891 government report on the railroad shipments that left the border counties details the kinds of agricultural commodities that were shipped to Kansas City. Cattle, hogs, and corn were the most commonly exported items, but flax, hay, oats, and wheat

---

26. Addie Aldridge Gordon's recollections reveal that the members of one antebellum southern family preferred to purchase their whiskey, paying twelve to thirteen cents a gallon at the river port of Lexington, rather than make it themselves (Gordon Papers, folder 1, Western Historical Manuscripts Collection, Kansas City).

27. Glaab, *Kansas City and the Railroads*, 169. For an excellent analysis of the symbiotic relationship between rural producers and urban consumers, see Cronon, *Nature's Metropolis*.

were also shipped in significant quantities. State reports did not usually account for some of the less common items exported by local settlers. In January 1880, for example, mounting debts forced John Dryden to harvest many of the large walnut trees growing on his farm and ship the wood overseas to buyers in England.[28]

Although Dryden was certainly not alone in turning to his woods for a quick profit—more than one-third of border farmers harvested forest products in 1880—corn remained the privileged cornerstone of the diversified farm economy.[29] Even before the initial settlement of westering Americans, corn had been a fixture in the successive rotation of crops that Osage women maintained to preserve soil fertility. The intuition of indigenous gardeners had not been lost on farmers who succeeded them in the Osage valley. "I am satisfied that farmers here will have to change their mode of farming or quit farming all together," wrote Dryden. "We will have to set up a system of rotation. Nature itself has taught me the fallacy of growing the same crop year after year on the same land." Like most farmers in the area, he adhered to a three-crop rotation of corn, wheat, and oats. Wheat cultivation, however, was a relatively new phenomenon among settlers in western Missouri, except for the few individuals, like Dryden, who had been planting it since before the Civil War. In 1860, fewer than one in every seven farmers living in Bates and Vernon Counties had reported harvesting any wheat. After the war, planting wheat became more common, thanks in large part to the considerable influx of northern immigrants. In 1870, wheat cultivation was more common in Kansas, where 58 percent of border farmers grew the crop, than in Missouri, where the proportion had increased to 46 percent. In 1880, however, the proportion of farmers raising wheat was higher in Missouri (48 percent) than in Kansas (35 percent).[30]

28. Falor, Crabb, and McGennis Families Collection, Collection 852kc, Western Historical Manuscripts Collection, Kansas City; Missouri Bureau of Labor Statistics, *Annual Report of the Bureau of Labor Statistics of Missouri for 1891*, 78; Dryden, January 7, 1880, *With Plow and Pen*, 129. A subsequent diary entry (March 30, 1880, 130) finds Dryden confessing his embarrassment at borrowing money in order to escape existing debts.

29. In Missouri border counties, 44 percent of farmers harvested forest products; in Kansas, 30 percent did so. Although census enumerators counted harvested timber as "forest products," local settlers almost never used the term *forest*, choosing instead to describe "the woods" behind their houses. See Dryden, *With Plow and Pen*, 85, 152; and Gordon Papers, folder 6 ("Farmers: 'Our Woods'"), Western Historical Manuscripts Collection, Kansas City.

30. Dryden, August 10, 1868, *With Plow and Pen*, 49; Census-Ag, Kansas, Bourbon, Linn, and Miami Counties, 1870, 1880; Census-Ag, Missouri, Bates, Cass, and Vernon Counties, 1860–1880. For contrasting northern and southern attitudes toward wheat cultivation, see Power, *Planting Corn Belt Culture*, 112.

For most border farmers, winter wheat—Kansas State Board of Agriculture's reports indicate that almost all farmers near the Missouri border grew winter but not spring wheat—remained a secondary or tertiary crop behind corn and oats. Table 16 (Acreage Ratios for Major Grain Crops, Kansas Farms, 1872–1896) illustrates the changing ratio of crop acreages that Kansas farmers dedicated to the major grain crops of corn, oats, and wheat from 1872 to 1896. These figures show that both the amount and the proportion of land that Kansas farmers used for winter wheat actually declined in all three border counties. The extent to which the decline in wheat cultivation resulted from environmental factors, such as unfavorable weather, or changing preferences among border farmers—or a combination of the two—remains unclear. During this same period, the acreage put into oats increased in each county, but the ratio of oats acreage declined slightly, as farmers in every county devoted a greater proportion of their land to corn cultivation. This growing emphasis on corn production was evident in both the amount and the proportion of acreage on which the crop was planted.

In the agricultural census of 1880, the first year when enumerators listed the amount of acres planted to each major crop, one finds a common emphasis on corn production on both sides of the state line. Table 17 (Proportion of Improved Land in Major Grain Crops, 1880) further demonstrates that corn was clearly the dominant grain crop in both western Missouri and eastern Kansas. Wheat remained a less important crop on both sides of the border. A few subtle differences between the farming strategies in each state can be apprehended from the figures in table 17. First, Missourians put slightly more of their improved acreage into major grain crops; Kansans presumably turned more of their land into improved pasture. In addition, the cultivation of oats was somewhat more prominent on the eastern side of the border. Overall, however, the obvious similarities were more important than the minor differences in farming strategies.

Specific examples, one from Missouri and another from Kansas, help to delineate the rise of Corn Belt agriculture by illustrating changing crop preferences and by shedding light on the process of intensification. Three successive enumerations revealed steady improvements on the Milo, Missouri, farm of Andrew J. Longacre, an early member of the local agricultural and mechanical society. In 1860, the Tennessee native had improved barely one-third of his 120 acres. Over the next decade, his improved acreage had nearly doubled, increasing the farm's value from $720 to $1,800, and in another ten years, the farm had grown to 195 acres, two-thirds of which had been improved, putting its value at $2,500. As a result of the improvements that Longacre made during the 1870s, his annual corn harvest increased from 300 to 650 bushels, and his oats production jumped from zero to 260 bushels. His livestock herd, usually consisting of about a dozen hogs and cattle, remained relatively small in all three decades.[31]

The farm operated by George and Barbara Karliskind in Marmaton, Kansas, offered an instructive example of intensive, diversified agriculture. The Karliskinds had improved nearly all of the land on their 160-acre farm in both 1870 and 1880. Although the amount of improved acreage did not change during the 1870s, the allocation of the family's farmland apparently underwent significant changes. Over the course of the decade, their annual corn harvest more than doubled, while their output of oats and wheat declined sharply. The Karliskinds also became more heavily involved in livestock production. In 1870, the New York immigrants had kept only three hogs and a small team of work animals, but ten years later, they owned ten dairy cows (which helped to quadruple their butter production), twice as many beef cattle, and a slightly larger drove of hogs. To feed this growing herd of stock, the family dedicated a larger amount of land to improved pasture, and by 1880 its annual hay harvest grew to forty tons. Many of these changes were made possible by a threefold increase in the family's investment in farm implements. In neither decade did the family's corn production match Hudson's first threshold of Corn Belt agriculture (in 1880, they came closest with a ratio of 6.3), yet even more than Longacre, the Karliskinds' crop choices clearly exemplify the farming strategy that prevailed across the countryside from Kansas City to Chicago.[32]

Farmers on the Osage plains occupied a unique geographical position, situated at the meeting ground of two different approaches to raising cattle. To the south and west, Texas cattle drovers fed longhorns on the open range before eventually driving them northward to Sedalia, which had been established as a station on the Missouri Pacific Railroad in 1857. Farmers to the north and east, however, adopted another system of ranching that was distinguished by greater attention to the welfare and quality of their stock. Several elements distinguished midwestern ranchers from their Texas and California counterparts. Midwesterners were more likely to employ selective breeding to improve the bloodlines of their herds, provide winter feed for their cattle, use some of their cows for milk and butter, and devote considerable attention to raising crops and

31. Census-Ag, Missouri, Bates and Vernon Counties, 1860–1880.
32. Census-Ag, Kansas, Bourbon County, 1870–1880.

other animals, such as hogs or sheep. Midwestern ranching, according to one geographer, thus could be more accurately described as "stock farming" or "mixed farming."[33]

The most intense controversy on the Osage plains involved the clash of local farmers with the Texas cattlemen who drove their livestock across the region's tallgrass prairies. By the early 1850s, Missouri farmers had begun to suspect that many of their own cattle had become infected with the Spanish, or Texas, fever brought into the area by migrating longhorns. Ranchers' fears seemed justified by the inordinate concentration of shorthorn deaths in areas near the major Texas cattle trails. As farmers' losses continued to mount, many citizens petitioned the Missouri legislature for relief. A law passed in 1855 imposed heavy fines for individuals who drove infected cattle into the state, but insufficient knowledge about the Texas fever made this measure difficult to enforce. Missouri farmers employed more direct actions in the summer of 1858, when farmers west of Clinton blocked the cattle crossing the South Grand River and forced Texas drovers to turn back. In February 1859, territorial legislators passed a law prohibiting the droving of infected livestock through Kansas, but this measure suffered widespread violations. Two years later, the Missouri legislature devised a stronger livestock law that authorized the removal of diseased cattle by local authorities.[34]

The Civil War temporarily halted cattle drives across the border, but old tensions resurfaced soon after the conflict ended. In early 1866, Texas veterans began driving 260,000 cattle northward toward the Pacific railroad at Sedalia. According to a Kansas statute passed that year, the state's borders were now fully opened to Texas cattle. Alarmed settlers in Missouri, however, blocked their passage across the state line. Many of the drovers who attempted to push through the state's southwestern counties were beaten or had their livestock stampeded.[35] Old-stock settlers would later recall that Texas cattlemen offered to pay John Atkinson, the sheriff of Bates County, ten thousand dollars if he would allow their livestock to pass; when Atkinson refused the bribe, the drovers allegedly withdrew their cattle and sought a rail connection farther south. The Texas cattlemen's reception in eastern Kansas, where the disease began to spread again quickly, was no more hospitable than it had been in western Missouri. Linn County had been among the first areas to report new

33. Hudson, *Making the Corn Belt*, 141; Jordan, *Cattle-Ranching Frontiers*, 269.
34. Cecil Kirk Hutson, "Texas Fever in Kansas, 1866–1930," 74–75; March, *The History of Missouri*, 2:1053.
35. Hutson, "Texas Fever in Kansas," 75–76; March, *The History of Missouri*, 2:1054–55; Hudson, *Making the Corn Belt*, 141.

outbreaks; to the south, almost half the cows in Bourbon County died when the Texans came through on their annual drive. Kansas vigilantes apprehended and killed at least two herds of southern cattle that were suspected of carrying Texas fever.[36] Although farmers living on opposite sides of the border may have sharply disagreed about secession or the expansion of slavery, many were of like minds when it came to protecting their livestock from the encroachment and infection of outsiders.

Not all Kansans favored the elimination of Texas cattle from their state, as many citizens near Abilene and other trailheads stood to profit from their dealings with cattle drovers. Kansas lawmakers tried to appease the critics and defenders of Texas cattlemen with an 1867 law that prohibited droving within five miles of an individual's ranch without first receiving that person's permission. This compromise measure, as its detractors pointed out, still allowed diseased cattle to be shipped through the state via railroad. Throughout the summer of 1868, farmers in Kansas and Missouri again took it upon themselves to address an issue that their elected officials could (or would) not solve. One Kansan described the violent strategy, a so-called Winchester quarantine, preferred by many border farmers. When Texas cattle approached, he explained, a local rancher "coolly loads his gun, and joins his neighbors, and they intend no scare either. They mean to kill, and do kill, and will keep killing until the drove takes the back track; and the drovers must be careful not to get between their cattle and the citizens either, unless they are bulletproof."[37]

Missourians strengthened their legal restrictions against Texas cattle in 1869. Empirical evidence indicated that the Texas fever usually occurred in areas where Texas cattle had been driven during warm weather. As a result, the legislature passed a law that prohibited Texas cattle from entering the state between March and December. Lawmakers further stipulated that animals brought into Missouri by railroad or steamboat could not be unloaded en route and that transportation companies could be held responsible for any damages that Texas fever might inflict near their line of travel. In addition to these regulations, expansion westward into the Great Plains ameliorated the threat that Texas fever posed to farmers along the Missouri-Kansas border. By the late 1860s, many Texas drovers were already taking their cattle farther west, either to Abilene and other new railheads or to grasslands in Colorado, Nebraska, and Wyoming.

36. Bates County Old Settlers Society, *Old Settlers' History*, 180–82; Hutson, "Texas Fever in Kansas," 76–77; Botkin, "Sixty Years in Kansas," 3, Botkin Papers, KSHS; McFadin, "Kansas in Early Times," box 55, McFadin Papers, KSHS.
37. Hutson, "Texas Fever in Kansas," 77.

Occasional bouts of Texas fever continued through the 1880s, but with the eventual discovery that ticks were responsible for transmitting the disease, farmers could begin to immunize their livestock with success.[38]

The sight of Texas cattle in years to come would evoke bitter memories for farmers whose herds had been affected by Texas fever. "A drove of Texas cattle passed through today," noted John Dryden. "Oh, but I hate them come, and their owners a great deal." Some—but certainly not all—local ranchers also believed that nearly wild Texas longhorns imperiled efforts to improve the bloodlines of their own stock. In addition to the dreaded fever, Texas cattle brought with them a reputation for aggressive behavior and poorer-quality beef, and they thus fetched comparatively low prices at market. The improvement of livestock bloodlines became increasingly popular after the war among Corn Belt farmers eager to earn a premium for higher-quality beef. Farmers realized such improvements primarily through the selective introduction of purebred shorthorn (Durham) cattle. For cattle, the improvement of a herd's bloodline was a relatively slow process, given the nine-month gestation for cows, which usually delivered only one live birth. With hogs, on the other hand, expansion could be achieved at a much quicker pace, as sows had a shorter gestation and delivered many live births within a single litter.[39]

The agricultural schedules of the federal census manuscripts from 1850 to 1880 do not enumerate specific breed types, but other primary sources indicate that the improvement of cattle herds did indeed proceed rather slowly. In 1873, fewer than 2 percent of the cattle in Linn and Miami counties were purebred shorthorns. (By contrast, nearly 22 percent of all hogs were one of several purebred varieties.) In addition, there were nearly ten times as many "southern" (or longhorn) cattle in both counties. The state board of agriculture described the vast majority of animals in each county as "native grades and crosses." A survey of farmer biographies in the local histories of Missouri counties also suggests that relatively few families dealt exclusively with purebred animals. Only a handful of the individuals who described themselves as farmers, ranchers, or stock traders made any mention of the specific breeds they handled. One exception was Ashby Hamilton, a well-educated farmer from Illinois who had traded cattle in Texas before migrating to Summit Township in eastern Bates

38. March, *The History of Missouri*, 2:1055; Hutson, "Texas Fever in Kansas," 80. The memoir of Joseph G. McCoy, *Historic Sketches of the Cattle Trade of the West and Southwest*, illustrates how he and other cattle barons utilized these railheads for great profit and helped to accelerate Kansas City's development as a major western livestock center.

39. Dryden, April 28, 1869, *With Plow and Pen*, 62; Bogue, *From Prairie to Corn Belt*, 89, 104; Hudson, *Making the Corn Belt*, 141–42.

County—one of the last stretches of open prairie to be settled—where he bred both shorthorn and Galloway cattle.[40]

Even after the major Texas cattle trails had moved farther west, farmers along the Missouri-Kansas border remained divided over their rights and responsibilities with respect to the open range that still prevailed throughout much of the Osage plains. Since the region's initial settlement, most farmers on both sides of the border had used the tallgrass prairies as a common pasture. Expressing the local faith in the nutritional value of prairie grasses, one settler wrote, "It is safe to say that . . . native herbage will put more flesh on cattle from the beginning of April to early autumn than any of the domestic grasses."[41] Continued immigration, however, had left fewer stretches of prairie unsettled, but even with the open range's shrinking size, most livestock owners were reluctant to abandon the traditional grazing strategy. Yet as the number of farms and livestock grew, so too did the likelihood that settlers' crops would be damaged or eaten by foraging animals. What's more, the increased grazing pressure caused by the ever growing numbers of cattle, horses, and sheep threatened to erode the quality of native grasses that so many ranchers preferred. By the early 1870s, a growing chorus of disenchanted farmers began to advocate a herd law that would require stock owners to restrain their wandering animals within a fenced pasture.

The early supporters of a herd law, which some observers referred to as a stock law or a fence law, may not have envisioned a complete end to public grazing on the grasslands of the Osage valley, but many clearly endorsed a reversal in the customary obligations of frontier agriculture. The traditional burden of putting up fences fell upon farmers who wished to protect their gardens and fields from wandering livestock. Herd-law proponents wished to shift this burden by forcing stock owners to assume the responsibility and expense of confining their cattle, hogs, and sheep. A great many farmers, however, strongly opposed such a law as a threat to both their property rights and their very way of life. The enclosure issue divided rural citizens along lines of class and residence, pitting small ranchers who wished to preserve customary grazing

40. Kansas State Board of Agriculture, *Abstracts of Statistical Rolls*, 1873, vol. 3. The Hamilton biography was found in O. Williams, *Cass and Bates Counties*, 1264–65. Conclusions about the topography and delayed settlement of Summit Township come from Schroeder, *Presettlement Prairie of Missouri*, 32; and James R. Shortridge, "The Expansion of the Settlement Frontier in Missouri," 88.

41. O. Williams, *Cass and Bates Counties*, 1005. The letters of John Everett provide anecdotal evidence of similar grazing customs in territorial Kansas. See Everett and Everett, "Letters of John and Sarah Everett," 25 (John Everett to Robert Everett, January 25, 1856).

rights against commerce-minded planters and wealthy town interests hoping to modernize rural property rights.[42]

Farmers who wished to erect fences for their fields or livestock could choose from several options. The majority of early settlers relied on Osage orange trees, a tough, disease- and insect-resistant species whose dense, thorny branches could be "plashed," or pruned, into hedge rows. Hedge fences were cheap, effective fences but were rather slow to establish. Other alternatives, such as fences made of sawed lumber, split rails, or stone, could be assembled in less time but with greater expense. Fencerows built with native limestone were durable but demanded considerable physical effort. The twisted, twin-strand variety of barbed-wire fencing developed by J. F. Glidden in 1873 seemed to offer myriad advantages that would someday render each of these other options almost obsolete. Constructed with relative ease, barbed-wire fences did not exhaust soil or shade crops from the sun, and although they could enclose vast acreages, they took up virtually no space. Most important, this new technology was durable and inexpensive, costing less than ten dollars for one hundred pounds.[43]

In spite of barbed wire's revolutionary potential, however, settlers in eastern Kansas were slow to adopt wire fences, as table 18 (Fencing Preferences of Kansas Settlers, 1883) illustrates. A full decade after Glidden had first sold his innovation, fewer than one-fourth of the farmers along the Missouri border were using barbed wire. The greatest number of settlers still depended on the hedge fences already planted. Split-rail fences were also fairly popular, but board and stone fences, given the high cost and uneven availability of building materials, appeared on only a small fraction of farms. The popularity of barbed wire may have been low because a large number of producers continued to rely on an even cheaper alternative—that of building no fences at all. This, too, was an imperfect alternative as well. Unfenced fields were vulnerable to foraging livestock, and maintaining a herd of wandering strays (or "cow hunting," as John Dryden called it) demanded considerable time and energy.

Farmers on both sides of the state line claimed that prairie grasses such as bluestem were more nutritious than domesticated species of hay. An 1873 survey of ranching strategies found that more than 95 percent of the pastureland in Bourbon, Linn, and Miami Counties was classified as prairie. In eleven of the counties' townships, none of the acreage had

---

42. Bogue, *From Prairie to Corn Belt*, 80–81; Hahn, *Roots of Southern Populism*, 239–68. For the impact of fencing laws on freed blacks who raised livestock, see Bercaw, *Gendered Freedoms*, 127.

43. Cutler, *History of Kansas*, 2:1072; Walter P. Webb, *The Great Plains*, 295–98; Bogue, *From Prairie to Corn Belt*, 78–81.

been put into bluegrass, timothy, or clover.[44] Except for the Bourbon County townships that kept a nighttime stock law in force, none of these counties maintained a general herd law, a fact that undoubtedly helped to preserve widespread access to the open prairie range. Producers justified their opposition to enclosure on the grounds that it interfered with stock raising. Noting the absence of a fence law in Linn County, one observer wrote, "It is held that the use of all unoccupied and uncultivated lands for free pasturage is more valuable than the advantage of protection to crops without fences." Fencing opponents elsewhere feared that the enclosure of the country's prairies might glut the market with surplus grain production or drive away potential immigrants seeking cheap pasture.[45]

The citizens who supported a herd law maintained that such a measure would actually promote greater immigration. Enclosure, its supporters contended, would stimulate, not retard, agricultural development. Ignoring their detractors' worries about overproduction, herd-law advocates agreed that fencing reforms would indeed promote increased grain production, as farmers would be able to spend more time tending crops and less time repairing broken fences. For one Miami County farmer, shifting the fencing burden from crop growers to livestock ranchers was a matter of economic justice. "The rich man has a large herd of cattle and horses; they break into the poor man's field, and destroy his crop," the correspondent wrote. "So you see the rich man's cattle get fat off the poor man's corn. Thus the rich get richer and the poor get poorer." Such pleas apparently failed to sway citizens who voted down petitions that would have instituted herd laws by resounding margins.[46]

Based on data published in the agricultural census of 1880, it is difficult to generalize about which farmers were putting up fences. A significant proportion—but fewer than half—of the farmers along the border invested in fencing. The amount of money that settlers spent varied a great deal, ranging from less than $10 to more than $600. The median investment for farmers who put up fences was $27.50 in Miami County but ran as high as $100 in Vernon County. There was no obvious pattern to the regional backgrounds of farmers who maintained fences. In Bates,

44. Kansas State Board of Agriculture, *Abstracts of Statistical Rolls, 1873*, vol. 3. For local opinions about the superior nutritional value of prairie grasses, see Bates County Old Settlers Society, *Old Settlers' History*, 133–34; and Cutler, *History of Kansas*, 2:881.

45. Kansas State Board of Agriculture, *First Biennial Report of the State Board of Agriculture to the Legislature of the State of Kansas for the Years 1877–78*, 119, 284, 315.

46. *Miami County Republican*, December 25, 1875. For examples of defeated herd-law proposals, see *Bates County Record*, November 14, 1874; and *Nevada Daily Mail*, November 6, 1886.

Bourbon, and Linn Counties, immigrants from northern states had a higher average investment than did natives of southern states, but in Vernon County southerners spent relatively more than their northern neighbors. The variables of age and tenure had the most influence in predicting the extent of fencing on border farms. Producers in their thirties, forties, and fifties spent more on fences than did settlers who were only in their twenties. In addition, as table 19 (Border Farmers Who Built Fences, by Tenure, 1880) indicates, farm owners were more likely to build fences than were cash or share tenants. Such findings seem to complicate the previously quoted assertion that the fencing issue was a fight between rich and poor farmers. Although this information does not detract from the moral forcefulness of that Miami County farmer's argument, fences were in fact more common among farm owners, who were generally wealthier than farm tenants.[47]

Several factors contributed to the decline of the open range in the final decades of the nineteenth century. During the 1870s, the total number of farms in the six border counties increased by nearly 60 percent. The majority of these new farms were located in the previously unsettled areas dominated by tallgrass prairies that had recently been used as common pasture. In turn, the increased number of livestock grazing on the prairies brought a significant decline in native plant species. With the decline in prairie plants, farmers then turned to domestic grasses to feed their cows.[48] Census data from the border indicate that well over half of Kansas and Missouri farms harvested hay in 1880. Those who produced hay harvested it in ever greater quantities, averaging twenty-six tons per farm in Bates County, fifteen in Cass County, twenty-two in Vernon County, twenty-one in Bourbon County, twenty-eight in Linn County, and twenty-three in Miami County. Changing attitudes also fostered a broader acceptance of the herd law, especially among inhabitants of towns where free-ranging hogs had become noisome pests. In the fall of 1886, for example, more than 54 percent of the voters in Bates County approved a petition that would force owners to restrain their livestock. As a result, the open range became little more than a memory in many

47. Census-Ag, Missouri, Bates, Cass, and Vernon Counties, 1880; Census-Ag, Kansas, Bourbon, Linn, and Miami Counties, 1880. The following percentages of farmers put up fences in each county: Bates, 47; Cass, 37; Vernon, 27; Bourbon, 40; Linn, 47; Miami, 40 (ibid.).

48. Willard Cochrane, *The Development of American Agriculture: An Historical Analysis*, 177–78. The suppression of prairie fires, which had checked the spread of woody vegetation beyond the stream valleys, was also responsible for this environmental transformation. See Schroeder, *Presettlement Prairie of Missouri*, 22.

parts of the borderland. "Open prairie in this neighborhood," wrote a Rich Hill editor in 1886, "is a thing of the past."[49]

Amid the economic and environmental changes taking place along the border, one primary institution, the family farm, remained the foundation of Corn Belt agriculture, for it was still the basic social, economic, and cultural building block of the rural community. Farming was both a commercial enterprise and a way of life for rural families. The family farm was at once many different things. To the naked eye, farms were physical places centered around the home, including the garden, pastures, fields, and outbuildings. They were also economic ventures that provided for their members' subsistence but were increasingly committed to the maximization of profit, in addition to being a social institution that nurtured its members and sought its own perpetuation across generations. Finally, the farm was a cultural touchstone that represented and transmitted the traditions, attitudes, and noneconomic values of localism, independence, and community that helped a family negotiate a competitive and often perilous marketplace. Amid the rapid changes that accompanied the industrial revolution in the United States, the family farm persisted as an institution of remarkable continuity and adaptability.[50]

The various labor strategies employed along the Kansas-Missouri border illustrate this dual nature of family farming, for although many farms occasionally relied on the contributions of farmhands or wage laborers, most rural households depended largely on the necessary assistance of family members and neighbors. Although the discussion of dairy production above illustrates the extent to which farm women stimulated local commerce, the capitalist marketplace did not place a high value on their domestic labor. Nineteenth-century census enumerators often described farmwives as "not gainfully employed" and thus failed to account for women's myriad responsibilities within the farm household, in the family garden and fields, and around the barn.[51] Enumerators listed "keeping house" as the occupation for the overwhelming majority of adult women in Missouri and Kansas; the few women who were identified as "farmers" were almost invariably widows. This trend suggests

49. Census-Ag, Kansas, Bourbon, Linn, and Miami Counties, 1880; Census-Ag, Missouri, Bates, Cass, and Vernon Counties, 1880; Bates County Court, Minutes, November 6, 1886; *Rich Hill Enterprise*, May 18, 1888.

50. The rich historiography on the "dual nature" of the family farm includes Hal S. Barron, *Mixed Harvest: The Second Great Transformation in the Rural North, 1870–1930*; Mary Neth, *Preserving the Family Farm: Women, Community, and the Foundations of Agribusiness in the Midwest, 1900–1940*; Osterud, *Bonds of Community*; and Rugh, *Our Common Country*.

51. Osterud, *Bonds of Community*, 12; Riley, "'Not Gainfully Employed,'" 238–39.

the extent to which an enumerator categorized women's economic roles based on their relationships to their husbands. Only with the death of a spouse could a woman gain greater recognition for the work she performed on the farm.

Neither "farmer" nor "keeping house" fully reflects the breadth of farm women's contributions. In addition to bearing and raising the family's children, farm women produced a wide array of goods, including eggs, poultry, butter, candles, linen, cloth, and soap. They also prepared, processed, and stored the family's food; washed and mended its clothing; furnished and cleaned the home; tended to sick children; and assisted in the fields and barn. To accomplish these tasks, a farmwife often depended on the assistance of her children. "Mother got along with the help of all of us," one border native would recall. "Each child did some certain task—washing or drying dishes, bringing in wood, chips, and corn cobs, churning, feeding chickens, gathering eggs, rocking the baby, or any one of the many things to be done." In families that had few children, husbands may have been more likely to assist with domestic chores. In the Dryden household, which had suffered the loss of eight children through miscarriage or death, Louisa and John both participated in canning, soap making, and most other household jobs.[52]

Although the patriarchal structure of rural households subordinated women and children to the authority of husbands and fathers, the success of each farm nevertheless depended on the essential cooperation of each family member. Men's and women's work spaces and rhythms were different. Men's labors, which mainly took place in the fields and barns, usually followed a sequential and seasonal pattern, whereas women's work, which usually occurred around the home and in the garden, was more simultaneous and repetitive in nature. Although this separation gave rural women and men a measure of independence, farmwives nurtured an ethic of mutuality with their husbands in the barnyard and other areas where their work routines overlapped, sharing in highly valued, labor-intensive work such as milking and caring for livestock. In the case of Louisa Dryden, such steady efforts, particularly on the Sabbath, did not go unappreciated. "[Sunday] is called a day of rest," wrote her husband, "but with many well meaning people it is the most laborious day of the seven at times; especially to women. They go to meeting, sit on an

52. Gordon Papers, folder 1 ("Entry into Missouri"), Western Historical Manuscripts Collection, Kansas City; McFadin, "Kansas in Early Times," 8, box 55, McFadin Papers, KSHS; Dryden, February 27, April 4, September 5, 1870, *With Plow and Pen*, 72–78. For the distribution of labor responsibilities within farm households, see Neth, *Preserving the Family Farm*, 17–39.

uncomfortable seat during the services, invite company home with them, cook a big dinner, wash the dishes, get the children tidy for the evening meeting, and where does *their* rest come in?"[53] This observation reveals that aside from their responsibilities on the farm, rural women also played a significant role in organizing the social gatherings that strengthened the ties of community among farm households.

Neighborliness, the sense of community that bound settlers within a rural neighborhood, also found expression within the flexible exchange of labor and tools among farms. Dryden's farm diary is filled with regular instances in which neighbors, friends, and extended kin provided and received assistance during harvest or peak work periods. Entries from a single week in the summer of 1869 illustrate the extent to which he and his neighbors traded work on each other's farms. On the morning of Monday, June 28, Dryden joined other settlers to help a local widow begin her harvest; the next day, several "hands" came to work at his place; and on Wednesday, he and other neighbors assisted in harvesting the Paynes' wheat. After spending the rest of the week helping to cradle and bind wheat for the Paynes and Mousers, the farmers living near Little Osage paused to celebrate Independence Day, but on Monday they resumed helping to bind and shock their oats. Many settlers occasionally "hired out" to individuals with specialized skills or machinery for capital-intensive tasks such as sod breaking.[54]

The decision to seek assistance from neighbors or hired hands was influenced by the size and structure of farm families. For households with several able-bodied sons, such as that of Daniel Graham, whose children, Finley, Jesse, and Albert, continued to live at home and work as farm laborers through their midtwenties, hiring out for assistance in the fields was less common. For families with young children or with few mature sons, a hired hand often became a vital part of the farm's operation, even though his wages may have absorbed much of its profits. "All our extra money goes to pay the hired men," explained one Missouri

53. Osterud, *Bonds of Community*, 4–7, 142–60; Neth, *Preserving the Family Farm*, 32–39; Jane Adams, *The Transformation of Rural Life: Southern Illinois, 1890–1990*, 84–107; Jane Marie Pederson, *Between Memory and Reality: Family and Community in Rural Wisconsin, 1870–1970*, 157–85; Rugh, *Our Common Country*, 66–67; Dryden, June 23, 1878, *With Plow and Pen*, 117.

54. Dryden, June 28–July 6, 1869, July 31, 1876, *With Plow and Pen*, 64–65, 100; Everett and Everett, "Letters of John and Sarah Everett," 280 (John Everett to Robert Everett, May 28, 1857). For neighborly assistance among farmers, see Bogue, *From Prairie to Corn Belt*, 185; Faragher, *Sugar Creek*, 133–35; and Neth, *Preserving the Family Farm*, 40–41.

mother pointedly. "If some of you girls had been born boys your Father could have field help like his brothers."[55]

As farms grew larger and produced corn and livestock in greater numbers, the proportion of households that employed wage laborers remained relatively low. In both 1870 and 1880, roughly one-third of the families in Missouri and Kansas kept a hired hand. It was quite uncommon for farms to employ a hired hand on a year-round basis, as only 15 percent of the Kansas and Missouri farms that paid wages to farm laborers retained a full-time farmhand in 1880. The uneven seasonal rhythm of corn cultivation offered a compelling explanation for these low percentages. On farms where corn was the primary grain crop—and on the Kansas-Missouri border, this included nearly all farms—there were two periods, planting and harvest, where the need for additional labor was greatest. There was simply little need to keep extra laborers during most of the growing season. Most families could not afford or justify the expense of paying a hand during winter months and other periods when labor demands slackened. Farmhands were generally paid around eighteen dollars per month, in addition to receiving free room and board from their employers. The median values for the annual wages that border farmers spent on hired hands in 1880 ranged from fifty to seventy-five dollars, the rough equivalent of what a farm laborer could expect to be paid for three to four months of work.[56]

Although many farm laborers came and went with the passing harvest, some families nevertheless regarded their hired hands with a kind of affection reserved for family and close friends. "We, and all our neighbors," recalled Addie Aldridge Gordon, "had our hired man eat with us. We treated them not unlike company." An exception to the hospitality extended by Aldridge's family occurred after her father reluctantly hired an African American man to help cut corn, as they agreed to feed the laborer in the front room but not at the table with the rest of the family. Other hired hands found their circumstances difficult to bear. Will Haskins, for example, described himself as an "inmate" of the Miami County home where he stayed. Some farm laborers helped several families over

55. Census-Ag, Missouri, Bates, Cass, and Vernon Counties, 1870; McFadin, "Kansas in Early Days," 8, box 55, McFadin Papers, KSHS; Gordon Papers, folder 32 ("Hired Help"), Western Historical Manuscripts Collection, Kansas City.

56. Missouri Bureau of Labor Statistics, *Sixth Annual Report of the Bureau of Labor Statistics of the State of Missouri for the Year Ending December 31, 1884*, 83; Census-Ag, Kansas, Bourbon, Linn, and Miami Counties, 1880; Census-Ag, Missouri, Bates, Cass, and Vernon Counties, 1880.

the course of a year. William A. Peele, for example, found work in and around Fort Scott, helping his father and other local settlers. According to Peele's diary, his various jobs—tending cattle, repairing fences, harvesting oats, hauling water, working as a carpenter—were broken up by long stretches in which he "done nothing," save for occasional trips to go "a hunting" or "a fishing."[57]

Like Peele's father, most households relied on the contributions of sons, cousins, and other young male kin, rather than hire full-time non-relative farmhands. Two statistical trends drawn from the population schedules of the federal census support such a conclusion. First, from 1860 to 1880, the average age of farm laborers declined in all six border counties. The mean age of antebellum farmhands in Cass County, for example, was 24 years; two decades later, the average age fell to 18.3 years. The second statistical trend identified within the census shows that during this same period the proportion of farm laborers who were also listed as heads of their respective households declined as well. Although many young men could realistically expect to move out of their parents' homes by the time they reached their early twenties, a large number would likely work as farm tenants, renting either from a family member or from another landlord, before becoming farm owners themselves. Since reliable census data regarding tenancy became available only with the 1880 enumeration, it is difficult to assess changes in farm tenure with great confidence. An assessment of that year's agricultural census indicates that at least 70 percent of the border counties' producers owned their own farms. For an individual under the age of 30, farm ownership could be a particularly elusive goal. In several counties, almost half of the farmers in their twenties were share or cash tenants. Across the six border counties, the average age of tenant farmers varied widely, though it usually fell close to 40 years, meaning that many renters might wait several years before they could hope to attain independent ownership.[58]

Yet even the economic independence that was long associated with farm ownership became somewhat illusory in the difficult financial circumstances of the late nineteenth century. Commodity prices suffered a significant decline during the thirty years after the Civil War. Most farms raised more crops and livestock to compensate for this drop, but overproduction merely made the situation worse. Much of this expansion was

57. Gordon Papers, folder 32 ("Hired Help"), Western Historical Manuscripts Collection, Kansas City; Haskins to S. P. Borders, April 16, 1882, Robert T. Rhea Papers (box 72), KSHS; Peele, diary, May 19–September 18, 1879, KSHS.

58. Census-Ag and Census-Pop, Kansas, Bourbon, Linn, and Miami Counties, 1880; Census-Ag and Census-Pop, Missouri, Bates, Cass, and Vernon Counties, 1880.

made possible by increased investments in land and technology, which pushed many families into debt. What's more, the dangerous cycle of debt that entrapped many farmers was made worse by the deflationary state of the national economy. John Dryden acknowledged as much in the fall of 1878. "It is a risky proposition going in debt these times," he confided to his diary after he had "bought himself poor" purchasing livestock and implements worth at least two hundred dollars. Unlike the grasshoppers that had fled the border just years earlier, neither his debts nor the anxieties they produced were to vanish soon.[59]

By the early 1880s, Dryden had endured a series of crushing losses. His infant daughter Pearl died in October 1881; of the family's ten children, she was the eighth to pass away before adolescence. Louisa, his wife of twenty-four years, died the following January. "O my God!" wrote the grieving widower. "I feel crushed to the earth. The future presents a dark and gloomy page to me. My children are the only ties that now bind me to earth. I *do* want to live, and pray that I may be spared to see them settled in life, but nothing seems sure to me but an unrelenting and cruel Fate." Money woes compounded Dryden's depression over the coming months. When the income he earned as a justice of the peace dwindled, he again turned to selling off timbered property for extra cash. Financial independence, the beleaguered farmer found, was tenuous and not easily maintained. On May 2, 1883, debt managed to do what waves of ravaging grasshoppers could not: push Dryden off the farm. His departure for the booming coal town of Rich Hill, where he expected to find work, was the last event recorded in his long journal.[60]

For well-to-do farmers who could afford to expand their operations without assuming dangerous levels of debt, the rise of the Corn Belt and the achievement of personal independence were indeed developments to be celebrated, a promising prelude to the so-called golden age of American agriculture that would arrive early in the twentieth century. A great many other producers, like Dryden, found less to celebrate in their dire financial predicaments. Frustrated by the indifference of elected officials and the exploitative behavior of railroads and middlemen, several of these disaffected farmers looked to forge a political solution to their economic hardships. These efforts of agrarian insurgents would soon culminate in the emergence of the Patrons of Husbandry, the Farmers' Alliance,

59. Bogue, *From Prairie to Corn Belt*, 283–86; Dryden, October 19, 1878, *With Plow and Pen*, 118.
60. Dryden, November 16, 1881, January 18, 1882, April 28, 29, May 1, 1883, *With Plow and Pen*, 118, 145, 154–56.

and eventually the Populist Party, organizations that would attract a large number of followers on both sides of the Missouri-Kansas border.

The appeal of populism would test long-standing political loyalties along the state line. The partisan identities of citizens in each state— mostly Republicans in Kansas and Democrats in Missouri—had been shaped in large part by their (or their families') own experiences during the long border war. In the fifteen years after that conflict, farmers throughout the Osage plains had helped to establish an agricultural region, the Corn Belt, that transcended state boundaries, but even though the Missouri-Kansas border was hardly a significant marker of regional farm ways, it remained a meaningful political divide. The concluding chapter reveals that although Kansans and Missourians were willing to forgive one another for the hostilities of decades past, citizens in both states were unlikely to forsake established partisan ties, even for the sake of agrarian reform.

THE BORDER RECONCILED AND REMEMBERED

A scattered army of more than fifty thousand Protestant women marched upon the saloons of the United States in early 1874, determined to combat liquor's pernicious influence in their homes and communities. Relying on the peculiar moral superiority that Victorian culture imbued in Christian women, most of these temperance advocates acted peaceably, gathering within or outside of bars to pray and sing hymns loudly. Such efforts produced immediate results in Butler, Missouri, where the daily prayer meetings of some two hundred women forced the closure of every saloon but one. Reformers pursued a bolder strategy across the border in Fort Scott. On Friday, March 27, Amanda Way and several other women paraded twenty-one "ragged, dirty, and forlorn-looking" children through the Capital Saloon in order to expose the drunkard fathers who spent their wages on drink rather than on their hungry families.[1] For two housewives in the eastern Kansas town of Burlingame, even more forceful action was necessary. When Mrs. Allen and Mrs. Wertz entered a local tavern and approached the bar, the latter reportedly informed the proprietor, "Mr. Schuyler, I have come down to show you how my husband acts when he comes home drunk with your whiskey." Brandishing tomahawks, the women then set

---

1. *Fort Scott Daily Monitor,* March 29, 1874; Bates County Old Settlers Society, *Old Settlers' History,* 194.

themselves to destroying mirrors, decanters, pitchers, jugs, and whatever glassware they could find.[2]

The assault on Schuyler's bar was one of the several examples of politicized violence that afflicted eastern Kansas and western Missouri during the nineteenth century, and it placed saloon keepers on a long list of people—slave owners, abolitionists, Texas cattlemen, railroad builders, and corrupt politicians—who had been targets of extralegal harassment. The Burlingame incident also stood as a precursor to the famous joint smashings that a daughter of the borderland would carry out in decades to come. Born in Kentucky in 1846, Carrie Amelia Moore had settled with her slaveholding family in Belton, Missouri, at the age of nine. Except for a brief sojourn to Texas during the Civil War, she had lived in or near Cass County through her early thirties. After a short and unhappy marriage to an alcoholic physician named Charles Gloyd, Carrie remarried and moved back to Texas with her new husband, David Nation. The couple eventually migrated to the south-central Kansas town of Medicine Lodge. There Carrie A. Nation would eventually gain national notoriety as a temperance crusader. Like thousands of other women in Kansas and Missouri, she would become an active member of the Women's Christian Temperance Union; by June 1900, she would be more commonly associated with the hatchet and stones that she used to smash up bars throughout Kansas.[3] Upon her death in 1911, Nation would be buried in Belton.[4]

The controversial actions of Nation, Allen, and Wertz were extreme examples of the increasingly aggressive stance that Kansas citizens adopted to address the vexing problem of alcohol. Kansas lawmakers had shown reformist inclinations on this issue even before statehood. The territorial legislature passed a dram-shop law in 1859 that prohibited the sale of alcohol to married men against the known wishes of their wives. An 1867 act promised to give Kansas women even greater influence over public drinking; to be fully licensed, vendors were required to present a

2. *Fort Scott Daily Monitor,* March 31, 1874; Nancy G. Garner, "'A Prayerful Public Protest': The Significance of Gender in the Kansas Woman's Crusade of 1874," 219–21. For the antebellum temperance efforts of middle-class women, see Mary Ryan, *Cradle of the Middle Class: The Family in Oneida County, New York, 1790–1865,* 116–45.

3. Local newspapers indicate that the WCTU was active in each of the border counties. See *Butler Free Press,* April 17, 1896; *Nevada Daily Mail,* October 6, 1884; and *Pleasant Hill Western Dispatch,* April 21, 1886. For the WCTU in Kansas and Missouri, see W. Smith, "Half Century of Struggle," 87–88; Thelen, *Paths of Resistance,* 153–54; and June O. Underwood, "Civilizing Kansas: Women's Organizations, 1880–1920," 293–300.

4. Carla Waal and Barbara Oliver Korner, eds., *Hardship and Hope: Missouri Women Writing about Their Lives, 1820–1920,* 185–92. Anecdotal evidence of Nation's fame comes from Gordon, folder 16 ("Holidays"), Gordon Papers, Collection KC068, Western Historical Manuscripts Collection, Kansas City.

petition endorsed by a majority of the residents, both male and female, within a community. Although both measures apparently suffered from lax and inconsistent enforcement, temperance advocates achieved a landmark accomplishment in 1880 when Kansas voters passed a state constitutional amendment prohibiting the sale of alcohol, making it the first state to do so.[5] For their part, voters near the Missouri line were divided over the prohibition amendment; only one of the three Kansas border counties approved the measure.[6] In 1887, when the state's women gained the right to vote in municipal elections, the *New York Times* concluded that Kansas was indeed "the great experimental ground of the nation."[7]

Grand experiments were not forthcoming in the neighboring state of Missouri, where most citizens, like their peers in the South, had long been reluctant to embrace abolitionism, feminism, and other major reform movements. Missourians preferred to regulate the sale and consumption of alcohol in at least two fashions. First, municipal and county authorities required that dram shops, saloons, groceries, and drugstores—the usual places where a person might purchase liquor by the drink—obtain an annual license and pay a substantial fee in order to sell alcohol. The fines levied against individuals who failed to acquire a license were usually steep; decades before the Civil War, lawbreakers in Cass County had paid as much as one hundred dollars apiece for violations. Second, local officials policed excessive drinking through the prosecution of morality crimes such as public drunkenness, disorderly behavior, Sabbath breaking, and gambling. Even amid the violent turmoil of Bleeding Kansas, morality prosecutions composed the overwhelming bulk of the criminal caseloads in the three border counties.[8] From 1858 to 1860, for example, more than 95 percent of the criminal prosecutions brought before the Bates County Circuit Court involved some kind of morality offense.[9] The

5. Goldberg, *Army of Women,* 46–53; W. Smith, "Half Century of Struggle," 87–88; Garner, "'Prayerful Public Protest,'" 218.

6. Cutler shows that 52 percent of Kansas voters approved the prohibition amendment. On the border, the amendment passed in Linn County (with a 54 percent majority), but it faltered in Bourbon (42 percent in favor) and Miami (46 percent) Counties (*History of Kansas,* 2:288–89).

7. McNall, *Road to Rebellion,* 63.

8. Cass County Circuit Court Records, 1845–1846, vol. A, 392–440, vol. B, 308, Missouri State Archives; Christopher Waldrep, *Roots of Disorder: Race and Criminal Justice in the American South, 1817–1880,* 15–59. For a comparative regional analysis of the prosecution of morality crimes, see John W. Quist, *Restless Visionaries: The Social Roots of Antebellum Reform in Alabama and Michigan,* 155–235.

9. Bates County Circuit Court Records, 1858–1860, vol. B, 75–341. See also ibid., 1865, vol. C, 390–403, 1866–1868, 6–355; Cass County Circuit Court Records, 1857–1859, vol. B, 287–419, 1859–1865, 21–359, vol. C, 1866–1867, 128; and Vernon

most significant piece of temperance legislation came in 1887 when Missouri legislators approved the Wood Local Option Law, which held that the male citizens of a local jurisdiction—Missouri women were still denied the ballot—could decide by popular vote whether to prohibit liquor sales. A survey of newspapers suggests that none of the counties or communities along the open Kansas border became dry jurisdictions. In a rare exception, Nevada mayor C. B. Ingels issued a proclamation in 1884 that prohibited the sale of alcohol on election day. One Vernon County editor noted that it was a common occurrence for Kansans to slip across the state line and buy their whiskey from Missouri proprietors.[10]

The different temperance reforms that were adopted in wet Missouri and dry Kansas were apt examples of the distinct political cultures that took shape on opposite sides of the state line. The Civil War and the changes it wrought, such as emancipation, industrial expansion, and extensive northern immigration, had eroded many of the differences between the communities along the border. In many respects, the Kansas-Missouri border was hardly a significant economic or social boundary as the nineteenth century drew to a close. At the same time, however, it remained a meaningful political divide, as the border war had served to reinforce competing partisan loyalties in each state. The Republican Party had dominated Kansas politics since the territorial period, when Democratic presidents Pierce and Buchanan had not only appointed a series of unpopular and ineffective governors but also tried to foist a proslavery government on a free-soil majority. The Civil War further galvanized the political identity of Kansas citizens and converted a large number of erstwhile Democrats, who were repulsed by their secessionist counterparts, into stalwart Republicans.[11]

Although voters in western Missouri had been more divided over the question of disunion, most had stayed loyal to the Democratic Party and associated Republicanism with moralizing abolitionists, murderous jayhawkers, and abusive federal soldiers. The vengeful policies implemented during the Radical Republicans' postwar reign reinforced the Democratic allegiances of reenfranchised Missourians. The Radicals' punitive agenda also produced a statewide partisan backlash that soon resulted in the political ascendance of many former rebels. Legislators

---

County Circuit Court Records, 1856–1866, vol. A, 17–461, Missouri State Archives. For southern wariness about nineteenth-century reform movements, see Faust, *Confederate Nationalism*, 29–30.

10. Thelen, *Paths of Resistance*, 154; *Nevada Daily Mail*, November 4, 1884, February 12, 1887.

11. Miner, *Kansas*, 56–63; Etcheson, *Bleeding Kansas*, 141.

sent Democrats Francis Cockrell, who had been a general in the Confederate army, and George Vest, a former member of the Confederate Congress, to the U.S. Senate in the late 1870s. The Confederate resurgence peaked in 1884, when a majority of Missouri voters cast ballots for gubernatorial candidate John Sappington Marmaduke, who was not only a former rebel general and the son of a previous governor but also a nephew of Claiborne Fox Jackson, the secessionist leader who had tried to steer Missouri out of the Union in 1861. Results from the rural Kansas border suggest that the revival of Confederate influence was less thorough in local elections. Democrats dominated the border counties from 1876 forward, but not all of the winning candidates had been dyed-in-the-wool Southern sympathizers. Local contests in Cass County provide a telling illustration. For every Hiram Bledsoe—a state senator, county collector, and three-time judge who had served under General Sterling Price—there seemed to be a George W. Stevens, a postwar immigrant of northeastern descent who was named both sheriff and county judge.[12]

A broad survey of postwar election results (table 20, Results of Presidential Elections, Missouri-Kansas Border Counties, 1868–1896) illustrates the dominance of Democrats in Missouri and Republicans in Kansas. In the three Kansas counties, Republican candidates captured the first six presidential elections held after the war; voters in the Missouri counties, on the other hand, endorsed the Democratic candidates in those same contests. This sharp contrast demonstrated that the politics of the "bloody shirt" and the "lost cause" resonated on either side of the border, at least during the immediate postwar period. Editors in both states were quick to remind partisan readers to vote as they or their fathers had shot. "Every man who wishes that none but loyal men should rule," instructed one Republican Missouri editor in 1870, "should see that he is duly registered as a voter, and then vote for the regular Republican nominees." With the shadow of the Civil War still looming and the politics of the past and present ever entangled, partisan editors were not above stoking old loyalties and animosities to win more votes.[13]

Over time, as immigration introduced new voters who had not been part of the border conflict, appeals to wartime allegiances became a less

12. Phillips, *Missouri's Confederate*, 247–63; O. Williams, *Cass and Bates Counties*, 318–22, 520, 533. The election of 1874, when a fusion ticket of Grangers, Republicans, and antimonopolists swept most races in Cass and Bates Counties, was a rare anomaly within a long stretch of Democratic dominance.

13. *Bates County Record*, October 1, 1870; Goldberg, *Army of Women*, 13; McNall, *Road to Rebellion*, 83; Cobb, *Away Down South*, 62–66, 98.

salient feature of local electioneering. Postwar immigration may account in part for the shrinking majorities of the dominant parties, but another plausible explanation for this decline lay with the two major parties' indifference toward the interests of disaffected rural citizens. The growing popularity of third-party presidential candidates offers a reasonable measure of such discontent. In addition to the Prohibition Party, which never obtained more than 1 percent or 2 percent of the votes in either state, the Greenback and Union Labor Parties attracted a significant number of followers, especially in Kansas. From 1876 to 1888, third-party candidates siphoned supporters from the Republican nominees in Missouri and from the Democrats in Kansas but failed to threaten either of the major parties. By 1892, however, the People's (or Populist) Party posed a serious challenge to the dominant parties in four of the six border counties. In fact, Populist candidate James Weaver defeated Republican incumbent President Benjamin Harrison in Bourbon and Miami Counties; Democratic candidate Grover Cleveland was left off the ballot in all three Kansas counties.

Weaver's statewide victory in Kansas was made possible by the Populists' fusion with the state's Democrats, but it also represented a significant triumph for the many agrarian reformers who had mobilized during the past two decades. Many of the nation's largest reform organizations attracted members on both sides of the Kansas-Missouri border. By the early 1870s, the Patrons of Husbandry (or Grange), a nonpartisan organization dedicated to the economic and social improvement of farm life, had chapters in both states, attracting both male and female members.[14] The similarly inclusive, nonpartisan character of the Farmers' Alliance helped to make it the largest reform movement of its era. Seeking to address the economic grievances of American farmers through positive government action and cooperation among producers, the Alliance boasted nearly 1.3 million members in twenty-two states; in July 1890, its national secretary reported that there were roughly 100,000 and 150,000 members in Kansas and Missouri, respectively.[15] The Wheel, the Farmers' Cooperative Union, the Labor Exchange, and the workers' colony at Freedom, Kansas, all developed cooperative institutions similar to the Alliance's subtreasury

14. *LaCygne Journal*, July 19, 1873; Dryden, July 8, 1876, *With Plow and Pen*, 99. For the Grange, see Donald B. Marti, *Women of the Grange: Mutuality and Sisterhood in Rural America, 1866–1920*; and D. Sven Nordin, *Rich Harvest: A History of the Grange, 1867–1900*.

15. *Goodrich Graphic*, March 14, 1890; W. P. Harrington, "The Populist Party in Kansas," 407; Homer Clevenger, "Agrarian Politics in Missouri, 1880–1896," 68–110; Lawrence Goodwyn, *Democratic Promise: The Populist Moment in America*; Robert C. McMath, *American Populism: A Social History, 1877–1898*, 83–148.

plan that aimed to expand farmers' profits by reducing the influence of merchants and middlemen.[16]

The eventual decision by agrarian reformers to enter the fray of party politics occasioned considerable dissent among insurgents who feared that such a course would compromise the independence and success of the farmers' movement. Populist leaders also recognized the difficulty of persuading farmers to break from their established partisan affinities. In Missouri, as in the South, it would be difficult to lure rural voters away from the Democratic Party, especially since its leaders claimed to support (although not enact) many of the agrarians' demands. The challenge for third-party organizers was just as great in Kansas, but there it entailed challenging the supremacy of the Republican Party. Rallying behind the twin reforms of currency expansion and railroad regulation, a great many farmers eventually broke from the major parties of each state. "We as the farmers and laborers of the country are seeking laws that will be to our own interest," wrote one citizen in Goodrich, Kansas. "The questions that are agitating the minds of the people today are not so much partisan as they are sectional, and what is good for the western democrat is good for the western republican."[17]

The People's (or Populist) Party was remarkably successful within Kansas, where support for the Alliance and populist reforms had been quite solid.[18] In 1890, Populists wrested control of the state House of Representatives from the Republican Party; two years later, they claimed the state senate, the governor's mansion, and four congressional seats, in addition to becoming one of the five western states that endorsed presidential candidate Weaver. The Populists drew their greatest strength from the wheat-growing settlers in central Kansas, but at the statewide level and in the corn-producing eastern counties, electoral success required the calculated fusion of the party's supporters with those of the Democrats. Third-party Populist candidates in Missouri were largely unsuccessful, winning only 61 of the state's 2,175 precincts in 1892.

16. *Miami County Republican,* January 10, 1874; W. Scott Morgan, *History of the Wheel and Alliance and the Impending Revolution,* 115; H. Roger Grant, "Portrait of a Workers' Utopia: The Labor Exchange and the Freedom, Kansas, Colony," 56–66.

17. Clevenger, "Agrarian Politics," 161–210; March, *The History of Missouri,* 2:1171; *Goodrich Graphic,* May 23, 1890.

18. The profusion of Populist scholarship in Kansas reflects the vitality and success of the state's agrarian reformers. Notable works include Peter H. Argersinger, "Pentecostal Politics in Kansas: Religion, the Farmers' Alliance, and the Gospel of Populism"; O. Gene Clanton, "Intolerant Populist? The Disaffection of Mary Elizabeth Lease"; Goldberg, *Army of Women,* 127–259; McNall, *Road to Rebellion;* and Jeffrey Ostler, *Prairie Populism: The Fate of Agrarian Radicalism in Kansas, Nebraska, and Iowa.*

Populism was unusually strong, however, in Bates County, which was the home to the party's state chairman, M. V. Carroll. Weaver claimed 27 percent of the county's votes—slightly less than the Republican Harrison—but won 9 of 24 townships. The Democratic nominee, former president Cleveland, captured the other 15 districts.[19]

The Populist Party's ascendance was a rather momentous opportunity to bridge the partisan divide along the Missouri-Kansas border. One observer from Butler expressed the view that populism could in fact transcend old differences and declared that a People's Party picnic in Mine Creek, Kansas, which attracted families from both sides of the state line, was emblematic of the movement's great success. "Populism is the same everywhere," he declared. The popularity of William Jennings Bryan, the presidential nominee of the Democratic-Populist fusion ticket in 1896, seemed to support such an assertion. Bryan not only won two-thirds of the vote in western Missouri but also became the first non-Republican candidate to sweep the three adjacent counties in Kansas. The nationwide defeat of the fusion ticket by William McKinley, however, signaled the demise of the People's Party, and with it vanished the common political ground that had been established on the border. In 1898 the Populists still retained a sizable following in Bates County, where the party's candidates won 14 percent of the vote. At the statewide level, however, the party was no longer a significant factor, as Populists won fewer than ten thousand votes in all of Missouri, or less than 3 percent of the total vote. As in Kansas, most of the former Populists returned to the parties of their fathers, and a good many others dropped out of politics altogether.[20] As a result, the Democrats maintained control of local politics in western Missouri, while the Republicans soon returned to power in Kansas.

The Populists' cross-border success, however brief, suggests that the long-standing differences between Kansans and Missourians were no longer as obvious or meaningful by the end of the nineteenth century. Rather than indulge the bitter memories of past feuds, citizens in each state exhibited a marked willingness to forgive old wartime foes. The *Cass News* of Harrisonville, Missouri, had articulated a growing distaste for the politics of the bloody shirt back in 1888, when it admonished a rival paper's willingness to resort to such once-provocative rhetoric. "We are sorry to see the Times persist in waving the bloody shirt. Will it never cease to prate of 'perpetuation of hostilities'?" asked the paper's editor.

19. McNall, *Road to Rebellion*, 263–76; Alexander A. Lesueur, *Official Directory of Missouri for the Years 1893–1894*, 21; March, *The History of Missouri*, 2:1177.

20. *Butler Free Press*, September 11, 1896, November 18, 1898; *Cass News*, November 11, 1898; March, *The History of Missouri*, 2:1204–5; McMath, *American Populism*, 206.

"There is no antipathy between the two sections, or between the men who fought in hostile ranks."[21]

Even the most ardent Civil War partisans could agree that a spirit of reconciliation had settled upon the communities of the postwar border. General Jo Shelby had fought Kansans first as a proslavery partisan in the 1850s and then during the Civil War as one of the Confederacy's most effective cavalry officers. Shelby became a folk hero to many Confederates by refusing to surrender at the end of the war and then fleeing to Mexico, where he offered the services of his "Iron Brigade" to Emperor Maximilian. Weeks before his death in 1898, Shelby spoke with Kansas historian William Connelly and expressed regret over his participation in the territorial conflict. "I went there to kill Free State men. I did kill them," he recalled.

> I am now ashamed of myself for having done so, but then times were different from what they are now. . . . I had no business there. No Missourian had any business there with arms in his hands. The policy that sent us there was damnable and the trouble we started on the border bore fruit for ten years. . . . I say John Brown was right. He did in his country what I would have done in mine in like circumstances. Those were the days when slavery was in the balance and the violence engendered made men irresponsible.[22]

Columbus C. Blankenbecker, a Missouri resident who had fought with Sterling Price at the battle of Wilson's Creek, also empathized with his former enemies. Expelled from his home by the Union army, Blankenbecker had returned after the war to find that a feeling of affection had quickly replaced much of the animosity that had lingered along the Kansas line. "I am proud to say," he noted in the late 1890s, "that now my warmest friends are those who wore the Blue, some of whom I met on the battlefield." A farmer named William Walton agreed that partisan tensions had largely faded. He attributed the decline in "the asperities incident to the war" to several factors. "For thirty years now the Northern and Southern people have lived here together, their children have intermarried and they are brothers in the lodge and the church. Our political beliefs that differed so widely when living apart have now after years of intimate social contact shaded into each other," wrote Walton. The passage of time was a critical factor in facilitating cross-border reconciliation; the expression of such warm sentiments was nearly unthinkable decades

---

21. *Cass News,* June 15, 1888.
22. William Elsey Connelly, *Quantrill and the Border Wars,* 288.

earlier. Kansas settler J. T. Botkin reflected upon his extended tenure along the border and enumerated the many positive changes he had seen. "No one carries arms, and I doubt if there are a half dozen men along the border, including both sides of the line from St. Joseph, Mo., to Galena, Kan., who know how to tie a hangman's knot. Peace and prosperity have taken the place of strife and bloodshed," he observed. "The border war is only a memory."[23]

Memories of the border war, however, continued to pervade public life and were an essential part of many citizens' social identity in the late nineteenth century. Among the Kansans and Missourians who took an active interest in preserving their social and cultural ties to the past were members of Union and Confederate veterans' organizations, such as Grand Army of the Republic and the United Confederate Veterans, and women's groups like the National Women's Relief Corps, the Ladies of the Grand Army of the Republic, and the United Daughters of the Confederacy (UDC).[24] The veterans' groups were social organizations that served a variety of purposes, such as honoring fellow comrades; providing charitable assistance to veterans' homes, widows, and orphans; and promoting better veterans' pensions. Women's associations fulfilled a similar charitable mission but also assumed a special responsibility for memorializing fallen soldiers. In an era when the public arena was considered a predominately masculine sphere, organized expressions of mourning were an uncontroversial civic opportunity for women. One UDC member from Missouri looked to the Bible in describing memorials as an appropriate feminine responsibility. "As woman was last at the cross and first at the tomb, 'twas fitting that she should be the first, not only to remember the living, but the dead; for them nothing could be done except to mark their resting places and keep alive the memories of their valor and bravery, and show by decorating their graves with flowers that 'though dead yet do they speak.'"[25]

Settlers on both sides of the border maintained an active interest in commemorating the service and sacrifice of those who had fought in the border war. Citizens from Franklin and Miami Counties, for example, erected a monument in 1877 that memorialized the men who had died defending the

23. Bates County Old Settlers Society, *Old Settlers' History,* 142, 193; Botkin, "Justice Was Swift," 493. For the role that time played in postwar reconciliation, see David W. Blight, *Race and Reunion: The Civil War in American Memory,* 64–97, 149–205; and Rubin, *Shattered Nation,* 215.

24. Brundage, *Where These Memories Grow,* 3–21; Blight, *Race and Reunion,* 140–70, 255–99.

25. United Daughters of the Confederacy, Missouri Division, *Reminiscences,* 7. See also Whites, *Crisis in Gender,* 166–200; Rubin, *Shattered Nation,* 233–39; and Brundage, *Where These Memories Grow,* 14.

town of Osawatomie from Missouri raiders. In addition to these fallen dead, a thirteen-foot marble shaft was dedicated to the memory of a man who was not buried on the site. The John Brown monument in Osawatomie, as the marker became commonly identified, had the primary effect of reiterating the heroic legend of the controversial abolitionist warrior within Kansas and beyond.[26] Across the state line, organizations of former Confederates and widows in Cass and Vernon Counties worked to fund a monument to honor the memory of Jefferson Davis. "It is true that many of us are poor, yet we all can contribute something," wrote one veteran. "Turn out and don't let us forget our illustrious dead." This and other Confederate monuments were tangible bonds between the past and present, but also signified that a distinctive southern identity endured throughout rural Missouri decades after the war's conclusion.[27]

Partisan commemorations were an important thread within the tapestry of historical memory that Americans began to weave during the postwar period. Collective memories were self-conscious creations in which reconciliation was often stressed as a central theme. Whether in organized commemorations or local histories, people actively tried to make sense of their shared history, both for themselves and for future generations, by emphasizing certain parts of the past while obscuring or even ignoring other more controversial elements.[28] At the ceremonial rituals that were carried out annually on Decoration Day and Independence Day, former combatants came together to honor their shared patriotism and national identity. Editors looked approvingly upon the poignant scenes that played out in cemeteries along the border, but carefully ignored the actual causes of the war and instead stressed the common courage of combatants on each side. "The sight of Federal soldiers decorating with flowers the graves of Confederate dead, and *vice versa*, against whom they had fought so hard, was often witnessed, and so great and sublime a thought was such forgiveness that it made our own petty trials sink into insignificance by comparison," wrote one Harrisonville editor.[29] Military reunions were also inclusive affairs that drew together former

26. Malin, *John Brown*, 351–69. Malin's critical assessment remains the most exhaustively researched account of Brown's time in Kansas and the legend that it inspired.

27. *Pleasant Hill Leader*, May 29, 1891; J. Johnson, *History of Vernon County*, 499; Brundage, *Where These Memories Grow*, 8; Phillips, *Missouri's Confederate*, 247–63.

28. Michael Kammen, *Mystic Chords of Memory: The Transformation of Tradition in American Culture*, 10–13, 101–21.

29. *Cass News*, June 7, 1889. For other examples, see *Belton Herald*, June 7, 1895; *Cass News*, June 8, 1888; and *Nevada Noticer*, July 7, 1887. For the significance of former soldiers as symbols of reunion, see Blight, *Race and Reunion*, 190–205.

partisans from opposite sides of the sectional divide. A Nevada observer applauded the efforts of citizens who had organized a reunion of Jo Shelby's old brigade and had extended an open invitation to Union veterans as well. The reunion, he wrote, demonstrated the "spirit of reconciliation so beautiful, patriotic, and appropriate to Americans."[30]

Discussions of slavery or secession, as well as the cultural, political, and personal tensions that had fueled the border war, were conspicuously absent from patriotic celebrations along the state line. By stripping away the causes of the war, citizens could instead infuse the conflict with a powerful symbolic meaning that was accessible to former partisans from each side, who were now reconciled—whether in life or death—by their mutual sacrifice. "The bitter sectional hate of a few years ago is gone," observed the Reverend O. P. Shrout of Belton, Missouri. "As we thus look upon the remnant of reunited heroes of other days, we feel in our hearts that they are indeed brethren and all loyal sons of a common country." Former bushwhacker Kit Dalton echoed this glowing regard for national unity. "I am glad there is no more north and south," wrote Dalton at the age of seventy-one. "We have shaken the right hand of fellowship and brotherly love and are all serving and living under the Stars and Stripes, the most glorious flag that ever fluttered over a free and courageous people."[31]

The old settlers' societies that were organized in Cass, Bates, and Bourbon Counties offered living proof of citizens' interest in their shared history and a commitment to minimizing the potentially divisive elements within that past. Organized in 1879, the Cass County Old Settlers' Society was a fraternal group whose membership was initially limited to persons who had come to the area before 1846, though the requirements were eventually broadened to include all antebellum settlers. Given the predominantly southern character of the county's prewar population, the organization was dominated by individuals who had been born in or emigrated from slave states. Citizens in Bourbon County formed a society known as the Border Tier Old Settlers Association in 1886 and opened its membership to men and women who had lived in Kansas for at least twenty years.[32]

Like the Cass County and Border Tier associations, the Bates County Old Settlers Society was established "to cultivate more friendly and fra-

---

30. *Nevada Daily Mail*, August 29, 1885. For similarly inclusive reunions in Missouri and Kansas, see ibid., February 16, 1885; and *Fort Scott Daily Monitor*, May 30, 1883.

31. *Belton Herald*, June 7, 1895; Dalton, *Under the Black Flag*, 251.

32. Society records indicate that more than 90 percent of the Cass County old settlers had been born in slave states (Glenn, *History of Cass County*, 228–51; Fulton Old Settlers Association, Constitution, and Member List, Bourbon County History, Collection 668, box 1, KSHS).

ternal relations" among the area's inhabitants, but it was organized in 1897 with an explicitly more apolitical purpose. At the meetings of the Bates County group, no member was permitted "to publicly discuss any political, religious, or other subject in manner calculated to injure the feelings or mar the enjoyment of other members there present." Because anyone who had lived within the county for more than twenty-five years could join the Old Settlers, the organization's mixed ranks included a large number of former Unionists and Confederates. Any discussion of slavery, secession, and border disputes, which could unnecessarily stir up hard feelings, was considered taboo, and offenders who engaged in such inappropriate behavior were to be struck from the Old Settlers membership rolls. "The past is behind us," wrote one old settler. "Our duty is to the future and as patriotic Americans we should turn our eyes in that direction."[33] A blanket proscription on such topics, however, suggested that raw feelings and wartime divisions nonetheless lingered among old-stock congregants.

Reunions and local histories were opportunities for longtime settlers to put their best historical faces forward. Long on self-congratulation and short on criticism, the histories that began appearing in the 1880s retold the border counties' past as their boosters preferred to see it. "The fact is that the fathers and mothers of the Civil War period were the best and purest and bravest men and women that ever lived in anybody's time or country," claimed one admiring Kansas writer. The pleasant reflections and flattering biographies contained within these volumes obscured more contentious elements of the border's history. Local authors recognized that the dispossession of the Osages, violent controversies over railroads, and ruthless guerrilla warfare were indelible parts of the recent past but maintained that these episodes, like the divisions they fostered, belonged to a bygone era. The experiences of African Americans were also conspicuously absent, perhaps because many black emigrants were long gone, having fled slavery in Missouri for freedom in Kansas and beyond. Citizens gladly heralded the Union that had been preserved through a devastating war but generally overlooked its other central accomplishment, the emancipation of million of black slaves.[34]

From the perspective of old-stock boosters, the communities that had developed on opposite sides of the open state line—overwhelmingly

33. Bates County Old Settlers Society, *Old Settlers' History,* 83, 142.
34. Mitchell, *Linn County,* 382; Bates County Old Settlers Society, *Old Settlers' History,* 32–199; Atkeson, *History of Bates County,* 135–43; J. Johnson, *History of Vernon County,* 223–337.

white, agrarian, native born, patriotic, and Protestant—seemed nearly indistinguishable. A reconciled border, one whose past had been depoliticized and cleansed of ugly tensions, was easily embraced by a wide swath of people in each state. Whether old-stock or new, Democrats or Republicans, farmers or merchants, Unionists or rebels, settlers of many different backgrounds preferred reunion over rancor, healing over hostility. A preference for social harmony and economic prosperity nurtured this carefully constructed historical memory. Reconciliation was good for business: it kindled cross-border commerce and stimulated economic growth, making the borderland a more attractive destination to potential immigrants.[35]

Like thousands of newcomers, for whom the border war was a bitter and unfamiliar part of someone else's past, boosters shared an active interest in seeing the embers of that conflict extinguished at last. Local promoters and developers in Missouri and Kansas had fashioned a new kind of border over the past quarter century, one that better fitted the needs of the postwar world they occupied together. By encouraging the erosion of old antagonisms and the establishment of commercial, political, and social ties, growth-minded citizens helped to refashion the state line, transforming the once-divisive boundary into a more benign relic of collective memory. Losing its once-powerful significance as an emblem of America at war with itself, the Kansas-Missouri border instead gained fresh meaning as an example of reconciliation.

Settlers whose experiences and memories did not readily fit the boosters' narrative of progress maintained a rather different view of the war along the state line. Former Confederates sympathizers, for example, cultivated an alternative memory of the war, sharing a perspective tinged with bitterness and regret that held that although the fighting was finished, hard feelings still remained. The southern identity of many old-stock Missourians likewise endured, having withstood both the demise of the Confederacy and the postwar developments that had brought together reconciliationists in each state. This defensive but proud identity was inextricably linked to memories of the war, as it had first taken shape during the struggle over Kansas Territory, when proslavery citizens were quick to define themselves in opposition to their free-state rivals. Southern identity continued to rest on the twin pillars of female virtue and male honor, but by the late nineteenth century it also mingled nostalgia for the antebellum past with outspoken American patriotism. Devotion to the Stars and Stripes was now universal along the state line, as were shared notions of white supremacy. Former

35. For the link between reconciliation and historical amnesia, see Kammen, *Mystic Chords of Memory*, 13.

slaveholders, however, stood apart in their steadfast defenses of chattel bondage and descriptions of loyal, contented slaves, most of whom purportedly abandoned the family farm only at the orders of federals and Kansans. "The slaves, as a rule, did not want to go," said Mrs. J. A. B. Adcock.[36]

The United Daughters of the Confederacy was an active vehicle for the preservation of southern identity in Missouri. Before and during the Civil War, newspapers and journals throughout the Confederate states had been the primary media through which southerners cultivated a distinctive regional identity. On the postwar Kansas border, however, most newspapers belonged to recent immigrants and people who had little interest in honoring the Confederacy or those who fought for it. The responsibility of celebrating southern valor and transmitting pride in the South's cause thus fell to private citizens and groups such as the UDC. In addition to memorializing the Confederate dead, the organization's Missouri Division endeavored to record the wartime contributions and experiences of southern women. "Teaching our children to love the dear old Southland" was a foremost responsibility of the group. Future generations, one member declared, needed "to become imbued with the right emotions, sentiments and principles, always remembering that their fathers were never *rebels nor traitors to their country.*"[37]

The hard feelings and divisions engendered by the border war did not dissipate quickly on either side of the state line. "The feeling of animosity that was engendered during that strife never died out among those who were engaged in it," explained one Missouri woman.[38] In spite of booster assertions to the contrary, many Kansans and Missourians understood that memories of the border between them, particularly the oft-told tales of bloodshed, destruction, and vengeance, were still a source of dissension. Survivors continued to cast blame as they saw fit; free-soil and proslavery partisans, Unionists and rebels, ruffians and jayhawkers, bushwhackers and red-legs, all had committed grievous wrongs, but the judgment that one rendered depended on a person's wartime loyalties. Even after several decades, inhabitants of each state reflected on the same events and people with vastly different perspectives.

When it came to the border war's most famous combatants, acclaim or notoriety rested in the eye of the beholder. James Montgomery and Charles "Doc" Jennison died in 1871 and 1884, respectively, but remained

36. United Daughters of the Confederacy, Missouri Division, *Reminiscences*, 91; Rubin, *Shattered Nation*, 50; Faust, *Confederate Nationalism*, 10–22.
37. United Daughters of the Confederacy, Missouri Division, *Reminiscences*, 5–6. See also Rubin, *Shattered Nation*, 208–11; and Whites, *Crisis in Gender*, 14.
38. United Daughters of the Confederacy, Missouri Division, *Reminiscences*, 93.

divisive long after their passing. Effusive tributes to Montgomery lined the pages of one Linn County history, which also described the physician-turned-guerrilla Jennison as a "young scamp" whose bright future was undone by "sinful habits" and "plundering proclivities." The Missourians affected by cross-border raids, meanwhile, deplored the Kansans as men of unsparing brutality. "The history of the world," wrote Mrs. N. M. Harris, "furnishes no parallel to the consummate, cruel, low-down, contemptible conduct of Jennison's band of Jayhawkers when they marched over our fair land." The guerrilla leader, she maintained, killed men in front of their families and even shot a woman who was trying to shield her husband, an extraordinary charge for an era in which all sides condemned the use of force upon women.[39]

There was likewise no middle ground when it came to describing John Brown, perhaps the most famous person associated with the territorial struggle in Kansas. While southern critics dismissed the executed abolitionist as a fanatic, his defenders hailed him as a martyr whose valor and self-sacrifice had saved Kansas, the West, and all of the United States from slavery's clutches. "John Brown was not a statesman, not a philosopher, not even a leader," said one Paola resident. "He was truly a hero."[40] Former Confederates were nearly as quick to praise the guerrillas who defended western Missouri against federal troops and Kansas raiders. "These Missourians were noble people," wrote W. L. Webb, "but they believed in slavery, and they were quick to resent anything like encroachment on the rights of slave property." Almost forty years after the war ended, however, at least one Kansan was still appalled by the reunions that drew together men who fought under William Quantrill. "The Quantrill reunions are the last wrigglings of the dying snake's tail," remarked George Martin.[41]

Decades after the fact, members of the Civil War generation earnestly questioned which incident was a more inexcusable tragedy, the 1861 attack on Osceola by James Lane's Kansans or the massacre of nearly two hundred Lawrence residents by Quantrill and his Missouri guerrillas. In January 1899, eighty-one-year-old newspaper editor John Speer stood before the annual gathering of the Kansas State Historical Society, a group of which he had been named president, and addressed the claim that the

39. Mitchell, *Linn County*, 15–24, 190–91; United Daughters of the Confederacy, Missouri Division, *Reminiscences*, 216–17.

40. Samuel J. Shively, address before meeting of KSHS, December 1, 1903, in Mitchell, *Linn County*, 77–79. See also Dalton, *Under the Black Flag*, 99.

41. Martin, *The First Two Years of Kansas; or, Where, When, and How the Missouri Bushwhacker, the Missouri Train Robber, and Those Who Stole Themselves Rich in the Name of Liberty, Were Sired and Reared*, 29 (both quotes).

destruction of Lawrence had been an act of justifiable retaliation for the devastation visited upon Osceola two years earlier. Speer had visited the Missouri town in 1897 to gather information for a biography he was writing on Lane. Observing that a small number of the settlers affected by the raid were still living, the visitor found little evidence to suggest lingering wartime animosities. "On the contrary," he reported, "it seemed to give people pleasure to relate the story of Osceola." Troops destroyed two large warehouses and nearly every other building within the town, whose location along the Osage River had made it an important trade center for settlers from southwest Missouri and northwest Arkansas. Relatively few people were in the town at the time, as most men had gone to fight in Sterling Price's pro-Confederate Missouri State Guard, and most of their families had scattered into the surrounding countryside.[42]

Prominent citizens also told Speer that Lane's men treated the wounded rebels, women, and noncombatants they had found with considerable kindness. The soldiers' conduct, the writer maintained, was a testament to "the wisdom, the honor and the humanity of the Kansas troops." The elderly speaker concluded that the attack on Osceola was a legitimate act of war, carried out to destroy supplies that inevitably would have fallen into Price's hands. He contrasted the raid with the "horrid murders" at Lawrence, where scores of unarmed men and boys died at the hands of dishonorable Missouri bushwhackers. Members of the audience no doubt supported the argument that there was no moral equivalence between the two attacks. For John Speer, it was a personal and painful question that had been settled long ago. On that dark morning in August 1863, Quantrill's raiders had killed two of his teenage sons, John and Robert, and had destroyed the family's home and newspaper office in Lawrence.[43] For thousands of people such as Speer, the memory of the border was a piercing ache that time served only to dull, but not fully eliminate.

At least one guerrilla who rode to Lawrence expressed regret for his actions that day. John McCorkle, a bushwhacker scout who eventually retired to a farm in central Missouri, concluded his memoirs by conveying his "hope that my enemies will forgive me for any wrong act of mine." Kit Dalton also participated in the slaughter at Lawrence but made few apologies for his fellow raiders. Quantrill's men had "many grievances to redress, many causes for the thirst for vengeance," he explained. "We fought to avenge the cruel murder of our loved ones," the guerilla continued,

42. Speer, "Burning of Osceola," 305–9; Martin, *First Two Years of Kansas*, 26. Support for the claim that women and children fled Osceola ahead of the Kansas raiders can be found in United Daughters of the Confederacy, Missouri Division, *Reminiscences*, 59–65.
43. Speer, "Burning of Osceola," 309–12.

perhaps alluding in particular to the jail collapse in Kansas City days before the raid, which killed the female family members of at least two guerrillas, or in general to the harassment of Missouri settlers by Kansas jayhawkers. (None of Dalton's relatives died in the jail accident, however, as the Kentucky native had arrived in Missouri only weeks earlier.) He derided the apparent cowardice of their victims in Lawrence, many of whom were roused out of bed, unarmed, and shot, saying, "We did expect the resistance of soldiers and men, instead of which we met with cowards, renegades and Kansas Red Legs, all pleading instead of shooting; begging instead of fighting." He acknowledged the thorough and shocking brutality of the attack and described it as "butchery of the bloodiest sort" and "merciless murder. . . of men too terror stricken to surrender and too wild with the fright that possessed them to offer any effective resistance." He attributed the bushwhackers' ruthlessness to the no-quarter policy of the Union army, which had vowed to execute captured guerrillas, but still believed their vengeful actions justified. "We erred? Yes, of course we did," he conceded. "We were human beings, outlawed by the national government and hunted like wild beasts—not permitted to surrender."[44]

No episode of the entire border war was as roundly questioned and defended as the Union army's controversial removal of Southern sympathizers from four Missouri counties. Many Confederate sympathizers denounced Order No. 11 as a vengeful effort by Unionists to punish Missourians for the attack on Lawrence. "Nothing could be more absurd," answered General John M. Schofield. "It was an act of wisdom, courage, and humanity by which the lives of hundreds of innocent people were saved and a disgraceful conflict brought to a summary close. Not a life was sacrificed nor any great discomfort inflicted in carrying out the order." R. H. Hunt, a veteran of the Fifteenth Kansas Cavalry, attributed the controversy surrounding the order to the "intense ignorance and disloyalty" of its critics, who failed to appreciate that the depopulation was justified by the necessities of war. Other former soldiers offered credulous descriptions of the order's impact. A Kansas veteran named W. C. Ransom recalled that Order No. 11—a policy that affected an area of more than twenty-five hundred square miles—displaced between sixty or seventy families and claimed their removal "was executed in no cruel or vindictive spirit."[45]

Thomas Ewing, the general who issued the order and a lightning rod for criticism from all quarters, certainly agreed. "Order No. 11 was issued

---

44. McCorkle, *Three Years with Quantrill,* 157; Dalton, *Under the Black Flag,* 8, 101–3.
45. Schofield to Thomas Ewing, January 25, 1877; Hunt, "General Orders No. 11," 4, box 212, folder A; Ransom to Ewing, January 10, May 30, 1871, box 212, folder D, Ewing Family Papers, Manuscript Division, Library of Congress, hereinafter cited as TE-LOC.

out of a spirit of mercy to the people whose homes were in the border counties. Those people were told that they must move, and they did so without any show of interference," he maintained. Speaking at a Kansas City reception in 1890, the general assured his audience that disloyal Missourians "were no more inconvenienced than any of you would be to-day who had to change your place of abode." Years of criticism had wounded Ewing, but he remained steadfastly unrepentant about his decision to evacuate the border counties. "The charge that I was cruel to my fellow-beings while in a position to command is galling. Yet, if I had to do it over again, I would do it in the same way."[46] The passage of time had certainly obscured the policy's harshness in the eyes of the men who carried it out. After the devastating total war that William Tecumseh Sherman, who happened to be Ewing's brother-in-law, waged against civilians in the Deep South, Order No. 11 seemed a less extraordinary measure and instead represented an early lesson in the army's sweeping attempts to subdue an entire society of disloyal persons.

Missourians who witnessed or suffered under the order rejected any assertion about the policy's leniency. "O, the misery!" exclaimed one witness, decades after the depopulation took place. "Old men, women, and children plodding the dusty roads barefooted, with nothing to eat save what was furnished by friendly citizens." Time did little to soften another woman's enduring contempt for Ewing, who passed away in 1896. "I try to forgive, but I cannot—no cannot forget," wrote Frances Fristoe Twyman. "If Tom Ewing is in heaven today his inner life must have been greatly changed." George Caleb Bingham, the federal officer and painter who had roundly condemned the order, flatly rejected the denials of fellow Union veterans. "It is well known that men were shot down in the very act of obeying the order, and their wagons and effects seized by their murderers," he contended. "Bare-footed and bare-headed women and children, stripped of every article of clothing except a scant covering for their bodies, were exposed to the heat of an August sun and compelled to struggle through the dust on foot. All their means of transportation had been seized by their spoilers, except an occasional dilapidated cart, or an old and superannuated horse." Ewing's order, Bingham concluded, was "an act of purely arbitrary power, directed against a disarmed and defenceless population. It was an exhibition of cowardice in its most odious and repulsive form."[47] Even the ranks of Union veterans, once bound

46. Ewing, statement, January 1890, box 212, folder A, TE-LOC.
47. United Daughters of the Confederacy, Missouri Division, *Reminiscences*, 27, 263; Bingham to editor of *Jefferson City Republican* (reprint), February 22, 1877, box 212, folder D, TE-LOC.

together by mutual devotion to their country, remained ever divided, Missourian against Kansan.

By the turn of the twentieth century, the Kansas-Missouri border war still held tremendous power over its survivors and their descendants. Industrialization, immigration, and decades of modernizing change had eroded the divisive significance of the state line, but the boundary nonetheless endured as a meaningful historical touchstone. For the great many people who were able to reconcile with old foes, the peaceful border was a testament to their own magnanimity. For the citizens who found that wartime identities and resentments were not easily relinquished, the border lingered on as a symbol of division. The shadow of guerrilla warfare continued to loom so heavily over the border counties that one member of the UDC found that writing a balanced history of the conflict was a nearly impossible task. "It will be a terrible chapter when finally written," said W. L. Webb. "This generation is too close to the horrible things done in those awful days. Too many private wrongs were avenged; too many unpardonable deeds were committed. These are fresh in the memory of those old enough to see them, and those of us born since then inherit a sort of abhorrent memory of the time."[48]

That cultural inheritance has persisted for yet another hundred years and today animates the athletic "Border Showdown" between the Jayhawks and Tigers, teams whose mascots can be traced, not surprisingly, back to the Civil War era.[49] Cross-border hostilities have long since been defused and channeled into socially appropriate outlets; grudges are settled now on a basketball court, not a battlefield. Yet partisans from each state nonetheless believe, as did citizens a century and a half earlier, that the border between them—a line that divides state from state and links the present and past—still matters.

48. United Daughters of the Confederacy, Missouri Division, *Reminiscences,* 272.
49. The Tigers were a militia unit that organized to defend Columbia and Boone County, home to the University of Missouri, from marauding bands.

APPENDIX: TABLES

TABLE 1. NATIVITY OF MISSOURI BORDER POPULATION, 1850

	TOTAL POPULATION	HEADS OF HOUSEHOLD
Missouri	44.2	8.0
Lower Midwest	13.2	12.5
Upper South	34.7	62.4
Northern	1.3	3.0
Southern	5.4	10.7
Foreign	0.8	3.0
Miscellaneous	0.5	0.7

Notes: The Lower Midwest group includes persons born in the states of Illinois, Indiana, Ohio, Pennsylvania, Iowa, and New Jersey; for the Upper South group, the states are Kentucky, Tennessee, Virginia, Maryland, Delaware, and Arkansas; for the Northern group, New York, Connecticut, Rhode Island, Massachusetts, Vermont, New Hampshire, Maine, Michigan, and Wisconsin; and for the Southern group, North Carolina, South Carolina, Georgia, Alabama, Mississippi, Florida, Louisiana, and Texas. The Miscellaneous group includes persons born in "Indian Territory" or individuals whose nativity was illegible. A similar regional nativity framework can be found in James R. Shortridge, *Peopling the Plains: Who Settled Where in Frontier Kansas*, 15–45.

The percentages listed above are averages of the nativity data gathered from Bates and Cass Counties. Vernon County had not yet been organized.

Source: Author's sample, U.S. Bureau of the Census, Manuscript Census, Missouri, Bates and Cass Counties, Schedule I (Population), 1850. For a detailed explanation of the sample and its methodology, see the Note on Statistical Tables and Methods.

TABLE 2. DISTRIBUTION OF OCCUPATIONS, MISSOURI HOUSEHOLD HEADS, 1850

OCCUPATION	BATES COUNTY	CASS COUNTY
Farmer	49.0	36.3
Tenant/Farm Laborer	41.3	54.1
Trade	1.5	2.7
Professional	2.5	3.3
Service	0.6	0.2
Skilled/Semiskilled	4.4	2.9
Other Laborer	0.8	0.4

Notes: The Tenant/Farm Laborer group includes individuals identified as "tenant farmers," "farm laborers," or "farmers" with zero real property; the Trade group includes merchants, grocers, traders, and dealers of various goods; the Professional group, ministers, attorneys, physicians, teachers, managers, and political officials; the Service group, clerks and hotel, saloon, and livery-stable keepers; the Skilled/Semiskilled group, artisans and apprentices.

Figures are percentages.

Source: Author's sample, U.S. Bureau of the Census, Manuscript Census, Missouri, Bates and Cass Counties, Schedule I (Population), 1850.

TABLE 3. NATIVITY OF HOUSEHOLDS WITH PARENTS OF KANSAS-BORN CHILDREN, 1854–1860

	PARENTS OF CHILDREN BORN IN KANSAS *from 1854 to 1856*	PARENTS OF CHILDREN BORN IN KANSAS *from 1857 to 1860*
% of households with both parents born in slave states	57.6	28.4
% of households with both parents born in slave and free states	15.2	20.9
% of households with both parents born in free states	27.3	50.7
	n = 33 households	n = 282 households

Note: This sample represents an imperfect expression of the changing population of southeastern Kansas. First, it must be noted that a person's place of birth did not determine his or her ideological outlook; not all southern immigrants supported slavery, and several northeastern natives in Missouri were themselves slave owners. Aside from the flaws that invariably hampered the census enumerations of the nineteenth century, there also are obvious methodological limitations in using data gleaned in 1860 to look backward at what happened in the preceding six years. After all, not every family who moved to Kansas and had children there stayed long enough to be counted in the decennial federal census. The structure of the sample here is also, by its very nature, limited. It does not account for the great many individuals and families who immigrated to Kansas but did not have children, nor does it include the families whose Kansas-born babies died in childbirth. Despite the relatively small size of the sample, its raw numbers nonetheless illuminate another important change in the territorial population. Whereas only 33 households had children born in Kansas during the early territorial period, that total jumped to 282 for the later period. Later immigrants were not only more likely to come from free states but also arriving in greater numbers and producing more children than the territory's earliest settlers.

Source: Author's sample, U.S. Bureau of the Census, Manuscript Census, Kansas, Bourbon, Linn, and Miami Counties, Schedule I (Population), 1860. For an assessment of nineteenth-century federal census enumerations, see Donald H. Parkerson, "Comments on the Underenumeration of the U.S. Census, 1850–1880," 509–15.

TABLE 4. NATIVITY OF SETTLERS, KANSAS BORDER COUNTIES, 1860

| | TOTAL POPULATION | | | HEADS OF HOUSEHOLD | | |
	BOURBON	LINN	MIAMI	BOURBON	LINN	MIAMI
Missouri	14.1	12.7	16.2	3.6	4.5	4.7
Kansas	7.1	7.7	11.7	0.0	1.0	0.0
Lower Midwest	46.0	48.7	30.4	44.0	45.2	33.2
Upper South	16.3	12.9	19.3	27.1	23.1	27.2
Northern	8.9	11.5	13.2	12.8	16.2	20.8
Southern	3.2	3.0	3.1	4.3	2.8	5.4
Foreign	4.5	3.4	6.1	8.7	7.2	8.7

Note: Figures are percentages.

Source: Author's sample, U.S. Bureau of the Census, Manuscript Census, Kansas, Bourbon, Linn, and Miami Counties, Schedule I (Population), 1860.

TABLE 5. NATIVITY OF TOTAL POPULATION, KANSAS AND MISSOURI BORDER COUNTIES, 1860

NATIVITY	MISSOURI COUNTIES	KANSAS COUNTIES
Missouri	42.5	12.8
Kansas	0.2	7.8
North	1.6	11.8
Lower Midwest	19.6	45.0
Upper South	31.5	15.0
Deep South	3.1	3.2
Foreign	1.5	4.3
Miscellaneous	0.0	0.0

Note: Figures are percentages.

Source: Author's sample, U.S. Bureau of the Census, Manuscript Census, Schedule I (Population), 1860: Missouri, Bates, Cass, and Vernon Counties; Kansas, Bourbon, Linn, and Miami Counties.

TABLE 6. DISTRIBUTION OF OCCUPATIONS, MISSOURI BORDER COUNTIES, 1850–1880

| | 1850 | | | 1860 | | |
	BATES	CASS		BATES	CASS	VERNON
Occupation						
Farmer	49.0	36.3		45.2	51.0	52.7
Tenant/Farm Laborer	41.3	54.1		28.0	13.3	31.3
Trade	1.5	2.7		3.3	2.8	0.9
Professional	2.5	3.3		3.7	7.7	4.2
Service	0.6	0.2		3.1	3.2	0.7
Skilled/Semiskilled	4.4	2.9		13.7	13.3	9.5
Other Laborer	0.8	0.4		3.1	8.6	0.7

| | 1870 | | | 1880 | | |
	BATES	CASS	VERNON	BATES	CASS	VERNON
Occupation						
Farmer	45.7	48.7	40.5	57.4	51.2	52.0
Tenant/Farm Laborer	29.1	21.0	23.7	16.1	14.1	21.2
Trade	4.3	2.8	5.0	3.0	3.7	1.7
Professional	2.6	4.2	3.6	4.1	4.4	5.2
Service	3.8	5.1	2.5	3.0	2.9	3.7
Skilled/Semiskilled	6.8	8.6	12.5	5.2	7.3	5.4
Other Laborer	7.7	9.6	12.2	11.2	16.5	10.8

Notes: Figures are percentages.

"Tenant/Farm Laborer" includes people listed as tenants and farmers whose real estate holdings equaled zero. Real estate values were not taken in the 1880 census. "Trade" includes grocers, merchants, "traders," shopkeepers, and "dealers" in various goods. "Professional" includes ministers, attorneys, physicians, teachers, managers, and political officials. "Service" includes clerks and hotel, saloon, and livery-stable keepers.

Source: Author's sample, U.S. Bureau of the Census, Manuscript Census, Missouri, Bates, Cass, and Vernon Counties, Schedule I (Population), 1850–1880.

TABLE 7. DISTRIBUTION OF OCCUPATIONS, KANSAS BORDER COUNTIES, 1860–1880

| | 1860 | | | 1870 | | |
	BOURBON	LINN	MIAMI	BOURBON	LINN	MIAMI
Occupation						
Farmer	8.3	45.2	44.6	27.0	35.3	30.8
Tenant/Farm Laborer	69.2	35.7	19.5	24.4	42.1	46.7
Trade	1.8	2.2	3.4	4.0	2.9	2.0
Professional	5.5	5.3	5.4	3.6	3.1	4.0
Service	2.5	1.1	2.0	4.9	1.0	2.5
Skilled/Semiskilled	8.8	7.2	13.7	17.7	10.2	7.9
Other Laborer	4.0	3.3	11.5	18.4	5.2	6.2

| | 1880 | | |
	BOURBON	LINN	MIAMI
Occupation			
Farmer	37.5	51.9	48.4
Tenant/Farm Laborer	18.8	26.0	17.5
Trade	3.1	3.0	1.8
Professional	6.4	4.3	7.1
Service	4.4	2.1	2.8
Skilled/Semiskilled	10.8	5.9	12.2
Other Laborer	19.0	6.8	10.4

Notes: Figures are percentages.

"Tenant/Farm Laborer" includes people listed as tenants and farmers whose real estate holdings equaled zero. Real estate values were not taken in the 1880 census. "Trade" includes grocers, merchants, "traders," shopkeepers, and "dealers" in various goods. "Professional" includes ministers, attorneys, physicians, teachers, managers, and political officials. "Service" includes clerks and hotel, saloon, and livery-stable keepers.

Source: Author's sample, U.S. Bureau of the Census, Manuscript Census, Kansas, Bourbon, Linn, and Miami Counties, Schedule I (Population), 1850–1880.

TABLE 8. NATIVITY OF SOUTHERN HEADS OF HOUSEHOLD, KANSAS BORDER COUNTIES, 1860

NATIVITY	TOTAL NUMBER	PERCENTAGE
Alabama	2	0.8
Arkansas	3	1.1
Georgia	1	0.4
Kentucky	98	37.5
Maryland	12	4.6
Missouri	37	14.2
Tennessee	54	20.7
Virginia	54	20.7

Source: Author's sample, U.S. Bureau of the Census, Manuscript Census, Kansas, Bourbon, Linn, Miami Counties, Schedule I (Population), 1860.

TABLE 9. RESULTS OF MISSOURI GUBERNATORIAL ELECTION, 1860

	STATEWIDE	BATES COUNTY	CASS COUNTY	VERNON COUNTY
Hancock Jackson (Breckinridge Democrat)	7	16	21	38
Claiborne Fox Jackson (Douglas Democrat)	47	65	31	44
Sample Orr (Constitutional Unionist)	42	19	48	18
James Gardenhire (Republican)	4	0	0	0

Note: Figures are percentages.

Source: Missouri Gubernatorial Election Results, Bates, Cass, and Vernon Counties, 1860, Missouri State Archives.

TABLE 10. RELIGIOUS AFFILIATION ALONG THE KANSAS-MISSOURI BORDER, 1870

	BAPTIST		METHODIST		PRESBYTERIAN		ALL DENOMINATIONS	
	ORGS.	MEMBERS	ORGS.	MEMBERS	ORGS.	MEMBERS	ORGS.	MEMBERSHIP
Kansas								
Bourbon Co.	4	400	12	425	5	385	27	1,970
Linn Co.	7	1,100	6	1,200	8	2,700	29	7,800
Miami Co.	5	800	2	400	0	0	9	1,375
Missouri								
Bates Co.	1	N/A	3	100	2	300	7	500
Cass Co.	13	3,250	30	4,500	13	4,500	68	15,325
Vernon Co.	4	N/A	6	300	3	N/A	17	600

Source: U.S. Bureau of the Census, Ninth Census: The Statistics of the Population of the United States. Other primary sources suggest that the striking disparities between the number of church organizations and church membership in some counties—Cass County had a total church membership of 15,325 people, while Bates County had only 500 members—can be attributed more to the work done by the census enumerator(s) in each county than to extraordinary differences in religious devotion. A Kansas state report from 1878, for example, found 46 church organizations in Miami County, while an 1883 local history of Missouri, for example, identified 73 and 58 churches in Cass and Bates Counties, respectively. See Kansas State Board of Agriculture, First Biennial Report of the State Board of Agriculture to the Legislature of the State of Kansas for the Years 1877–78, 316; and O. P. Williams, The History of Cass and Bates Counties, Missouri.

TABLE 11. NATIVITY OF MISSOURI BORDER POPULATION, 1870–1880

1870	TOTAL POPULATION				HEADS OF HOUSEHOLD			
	ALL COUNTIES	BATES	CASS	VERNON	ALL COUNTIES	BATES	CASS	VERNON
Missouri	33.6	31.2	32.1	39.9	11.3	10.7	10.6	13.5
Kansas	1.3	1.4	0.9	1.9	0.0	0.0	0.0	0.0
Lower Midwest	34.8	41.2	31.6	30.5	33.3	38.9	30.6	30.0
Upper South	20.1	15.3	24.7	17.6	38.3	32.9	41.7	40.1
Northern	3.7	4.0	2.8	4.7	6.8	7.4	4.7	9.6
Southern	2.1	1.1	2.4	3.3	3.4	1.7	4.7	3.4
Foreign	3.5	5.0	3.6	1.4	6.9	8.4	7.8	3.4
Miscellaneous	1.0	0.9	1.3	0.7	0.0	0.0	0.0	0.0

1880	TOTAL POPULATION				HEADS OF HOUSEHOLD			
	ALL COUNTIES	BATES	CASS	VERNON	ALL COUNTIES	BATES	CASS	VERNON
Missouri	49.4	49.8	47.6	50.7	23.6	27.5	16.6	26.8
Kansas	2.2	3.0	1.8	1.5	0.5	0.6	0.3	0.4
Lower Midwest	28.5	29.0	27.3	29.1	35.9	37.3	35.5	33.7
Upper South	14.1	13.6	15.9	12.5	26.9	24.0	31.4	26.0
Northern	1.7	1.0	1.9	2.2	3.5	2.1	4.8	4.1
Southern	1.5	1.4	1.6	1.4	3.3	3.3	3.5	3.3
Foreign	2.3	1.8	3.3	1.9	6.2	5.3	7.6	5.7
Miscellaneous	0.5	0.4	0.5	0.8	0.1	0.0	0.3	0.0

Note: Figures are percentages.

Source: Author's sample, U.S. Bureau of the Census, Manuscript Census, Missouri, Bates, Cass, and Vernon Counties, Schedule I (Population), 1870–1880.

TABLE 12. NATIVITY OF KANSAS BORDER POPULATION, 1870–1880 (AS A PERCENTAGE)

1870	TOTAL POPULATION				HEADS OF HOUSEHOLD			
	ALL COUNTIES	BOURBON	LINN	MIAMI	ALL COUNTIES	BOURBON	LINN	MIAMI
Missouri	8.5	6.8	10.6	8.6	5.9	5.5	6.5	5.9
Kansas	19.4	16.6	22.3	20.1	0.5	1.1	0.0	0.5
Lower Midwest	43.1	43.1	43.1	43.0	41.1	38.4	44.8	40.3
Upper South	11.6	12.9	10.6	10.8	21.3	21.4	22.8	19.5
Northern	9.0	10.9	7.8	7.5	15.6	17.0	15.1	14.5
Southern	2.0	1.7	2.3	2.0	3.4	3.0	3.5	4.0
Foreign	5.9	7.5	2.5	7.5	11.7	13.3	6.9	14.9
Miscellaneous	0.6	0.6	0.8	0.4	0.4	0.4	0.4	0.5

1880	TOTAL POPULATION				HEADS OF HOUSEHOLD			
	ALL COUNTIES	BOURBON	LINN	MIAMI	ALL COUNTIES	BOURBON	LINN	MIAMI
Missouri	8.5	8.9	9.0	7.6	8.0	8.3	8.3	7.3
Kansas	30.3	30.2	32.1	28.9	0.8	0.0	0.0	2.8
Lower Midwest	39.1	36.3	39.4	42.1	47.8	43.5	47.0	53.8
Upper South	9.3	10.8	9.3	7.7	17.0	18.2	18.6	13.8
Northern	5.7	6.0	6.4	4.6	11.9	12.3	13.8	9.2
Southern	1.9	1.0	1.0	2.7	3.3	2.8	5.5	1.4
Foreign	5.0	6.6	2.3	6.4	11.1	15.0	6.7	11.9
Miscellaneous	0.3	0.2	0.6	0.0	0.0	0.0	0.0	0.0

Note: Figures are percentages.

Source: Author's sample, U.S. Bureau of the Census, Manuscript Census, Kansas, Bourbon, Linn, and Miami Counties, Schedule I (Population), 1870–1880.

TABLE 13. AFRICAN AMERICAN BORDER POPULATION, 1860–1870

| | 1860 | | 1870 | |
	POPULATION	% TOTAL POPULATION	POPULATION	% TOTAL POPULATION
Kansas				
Bourbon	65	1.0	770	5.1
Linn	1	0.02	655	5.4
Miami	0	0	466	4.0
Total	66		1891	
Missouri				
Bates	450	6	120	0.8
Cass	1013	10	502	2.6
Vernon	138	3	82	0.7
Total	1601		704	

Sources: U.S. Bureau of the Census, *Eighth Census: Population of the United States, Compiled from the Original Returns,* 162–65; 286–98; U.S. Bureau of the Census, *Ninth Census: The Statistics of the Population of the United States,* 29–30, 43–45, 143–145, 187–95.

TABLE 14. SCHOOL ATTENDANCE RATES, KANSAS AND MISSOURI CHILDREN, 1850–1880

	1850	1860	1870	1880
Kansas				
Bourbon County		32.4	38.4	43.3
Linn County		28.3	46.9	46.3
Miami County		29.0	39.5	49.2
Boys		31.0	40.8	46.2
Girls		28.6	42.4	46.2
Black Children		0.0	36.0	34.4
Missouri				
Bates County	22.7	36.5	39.4	44.6
Cass County	31.0	41.6	43.0	48.0
Vernon County		36.6	36.1	41.5
Boys	29.2	40.2	42.7	44.7
Girls	24.5	36.2	37.2	45.2
Black Children	0.0	0.0	15.4	34.3

Note: Figures are percentages.

Source: Author's sample, U.S. Bureau of the Census, Manuscript Census, Kansas, Bourbon, Linn, and Miami Counties, Schedule I (Population), 1860–1880; and Missouri, Bates, Cass, and Vernon Counties, Schedule I (Population), 1850–1880.

TABLE 15. AVERAGE ANNUAL INVESTMENT IN IMPLEMENTS, 1850–1880

	1850	1860	1870	1880
Kansas				
Bourbon Co	N/A	N/A	111.49	188.21
Linn Co.	N/A	N/A	119.44	90.36
Miami Co.	N/A	N/A	107.24	100.79
Missouri				
Bates Co.	51.27	145.78	50.74	112.81
Cass Co.	62.66	108.86	141.54	116.35
Vernon Co.	N/A	106.33	139.95	104.94

Note: Figures are in dollars.

Source: Author's sample, U.S. Bureau of the Census, Manuscript Census, Kansas, Bourbon, Linn, and Miami Counties, Schedule II (Agriculture), 1850–1880; and Missouri, Bates, Cass, and Vernon Counties, Schedule II (Agriculture), 1850–1880.

TABLE 16. ACREAGE RATIOS FOR MAJOR GRAIN CROPS, KANSAS FARMS,
1872–1896

COUNTY, YEAR	CORN ACRES	% CORN	OATS ACRES	% OATS	WHEAT ACRES	% WHEAT
Bourbon, 1872	33,661	56	15,148	25	11,292	19
Bourbon, 1887	74,052	78	19,151	20	1,422	2
Bourbon, 1896	89,127	79	20,947	18	3,194	3
Linn, 1872	28,314	73	8,098	21	2,307	6
Linn, 1887	88,241	80	20,382	18	2,085	2
Linn, 1896	104,402	82	20,371	16	1,862	1
Miami, 1872	54,070	74	12,285	17	6,731	9
Miami, 1887	82,323	75	26,422	24	1,101	1
Miami, 1896	123,385	83	21,004	14	3,736	3

Source: Kansas State Board of Agriculture, *Records of the Kansas State Board of Agriculture: Abstracts of Statistical Rolls, 1873,* vol. 3; Kansas State Board of Agriculture, *Tenth Biennial Report of the Kansas State Board of Agriculture to the Legislature of the State for the Years 1895 and 1896.*

TABLE 17. PROPORTION OF IMPROVED LAND IN MAJOR GRAIN CROPS,
1880

COUNTY	% IMPROVED LAND IN MAJOR GRAIN CROPS	% IN CORN	% IN OATS	% IN WHEAT
Kansas				
Bourbon	58	50	3	5
Linn	58	49	6	3
Miami	54	45	5	4
Missouri				
Bates	63	53	6	4
Cass	70	53	12	5
Vernon	61	46	9	6

Note: Unlike table 16, which focuses only on the improved acreage that was planted in corn, oats, and wheat, this table examines all improved acreage, including lands that were used for pasture and for lesser crops.

Source: Author's sample, U.S. Bureau of the Census, Manuscript Census, Kansas, Bourbon, Linn, and Miami Counties, Schedule II (Agriculture), 1880; and Missouri, Bates, Cass, and Vernon Counties, Schedule II (Agriculture), 1880.

TABLE 18. FENCING PREFERENCES OF KANSAS SETTLERS, 1883

FENCING TYPE	BOURBON COUNTY	LINN COUNTY	MIAMI COUNTY	MAINTENANCE COST
Board	2.2	3.8	5.2	$3.00/hundred
Split Rail	24.1	29.2	16.6	$3.25/hundred
Stone	11.1	7.0	2.3	$1.75/rod
Hedge	49.4	41.2	46.8	$0.60/rod
Wire	13.0	18.8	29.1	$0.40/rod
Total	99.8	100.0	100.0	

Note: Figures are percentages. Any variance from 100 percent in the percentage totals resulted from rounding.

Sources: William G. Cutler, *History of the State of Kansas*, 2:881, 1072, 1108; Kansas State Board of Agriculture, *Second Biennial Report*, 264.

TABLE 19. BORDER FARMERS WHO BUILT FENCES, BY TENURE, 1880

TENURE	BATES CO.	CASS CO.	VERNON CO.	BOURBON CO.	LINN CO.	MIAMI CO.
Owner	54	48	31	47	52	42
Cash Tenant	39	20	0	17	56	33
Share Tenant	25	6	15	13	14	31

Note: Figures are percentages.

Note on how to read the table: In Bates County, 54 percent of farm owners built fences, as did 39 percent of cash tenants and 25 percent of share tenants.

Source: Author's sample, U.S. Bureau of the Census, Manuscript Census, Missouri, Bates, Cass, and Vernon Counties, Schedule II (Agriculture), 1880; and Kansas, Bourbon, Linn, and Miami Counties, Schedule II (Agriculture), 1880.

TABLE 20. RESULTS OF PRESIDENTIAL ELECTIONS, MISSOURI-KANSAS BORDER COUNTIES, 1868–1896 (AS A PERCENT)

COUNTY	1868 DEM.	1868 REP.	1872 DEM.	1872 REP.	1876 OTHER	1876 DEM.	1876 REP.	1876 GREENBACK
Missouri								
Bates	45	55	53	46	1	58	42	0
Cass	53	47	57	41	1	61	39	0
Vernon	63	37	68	31	1	71	29	0
Kansas								
Bourbon	25	75	41	59		24	57	20
Linn	24	76	27	73		23	68	9
Miami	33	67	35	65		30	57	12

COUNTY	1880 DEM.	1880 REP.	1880 GREENBACK	1884 DEM.	1884 REP.	1884 PROHIB.	1884 GREENBACK
Missouri							
Bates	58	37	5	55	44	1	0
Cass	58	36	6	58	40	1	0
Vernon	64	26	10	65	34	1	0
Kansas							
Bourbon	30	60	9	36	63	1	0
Linn	22	60	17	28	57	1	15
Miami	35	53	12	40	50	1	9

COUNTY	1888 DEM.	1888 REP.	1888 PROHIB.	1888 UNION LABOR	1892 DEM.	1892 REP.	1892 PEOPLE'S	1892 PROHIB.
Missouri								
Bates	51	38	2	9	43	28	27	2
Cass	58	40	2	0	56	35	8	1
Vernon	61	34	1	4	57	29	12	2

(continued)

TABLE 20. RESULTS OF PRESIDENTIAL ELECTIONS, MISSOURI-KANSAS BORDER COUNTIES, 1868–1896 (AS A PERCENT) (CONTINUED)

COUNTY	1888				1892			
	DEM.	REP.	PROHIB.	UNION LABOR	DEM.	REP.	PEOPLE'S	PROHIB.
Kansas								
Bourbon	30	58	0	13	0	49	51	0
Linn	20	54	0	26	0	51	49	0
Miami	38	53	0	9	0	49.7	50.3	0

COUNTY	1896		
	DEM./PEOPLE'S	REP.	PROHIB.
Missouri			
Bates	66	33	1
Cass	63	35	1
Vernon	69	30	1
Kansas			
Bourbon	54	45	0
Linn	53	47	0
Miami	53	47	0

Note: Dem. = Democratic Party; Rep. = Republican Party; Prohib. = Prohibition Party; People's Prohib. = People's Prohibition Party.

Sources: Fort Scott Monitor, November 11, 1868, November 7, 1872, November 11, 1876, November 11, 1880, November 10, 1884, November 15, 1888, November 11, 1892; *Miami County Republican,* November 14, 1868, November 9, 1872, November 14, 1884, November 16, 1888, November 11, 1892, November 13, 1896; *Fort Scott Daily Monitor,* November 7, 1872; *LaCygne Journal,* November 9, 1872, November 18, 1876; *LaCygne Weekly Journal,* November 13, 1880; *Linn County Clarion,* November 16, 1888; *Mound City Torch of Liberty,* November 17, 1892; *Linn County Republic,* November 13, 1896; Michael K. McGrath, *Official Directory of Missouri for 1881,* 37–64; *Official Directory of Missouri for 1885,* 40–69; Alexander A. Lesueur, *Official Directory of Missouri for the Years 1891–92,* 12–28; *Official Directory of Missouri for the Years 1893–94,* 21–38; *Official Directory of Missouri for the Years 1897–1898,* 14–33.

BIBLIOGRAPHY

MANUSCRIPT COLLECTIONS

Duke University, Rare Book, Manuscript, and Special Collections Library, Durham, North Carolina
>   Missouri Volunteer Militia Papers
Fort Scott National Historic Site, Fort Scott, Kansas
>   Burchard, Al. Correspondence, 1858.
>   Campbell, Gene. Correspondence, 1858.
Kansas State Historical Society, Topeka
>   Abbott, James B. Reminiscences, 1896.
>   Adair, Samuel L. Family Papers, 1854–1867.
>   Blood, James. Papers, 1855–1858.
>   Botkin, J. T. Papers. "Sixty Years in Kansas." Miscellaneous, box 8.
>   Caine, William W. Correspondence, 1889.
>   Cobb, David G. Correspondence, 1858–1864.
>   Connelly, William Elsey. Correspondence, 1905–1908.
>   Ewing, Thomas, Jr. Papers, 1860.
>   Fulton Old Settlers Association. Constitution and list of members, 1886.
>   Hamilton, John. Papers, 1872.
>   Hamilton, Nancy McCrum. Papers, 1857–1858.
>   Hutchinson, William. Papers, 1858.
>   Hyatt, Thaddeus. Collection. 1860.
>   Kelley, Harry E. Papers, 1887–1905.
>   Linn County Old Settlers' Association. Register of meetings, 1888–1889.
>   McFadin, George Edwin. Papers, 1854–1874.

Palmer, H. E. "The Border War—When—Where." Civil War Narratives, Military History Collection, n.d.

Peele, William J. Diary, 1879–1888.

Poinsett, William B. Papers, 1871–1884.

Smith, William. Papers, 1859.

Stark, Andrew. Reminiscences, 1881.

Stearns, George L. Papers, 1860.

Trego, Joseph Harrington. Diaries, 1861–1863.

Walker, Frank. Papers, 1858–1859.

Ward, Allen T. Papers, 1850–1861.

Woman's Suffrage Collection, 1867.

Library of Congress, Manuscript Division, Washington, D.C.

Brown, John. Papers.

Ewing, Thomas. Family Papers.

Schofield, John McAllister. Papers.

Stanton, Elizabeth Cady. Papers.

Missouri State Archives, Jefferson City

Keith and Perry Mining Company. Corporation Files, 1880–1905.

Missouri Gubernatorial Election Results, 1856, 1860. Capitol Fire Documents, microfilm.

Missouri-Kansas Border War Collection.

Rich Hill Coal Mining Company. Corporation Files, 1880–1912.

University of Kansas, Kenneth Spencer Research Library, Lawrence

Vansickle, John Henry. Collection, 1859–1863.

Walker, Frank. Correspondence, 1859.

Vernon County Historical Society, Nevada, Missouri

Badger, Albert. Papers, 1852–1890.

Baker, Augustus. Papers, 1860–1865.

Ball, Cecil. Papers, 1859–1860.

Dryden, John G. Papers, 1858–1883.

Lawrence, James. Papers, 1858.

Little Osage Literary Association. Papers, 1839–1858.

Miscellaneous Papers, Slavery File, 1860.

Moore, James. Papers, Slavery File, n.d.

Western Historical Manuscripts Collection, Columbia, Missouri

Kansas City, Nevada, and Fort Smith Railroad Company. Papers (C3205).

King, Henry, to Missouri Legislature. "Report of a Geological Reconnaissance," 1839.

Mahin, Milton Fletcher. Memoirs, 1933 (C701).

Pike, Joshua A. Reminiscence, 1917 (C2704).

Vernon County School District no. 2. Record Book, 1858–1860. Collection 2467.
Western Historical Manuscripts Collection, Kansas City, Missouri
    Falor, Crabb, and McGennis Families. Collection (852kc SHS).
    Gordon, Addie Aldridge (1887–1973). Papers (KC068).

NEWSPAPERS

Kansas

Daily Kansas State Journal, 1867.
Fort Scott Colored Citizen, 1878.
Fort Scott Democrat, 1858–1861.
Fort Scott Pioneer, 1876–1878.
Fort Scott Union Monitor, 1863–1865.
Fort Scott Weekly Monitor, 1864–1878.
Fort Scott Western Volunteer, 1862.
Goodrich Graphic, 1890–1891.
LaCygne Journal, 1873.
LaCygne Visitor, 1890–1891.
Lawrence Journal-World, 2004.
Miami County Republican, 1866–1880.
Mound City Border Sentinel, 1865–1867.
Mound City Report, 1860.
Paola Union Crusader, 1864.
Southern Kansas Herald (Osawatomie), 1858–1865.

Missouri

Bates County Advocate, 1878.
Bates County Democrat, 1872.
Bates County Record, 1869–1896.
Belton Herald, 1895.
Butler Free Press, 1896–1898.
Cass County News (Belton), 1893.
Cass News (Harrisonville), 1888–1895.
Columbia Daily Tribune, 2004.
Liberty Weekly Tribune, 1855.
Nevada Mail, 1884–1887.
Nevada Noticer, 1886–1887.

Pleasant Hill Leader, 1869–1873.
Pleasant Hill Local, 1886–1895.
Western Dispatch (Pleasant Hill), 1886.
Western Enterprise (Rich Hill), 1886–1890.

GOVERNMENT DOCUMENTS

Bates County Circuit Court. Civil and Criminal Docket, 1858–1868, microfilm. Missouri State Archives, Jefferson City.

Bates County Court. Minutes of the Bates County Court, 1854–1888. Bates County Courthouse, Butler, Missouri.

Cass County Circuit Court. Civil and Criminal Docket, 1858–1868, microfilm. Missouri State Archives, Jefferson City.

Kansas Agriculture Board. Grasshopper Report, Spring 1877. Kansas State Historical Society, Topeka.

Lesueur, Alexander A. *Official Directory of Missouri for the Years 1893–1894.* St. Louis: J. Daly, 1895.

Missouri, State of. *The General Statutes of the State of Missouri.* Jefferson City: Emory Foster, Printer, 1866.

Missouri Bureau of Labor Statistics. *Annual Reports of the Bureau of Labor Statistics of Missouri for 1884, 1885, 1886, 1889, 1891, and 1893.* Jefferson City: Tribune Printing, 1885, 1886, 1887, 1890, 1891, 1894.

Missouri Secretary of State. *Official Directory of the State of Missouri.* Jefferson City: Tribune Printing, 1879, 1881, 1883, 1889, 1892, 1894, 1896, 1898.

Smith, W. J., Bates County Clerk. Bates County Election Results, 1872. Missouri State Archives, Jefferson City.

State Mine Inspector of Missouri. *Annual Reports of the State Mine Inspector for 1891, 1894, 1897, and 1901.* Jefferson City: Tribune Printing, 1891, 1895, 1898, 1902.

U.S. Bureau of the Census. *Seventh Census of the United States: Appendix.* Washington, D.C.: Robert Armstrong, Public Printer, 1853.

———. Manuscript Census. Kansas, Bourbon, Linn, and Miami Counties. Schedule I (Population), 1860, 1870, 1880, microfilm.

———. Manuscript Census. Kansas, Bourbon, Linn, and Miami Counties. Schedule II (Agriculture), 1870, 1880, microfilm.

———. Manuscript Census. Missouri, Bates, Cass, and Vernon Counties. Schedule I (Population), 1850, 1860, 1870, 1880, microfilm.

———. Manuscript Census. Missouri, Bates, Cass, and Vernon Counties. Schedule II (Agriculture), 1850, 1860, 1870, 1880, microfilm.

————. *Eighth Census: Population of the United States, Compiled from the Original Returns.* Washington, D.C.: Government Printing Office, 1865.

————. *Ninth Census: The Statistics of the Population of the United States.* Washington, D.C.: Government Printing Office, 1872.

————. *Ninth Census: The Statistics of Wealth and Industry of the United States.* Washington, D.C.: Government Printing Office, 1872.

————. *Statistics of the Population of the United States at the Tenth Census.* Washington, D.C.: Government Printing Office, 1883.

————. *Compendium of the Eleventh Census.* Washington, D.C.: Government Printing Office, 1892.

————. *Eleventh Census: Report on the Mineral Industries in the United States.* Washington, D.C.: Government Printing Office, 1892.

————. *Eleventh Census: Report on the Population of the United States, Part I.* Washington, D.C.: Government Printing Office, 1892.

————. *Eleventh Census: Report on the Statistics of Agriculture in the United States.* Washington, D.C.: Government Printing Office, 1895.

U.S. War Department. Letters received, 1861–1867. Record Group 393, File 2593. Records of the U.S. Army Continental Commands, Department of the Missouri, 1821–1920. National Archives Building, Washington, D.C.

————. Union Provost Marshal Papers. Missouri State Archives, Jefferson City.

————. *The War of the Rebellion: A Compilation of the Official Records of the Union and the Confederate Army.* 4 series. 128 vols. Washington, D.C.: Government Printing Office, 1880–1901.

Vernon County Circuit Court. Civil and Criminal Docket, 1858–1868, microfilm. Missouri State Archives, Jefferson City.

OTHER SOURCES

Abing, Kevin J. "Before Bleeding Kansas: Christian Missionaries, Slavery, and the Shawnee Indians in Pre-territorial Kansas, 1844–1854." *Kansas History* 24, no. 1 (Spring 2001): 54–70.

Adams, Jane. *The Transformation of Rural Life: Southern Illinois, 1890–1990.* Chapel Hill: University of North Carolina Press, 1994.

Argersinger, Peter H. "Pentecostal Politics in Kansas; Religion, the Farmers' Alliance, and the Gospel of Populism." *Kansas Quarterly* 1 (1969): 24–35.

Aron, Stephen. *How the West Was Lost: The Transformation of Kentucky from Daniel Boone to Henry Clay.* Baltimore: Johns Hopkins University Press, 1996.

Athearn, Robert G. *In Search of Canaan: Black Migration to Kansas, 1879–1880.* Lawrence: Regents Press of Kansas, 1978.

Atherton, Lewis. *Main Street on the Middle Border.* Bloomington: Indiana University Press, 1984.

Atkeson, W. O. *History of Bates County, Missouri.* Topeka: Historical Publishing, 1918.

Atkins, Annette. *Harvest of Grief: Grasshopper Plagues and Public Assistance in Minnesota, 1873–78.* St. Paul: Minnesota Historical Society Press, 1984.

Ayers, Edward L., Patricia Nelson Limerick, Stephen Nissenbaum, and Peter S. Onuf. *All Over the Map: Rethinking American Regions.* Baltimore: Johns Hopkins University Press, 1996.

Bailey, Anne J. *War and Ruin: William T. Sherman and the Savannah Campaign.* Wilmington, Del.: Scholarly Resources, 2003.

Bannon, John F. "Missouri, a Borderland." *Missouri Historical Review* 63 (1969): 227–40.

Barron, Hal S. "Listening to the Silent Majority: Change and Continuity in the Nineteenth-Century Rural North." In *Agriculture and National Development,* ed. Lou Ferleger, 3–23. Ames: Iowa State University Press, 1990.

———. *Mixed Harvest: The Second Great Transformation in the Rural North, 1870–1930.* Chapel Hill: University of North Carolina Press, 1997.

Barry, Louise. "The Fort Leavenworth–Fort Gibson Military Road and the Founding of Fort Scott." *Kansas Historical Quarterly* 11 (1942): 115–29.

Bates County Old Settlers Society. *The Old Settlers' History of Bates County, Missouri: From Its Settlement to the First Day of January, 1900.* Amsterdam, Mo.: Tathwell and Maxey, 1897.

Bensel, Richard Franklin. *Yankee Leviathan: The Origins of Central State Authority in America, 1859–1877.* Cambridge: Cambridge University Press, 1990.

Bercaw, Nancy. *Gendered Freedoms: Race, Rights, and the Politics of the Household in the Delta, 1861–1875.* Gainesville: University Press of Florida, 2003.

Berlin, Ira. *Many Thousands Gone: The First Two Centuries of Slavery in North America.* Cambridge: Harvard University Press, Belknap Press, 1998.

Berwanger, Eugene H. *The Frontier against Slavery: Western Anti-Negro Prejudice and the Slavery Extension Controversy.* Urbana: University of Illinois Press, 1967.

———. *The West and Reconstruction.* Urbana: University of Illinois Press, 1981.

Billingsley, Carolyn Earle. *Communities of Kinship: Antebellum Families and the Settlement of the Cotton Frontier.* Athens: University of Georgia Press, 2004.

Blackmar, Frank W., ed. *Kansas: A Cyclopedia of State History, Embracing Events, Institutions, Industries, Counties, Cities, Towns, Prominent Persons, Etc.* Vol. 2. Chicago: Standard Publishing, 1912.

Blight, David. *Race and Reunion: The Civil War in American Memory.* Cambridge: Harvard University Press, Belknap Press, 2001.

Bogue, Allan G. *From Prairie to Corn Belt: Farming on the Illinois and Iowa Prairies in the Nineteenth Century.* Chicago: University of Chicago Press, 1963.

Bolton, Charles C. *Poor Whites of the Antebellum South: Tenants and Laborers in Central North Carolina and Northeast Mississippi.* Durham: Duke University Press, 1994.

Botkin, J. T. "Justice Was Swift and Sure in Early Kansas," ed. William Elsey Connelly and Clara Francis Shelton. *Collections of the Kansas State Historical Society* 16 (1923–1925): 488–93.

Bowen, Don R. "Guerrilla War in Western Missouri, 1862–65: Historical Extensions of the Relative Deprivation Hypothesis." *Comparative Studies in History and Society* 19 (January 1977): 30–51.

Brophy, Dixie, comp., and Patrick Brophy, ed. *Vernon County Confederates: Soldiers, Bushwhackers, Sympathizers, Victims, and Veterans of the Southern Cause with Connections to Vernon County, Missouri.* Nevada, Mo.: Bushwhacker Museum, 1991.

Brophy, Patrick. *Bushwhackers of the Border: The Civil War Period in Western Missouri.* Nevada, Mo.: Vernon County Historical Society, 2000.

Brown, Al Theodore. "Business 'Neutralism' on the Kansas Border: Kansas City, 1854–1857." *Journal of Southern History* 29, no. 2 (1963): 229–40.

Brownlee, Richard S. *Gray Ghosts of the Confederacy.* Baton Rouge: Louisiana State University Press, 1958.

Brundage, W. Fitzhugh, ed. *Where These Memories Grow: History, Memory, and Southern Identity.* Chapel Hill: University of North Carolina Press, 2000.

Burch, Paul W. "Kansas: Bushwhackers vs. Jayhawkers." *Journal of the West* 14, no. 1 (1975): 83–104.

Camp, C. Rollin. *Camp's Emigrants Guide to Kansas.* Kansas City, Mo., 1880.

Campbell, Jacqueline Glass. *When Sherman Marched North from the Sea.* Chapel Hill: University of North Carolina Press, 2003.

Carper, James C. "The Popular Ideology of Segregated Schooling: Attitudes toward the Education of Blacks in Kansas, 1854–1900." *Kansas History* 1, no. 4 (1978): 254–66.

Carroll, Mark M. *Homesteads Ungovernable: Families, Sex, Race, and the Law in Frontier Texas, 1823–1860.* Austin: University of Texas Press, 2001.

Cashin, Joan. *A Family Venture: Men and Women on the Southern Frontier.* Baltimore: Johns Hopkins University Press, 1991.

Cassity, Michael. *Defending a Way of Life: An American Community in the Nineteenth Century.* Albany: SUNY Press, 1989.

Castel, Albert E. *A Frontier State at War: Kansas, 1861–1865.* Ithaca: Cornell University Press, 1958.

———. "Order Number 11 and the Civil War on the Border." *Missouri Historical Review* 57 (1963): 357–86.

———. *William Clarke Quantrill: His Life and Times.* Norman: University of Oklahoma Press, 1999.

Cayton, Andrew R. L, and Susan E. Gray, eds. *The American Midwest: Essays on Regional History.* Bloomington: Indiana University Press, 2001.

Cayton, Andrew R. L., and Peter S. Onuf, eds. *The Midwest and the Nation: Rethinking the History of an American Region.* Bloomington: Indiana University Press, 1990.

Cecil-Fronsman, Bill. "'Death to All Yankees and Traitors in Kansas': The *Squatter Sovereign* and the Defense of Slavery in Kansas." In *Kansas and the West: New Perspectives,* ed. Rita Napier, 140–56. Lawrence: University Press of Kansas, 2003.

Cheatham, Gary L. "'Desperate Characters': The Development and Impact of the Confederate Guerrillas in Kansas." *Kansas History* 14 (1991): 144–61.

———. "Divided Loyalties in Civil War Kansas." *Kansas History* 11 (1988): 93–107.

Christensen, Donald. "A Vignette of Missouri's Native Prairie," *Missouri Historical Review* 61 (1966): 166–86.

Christensen, Lawrence O., and Gary R. Kremer. *A History of Missouri: Volume IV, 1875–1919.* Columbia: University of Missouri Press, 1997.

Christian, Shirley. *Before Lewis and Clark: The Story of the Chouteaus, the French Dynasty That Ruled America's Frontier.* New York: Farrar, Straus, and Giroux, 2004.

Christianson, James R. "The Early Osage—'Ishmaelites of the Savages.'" *Kansas History* 11, no. 1 (1988): 2–21.

Clanton, O. Gene. "Intolerant Populist? The Disaffection of Mary Elizabeth Lease." *Kansas Historical Quarterly* 34 (1968): 189–200.

Clark, Christopher. *The Roots of Rural Capitalism: Western Massachusetts, 1780–1860.* Ithaca: Cornell University Press, 1990.

Clemens, Russell J. "The Development of a Market Economy: Bates County, Missouri, 1875–1890." *Missouri Historical Society Bulletin* 35 (October 1978): 28–35.

Clevenger, Homer. "Agrarian Politics in Missouri, 1880–1896." Ph.D. diss., University of Missouri–Columbia, 1940.

Cobb, James. *Away Down South: A History of Southern Identity.* New York: Oxford University Press, 2005

Cochrane, Willard W. *The Development of American Agriculture: An Historical Analysis.* Minneapolis: University of Minnesota Press, 1979.

Conkright, James D. "A Social History of Fort Scott, Kansas, at the Turn of the Century." Master's thesis, Pittsburg (Kans.) State University, 1973.

Connelly, William Elsey. *Quantrill and the Border Wars.* Cedar Rapids, Iowa: Torch Press, 1910.

Crenshaw, Ollinger. *The Slave States in the Presidential Election of 1860.* Baltimore: Johns Hopkins University Press, 1945.

Cronon, William. *Changes in the Land: Indians, Colonists, and the Ecology of New England.* New York: Hill and Wang, 1983.

———. *Nature's Metropolis: Chicago and the Great West.* New York: W. W. Norton, 1991.

Cutler, William G. *History of the State of Kansas.* Vols. 1–2. Chicago: A. T. Andreas, 1883.

Dalton, Kit. *Under the Black Flag.* Memphis: Lockard Publishing, 1914.

Danhof, Clarence. *Changes in Agriculture: The Northern United States, 1820–1870.* Cambridge: Harvard University Press, 1969.

de Mun, Jules. *Journals of Jules de Mun.* Trans. Nettie Harney Beauregard. Ed. Thomas M. Marshall. Comp. Marquis de Mun and N. H. Beauregard. Reprint from *Missouri Historical Society Collections* 5, no. 3 (1928).

Diggs, Annie L. "Women in the Alliance Movement." *Arena* 6, no. 2 (July 1892): 161–79.

Dobak, William A., ed. "Civil War on the Kansas-Missouri Border: The Narrative of Former Slave Andrew Williams." *Kansas History* 6 (1983): 237–42.

Donaldson, Alice. "Rhetoric of a Small Midwestern Town." *Missouri Historical Review* 75, no. 4 (1981): 448–63.

Dryden, John G. *With Plow and Pen: The Diary of John G. Dryden, 1856–1883.* Ed. Patrick Brophy. Nevada, Mo.: Vernon County Historical Society, 2001.

Dupre, Daniel. *Transforming the Cotton Frontier: Madison County, Alabama, 1800–1840*. Baton Rouge: Louisiana State University Press, 1997.

Eakin, Joanne Chiles. *Tears and Turmoil: Order #11*. N.p., 1996.

Edwards, John N. *Noted Guerrillas; or, The Warfare of the Border*. St. Louis: Bryan, Brand, 1877.

Ellis, James Fernando. *The Influence of Environment on the Settlement of Missouri*. St. Louis: Webster Publishing, 1929.

England, J. Merton. "A Hard Times Chronicler—an Ohio Teacher in Western Missouri, 1879–1881." *Missouri Historical Review* 89, no. 3 (1989): 311–29.

Entz, Gary R. "Image and Reality on the Kansas Prairie: 'Pap' Singleton's Cherokee County Colony." *Kansas History* 19:2 (1996): 124–39.

Epstein, Leslie. *The Politics of Domesticity: Women, Evangelism, and Temperance in Nineteenth-Century America*. Middletown, Conn.: Wesleyan University Press, 1981.

Etcheson, Nicole. *Bleeding Kansas: Contested Liberty in the Civil War Era*. Lawrence: University Press of Kansas, 2004.

———. *The Emerging Midwest: Upland Southerners and the Political Culture of the Old Northwest, 1787–1861*. Bloomington: Indiana University Press, 1996.

———. "The Great Principle of Self-Government: Popular Sovereignty and Bleeding Kansas." *Kansas History* 27 (Spring–Summer 2004): 16–17.

———. "'Labouring for the Freedom of This Territory': Free-State Kansas Women in the 1850s." *Kansas History* 21 (Summer 1998): 68–87.

Everett, John, and Sarah Everett. "Letters of John and Sarah Everett, 1854–1864, Miami County Pioneers." *Kansas Historical Review* 8, no. 1–4 (1939): 3–34, 143–74, 279–310, 350–83.

Ewy, Marvin. "The United States Army in the Border Troubles, 1855–1856." *Kansas Historical Quarterly* 32, no. 4 (Winter 1966): 385–400.

Faragher, John Mack. *Sugar Creek: Life on the Illinois Prairie*. New Haven: Yale University Press, 1986.

———. *Women and Men on the Overland Trail*. New Haven: Yale University Press, 1979.

Faragher, John Mack, ed. *Rereading Frederick Jackson Turner: "The Significance of the Frontier in American History" and Other Essays*. New York: Holt, 1994.

Faust, Drew Gilpin. *The Creation of Confederate Nationalism: Ideology and Identity in the Civil War South*. Baton Rouge: Louisiana State University Press, 1988.

Fellman, Michael. *Inside War: The Guerrilla Conflict in Missouri during the American Civil War.* New York: Oxford University Press, 1989.

Fleming, Walter L. "The Buford Expedition to Kansas." *American Historical Review* 6, no. 1 (October 1900): 38–48.

Flora, S. D. "The Great Flood of 1844 along the Kansas and Marais des Cygnes Rivers." *Kansas Historical Quarterly* 20, no. 2 (May 1952): 73–81.

Foner, Eric. *Free Soil, Free Labor, Free Men: The Ideology of the Republican Party before the Civil War.* New York: Oxford University Press, 1970.

———. *Reconstruction: America's Unfinished Revolution, 1863–1877.* New York: Harper and Row, 1988.

Fox-Genovese, Elizabeth. "Women in Agriculture during the Nineteenth Century." In *Agriculture and National Development: Views on the Nineteenth Century,* ed. Lou Ferleger, 267–300. Ames: Iowa State University Press, 1990.

Fuller, Wayne E. *The Old Country School: The Story of Rural Education in the Middle West.* Chicago: University of Chicago Press, 1982.

Gambone, Joseph G. "Economic Relief in Territorial Kansas, 1860–1861." *Kansas Historical Quarterly* 36, no. 2 (1970): 149–74.

Garner, Nancy. "'A Prayerful Public Protest': The Significance of Gender in the Kansas Woman's Crusade of 1874." *Kansas History* 20, no. 4 (1997–1998): 215–29.

Gastil, Raymond D. *Cultural Regions of the United States.* Seattle: University of Washington Press, 1975.

Gates, Paul Wallace. *Fifty Million Acres: Conflicts over Kansas Land Policy, 1854–1890.* Ithaca: Cornell University Press, 1954.

———. *History of Public Land Law Development.* Washington, D.C.: Government Printing Office, 1968.

Gerlach, Russell L. "Population Origins in Rural Missouri." *Missouri Historical Review* 71 (1976): 1–21.

———. *Settlement Patterns in Missouri: A Study of Population Origins.* Columbia: University of Missouri Press, 1986.

Gihon, John H. *Geary and Kansas: Governor Geary's Administration in Kansas, with a Complete History of the Territory until July 1857.* Philadelphia: Chas. C. Rhodes, 1857.

Gjerde, Jon. *The Minds of the West: Ethnocultural Evolution in the Rural Middle West, 1830–1917.* Chapel Hill: University of North Carolina Press, 1997.

Glaab, Charles N. *Kansas City and the Railroads: Community Policy in the Growth of a Regional Metropolis.* Madison: State Historical Society of Wisconsin, 1993.

Gladstone, Thomas H. *The Englishman in Kansas; or, Squatter Life and Border Warfare.* New York: Miller, 1857.

Glauert, Ralph E. "Stereotypes and Clichés: The Pioneer Teacher in Missouri." *Missouri Historical Review* 72, no. 2 (1978): 136–53.

Glenn, Allen. *History of Cass County.* Topeka: Historical Publishing, 1917.

Goldberg, Michael. *An Army of Women: Gender and Politics in Gilded Age Kansas.* Baltimore: Johns Hopkins University Press, 1997.

Goodlander, Charles W. *Memoirs and Recollections of Charles W. Goodlander of the Early Days of Fort Scott.* Fort Scott, Kans.: Monitor Printing, 1899.

Goodrich, Thomas. *Black Flag: Guerrilla Warfare on the Western Border, 1861–1865.* Bloomington: Indiana University Press, 1995.

Goodwyn, Lawrence. *Democratic Promise: The Populist Moment in America.* New York: Oxford University Press, 1976.

Grant, H. Roger. "Portrait of a Workers' Utopia: The Labor Exchange and the Freedom, Kan., Colony." *Kansas Historical Quarterly* 43, no. 1 (1977): 56–66.

Graves, W. W., Mrs. "In the Land of the Osages—Harmony Mission." *Missouri Historical Review* 19 (April 1925): 409–19.

Hahn, Steven. "Hunting, Fishing, and Foraging: Common Rights and Class Relations in the Post-bellum South." *Radical History Review* 26 (1982): 37–64.

———. *The Roots of Southern Populism: Yeoman Farmers and the Transformation of the Georgia Upcountry, 1850–1890.* New York: Oxford University Press, 1983.

Harrington, W. P. "The Populist Party in Kansas." Master's thesis, University of Kansas, 1924.

Harris, Charles F. "Catalyst for Terror: The Collapse of the Women's Prison in Kansas City." *Missouri Historical Review* 89, no. 3 (1995): 290–306.

Hart, John Fraser. *The Rural Landscape.* Baltimore: Johns Hopkins University Press, 1998.

Hatley, Paul B., and Noor Ampssler. "Army General Orders Number 11: Final Valid Option or Wanton Act of Brutality? The Missouri Question in the American Civil War." *Journal of the West* 33, no. 3 (1994): 77–87.

Henretta, James A. "Families and Farms: *Mentalité* in Pre-industrial America." *William and Mary Quarterly* 35 (1978): 3–32.

Hicks, John D. *The Populist Revolt: A History of the Farmers' Alliance and the People's Party.* Lincoln: University of Nebraska Press, 1959.

Hinds, Henry. *The Coal Deposits of Missouri.* Vol. 11, 2d ser. Jefferson City: Stephens Printing, 1912.

History of Vernon County, Missouri. St. Louis: Brown, 1887.

Hofstadter, Richard. *The Age of Reform: From Bryan to F.D.R.* New York: Vintage Books, 1955.

Holder, Daniel J., and Hal K. Rothman. *The Post on the Marmaton: An Historical Resource Study of Fort Scott National Historic Site.* Omaha: U.S. Department of the Interior, National Park Service, Midwest Regional Office, 2001.

Holman, Tommy L. "James Montgomery in Kansas, 1854–1863." Master's thesis, Pittsburg (Kans.) State University, 1959.

Hudson, John C. *Making the Corn Belt: A Geographical History of Middle-Western Agriculture.* Bloomington: Indiana University Press, 1994.

———. "North American Origins of Middlewestern Frontier Populations." *Annals of the Association of American Geographers* 78, no. 3 (1988): 395–413.

Hurst, James Willard. *Law and the Conditions of Freedom in the Nineteenth-Century United States.* Madison: University of Wisconsin Press, 1950.

Hurt, R. Douglas. *Agriculture and Slavery in Missouri's Little Dixie.* Columbia: University of Missouri Press, 1992.

Hutson, Cecil Kirk. "Texas Fever in Kansas, 1866–1930." *Agricultural History* 68 (Winter 1994): 74–104.

Hyatt, Thaddeus. *The Prayer of Thaddeus Hyatt to James Buchanan, President of the United States, in Behalf of Kansas, Asking for a Postponement of All the Land Sales in That Territory, and for Other Relief.* Washington, D.C.: H. Polkinhorn, Printer, 1860.

Hyslop, Stephen G. "One Nation among Many: The Origins and Objectives of Pike's Southwest Expedition." *Kansas History* 29 (Spring 2006): 2–13.

Johnson, Hildegard Binder. "Rational and Ecological Aspects of the Quarter Section." *Geographical Review* 47 (1957): 330–48.

Johnson, J. B., ed. *The History of Vernon County, Missouri, Past and Present.* Vol. 1. Chicago: C. F. Cooper, 1911.

Jordan, Terry G. "Between the Forest and the Prairie." *Agricultural History* 38 (1964): 205–16.

———. "The Imprint of the Upper and Lower South on Mid-Nineteenth-Century Texas." *Annals of the Association of American Geographers* 57 (1967): 667–90.

———. *North American Cattle-Ranching Frontiers: Origins, Diffusion, and Differentiation.* Albuquerque: University of New Mexico Press, 1993.

Kammen, Michael. *Mystic Chords of Memory: The Transformation of Tradition in American Culture.* New York: Alfred A. Knopf, 1991.

Kleppner, Paul. *The Cross of Culture: A Social Analysis of Midwestern Politics, 1850–1900.* New York: Free Press, 1970.

Koch, William E. "Campaign and Protest Singing during the Populist Era." *Journal of the West* 22, no. 3 (July 1983): 47–57.

Kulikoff, Allan. *The Agrarian Origins of American Capitalism.* Charlottesville: University Press of Virginia, 1992.

———. "The Transition to Capitalism in Rural America." *William and Mary Quarterly* (January 1989): 120–44.

Lang, William L. "From Where We Are Standing: The Sense of Place and Environmental History." In *Northwest Lands, Northwest Peoples,* ed. Dale D. Goble and Paul W. Hirt, 79–94. Seattle: University of Washington Press, 1999.

Larson, Lawrence H. *Federal Justice in Western Missouri: The Judges, the Cases, the Times.* Columbia: University of Missouri Press, 1994.

Leslie, Edward E. *The Devil Knows How to Ride: The True Story of William Clarke Quantrill and His Confederate Raiders.* New York: Random House, 1996.

Lewis, Lloyd. "Propaganda and the Kansas-Missouri War." *Missouri Historical Review* 92, no. 2 (1998): 135–49.

Lopata, Edward. *Local Aid to Railroads in Missouri.* New York: Parnassus Press, 1937.

Madden, John L. "An Emerging Agricultural Economy: Kansas, 1860–1880." *Kansas Historical Quarterly* 39, no. 1 (1973): 101–14.

Madison, James H., ed. *Heart Land: Comparative Histories of the Midwestern States.* Bloomington: Indiana University Press, 1988.

Malin, James C. *John Brown and the Legend of Fifty-six.* Philadelphia: American Philosophical Society, 1942.

———. "Judge Lecompte and the 'Sack of Lawrence,' May 21, 1856." *Kansas Historical Quarterly* 20, no. 7 (August 1953): 465–94.

———. "The Proslavery Background of the Kansas Struggle." *Mississippi Valley Historical Review* 10, no. 3 (December 1923): 285–305.

Mann, Charles J., Allen L. Higgins, and Lawrence A. Kolbe. *Soil Survey of Bates County, Missouri.* Washington, D.C.: Government Printing Office, 1910.

Manring, Randall C. "Population and Agriculture in Nodaway County, 1850–1860." *Missouri Historical Review* 72 (1977): 388–411.

March, David D. *The History of Missouri.* Vols. 1–2. New York: Lewis Historical Publishing, 1967.

Marti, Donald B. *Women of the Grange: Mutuality and Sisterhood in Rural America, 1866–1920*. New York: Greenwood Press, 1991.

Martin, George. *The First Two Years of Kansas; or, Where, When, and How the Missouri Bushwhacker, the Missouri Train Robber, and Those Who Stole Themselves Rich in the Name of Liberty, Were Sired and Reared.* Topeka: State Printing Office, 1907.

Mathews, John Joseph. *The Osages: Children of the Middle Waters.* Norman: University of Oklahoma Press, 1961.

McCorkle, John. *Three Years with Quantrill: A True Story Told by His Scout.* Armstrong, Mo.: Armstrong Herald Printing, 1914.

McCoy, Joseph G. *Historic Sketches of the Cattle Trade of the West and Southwest.* 1874. Reprint, Washington, D.C.: Rare Book Shop, 1932.

McCurry, Stephanie. *Masters of Small Worlds: Yeoman Households, Gender Relations, and the Political Culture of the Antebellum South Carolina Low Country.* New York: Oxford University Press, 1995.

McManis, Douglas R. *The Initial Evaluation and Utilization of the Illinois Prairies, 1815–1940.* Research Paper no. 94. Chicago: University of Chicago Department of Geography, 1964.

McMath, Robert C. *American Populism: A Social History, 1877–1898.* New York: Hill and Wang, 1993.

McMillen, Margot Ford, ed. "*Les Indiens Osages:* French Publicity for the Traveling Osage." *Missouri Historical Review* 97, no. 4 (2003): 294–333.

McNall, Scott G. *The Road to Rebellion: Class Formation and Kansas Populism, 1865–1900.* Chicago: University of Chicago Press, 1988.

McPherson, James. *Battle Cry of Freedom: The Civil War Era.* New York: Oxford University Press, 1988.

McQuillan, D. Aidan. *Prevailing over Time: Ethnic Adjustment on the Kansas Prairies, 1875–1925.* Lincoln: University of Nebraska Press, 1990.

Meinig, Donald W. "American Wests: Preface to a Geographical Interpretation." *Annals of the Association of American Geographers* 62 (1972): 159–85.

———. *The Shaping of America: A Geographical Perspective on 500 Years of History.* Vol. 2, *Continental America, 1800–1867.* Vol. 3, *Transcontinental America, 1850–1915.* New Haven: Yale University Press, 1993, 1998.

Merchant, Carolyn. *Ecological Revolutions: Nature, Gender, and Science in New England.* Chapel Hill: University of North Carolina Press, 1989.

Merrill, Michael. "Putting 'Capitalism' In Its Place: A Review of Recent Literature." *William and Mary Quarterly* 52 (1995): 315–26.

Miles, Kathleen White. *Bitter Ground: The Civil War in Missouri's Golden Valley*. Clinton, Mo.: Printery, 1971.

Miner, H. Craig. "Border Frontier: The Missouri River, Fort Scott and Gulf Railroad in the Cherokee Neutral Lands, 1868–1870." *Kansas Historical Quarterly* 35, no. 2 (1969): 105–29.

———. *The End of Indian Kansas*. Lawrence: Regents Press of Kansas, 1978.

———. *Kansas: The History of the Sunflower State, 1854–2002*. Lawrence: University Press of Kansas, 2002.

———. "The Kansas and Neosho Valley Railroad: Kansas City's Drive for the Gulf." *Journal of the West* 17, no. 4 (1978): 75–85.

Mitchell, William A. *Linn County, Kansas: A History*. Kansas City, Kans.: Campbell-Gates, 1928.

Monaghan, Jay. *Civil War on the Western Border, 1854–1865*. Boston: Little, Brown, 1955.

Morgan, W. Scott. *History of the Wheel and Alliance and the Impending Revolution*. Fort Scott, Kans.: Rice, 1889. Located in Miller Nichols Library Special Collections, University of Missouri–Kansas City.

Morrison, Michael A. *Slavery and the American West*. Chapel Hill: University of North Carolina Press, 1997.

Murphy, Bonnie. "Missouri: A State Asunder." *Journal of the West* 14, no. 1 (1975): 105–29.

Myres, Sandra L. *Westering Women and the Frontier Experience, 1800–1915*. Albuquerque: University of New Mexico Press, 1982.

Napier, Rita, ed. *Kansas and the West: New Perspectives*. Lawrence: University Press of Kansas, 2003.

Neely, Jeremy. "Bates County, Missouri: The Transformation of a Middle Western Frontier, 1855–1895." Master's thesis, University of Missouri–Columbia, 2000.

Neely, Mark E. *The Fate of Liberty: Abraham Lincoln and Civil Liberties*. New York: Oxford University Press, 1991.

Neth, Mary. *Preserving the Family Farm: Women, Community, and the Foundations of Agribusiness in the Midwest, 1900–1940*. Baltimore: Johns Hopkins University Press, 1995.

Niceley, Wilson. *The Great Southwest; or, Plain Guide for Emigrants and Capitalists: Embracing a Description of the States of Missouri and Kansas*. St. Louis: R. P. Studley, 1867.

Nichols, Alice. *Bleeding Kansas*. New York: Oxford University Press, 1954.

Niepman, Ann Davis. "General Orders No. 11 and Border Warfare during the Civil War." *Missouri Historical Review* 66 (1972): 185–210.

Nordin, Sven. *Rich Harvest: A History of the Grange, 1867–1900*. Jackson: University Press of Mississippi, 1974.

Nugent, Walter. *The Tolerant Populists: Kansas, Populism, and Nativism.* Chicago: University of Chicago Press, 1963.

Oates, Stephen B. *To Purge This Land with Blood: A Biography of John Brown.* Amherst: University of Massachusetts Press, 1984.

O'Brien, Michael, ed. *Grassland, Forest, and Historical Settlement.* Lincoln: University of Nebraska Press, 1984.

Oertel, Kristen Tegtmeier. "'The Free Sons of the North' versus 'The Myrmidons of Border-Ruffianism': What Makes a Man in Bleeding Kansas?" *Kansas History* 25, no. 3 (2002): 174–89.

O'Flaherty, Daniel. *General Jo Shelby: Undefeated Rebel.* Chapel Hill: University of North Carolina Press, 1954.

Opie, John. *The Law of the Land: Two Hundred Years of American Farmland Policy.* Lincoln: University of Nebraska Press, 1994.

Osterud, Nancy Grey. *Bonds of Community: The Lives of Farm Women in Nineteenth-Century New York.* Ithaca: Cornell University Press, 1991.

Ostler, Jeffrey. *Prairie Populism: The Fate of Agrarian Radicalism in Kansas, Nebraska, and Iowa.* Lawrence: University Press of Kansas, 1993.

Otto, John S., and Nain Estelle Anderson. "The Diffusion of Upland South Folk Culture, 1790–1840." *Southeastern Geographer* 20 (1982): 89–98.

Painter, Nell. *Exodusters: Black Migration to Kansas after Reconstruction.* New York: Alfred A. Knopf, 1977.

Parkerson, Donald H. "Comments on the Underenumeration of the U.S. Census, 1850–1880." *Social Science History* 15 (Winter 1991): 509–15.

Parrish, William E. *David Rice Atchison of Missouri: Border Politician.* Columbia: University of Missouri Press, 1961.

———. *A History of Missouri.* Vol. 3, *1860 to 1875.* Columbia: University of Missouri Press, 1973.

———. *Missouri under Radical Rule, 1865–1870.* Columbia: University of Missouri Press, 1965.

Peavy, Linda, and Ursula Smith. *Women in Waiting in the Westward Movement.* Norman: University of Oklahoma Press, 1994.

Pederson, Jane Marie. *Between Memory and Reality: Family and Community in Rural Wisconsin, 1870–1970.* Madison: University of Wisconsin Press, 1992.

Perkins, Elizabeth A. *Border Life: Experience and Memory in the Revolutionary Ohio Valley.* Chapel Hill: University of North Carolina Press, 1998.

Perry, Lewis, and Michael Fellman. *Antislavery Reconsidered: New Perspectives on the Abolitionists.* Baton Rouge: Louisiana State University, 1979.

Phillips, Christopher. "Calculated Confederate: Claiborne Fox Jackson and the Strategy for Secession in Missouri." *Missouri Historical Review* 94, no. 4 (2000): 389–414.

———. "'The Crime against Missouri': Slavery, Kansas, and the Cant of Southernness in the Border West." *Civil War History* 48, no. 1 (2002): 60–81.

———. *Damned Yankee: The Life of General Nathaniel Lyon.* Baton Rouge: Louisiana State University Press, 1996.

———. *Missouri's Confederate: Claiborne Fox Jackson and the Creation of Southern Identity in the Border West.* Columbia: University of Missouri Press, 2000.

Pike, Zebulon Montgomery. *The Journals of Zebulon Montgomery Pike, with Letters and Related Documents.* Ed. Donald Jackson. 2 vols. Norman: University of Oklahoma Press, 1966.

Porter, Charles W. *In the Devil's Dominions: A Union Soldier's Adventures in "Bushwhacker Country."* Ed. Patrick Brophy. Nevada, Mo.: Vernon County Historical Society, 1998.

Potter, David. *The Impending Crisis, 1848–1861.* Ed. Don E. Fehrenbacher. New York: Harper and Row, 1976.

Power, Richard Lyle. *Planting Corn Belt Culture: The Impress of the Upland Southerner and Yankee in the Old Northwest.* Indianapolis: Indiana Historical Society, 1953.

Preston, George H. *A History of the Cass County, Missouri, Bond Swindle.* St. Louis: Southwestern Book and Publishing, 1873.

Quist, John W. *Restless Visionaries: The Social Roots of Antebellum Reform in Alabama and Michigan.* Baton Rouge: Louisiana State University Press, 1998.

Rawley, James A. *Race and Politics: "Bleeding Kansas" and the Coming of the Civil War.* Philadelphia: J. B. Lippincott, 1969.

Reynolds, David S. *John Brown, Abolitionist: The Man Who Killed Slavery, Sparked the Civil War, and Seeded Civil Rights.* New York: Alfred A. Knopf, 2005.

Richardson, Albert D. *Beyond the Mississippi: From the Great River to the Great Ocean.* Hartford: American Publishing, 1869.

Riley, Glenda. *The Female Frontier: A Comparative View of Women on the Prairie and the Plains.* Lawrence: University Press of Kansas, 1988.

———. "'Not Gainfully Employed': Women on the Iowa Frontier, 1833–1870," *Pacific Historical Review* 49 (May 1980): 237–64.

Robbins, William G. *Colony and Empire: The Capitalist Transformation of the American West.* Lawrence: University Press of Kansas, 1994.

Rollings, Willard H. *The Osage: An Ethnohistorical Study of Hegemony on the Prairie-Plains.* Columbia: University of Missouri Press, 1992.

———. *Unaffected by the Gospel: Osage Resistance to the Christian Invasion (1673–1906), a Cultural Victory.* Albuquerque: University of New Mexico Press, 2004.

Rosenzweig, Roy. *Eight Hours for What We Will: Workers and Leisure in an Industrial City, 1870–1920.* Cambridge: Cambridge University Press, 1983.

Rubin, Anne Sarah. *A Shattered Nation: The Rise and Fall of the Confederacy.* Chapel Hill: University of North Carolina Press, 2005.

Rugh, Susan Sessions. *Our Common Country: Family Farming, Culture, and Community in the Nineteenth-Century Midwest.* Bloomington: Indiana University Press, 2001.

Ryan, Mary. *Cradle of the Middle Class: The Family in Oneida County, New York, 1790–1865.* Cambridge: Cambridge University Press, 1981.

Ryden, Kent C. "Writing the Midwest: History, Literature, and Regional Identity." *Geographical Review* 89, no. 4 (1999): 511–32.

Rydjord, John. *Kansas Place Names.* Norman: University of Oklahoma Press, 1972.

Sampson, Francis A. "Glimpses of Old Missouri by Explorers and Travelers." *Missouri Historical Review* 68, no. 1 (1973): 74–93.

Sanborn, Franklin B. "Colonel Montgomery and His Letters." In "Notes on the Territorial History of Kansas." *Kansas Historical Collections* 13 (1913–1914): 258–65.

Sauer, Carl O. *The Geography of the Ozark Highland of Missouri.* Chicago: University of Chicago Press, 1920.

Saville, Julie. *The Work of Reconstruction: From Slave to Wage Labor in South Carolina, 1860–1870.* New York: Cambridge University Press, 1994.

Schroeder, Walter A. "The Civil War and Regional Distribution of Wealth in Missouri." *Missouri Geographer* 20, no. 3 (1974): 33–47.

———. "The Geographical Configuration." In *Encyclopedia of Missouri,* ed. Frank H. Gille, 15–26. St. Clair Shores, Mich.: Somerset Publishers, 1985.

———. *Opening the Ozarks: A Historical Geography of Missouri's Ste. Genevieve District, 1760–1830.* Columbia: University of Missouri Press, 2002.

———. "Populating Missouri, 1804–1821." *Missouri Historical Review* 97, no. 4 (July 2003): 263–94.

———. *Presettlement Prairie of Missouri.* Natural History Series, no. 2. Jefferson City: Missouri Department of Conservation, 1983.

————. "Spread of Settlement in Howard County, Missouri, 1810–1859." *Missouri Historical Review* 63 (1968): 1–37.

Schultz, Duane. *Quantrill's War: The Life and Times of William Clarke Quantrill, 1837–1865*. New York: St. Martin's Press, 1996.

Schultz, Gerard. "Steamboat Navigation on the Osage River before the Civil War." *Missouri Historical Review* 29 (1934): 175–85.

Sellers, Charles. *The Market Revolution: Jacksonian America, 1815–1846*. New York: Oxford University Press, 1991.

SenGupta, Gunja. "Bleeding Kansas." Review Essay Series. *Kansas History* 24 (2001–2002): 318–41.

————. *For God and Mammon: Evangelicals and Entrepreneurs, Masters and Slaves in Kansas, 1854–1860*. Athens: University of Georgia Press, 1996.

Shackleton, Bernice C. *Handbook on the Frontier Days of Southeast Kansas*. N.p.: by the author, 1961.

Shaw, Robert Gould. *Blue-Eyed Child of Fortune: The Civil War Letters of Colonel Robert Gould Shaw*. Ed. Russell Duncan. Athens: University of Georgia Press, 1992.

Sheridan, Richard. "From Slavery in Missouri to Freedom in Kansas: The Influx of Black Fugitives and Contrabands into Kansas, 1854–1865." In *Kansas and the West: New Perspectives*, ed. Rita Napier, 157–80. Lawrence: University Press of Kansas, 2003.

Shoemaker, Earl Arthur. *The Permanent Indian Frontier: The Reason for the Construction and Abandonment of Fort Scott, Kansas, during the Dragoon Era*. Omaha: National Park Service, 1986.

Shoemaker, Floyd C. *Early History of Halley's Bluff, Osage Indian Villages, and Harmony Mission*. Nevada, Mo.: Osage-Halley's Bluff Park Association, 1953.

————. "Missouri's Proslavery Fight for Kansas, 1854–1855." *Missouri Historical Review* 48 (1954): 221–36, 325–40.

Shortridge, James R. "The Expansion of the Settlement Frontier in Missouri." *Missouri Historical Review* 75 (1980): 64–90.

————. *Peopling the Plains: Who Settled Where in Frontier Kansas*. Lawrence: University Press of Kansas, 1995.

Smith, Martha William. "Missouri, State, and National Election of 1860." Master's thesis, University of Missouri–Columbia, 1924.

Smith, Wilda M. "A Half Century of Struggle: Gaining Woman Suffrage in Kansas." *Kansas History* 4, no. 2 (1981): 74–95.

Snyder, Edwin. "The Farmers' Alliance." In *Kansas State Board of Agriculture*, 64. Nineteenth Annual Meeting, Topeka, 1890. N.p.

Socolofsky, Homer E. *Kansas Governors*. Lawrence: University Press of Kansas, 1990.

Speer, John. "The Burning of Osceola, Mo., by Lane, and the Quantrill Massacre Contrasted." *Kansas Historical Collections* 6 (1897–1900): 305–12.

Stiles, T. J. *Jesse James: Last Rebel of the Civil War.* New York: Alfred A. Knopf, 2002.

Stock, Catherine McNicol. *Main Street in Crisis: The Great Depression and the Old Middle Class on the Northern Plains.* Chapel Hill: University of North Carolina Press, 1992.

Stone, David. "Border Disputes in Southeast Kansas, 1856–1858." Master's thesis, Southwest Missouri State University, 2002.

Stratton, Joanna L. *Pioneer Women: Voices from the Kansas Frontier.* New York: Simon and Schuster, 1981.

Strickland, Arvarh E. "Toward the Promised Land: The Exodus to Kansas and Afterward." *Missouri Historical Review* 69 (1975): 376–412.

Tabor, Chris. *The Skirmish at Island Mound, Mo.* Independence, Mo.: Blue and Grey Book Shoppe, 2001.

Thelen, David. *Paths of Resistance: Tradition and Democracy in Industrializing Missouri.* Columbia: University of Missouri Press, 1991.

Transeau, Edgar Nelson. "The Prairie Peninsula." *Ecology* 16 (1935): 423–37.

Trego, Joseph H. "The Letters of Joseph H. Trego, 1857–1864, Linn County Pioneer." Ed. Edgar Langsdorf. *Kansas Historical Quarterly* 19, no. 2–4 (1951): 113–32, 287–308, 381–400.

Tucker, Phillip T. "'Ho, for Kansas': The Southwest Expedition of 1860." *Missouri Historical Review* 86, no. 1 (1991): 22–36.

Turner, Frederick Jackson. *The Frontier in American History.* New York: Holt, 1921.

Twain, Mark, and Charles Dudley Warner. *The Gilded Age: A Tale of Today.* New York: Grosset and Dunlap, 1915.

Underwood, June O. "Civilizing Kansas: Women's Organizations, 1880–1920." *Kansas History* 7, no. 4 (1984–1985): 291–306.

United Daughters of the Confederacy, Missouri Division. *Reminiscences of the Women of Missouri during the Sixties.* Jefferson City: Stephens, 192?.

Vinovskis, Maris A. *Toward a Social History of the American Civil War: Exploratory Essays.* New York: Cambridge University Press, 1990.

Waal, Carla, and Barbara Oliver Korner, eds. *Hardship and Hope: Missouri Women Writing about Their Lives, 1820–1920.* Columbia: University of Missouri Press, 1997.

Waldrep, Christopher. *Roots of Disorder: Race and Criminal Justice in the American South, 1817–1880.* Urbana: University of Illinois Press, 1998.

Walter, Joseph B. "Distribution of African-Americans in Missouri from 1860 to 1990." Master's thesis, University of Missouri–Columbia, 1996.

Ware, Eugene F. "The Neutral Lands." *Transactions of the Kansas State Historical Society* 6 (1900): 147–69 (microfilm reel LM 934).

Watts, Dale E. "How Bloody Was Bleeding Kansas? Political Killings in Kansas Territory, 1854–1861." *Kansas History* 18 (1995): 116–29.

Webb, Walter P. *The Great Plains.* New York: Houghton Mifflin, 1931.

Welch, G. Murlin. *Border Warfare in Southeastern Kansas, 1856–1859.* Ed. Dan Smith. Pleasanton, Kans.: Linn County Historical Society, 1977. Reprint of master's thesis, University of Kansas, 1938.

West, Elliott. *The Way to the West.* Albuquerque: University of New Mexico Press, 1995.

West, J. S. "Early Days in Drywood." In *Collections of the Kansas State Historical Society, 1926–1928,* 352–61. Topeka: B. P. Walker, State Printer.

White, Richard. *The Middle Ground: Indians, Empires, and Republics in the Great Lakes Region, 1650–1815.* Cambridge: Cambridge University Press, 1991.

———. "Outlaw Gangs of the Middle Border: American Social Bandits." *Western Historical Quarterly* 12 (October 1981): 387–408.

Whites, LeeAnn. *The Civil War as a Crisis in Gender.* Athens: University of Georgia Press, 1995.

Whites, LeeAnn, Mary C. Neth, and Gary R. Kremer, eds. *Women in Missouri History: In Search of Power and Influence.* Columbia: University of Missouri Press, 2004.

Wiebe, Robert. *The Search for Order, 1877–1920.* New York: Hill and Wang, 1967.

Williams, Betty Harvey. *Bates County, Missouri, Swamp Land Sales, 1854–1855.* Warrensburg, Mo.: by the author, 1977.

Williams, Henry. "Letters of a Free-State Man in Kansas, 1856." Ed. Nathan Smith. *Kansas Historical Quarterly* 21 (1954): 166–72.

Williams, O. P. *The History of Cass and Bates Counties, Missouri.* St. Joseph, Mo.: National Historical Company, 1883.

Woodrell, Daniel. *Woe to Live On.* New York: Holt, 1987.

Wyatt-Brown, Bertram. *Yankee Saints and Southern Sinners.* Baton Rouge: Louisiana State University Press, 1985.

Younger, Cole. *The Story of Cole Younger by Himself: Being an Autobiography of the Missouri Guerrilla Captain and Outlaw.* St. Paul: Minnesota Historical Society Press, 2000.

Zelinsky, Wilbur. *The Cultural Geography of the United States.* Englewood Cliffs, N.J.: Prentice-Hall, 1973.

Zilhart, William H. "Ledger of My Travels from Missouri to California." 1853. Available online at http://cotati.sjsu.edu/cockrill/d0001/d0001notes/ZilhartDiaryIndex.html.

INDEX

Abilene, Kansas, 220

Abolitionists, 55, 85; characterized as fanatics, 58–59; in Kansas antislavery movement, 47–48; Missouri denigrated by, 40–41; Montgomery as self-proclaimed, 93–94; outrage at Kansas-Nebraska Act, 38–39; slaveholders' fear of free-soilers as, 37, 42–44, 76, 84. *See also* Antislavery faction

Adair, Florella Brown, 55, 79, 85, 122

Adair, Samuel, 48, 55, 80, 85, 121–22

Adcock, Mrs. J. A. B., 247

African Americans, 245; border losing significance for, 153–54, 156–57; civil rights for, 157, 162–63; communities of, 144, 152–53; education for, 155–56; equality for, 48, 118n54; free, 4, 34, 48–49, 75, 92, 150–51; in Missouri, 153–54; postwar status of, 131, 133; social relations with whites, 154–55; Union army and, 117–18, 162–63; vote for, 134, 161–66, 168, 180

Agrarian capitalism, 4, 192, 206. *See also* Corn Belt agriculture

Agrarian reform, 238–39

Agriculture, 37, 42, 216, 223; crop prices in, 199, 230–31; development of markets in, 206–10, 213–14; homogeneity of crops, 29, 216–17; intensification of, 217–18, 230–31; investment in implements for, 212, 218, 230–31; mixed-crop strategy, 206–7, 218–19; railroad expansion and, 171–72, 200; threats to,

78, 96, 199, 202–6. *See also* Corn Belt agriculture; Farm economy; Farms

Alcohol, 21, 215; temperance movement against, 232–36

Amnesty: for former Confederates, 158; for guerrilla warfare, 71–72, 77

Anderson, Bill, 120–21

Anderson, Frank, 179

Anderson, J. C., 45

Anthony, Susan B., 166

Antislavery faction, 51; aid for, 39–40, 80; constituent elements of, 47–48; determination of, 59, 62–63; emigrants of, 39–40, 53; forced to flee to Kansas, 99–100; in Missouri, 88, 99–100; motives for, 55, 61; in politics, 62–63, 65–66. *See also* Abolitionists; Free-soil settlers

Arkansas River valley, 17

Armstrong, J. M., 138–39

Atchison, David Rice, 37, 45, 51, 54, 56–57, 88

Atchison, Kansas, 152, 179

Atkinson, John, 130, 219

Austin, Daniel, 25

Austin, Josiah, 117

Austin, Missouri, 72

Austin, O. D., 176, 196

Badger, Sarah, 154

Bailey, Joseph, 139–40, 159

Ball, Cecil, 24–25, 30–32, 76

Balltown, Missouri, 25, 95, 112, 155

Bartlett, Sidney, 186–87

Baskerville, T. J., 180
Bates County, Missouri: agriculture,
    30–31, 33, 214, 219, 224–25; in border
    war, 72, 75, 110, 130; in Civil War, 107,
    122–23, 132, 135; coal mining in,
    199–200; county government in, 124,
    135, 136–37, 140, 235; demographics
    of, 147, 151; old settlers' society in,
    244–45; political parties in, 90, 240;
    population of, 146–47; railroad expan-
    sion in, 179, 181–83, 189–91; slavery
    in, 33, 151
Bates County Record, 176, 191
Battle of the Mules, 105
Beaver, Henry, 35
Belcher, George W., 159
Bell, John, 89
Benton Democrats, Missouri, 47
Bingham, George Caleb, 125, 251
"Black Brigade," with Lane's force, 106
"Black Law," Kansas, 48–49
Blair, Charles, 124
Blankenbecker, Columbus C., 241
Bledsoe, Hiram, 238
"Bleeding Kansas," 85, 98; origin of, 4–5.
    See also Border war; Guerrilla warfare
Blue Lodges, 44
Blunt, Allen, 145
Boggs, Lilburn W., 10
Boosterism, 201; by newspaper editors,
    6, 175–76; for railroad expansion,
    172–73, 175–76, 179–80, 190–93
Border, Missouri/Kansas, 141, 145;
    breached, 59; changing meaning of,
    134, 246; cooperation across, by rail-
    road boosters, 173, 178–80; cultural
    differences across, 237; lack of geo-
    graphical features in, 81; losing signif-
    icance, 144, 153–54, 156–57, 207;
    militias told not to cross, 73–74, 94,
    126; setting of, 3; between slave and
    free societies, 66, 81, 150. *See also* Per-
    manent Indian Frontier
Border counties, Missouri, 184, 238; coal
    mining in, 199–200; depopulation of,
    5, 72–73, 119–24; devastation of, 72–73,
    95, 110, 134; Order No. 11 evacuating,
    122–24, 250–51; population of, 95,
    146–47; postwar changes in nativity,
    146–47; reputation for violence,
    195–96; return of exiled residents to,
    127–28, 137, 145–46; Union Army
    efforts to pacify, 112–13; Unionists

driven out of, 107–8; voting patterns
    in, 87–90, 237–40
Border country, 235; coal in, 199; demo-
    graphics of, 245–46; economic devel-
    opment of, 169–70, 173; effects of
    guerrilla warfare on, 132, 139–40, 171;
    family farm culture in, 205; land sold
    for back taxes in, 136–37; local histo-
    ries of, 245; Osage plains of, 28; per-
    sistence of settlers in, 111, 205–6;
    Populist Party in, 240; railroad expan-
    sion in, 177, 200; reconciliation in, 133,
    240–42; violence and lawlessness in,
    90–91, 139–40
Borders, malleability of, 11
Border war, Kansas/Missouri, 91, 142,
    209; commemoration of casualties of,
    242–43; continued influence of,
    247–49, 252; effects on reputations of,
    143–44; end of, 130–31, 250; Kansas
    not suffering as much damage from as
    Missouri, 132; national Civil War and,
    95, 98; as open war, 56, 58, 73–74, 91,
    95, 103; reconciliation of, 240–42, 245
Botkin, J. T., 205–6, 242
Bourbon County, Kansas, 62, 152, 244;
    agriculture in, 210, 219–20, 223–25;
    appeal to veterans by, 148–49; forma-
    tion of militias from, 102–3; political
    parties in, 87, 238; railroad expansion
    and, 183–85
Bowen, John S., 103
Boxley, Calvin, 137
Boydston, 75
Breckinridge, John C., 89–90
Briant, A. C., 194
Brockman, Thomas, 141
Brooks, Preston, 58
Brown, B. Gratz, 195
Brown, E. B., 126–28, 199
Brown, John, 3, 57, 75, 77, 243; acclaim
    vs. notoriety of, 248; assault at
    Harpers Ferry, 80; effects of attack on
    Lawrence on, 54, 56; executed, 91;
    murders at Pottawatomie Creek and,
    4, 56, 58–59; prepared for violence,
    55–56; raids on slaveholders, 75, 152
Brown, O. C., 52
Brown, Olympia, 166
Brown, Robert, 138
Brown, William, 145
Browning, Orville, 186
Bryan, William Jennings, 240

Buchanan, James: Kansans' dissatisfaction with, 86–87, 237; Kansas land sale and, 79–80; Kansas territorial government and, 58, 66, 99

Buford, Jefferson, 52–53, 57, 67, 84

Burchard, Al, 69–70

Burlingame, Kansas, 233–34

"Burnt District," 132; origin of term, 5; return of exiled settlers to, 137, 145–46. *See also* Border counties, Missouri; Order No. 11

Bushwhackers (pro-Southern guerrillas), 107–8, 130, 159; amnesty for, 122–23; attacks on Missouri Unionists, 118, 128–29, 145; Confederate authorities and, 116–17; demographics of, 109–10; enrolled Missouri Militia organized to fight, 114–15; Missouri disenfranchising, 157–58; motives of, 108–10; reputation of, 141–42, 248; support for, 99, 113, 119–20; Union army expelling sympathizers of, 119–23, 128; Union army's ineffectiveness against, 112–13, 119, 126. *See also* Guerrilla warfare

Butler, Andrew P., 58

Butler, Missouri, 72, 110, 233; as county seat, 135, 192–93; demographics of, 147, 154; railroad expansion and, 180–81, 190–93

California, 35–36, 96–97

California Trail, 34–35

Campbell, Gene, 74

Camp Daniel Boone, of Southwest Expedition, 95

Capitalism: in free-soil ideology, 40–41. *See also* Agrarian capitalism

Carondelet, Baron de, 16

Carroll, M. V., 240

Cass, Lewis, 21, 37

Cass County, Missouri, 146; agriculture in, 31, 214, 225; demographics of, 147, 151; General Order No. 11 evacuating, 122, 132; law enforcement in, 140, 235; old settlers in, 138, 244; politics of, 37, 107, 238; Quantrill's band hiding in, 121–22; railroad expansion and, 177, 179, 193–96, 198; slavery in, 32–33

Cattle: approaches to raising, 218–26; frontier farms raising, 29–30. *See also* Livestock

Census data: as primary source, 6

Cherokee Land League, 186–89

Cherokee Neutral Tract, 185–89

Chicago: as rail hub, 36, 184, 215

Chillicothe, Lexington, and Fort Scott Railroad, 177–78

Chilton, Frank, 32, 138–39, 208

Chouteau, Auguste, 15–16, 18

Chouteau, Pierre, 15–16, 18

Chrisman, John, 140

Christian, John, 113

Christopher, Joseph and America, 27

Citizenship: postwar debates about, 133, 157, 169; property ownership and, 25–26; swearing loyalty oath for, 159

Civil rights, 49; for African Americans, 157, 162; postwar debates over, 133, 157. *See also* Suffrage

Civil War: beginning of, 97–98, 100–101; effects of, 138, 143–44, 148, 179, 219, 237; forgiveness after, 240–42; influence of loyalties in, 197, 237–38, 246; preservation of Union through, 245; uniting in commemorations of, 243–44. *See also* Confederate army; Union army

Civil war, along border. *See* Border war, Kansas/Missouri

Clark, C. S., 127

Clark, Samuel, 153

Clark, William, 18

Clarke, George W., 57

Class, social, 4, 155, 192; on fence law *vs.* open range, 222–24; race and, 34, 153

Clement, Archie, 130

Cleveland, Grover, 238, 240

Cline, James, 194

Coal: in border region, 199–200

Cockrell, Francis, 238

Cockrill, James, 35

Cockrill, Larkin, 35

Collins, Thomas, 141–42

Comanche, 13

Compromise of 1850, 36–37

Confederacy, 148; bushwhackers and, 116–17; formation of, 98, 102; Union loyalty oaths and, 113–14

Confederate army, 108, 148, 159–60; monuments to, 243

Confederates, former, and sympathizers, 130, 197; ascendance as backlash against Radicals, 237–38; effects of war on, 132, 144; Kansas measures against, 158–59; Lane wanting to punish, 105–6; in Missouri, 3, 99, 117, 124;

Missouri disenfranchising, 133–34, 157–58; not forgiven after war, 136, 141; Radical regime campaign against, 160–61; on railroad expansion, 181–82; regaining status, 160, 182; reinstatement of vote for, 159–60, 162, 182; resentments about war, 246, 250–51; women's organizations of, 242, 247, 252

Confederate veterans, 145. *See also* Veterans

Congress, U.S., 80, 85; on Kansas territorial governments, 47, 65–66; sympathy for Kansas Lecompton government, 58

Connelly, William, 241

Constitutional Union Party, 89

Constitutions, Kansas, 235; Leavenworth, 66; Lecompton government and, 65–66, 85; Topeka government and, 47; Wyandotte, 80, 165, 174–75

Constitutions, Missouri: 1865, 155–62, 158, 174; 1875, 198

Constitutions, U.S.: Fifteenth Amendment to, 161–62, 169; Fourteenth Amendment to, 169; Thirteenth Amendment to, 161

Cook, Henry, 27, 29–30

Cook, Sarah, 30

Cooperative institutions, farmers', 238–39

Copeland, J. C., 194

Corn, 204, 215–17, 229; frontier farms raising, 28–30; livestock and, 213–14

Corn Belt agriculture: development of, 30–31, 201, 213–14, 217–19; importance of family farms in, 226–30; mixed-farming strategy in, 206–7

Coughenour, John, 113

Cowles, M. S., 180

Crawford, Samuel, 158–59

Crime against Kansas, The (Sumner), 58

Currency expansion, 239

Curry, James, 141–42

Dairy production, 208–11, 213

Dalton, Kit, 121, 244, 249–50

Daniel, John, 145

"Dark lantern lodges," 51

Davis, Jefferson, 58, 117, 243

Dayton, Kansas, 77

Dean, Abner, 160

Deer, 14, 16

DeJarnett, Richard, 180

Delawares, 20–21

Democracy: economic development and, 192–93, 200

Democratic Party: considering secession, in Missouri, 100–101; dominance of, in Missouri, 86–87, 237, 239; Kansans' dissatisfaction with presidents from, 86–87; in Kansas, 86, 238–40, 240; losing members over slavery, 38, 237; populism and, 232, 238–40; postwar revival of, 160, 182; sectional split in, 36, 85

Demographics: of border country, 144, 146–47, 245–46; of bushwhackers, 109–10; of Missourians *vs.* Kansans, 4, 81–84, 143–52. *See also* Nativity

Denver, Colorado, 73

Denver, James, 71–72

Doak, William, 77

Dobbins, Ann, 27

Dodge, Kansas, 24

Dodge, Leonard, 7–10, 117

Dodge, Nathaniel, Jr., 10

Dodge, Nathaniel B., 7–8, 19–20

Dodge, Samuel Newitt, 7–10

Douglas, Stephen A., 36–38, 89

Douglass, George, 22–23, 30–33, 207–8

Dred Scott case, 80

Drought, 78–80, 92, 96

Dryden, John, 98, 131, 183; on agriculture, 96, 221; attacks on, 99–100, 111, 118, 128–29, 142–43; death of children, 227, 231; on farm life, 227–28; fear of debt, 205, 231; finances of, 137–38, 202, 216, 231; land of, 97, 231; on locust invasion, 202, 204; on politics, 97, 114, 123, 158, 161; as Unionist, 5, 113, 128–29

Dryden, Louisa, 137–38; death of, 231; death of children, 227, 231

Dutch Henry's Crossing: murders at, 56

Du Tisne, Charles Claude, 13–14

Dutroe, T. E., 194

Eads, James, 107

Economic development, 129, 173, 197; market agriculture in, 206; Missouri's desire for neighboring territories', 36–37; railroad expansion in, 171, 176; reconciliation encouraging, 169–70, 200–201, 246; similarity of Missourians and Kansans concern for, 82–83; subverting democracy, 192–93, 200; voters given more control over, 198, 200

Economy, 173; boosted by western expansion, 34–35; of county and local governments, 135; effects of Civil War on, 122, 148; effects of drought on, 78–79; effects of guerrilla warfare on, 95, 135, 171, 196; farmers' grievances in, 238; free-labor *vs.* slave systems, 41, 49, 61; manufactured goods in, 212–13; in motives for migration, 24–26, 35, 39–40, 54–55; panic of 1857, 78; panic of 1873, 198–99; postwar reconstruction of, 173; railroad expansion and, 172, 198–99; of returning exiled settlers, 136–38; similarity of Missourians and Kansans, 82–83. *See also* Farm economy

Education: for Native Americans, 18, 19; postwar expansion of schools, 155–56

Elections: 1860 presidential, 85, 89–91; cross-border similarities, 173; irregularities in, 45, 65, 88, 90–91; Kansas, 44–45, 47, 65, 87; Missouri, 87–88, 101; Missourians voting in Kansas, 44–45; postwar presidential, 237–38, 240; on railroad bonds, 175, 181; voice vote in, 90

Ellis, James and Allen, 32

Emigrant-aid societies, 39–40, 42, 44. *See also* Immigrants

English, John, 66

English bill, 66

Enrolled Missouri Militia (EMM), 114–15

Equality: for African Americans, 48, 118n54

Everett, John and Sarah, 5, 41–42, 57n86, 85; butter and cheese production by, 208–9; on free-soil issue, 47, 48, 51, 62–63, 129; land claim jumped, 51–52; on murders, 69–70

Everett, Robert, 41

Ewing, Thomas, Jr., 119, 127, 130; blamed for Lawrence massacre, 121–22, 126; defense of, 125–26, 250–51; on opportunities for African Americans in Kansas, 152; Order No. 10 by, 121; Order No. 11 by, 119–24, 123, 126–27; residents petitioning to return, 127–28

Exodusters, 151–52

Fairchild, D. S., 180

Falor, Charles, 215

Falor, Elias, 215

Families, 26–27, 64, 226–28. *See also* Households; Kinship

Farm economy: butter, cheese, and egg production in, 208–11; cash production in, 22, 27, 209–10; cooperative institutions in, 238; cost of fencing *vs.* not, 222–25; difficulties of, 202, 231–32; effects of locust invasion on, 202–6; fear of debt, 205, 216n28, 231; household manufactures on, 212–13; lack of cash for taxes, 137–38, 198–99; pioneer, 22, 27, 29, 192; profitability of, 30–31, 230–31

Farmers' Alliance, 231–32, 238

Farms, 82, 106, 191, 216, 239; African Americans lacking capital for, 152; and burden of building fences, 222–25; butter and cheese production on, 208–11, 213; communities of, 227–28; culture of, 214–15; effects of Texas cattle drives on, 219–21; in guerrilla warfare, 95, 111, 134; importance of family, 226–30; increasing number of, 225; markets for, 215–16; merchants *vs.* farmers, 192–93, 201; Osage, 12, 18–19, 27–28; ownership of, 25, 230; persistence of settlers on, 205–6; pioneer, 22, 27; preferred sites for, 27–28; railroads and, 172–73, 206; value of, 205–6, 217–18; women's contributions on, 26–27, 30, 209–10. *See also* Agriculture; Corn Belt agriculture

Finney, Hamilton, 113

Fisher, H. D., 106

Fleming, Violine, 31

Fletcher, Thomas, 130

Forest products, 216, 231

Forgiveness: in border country, 142–43, 240–42

Forsythe, Robert W., 193–95

Fort Carondelet, 15–17

Fort Osage, 18

Fort Scott, Kansas, 21–23, 50, 155, 177; African Americans in, 75, 152; economy of, 30, 129, 184, 199; in guerrilla warfare, 71, 74–75, 95, 104, 116; reconciliation in, 78; temperance movement in, 233; Union rally in, 102

Fort Scott Democrat, 91, 93

Foster, Elias, 141

Foster, Robert, 138–39

Franklin County, Kansas, 242–43

Free-soil ideology, 40–41, 206; postwar immigrants reinforcing, 144, 148. *See also* Topeka government

Free-Soil Party, 37, 86

Free-soil settlers, 3, 48, 61; attacks by proslavery faction on, 51, 57, 69–71, 110; attacks on proslavery faction by, 56, 67–68, 93; exiles retaking land claims, 62–63, 67; immigration by, 38–39, 59, 63–65, 86; as minority, 51–52, 58, 65–66; postwar activism for women's suffrage by, 165; proslavery faction *vs.*, 46, 56–57, 59, 65–66; state government and, 46–47, 52, 66; working with proslavery faction, 82–83, 178–79

Free state, Kansas as, 60–61, 82–84; meaning of, 37, 81; opposition to, 36, 84

Free State Party, 68

Frémont, John C., 104, 112

French, 15; Indians and, 13, 31; Osages and, 10, 12–14

Friends of Society, 44

Frontier culture, 37–38, 197

Frontier Guards, 102

Frontier Military Road, 177

Frost, Daniel, 94, 101

Fugitive Slave Law, 46, 93. *See also* Slaves, fugitive

Fur trade: of Osages, 9, 14–15, 17, 19

Gabbert family, 109

Gamble, Hamilton, 102, 114, 126

Gardenhire, James, 87–89

Gardens: on pioneer farms, 30

Garwood, Gibson and Eliza, 137

Geary, John, 61

Gender, 156, 169, 246

Gender roles, 32, 120; in debate over vote for women, 166–67; on farms, 24, 212, 226–27, 242

General Order No. 11. *See* Order No. 11

Germantown, Missouri, 124

Gill, George, 74

Gladstone, Thomas, 51

Glidden, J. F., 223

Gold Rush, California, 35, 96–97

Goodlander, Charles, 86

Gordon, Addie Aldridge, 210–12, 215n26, 229

Gould, Jay, 199–200

Government, civil: county, 135, 139, 198; courts controlling railroad investments, 181–82, 189–90, 193–95, 198; importance of county seats *vs.* rural areas, 191–93; restoring postwar, 135, 139–40; violence against officials, 195–97

Government, local: Missouri, 133, 135, 158–60; railroad expansion and, 172, 174–75, 177–78, 181–82; state, 133–34, 198. *See also* Constitutions, Kansas; Constitutions, Missouri; Legislature, Missouri; Legislatures, Kansas

Government, U.S.: blamed for deaths in St. Louis riot, 101–2; helping farmers, 205, 238; regulation of alcohol sales by, 235–37; squatters feeling sold out by, 188–89. *See also* Congress, U.S.

—Native Americans and: getting land from, 17–18, 50, 185–86; Osage, 8–9, 22; treaties with, 8–9, 17–18, 43, 50; trying for separation from, 20–21; trying to keep peace among, 17–18

Governments, state: Missouri's two competing, 102

Graham, Daniel, 228

Grains, 122; in Corn Belt agriculture strategy, 206–7; farmers experimenting with, 78, 216–17; frontier farms raising, 29–30; markets for, 30–31, 184; wheat, 216–18. *See also* Corn

Gray, Nellie, 154

Greeley, Horace, 87

Greenback Party, 238

Griffith, William, 69

Guerrilla warfare, 2, 57; effects of, 78–79, 171; fear of, 72, 89; flight, 95, 97, 107–8, 111; in frontier culture of violence, 197; influences on, 71, 77, 91; lack of natural border prohibiting, 4; lasting attitudes, 139–40, 159; levels of, 66, 77, 80–81, 83, 107, 110–11, 179; minimizing, 69–70, 97; motives for, 68, 104, 108–9, 116; postwar feelings about, 245, 249; proslavery raids into Kansas, 57; reprisal raids into Kansas, 110; support for, 99, 108, 117; tactics in, 75, 110, 112, 116; troops *vs.*, 71, 99, 117, 119; women and, 74–75. *See also* Border war, Kansas/Missouri; Bushwhackers; Jayhawkers

Gunn City, Missouri, 194–96

Guns: trade in, 14–15, 21

Habeas corpus, 112

Hagans, Oscar, 35

Hagans, William Boyd, 35
Hall, Willard, 126
Halleck, Henry, 107, 112
Hamilton, Ashby, 221–22
Hamilton, Charles, 68–70, 91
Hamilton, John, 22, 45
Hamilton, Thomas and Nancy, 64
Hannibal and St. Joseph Railroad, 184
Hannibal Bridge, in Kansas City, 184
Hansborough, Gilford D., 43
Harbison, James, 160
Hardin, Charles Henry, 204
Harmony Mission, 7–8, 20, 145–46; establishment of, 18–19; founders of, 23–24
Harpers Ferry: Brown's assault at, 80
Harris, A. A., 154–55
Harris, Mrs. N. M., 248
Harrison, Benjamin, 238
Harrisonville, Missouri, 72, 112, 154; as county seat, 135; railroad expansion and, 177, 194–95
Haskins, Will, 229
Hay, 209, 218, 225
Herald of Freedom (Lawrence newspaper), 54
Hinds, Russell, 92–93
Hines, J. D., 194
Hobson, George and Ada, 63
Hogan, R. H., 35
Hogs, 221, 225; corn and, 213–14; frontier farms raising, 28–29. *See also* Livestock
Holcomb, Joseph, 159
Holderman, Scott, 141
Hollaway, Fleming, 138–39
Homestead Act (1862), 148, 185–86
Horses, stealing, 56, 70–71, 75, 139, 141
Households: economy of, 24, 172, 205, 211–13; guerrilla attacks on, 57, 61–62, 74–75, 106–7, 111, 129, 134; joint contributions within Corn Belt agriculture, 207, 209–10; makeup of, 153–54, 228–30. *See also* Farm economy; Farms
Hudson, John C., 213–14, 218
Hudson Township, Missouri, 182
Humboldt, Kansas, 110
Hunt, R. H., 124, 250
Hunter, D. C., 35
Hunting, 8–9, 12, 17–19, 28
Hyatt, Thaddeus, 79–80

Illinois, 48–49, 64, 84
Illiteracy, 5

Immigrants: agriculture and, 208, 216; demographics of, 143–44; effects of border war on, 42, 69–70, 196, 237–38; emigrant-aid settlers *vs.* independent, 42, 53; Exodusters, 151–52; foreign, 147, 149–50; free-soil, 46–47, 59, 63–64; to Kansas, 41–42, 84; land for, 138, 222, 224; from Missouri to Kansas, 53, 63–64, 81–82, 84; nativity of, 81–84; postwar, 133, 146, 148; railroad expansion and, 173, 179–80; settling in quickly, 41–42. *See also* Settlers
Impartial Suffrage Association (ISA), 164–67
Indiana, 48–49, 64, 84
Indian Territory, 8, 11, 21, 36, 50. *See also* Permanent Indian Frontier
Industrialization: free-soil ideology on, 40–41
Ingels, C. B., 237
Ingram, Tom, 140
Iowa, 49
Ironclad Oath, 157–58
Island Mound, Battle of, 118

Jack, William, 113
Jackson, Andrew, 86
Jackson, Claiborne Fox, 45, 87, 91, 100–102, 238
Jackson, Hancock, 87–89
Jackson, Isaiah, 114
Jackson, Jerry, 30–31, 75
Jackson County, Missouri, 10, 122, 130, 136
James, Frank, 108, 114
James, Jesse, 114, 130, 197
Jayhawkers, 125; acclaim *vs.* notoriety of, 247–48; attacks on Missouri, 72, 94–95, 126; cross-border trade by, 178; declining activity by, 77, 91, 103; effects of, 92, 144; fear of, 72–73, 94–95, 116; responses to, 76–77, 93, 110; tactics of, 93–94, 110–11, 115–16. *See also* Antislavery faction; Border war; Guerrilla warfare
Jennison, Charles "Doc": acclaim *vs.* notoriety of, 107, 247–48; tactics of, 66, 91–92, 103–4, 115–16
Johnson, Mrs. R. K., 129
Jones, Samuel J., 53–54, 56
Joplin, Missouri, 199
Joy, James F., 186–88

Kagi, J. H., 74

Kalloch, I. S., 167

Kansas. *See* Border country; Missouri *vs.* Kansas

Kansas and Neosho Valley railroad project, 185–87. *See also* Missouri River, Fort Scott, and Gulf Railroad

Kansas Anti-Suffrage Movement, 180

Kansas City: becoming agricultural market center, 184, 215–16; families of bushwhackers in, 120–21; growth of, 184–85, 199; railroad expansion and, 184–85, 189

Kansas Equal Suffrage Association (KESA), 169

Kansas Free State (Lawrence newspaper), 54

Kansas-Nebraska Act, 36–38, 46, 49–50, 85

Kansas State Central Committee, 68

Kansas Women's Christian Temperance Union (WCTU), 169

Karliskind, George and Barbara, 218

Kaw (Kansas) River, 184

Kentucky, 82–83, 146–47

Kinship, 146; of bushwhackers, 119; in makeup of households, 228–30; in motives for migration, 24, 26, 55, 64, 70

Know-Nothing Party, 86

Knox County, Missouri, 196

Labor: on border farms, 31–32; on family farms, 27, 212, 226–30; on farms, 30, 209–10, 226–28; in free-labor *vs.* slave systems, 40–41, 61; jobs, 152–54, 157–58, 191–92; maximizing in establishment of farms, 27–28; in pioneer households, 27–29; use of slaves', 31–32; women's, 26–27, 153, 216

Lacy, Henry, 152–53

Lafayette County, Missouri, 10, 128

Lamar, Missouri, 128, 135

Lamb, Reuben, 78

Land: competition for, 38–39, 49–50, 150; farm size, 29–30; fear of dispossession of, 192; homesteading on, 24, 148; in Kansas, 43–44, 49–50, 58–59, 79–80, 175; Native Americans', 8, 17–18, 50; public sales of, 79–80, 87, 136–37; taxes on, 136–37, 204. *See also* Property ownership

Land claims: claim jumping on, 51–52; conflicts over, 50–52, 83; of exiled settlers, 59, 62–63, 67–68; farmers' ownership of, 78–80

Land prices, 95, 185–89

Land speculation, 138–39, 185–89

Lane, James, 102, 152; in guerrilla warfare, 68, 104, 122, 126, 248–49; race and, 48, 118n54; on reconciliation *vs.* punishment, 100, 105–6; in Union army, 104–5, 115, 117–18

Langston, Charles, 163

Lapsley, James, 160

Larue, Isaac, 75

Law and Order Party (proslavery), 47, 56–57

Lawrence, Amos A., 48

Lawrence, James, 75

Lawrence, Kansas, 83, 152, 179; massacre in, 2, 121–22, 126, 248–50; sacking of, 53–54, 56, 58

Leavenworth, Kansas, 152, 177, 179, 184

Lecompton government, Kansas (proslavery), 52, 86; constitutions and, 65–66, 80, 85; federal government and, 58, 65, 85, 87; illegitimacy of, 47, 65; Topeka government and, 56, 80. *See also* Legislatures, Kansas

Legislature, Missouri, 77, 174, 198, 219–20. *See also* Constitutions, Missouri

Legislatures, Kansas: antislavery faction winning, 65; election irregularities in, 45–46; free-soil alternative to "Bogus," 47, 66; offering amnesty, 77; proslavery "Bogus Legislature," 46–47, 57–58; temperance movement and, 234–35. *See also* Constitutions, Kansas; Lecompton government, Kansas (proslavery)

Lexington, Missouri, 43

Lexington and Southern Railroad, 199–200

Liberty Party, 86

Lincoln, Abraham, 101; border states and, 99, 112; election of, 90–91; Lane and, 102, 107; support for, 86, 90, 102

Linn County, Kansas, 87, 155; agriculture in, 219–20, 223–25; in Civil War, 100n9, 130; demographics of, 149, 152; free-soilers in, 61–63; guerrilla warfare in, 75, 77, 248; railroad expansion and, 179, 185

Linn County Border Sentinel, 168

Lisa, Manuel, 16

Little, John, 74
Little Osage, Missouri, 25, 62
Little Osage River, 11, 103
Livestock, 138, 152, 209; approaches to raising, 218–26; border country, 218–21; in Corn Belt agriculture, 206–7, 213–14; increasing number of, 218, 225; markets for, 30–31, 35, 184, 207–8; settlers competing for, 38–39; stealing of, 67, 115, 127, 144; Texas cattle drives and, 35, 219–21; threats to, 9, 78, 204–5. *See also* Cattle; Hogs
Locust/grasshopper invasions, 199, 202–6
Long, Stephen, 37
Longacre, Andrew J., 217–18
Louisiana Territory, 3; French administration of, 13, 15; Spanish administration of, 15–16; U.S. and, 16–17
Lowe, George, 137
Loyalty oaths, 113–14, 122, 157–61
Lykins County, Kansas (renamed Miami County), 65
Lynchings. *See* Murders/lynchings
Lyon, Nathaniel, 71, 101–2

Marais des Cygnes River, 18; Harmony Mission at, 7–8; massacre at, 4, 69–71; Osage village at, 11, 17, 20, 22
Marchbanks, N. R., 144
Margraves, William, 45
Marmaduke, John Sappington, 238
Marmaton League, 140
Marmaton River, 8, 11, 13–14, 21
Martial law: Missouri under, 112, 133, 135
Martin, George, 248
Mason-Dixon line: Missouri-Kansas border compared to, 81
Massey, R. W., 166
McClellan, George, 115
McCorkle, John, 120–21, 139, 249
McFadin family, 110–11
McKinley, William, 240
Means, Robert D, 32
Medary, Samuel, 77
Medicine Lodge, Kansas, 234
Memphis, Tennessee, 189
Merchants, farmers *vs.*, 192–93, 238–39
Mexican War, 22
Miami County, Kansas, 152, 185; agriculture in, 223–25; commemoration of border war, 242–43; political parties in, 87, 238

Miami County Republican, 166–67, 195, 200–201
Miami Indians, 50
Migration, 148; dissuaded due to danger, 70; out of Kansas, 42; out of region, 35, 111. *See also* Immigrants
—motives for: financial improvement, 24–26, 35, 54–55; kinship, 24, 26, 55, 64
Militias: local Kansas, 100, 102; local Missouri, 10, 71–72, 76–77, 94, 101; not allowed to cross border, 73, 126. *See also* Missouri Militia; Missouri State Guard
Mine Creek, Kansas, 130
Missionaries/evangelists, 7–8, 10–11
Mississippi River, 30
Missouri. *See* Border counties; Border country; Missouri *vs.* Kansas
Missouri Bible Society, 76
Missouri Colonization Society, 76
Missouri Compromise: abrogation of, 36–39; popular sovereignty *vs.*, 37–38; setting of border under, 3, 11, 36
Missouri/Kansas athletic rivalry, 1–3, 252
Missouri, Kansas, and Texas (MKT) Railroad, 182–83, 184, 190–93
Missouri Militia, 73, 77, 157–58, 195
Missouri Pacific Railroad, 37, 136, 184, 218; Cass County bonds to, 193–96
Missouri River, 184; closed to free-soil traffic, 56–57; transportation by, 30, 176–77
Missouri River, Fort Scott, and Gulf Railroad, 187, 199–200
Missouri River valley, 11, 17
Missouri State Guard, 102, 104–5, 108
Missouri *vs.* Kansas, 64, 132, 155; African Americans in, 150–54; agriculture in, 210, 216–19, 222–24, 229; foreign immigrants in, 149–50; intermingling of populations, 145, 241; land prices in, 185; Missourians' differences from Kansans, 81–85; Missourians' similarities with Kansans, 82–83; political parties in, 232, 237, 239–40; similarities between, 143, 207, 229, 238; on social experiments/reform movements, 235–36; temperance movement and, 235–36
Mitchell, David, 34
Moneka Women's Rights Society, 165
Montgomery, James, 116; as abolitionist, 60–61, 93–94; attack on home of,

61–62; ceasing hostilities, 72, 77; fear of, 68, 76–77, 94–95; guerrilla warfare by, 66, 69, 70–71, 74–75, 91–93, 95, 104; guns for, 68, 92, 103; reputation of, 74, 247–48

Mooney, James, 76–77

Moore, H. H., 106

Moore, James, 34

Moore, Lester, 92

Morals: abolitionists' assertions of superiority, 44; "border ruffians" criticized for, 51; Missourians' criticized, 40–41; temperance movement and, 232–35

Morgan, Shubel (as Brown alias), 55–56

Moses, Webster, 117

Mound City, Kansas, 152, 180

Mound City Border Sentinel, 180, 195

Mound City Report, 93

Murders/lynchings: to block railroad construction, 188; by bushwhackers, 119, 145; of Cass County judges, 194–96; in culture of lawlessness, 139–41; by jayhawkers, 92–93, 110–11; responses to, 56, 93, 140

Nation, Carrie A., 234

National Kansas Relief Committee, 80

Native Americans, 31; government trying to keep peace among, 17–18, 22; Kansas land of, 50, 79–80; Missouri border as "Indian frontier," 3, 11; moved west, 17, 43; U.S. getting land from, 185–86; western, 13, 15–16; whites' efforts to separate from, 20–21. *See also* Osages

Nativity, 210–11, 244; judging slavery stance from, 31, 85, 110; of Missouri merchants, 138–39; of Missourians *vs.* Kansans, 39–40, 81–85; of postwar immigrants, 146–48; studying immigration patterns through, 63, 84, 149

Nebraska, 36–38

Nevada, Missouri, 44, 135, 154; railroad expansion and, 177, 183

Newberry, Jonathan, 35

New England Emigrant Aid Company, 39, 53–54

New Englanders, in Kansas, 39–40, 84–85

Newspapers: advocating forgiveness, 240–41; editors as primary source, 5–6; lack of extant in Missouri, 82n55; on murders of Cass County judges, 195–96; political bent of editors, 53–54,

82, 247; railroad boosters controlling, 175–76, 189–90; stirring partisan feelings, 237, 240

Newton, Samuel, 28

New Yorkers: in Kansas, 84–85

North, 86; Civil War and, 90, 148; nativity in, 84–85, 144, 146–48; support for free-soilers in, 68, 92

Northwest Ordinance, 38

Ohio, 64, 84

Ohio valley, 20–21, 84

Oldham, Stephen and Ann, 124–25

Old Northwest, 86, 214–15

Old settlers' societies, 244–45

Order No. 10, 121

Order No. 11, 128; amendment of, 126–27; effects of, 5, 122–24, 139, 144, 250–51; Ewing's defense of, 125–26, 250–51; refugees from, 124–25, 145; resistance to, 125, 159–60, 251; survival of Pleasant Hill under, 135–36; Union army enforcing, 123–24, 251

Order No. 11 (Bingham painting), 125

Oregon Trail, 34–35

O'Reilly, Alejandro, 15

Orr, Sample, 87–89

Osage country: beauty of, 17; Pike expedition to, 16–17

Osage plains, 28, 199, 214; cattle raising on, 218–26; grasshopper/locust invasions, 202–6

Osage River, transportation by, 30, 176–77

Osages, 21, 31; destabilization of, 14–16; dispossession of, 22, 245; relations with missionaries/evangelists, 8, 10–11, 18–20; relations with neighboring tribes, 15–16; relations with whites, 7–14; Spanish trying to control, 15–16; subsistence strategies of, 9, 11–12, 27–28, 216; territory of, 11–14; villages of, 11–12, 17, 20

Osage valley, 8, 23, 222; evacuated, 123–24, 132; isolation of, 30, 172; land claims in, 25, 67, 150; Native Americans and whites in, 10–11, 19, 50; railroads in, 172, 184; slavery in, 33, 117; Southern sympathizers from, 105–6

Osawatomie, Kansas, 75, 87; demographics of, 85, 152; guerrilla warfare in, 56–58, 122; John Brown and, 56, 243; memorial to defenders of, 242–43

Osborne, Christina, 26
Osceola, Missouri, 135, 177; attack on, 105–6, 110, 248–49
Outlaws/ruffians, 86, 141; with bushwhackers, 109–10; partisans called, 73, 75; taking advantage of guerrilla warfare, 57, 68

Palmer, William, 31
Paola, Kansas, 192, 195
Parks, Sophy, 154
Parsons, Gustavus, 72–73, 77, 95
Partisan Ranger Act (Confederate), 117
Pasture, 28; increasing acreage as, 217–18; prairie as, 29, 222–26
Patriotism, 148, 246
Patrons of Husbandry (Grange), 231–32, 238
Patterson, Wiley, 67
Pawnees, 13
Peace, 77. *See also* Reconciliation
Pea Ridge, Battle of, 108
Peele, William A., 229–30
People's (Populist) Party, 232; fusing with Democrats in Kansas, 238–40; in Missouri, 239–40
Permanent Indian Frontier, 3, 11, 21–22, 43; as division between Indian Territory and whites, 8; of Indian Territory, 8, 36
Petrie, Harriet, 165
Phelan, Thomas, 160
Pierce, Franklin: Kansans' dissatisfaction with, 86–87, 237; Kansas territorial government and, 45–46, 58; signing Kansas-Nebraska Act, 38, 49–50
Pike, Zebulon, 16–17
Pilot Knob, Missouri, 130
Pixley, Perry and Lewis, 139–40
Plantation system: *vs.* frontier farms, 31–32
Pleasant Hill, Missouri, 72, 112, 154, 184; jobs in, 191–92; Richland County and, 135–36
Pleasant Hill Leader, 177–78, 189, 194
Plundering: in guerrilla attacks, 105–6, 111, 144; by Union army, 115, 123, 129
Political parties: persistent differences along border, 237–38; sectional splits in, 85; third-party candidates of, 239. *See also* Democratic Party; Republican Party

Politics: agrarian reformers entering, 239; divergent cultures of, 237; farmers looking for relief through, 231–32
Popular sovereignty: in Kansas, 47, 66; Kansas-Nebraska Act allowing, 36–38
Populism, 232, 240. *See also* People's (Populist) Party
Potosi, Kansas, 110, 192
Pottawatomie Creek: murders at, 4, 56, 58–59
Pottawatomis, 17, 20–21, 50
Poverty: of new settlers, 27
Prairie, 78, 209, 219, 222–26; subsistence farming on, 27–29
Prairie City Township, Missouri, 183
Prairie Peninsula, 28, 213
Preemption Act (1841), 185–86
Price, Sterling, 104–5, 130, 249
Prince, W. E., 105
Prohibition Party, 238
Property: of bushwhackers, 126–27; of rebels, 112
Property ownership, 137, 148, 186; importance of, 25–26, 188; to prove residency, 44; tenancy *vs.,* 230; by women, 26, 165. *See also* Land
Proslavery faction: attacks by, 51, 54, 57, 68–70, 74–75, 110, 241; attacks on, 56–57, 62, 70, 92; defeated in Kansas, 65–66, 77, 102; dominance in Kansas, 44–46, 57–59, 66; immigrants as, 44, 52–53; Kansans moving to Missouri, 62, 67–68, 73, 95; leaving Kansas, 71, 84, 158–59; Missourians of, voting in Kansas, 44–45; numbers of free-soil settlers *vs.,* 38–39, 45; working with free-soilers, 82–83, 178–79
Proslavery legislature. *See* Lecompton government, Kansas (proslavery)

Quantrill, William C., 117; raids by, 128, 249–50; reputation of, 109–10
Quantrill's raiders, 3, 119, 248; Lawrence massacre by, 121–22, 248–50; as revered and reviled simultaneously, 109–10, 159

Racism, 118, 131; former Confederates' white supremacy, 246–47; pervasiveness of, 34, 48–49; in social relations, 154–55; vote for African Americans and, 134, 161–62

Radical Republicans, Missouri, 157, 197; backlash against, 182, 237–38; campaign against former Confederates by, 160–62; railroad expansion and, 173–74, 182

Railroad expansion: ambivalence about, 171–72, 181–82; boosters of, 173, 175–76, 178–80, 190–93, 200; divisiveness over, 36, 245; economic development tied to, 171, 184–85; funding for, 189–90, 198, 199; land for, 185–89; local governments competing for, 177–78, 180–81; obstacles to, 30, 179, 180–81, 189–91, 198–99; opposition to, 4, 174, 181–83, 188–90, 196–97; pro- and antislavery factions working together for, 178–79; routes for, 37, 199; support for, 173–75, 177–79; voters given more control in, 198, 200

Railroads, 170; in development of market agriculture, 206, 212, 215; in growth of towns, 136, 184; increasing availability of manufactured goods from, 212–13; regulation of, 239; relationships with local governments, 174–75; resistance to, 187–88, 197

Ransom, W. C., 250

Reconciliation, 83, 100, 240–42, 246, 252; cross-border cooperation for railroad expansion in, 173, 178–80; efforts toward, 56, 133–34, 246; need for forgiveness in, 142–43; postwar, 2–3, 169–70, 243–44; railroad controversy changing divisions and alliances, 200–201; veterans and, 141, 169–70

Reconstruction: of Burnt District, 146; postwar economic, 173

Reconstruction era, 131, 134; need for forgiveness in, 142–43

Reeder, Andrew H., 45–46

Reese, David, 78–79

Regional identity, Missouri's, 40, 89–90, 143–52, 206–7, 243, 246–47

Reid, John, 57

Relief: during drought, 79–80; during locust invasion, 204–5

Religion, 55, 143, 204, 233; at Harmony Mission, 19–20; loyalty oaths and, 160–61

Renault, Philippe, 14

Republican Party: dominance of, 237, 239; in Kansas, 86–87; in Missouri, 90, 240; slavery as key issue for, 38, 86; third-party candidates and, 232, 238; on vote for African Americans, 163–64, 168–69; on vote for women, 164–66, 168–69. See also Radical Republicans

Requa, George, and family, 145–46

Residency, Kansas, 44, 65

Revenge: efforts to break cycle of, 56, 71–72, 77; for Lawrence massacre, 122, 125–26; as motive in guerrilla warfare, 56, 68, 80–81, 104, 108–9, 111

Rice, Benjamin, 74

Rice, John, 200–201

Richardson, Albert, 46, 48

Rich Hill, Missouri, 199–200, 231

Richland County: attempt to create, 135

Riggins, B. L., 111

Riley, Charles, 204–5

Robberies: in guerrilla warfare, 56, 70–71, 75, 145; by outlaws, 57; responses to, 140–41. See also Plundering

Roberts, Tom, 86

Robinson, Charles, 54; formation of militias and, 100n9, 102; in Kansas free-soil government, 47–48, 56; Lane and, 104–5

Rollins, James, 87

Runk, John, 187–88

Russell, W. H., 43

Sabine, Thomas, 139

Samuels, Zerelda, 114

Santa Fe Trail, 34–35

Schofield, John, 114–15, 118, 125; on Order No. 11, 119–20, 126, 250–51

Scott, Kansas, 192

Scott, Samuel, 92

Sears, George, 154

Secession, 85, 91, 98; Missouri considering, 99–101; postwar discussion of, 244–45

Sedalia, Missouri, 218

Segregation, 154–56

Self-government, local, 37

Self-Protective Association, 62, 68

Senate Committee on Territories, 36

Serpel, John, 51–52

Settlers: African American, 131, 151, 154–55; antebellum, 244–45; approval of vigilantism by, 73, 104, 113, 140; criticisms of railroad boosters by, 190–93; demographics of, 63–64;

harassed by both sides, 110–11; lack of documentation about, 142, 143; land for, 79–80, 137–38; leaving border country, 75, 79, 96–97, 111; persistence of, 144, 205–6; postwar reconstruction by, 131, 146; railroads and, 171–72, 185, 187–88; relief for, 204–5; return of exiled, 132, 136–38, 142, 144–46. *See also* Immigrants

Settlers' organizations, 50–51; antebellum, 244–45

Seventh U.S. Dragoons, 10

Seward, William, 38

Shaw, Robert Gould, 116

Shawnees, 20–21, 50

Shelby, Jo, 241

Sherman, William, 134, 251

Shortridge, James R., 81n54

Shortridge, Thomas, 124

Shrout, O. P., 244

Sigel, Albert, 195

Simpson, James M., 31

Singleton, Benjamin "Pap," 151–52

Slaveholders: attacks on, 75, 91–92; bushwhackers as, 109; fear of Kansas abolitionists, 43, 76; in Missouri, 37, 46–47, 89, 91–92, 207–8; percentage of households as, 32–33; rights of, 37, 49, 89; status of, 32; Unionists as, 118

Slavery: border and, 11, 33; expansion of, 37, 76; federal government and, 80, 85; foreign immigrants' opposition to, 149–50; free African Americans returned to, 92; influence of, 23, 31, 117, 207–8, 213; judging stance on, from nativity, 31, 85, 110; in Kansas, 38, 46–47; in Kansas constitutions, 65–66, 80, 82–83; Kansas laws about, 46–47; Kansas settling issue, 66, 179; as key issue, 38–39, 48, 86; Missouri Compromise limiting, 3, 36; Missourians' acceptance of, 76, 97, 131; poor whites' support for, 34, 44; postwar discussions of, 244–47; preservation of, 48, 58–59, 99; racism and, 34. *See also* Free-soil settlers; Proslavery faction

Slaves, 80, 247; abolitionists stealing, 37, 43, 75, 93; demographics of, 31–32; emancipation of, 161; freed, 34, 75, 106, 151–52; in Kansas, 84; in Missouri population, 31, 151; of rebels, 112; revolts by, 58

—fugitive: free-soilers helping, 43, 46, 93–94; in Kansas, 4, 150–52; return of, 92–93

Slave states, 65

Slave trade, 15, 67–68

Sloan, Jeremiah, 145

Smith, Elijah, 159–60

Smith, Mrs. W. O., 210

Smith, Sophia, 167

Smith, William, 68

Snoddy, James D., 180

Social experiments/reform movements: in Kansas *vs.* in Missouri, 235–36

Sons of the South, 44

Sorghum, 78

South, 54, 101, 120, 148; characterizations of, 44, 58; in 1860 presidential election, 89–91; on expansion of slavery, 36, 38, 66; immigration to Kansas from, 52–53, 63–64, 81–84; influence in Missouri identity, 89–90, 243, 246–47; nativity in, 23, 31, 146–47, 149; political parties in, 85–86; secession by, 85, 98. *See also* Confederates, former, and sympathizers

Southern Aid Society, 76

Southwest Battalion, 95, 103

Southwest Expedition, 94–95

Southwood, Reverend, 67

Spain, 10, 15–16

Speer, John, 248–49

Sports: Missouri/Kansas rivalry in, 1–3, 252

Squatters: on Cherokee Neutral Tract, 185–89

Squatter Sovereign (newspaper), 42

Squatter sovereignty. *See* Popular sovereignty

"Squatters courts," 52

Stanton, Elizabeth Cady, 166, 169

Statehood, Kansas, 47, 65–66, 80

Status, social, 109; expanding suffrage and, 162–69; of railroad boosters, 172, 175–76, 179–80; slavery and, 32, 44, 49

St. Clair County, Missouri, 189, 196–97

Stearns, George, 92, 103

Stevens, George W., 238

Stevenson, J. C., 193–95

Stewart, Robert M., 72–73, 77, 87, 94–95

St. Louis, Missouri, 15, 101–2, 174, 184

Stone, Lucy, 166–67

Stone family, 67

Stringfellow, Benjamin, 42, 54

Subsistence farming, 25, 82; cash-pro-
    ducing items in, 30, 209–10; crops of,
    28–30; evolving to market agriculture,
    206–7; in Osage valley, 22–23; prairie
    environment conducive to, 27–29
Suffrage: for African Americans, 4,
    161–64, 168–69, 180; Confederates and
    sympathizers losing, 157–59; postwar
    debates over, 133–34; reinstated for
    Confederates and sympathizers,
    159–60, 162, 182; residency required for,
    44, 65; for women, 134, 164–69, 235–36
Sugar Mound, Kansas, 57, 61
Sumner, Charles, 58
Sumner, E. V., 10
Supreme Court, U.S., 80
Synder, J. F., 73

Tarkington, Hannah, 31
Taxes, 136; adjustments of assessments
    for, 113, 204; farmers' lack of cash for,
    136–37, 192, 199; railroad expansion
    and, 4, 170, 172, 174, 181–82, 198
Taylor, Zachary, 21
Tebo and Neosho railroad. *See* Missouri,
    Kansas, and Texas (MKT) Railroad
Temperance movement, 233–36
Tennessee, 83, 146–47
Texas cattle drives, 218–21, 219
Thayer, Eli, 39, 53
Thayer, Nathaniel, 186–87
Timber: establishment of farms near, 28
Topeka government (free-soil), 47–49,
    56, 58–59, 86
Toppin, Henry, 113
Total war, 106–7, 251
Toussaint-Louverture revolution, 58
Towns, 223; boosters in, 190–93, 201;
    influence of, 190–93, 238
Trade, 15, 37; in butter, cheese, and eggs,
    210–11; cross-border, 135, 178, 209,
    237; with Indians, 12, 14, 21. *See also*
    Economy; Fur trade; Slave trade
Trade and Intercourse Acts (1834), 21–22
Transportation, 213, 215; by rivers *vs.*
    railroads, 30, 176–77
Trego, Joseph, 67, 105–6
Turner, Nat, 58
Twyman, Frances Fristoe, 251

Underground Railroad, 55, 75, 150, 152
Union, 148; Kansas loyalty to, 3, 98,
    102–3; lessening support for in Mis-

souri, 101–2, 107; preservation of, 89,
    99, 245; unraveling of, 91, 98
Union army: abusing Missouri civilians,
    108–9, 115–16, 127; African Americans
    in, 117–18, 152, 162–63; demobiliza-
    tion of, 133; Enrolled Missouri Militia
    as alternative to, 114–15; former Con-
    federates enlisting in, 159–60; ineffec-
    tiveness of, 108, 112–13, 119, 126;
    Kansans in, 115–16, 118, 127, 130; Lane
    and, 107, 248–49; martial law by, 133;
    occupation of Missouri by, 99, 101,
    129; not occupied postwar, 133; resist-
    ance to, 109, 115, 119; trying to impose
    order, 112, 119; *vs.* bushwhackers and,
    113, 116–17, 119–20, 250. *See also* Order
    No. 11
Unionists, 109; bushwhacker attacks on,
    118–19, 127; driven out of western
    Missouri, 107–8, 128–29, 131, 149;
    financial position postwar, 138–39; in
    Missouri, 113, 131; not safe from jay-
    hawker violence, 106–9; Order No. 11
    and, 122–23, 126; Radical Republicans
    and, 157; as slaveholders, 118
Union Labor Party, 238
Union veterans, 136, 152, 160, 186, 188
United Daughters of the Confederacy
    (UDC), 242, 247, 252
United Foreign Mission Society, 18, 20
Updegraff, Mary, 165
U.S. Army, 23, 93; Kansas land sales and,
    80, 188; Native Americans and, 21–22;
    vs. guerrilla warfare, 58, 71. *See also*
    Union army

Van Buren, Martin, 37
Van Buren County, Missouri, 37
Vansickle, John, 68, 70
Vaughn, Richard, 125
Vernon County, Missouri, 25, 44, 140;
    agriculture in, 204–5, 210, 214, 224–25;
    civil government in, 135–37, 139–40;
    demographics of, 146, 151; jayhawker
    raids on, 75–77, 94; Order No. 11 evac-
    uating, 122–23; politics in, 88–89, 90;
    railroad expansion and, 177, 183
Vesey, Denmark, 58
Vest, George, 238
Veterans, 141, 148, 169, 242, 243–44
Vigilantism, 140–41, 197; blocking rail-
    road construction, 187–88; blocking
    Texas cattle drives, 219–20; against

Cass County judges, 194–96. *See also* Guerrilla warfare

Violence: frontier culture of, 197; Missouri's reputation for, 139–40, 170, 195–96; against officials subverting public wishes, 195–97; postwar, 139–40; remorse for, 241; by settlers blocking railroad construction, 187–88; in temperance movement, 233–34. *See also* Border war, Kansas/Missouri; Guerrilla warfare

Virginia, 83, 91, 146–47

Walker, Frank, 68, 87
Walker, John R., 180–81
Walker, Morgan, 110
Walker, Robert, 65
Walton, William, 241
Ward, Allen, 25
Washburne, Jacob and Anna, 84
Water, 28, 38–39
Wealth, 34, 138; expectation of acquiring, 24–25; of frontier households, 24–25, 33; making farms targets, 144; of railroad boosters, 175–76, 179–80; relation to slave ownership, 24–25, 31; subverting democracy, 193
Weaver, James, 238, 239–40
Webb, W. L., 248, 252
Webster, Martin, 153
Wells, William F., 186–87
West, 89, 124, 172, 177; agriculture in, 184–85, 213; as common heritage of Missourians and Kansans, 64, 82; restrictions on African American settlement in, 48–49

West, G. S., 155
West Point, Missouri, 69, 134–35
Westport, Battle of, 130
Westport, Missouri, 177
Westward expansion, 34–35, 143–44, 148, 208
Wheat, 216–18
Whig Party, 47, 85
Whitfield, J. W., 44–45
Williams, Henry, 56
Williams, Joseph, 52
Williams, S. A., 45
Williams, Thomas and Sarah, 149
Williams, William Shirley, 20
Wilson, Hiero T., 22
Wilson's Creek, Battle of, 104
Wiseman, F. J., 199–200
Women: African American, 153; associated with veterans' groups, 242, 247; contributions on farms, 30, 209–10, 226–28; families of bushwhackers, 120–21; guerrilla warfare and, 74–75, 248; Osage, 216; property ownership by, 26; vote for, 134, 164–69, 235–36
Women's Christian Temperance Union (WCTU), 234
Wood, Samuel Newitt, 164–66
Wood Local Option Law, 236
Wyandots, 20–21
Wyandotte constitution. *See* Constitutions, Kansas

Yoder, Solomon and Sarah, 145
Younger, Coleman, 108–9
Younger, Jim, 109